'Based on rigorous fieldwork, this well-argued volume brings together leading scholars of Nigeria and Islam in Africa. What makes it stand out in the crowded field of "Boko-Haramology" is the sophisticated analysis of the social and political processes explaining the emergence of the most violent insurgency led by a non state actor in West African post-colonial history.' – **Ousmane Kane, Prince Alwaleed Bin Talal Professor of Contemporary Islamic Religion and Society, Harvard Divinity School**

'a brilliant and trenchant inquiry into the contradictory causes of radicalization among Muslim youth in greater Nigeria. Its original field data alone will enlighten scholars and policy-makers struggling to grasp this movement's continuing enigmatic appeal.' – **Paul M. Lubeck, Johns Hopkins University, SAIS**

'Ten years on from the Boko Haram insurgency, the inability of successive governments to bring its potency to an end remains a tragic indictment on the Nigerian state at all levels. ...The collection of essays offer illuminating and thought provoking analytical descriptions of the social, political ...and religious processes that gave rise to Boko Haram. ...Crucially it contributes to a growing number of studies on the role of and impact the group has had on women and usefully examines previous religious insurgencies for insights on how to end Boko Haram's violent conflict. For policy-makers, this book offers a whole-of-society perspective on Boko Haram's rise which could help better shape responses to ending the insurgency. Finally, this book is a thoughtful memorial to the late Abdul Raufu Mustapha. His students and colleagues have faithfully preserved his scholarly endeavours to look beyond the motives and destructive impact of Boko Haram to provide an understanding of why northern Nigeria succumbed to Islamic extremism.' – **Comfort Ero, Program Director for International Crisis Group**

'Overcoming Boko Haram is a fitting completion of the late Raufu Mustapha's trilogy...on religion and identity in Nigeria. ...This book concludes on a hopeful note: Boko Haram and violent extremism, despite the damage and destruction which they continue to inflict on the people, can be overcome. ...The book should be required reading for policy makers and other stakeholders who are serious in finding ways to combat and defeat Boko Haram and violent extremism in Nigeria.' – **Ibrahim Gambari, Founder/Chair of Savannah Centre for Diplomacy, Democracy and Development, Abuja, and former UN Under-Secretary General**

'a very important contribution to the study of radicalisation in Nigeria and more generally.' – **Benjamin Soares, Department of Religion & Center for African Studies, University of Florida**

WESTERN AFRICA SERIES

The Economics of Ethnic Conflict:
The Case of Burkina Faso
Andreas Dafinger

Commercial Agriculture, the Slave Trade
& Slavery in Atlantic Africa
Edited by Robin Law, Suzanne Schwarz
& Silke Strickrodt

Sects & Social Disorder:
Muslim Identities & Conflict in Northern Nigeria
Edited by Abdul Raufu Mustapha

Afro-European Trade in the Atlantic World:
The Western Slave Coast c. 1550–c. 1885
Silke Strickrodt

The Politics of Peacemaking in Africa:
Non-State Actors' Role in the Liberian Civil War
Babatunde Tolu Afolabi

Creed & Grievance:
Muslim-Christian Relations & Conflict Resolution in Northern Nigeria
Edited by Abdul Raufu Mustapha & David Ehrhardt

The Politics of Work in a Post-Conflict State:
Youth, Labour & Violence in Sierra Leone
Luisa Enria

African Women in the Atlantic World:
Property, Vulnerability & Mobility, 1660–1880
Edited by Mariana P. Candido & Adam Jones

Overcoming Boko Haram:
Faith, Society & Islamic Radicalization in Northern Nigeria
Edited by Abdul Raufu Mustapha & Kate Meagher

Political Legitimacy in Postcolonial Mali
Dorothea E. Schulz

Order & Disorder in Northern Nigeria:
*Armed groups, Insurgency & Resistance**
Edited by Adam Higazi & Laurens Bakker

* forthcoming

Overcoming Boko Haram

FAITH, SOCIETY & ISLAMIC RADICALIZATION IN NORTHERN NIGERIA

Edited by
Abdul Raufu Mustapha & Kate Meagher

PREMIUM Times BOOKS

JAMES CURREY

James Currey
is an imprint of
Boydell & Brewer Ltd
PO Box 9, Woodbridge
Suffolk IP12 3DF (GB)
www.jamescurrey.com
and of
Boydell & Brewer Inc.
668 Mt Hope Avenue
Rochester, NY 14620-2731 (US)
www.boydellandbrewer.com

Nigerian paperback edition published in 2020 by
Premium Times Books, Abuja
53, Mambolo Street, Zone 2,
Wuse, Abuja, Nigeria
www.ptbooksglobal.com

First published in hardback 2020
Paperback edition 2022

British Library Cataloguing in Publication Data
A catalogue record for this book is available on request from the British Library

ISBN 978-1-84701-239-5 (James Currey hardback)
ISBN 978-0-9995584-6-1 (Premium Times Books Nigerian edition paperback)
ISBN 978-1-84701-328-6 (James Currey paperback)

This publication is printed on acid-free paper

Typeset in 11/13 Bembo with Albertus MT display
by Avocet Typeset, Bideford, Devon, EX39 2BP

Printed and bound in Great Britain by
TJ Books Ltd, Padstow, Cornwall

MIX
Paper from responsible sources
FSC® C013056

To Mahmoud, Ma'u, Yahaya
and families
for a lifetime of friendship

Contents

List of Maps, Figures & Tables

MAP

FIGURES

TABLES

Notes on Contributors

David Ehrhardt is an Assistant Professor in International Development at Leiden University College, where he teaches development studies and African politics. David conducted his doctoral research at the Department of International Development, University of Oxford. He specializes in the use of mixed methods to study religious politics and inter-faith conflict, citizenship and horizontal inequalities, and conflict resolution, with a focus on Nigeria. His current project focuses on the role of traditional authorities in conflict resolution in eight different cities in Nigeria. David is a fellow of Leiden's African Studies Centre and a member of the Nigeria Research Network and the Leiden Centre for the Study of Islam and Society. His articles have been published in journals such as *African Affairs*, *Contemporary Islam*, and the *Canadian Journal of African Studies*, and he appears regularly in Dutch news media to talk about Nigeria. He is the co-editor of *Creed and Grievance: Muslim-Christian Relations and Conflict Resolution in Northern Nigeria* (James Currey 2018) and *Food and Sustainability* (OUP 2019).

Sherine El Taraboulsi-McCarthy is Interim Senior Research Fellow with the Humanitarian Policy Group at the Overseas Development Institute. She recently completed a DPhil in Development Studies from the University of Oxford, and specializes in aid, conflict and security in the Middle East, North Africa and Europe. With over a decade of experience in the sector, she focuses on development and humanitarian policy and practice in the Arab region, with a strong focus on Libya, Yemen, Tunisia, Egypt and the Gulf. Her research interests include state formation and fragility, terrorism and extremist violence, humanitarian action in complex emergencies, state donors and non-state philanthropy in conflict regions, and the politics of communal loyalty and transnational networks in peace building and protection. She is a member of the Yemen Safe Passage Group.

Ibrahim Haruna Hassan is a Professor of Islamic Studies at the University of Jos, Nigeria. He obtained degrees in Civil Engineering and Development Studies, and worked as a civil engineer before undertaking a PhD in Islamic Studies. His research focuses on Islamic sciences and Islam in the modern world. Hassan was awarded a Post-Doctoral fellowship of the African Humanities Programme (AHP) by the American Council of Learned Societies (ACLS) 2009/2010, and was a Fulbright African visiting scholar (2014–15) at the Northwestern University, Evanston. He has participated in many international research projects including the Religion and Development (RaD) Research Project of Birmingham University (UK) and the Minnerva project of the Arizona State University. Hassan has published widely, including *Towards an Islamic Theory of Development* (Lambert, Germany, 2013) and 'Weathering the Storm: Shari'a in Nigeria from the Earliest Times to the Present' in *Law, Religion and Love: Seeking Eccumenical Justice for the Other* (Routledge 2018).

Khadija Gambo Hawaja is a Nigerian activist and founder of the Muslim Women Peace Forum in Plateau State. She studied Islam in the traditional as well as the Western system up to postgraduate level. From 2005 to 2009 she was a teacher of Islamic Studies, and from 2013 to 2016 she was a Political and Gender Adviser for the Center for Humanitarian Dialogue . In 2016, she was appointed as a Commissioner in the Judicial Commission of Inquiry over the December 2015 clashes between the Nigerian Army and the Shi'ite 'Islamic Movement in Nigeria'. She is involved in countering violent extremism, and in deradicalization activities through media campaigns, interviews, lectures, conferences and workshops both locally and internationally. She is a member of Sisters Against Violent Extremism (SAVE) and Women Without Borders, both based in Vienna, Austria.

Rahmane Idrissa is a political scientist at the African Studies Centre, Leiden University, where he is senior researcher and assistant professor in Islam in Contemporary Sub-Saharan Africa. His main interests are the political economy of state-building and the politics of Islam in Africa. His recent book, *The Politics of Islam in the Sahel: Between Persuasion and Violence* (Routledge 2017) offers a comparative analysis of the varied role of Islam in politics and state formation in West African Muslim majority countries.

Murray Last is Professor Emeritus in the Department of Anthropology, University College London. His PhD in 1964 was the first to be awarded by a Nigerian university (University College Ibadan), and his previous degrees are from Cambridge (1959) and Yale (1961). He specializes in both the pre-colonial history of Muslim northern Nigeria and the ethnography of illness and healing. He has been working in or on northern Nigeria since 1961, researching a wide variety of subjects especially with colleagues in Bayero University, Kano (where he was Professor of History 1978–80). He visits Nigeria every year for a month at least. He has been a 'traditional' Muslim student in Zaria City, and lived for two years in a non-Muslim Hausa farmstead. He is the author of *The Sokoto Caliphate* (Longmans Green 1967, also published in Hausa as *Daular Sakkwato*). He also edited (with G.L. Chavunduka) *The Professionalisation of African Medicine* (Manchester University Press for the International African Institute 1986). In addition he has over a hundred publications on African history and anthropology. He was sole editor of the International African Institute's journal *AFRICA* from 1986 to 2001.

Kate Meagher is an Associate Professor in Development Studies at the Department of International Development, London School of Economics and Political Science. She has published widely on various aspects of African informal economies, from the changing dynamics of cross-border trade, and the economic governance of informal enterprise clusters, to the political economy of informal economic inclusion. Her publications include *Identity Economics: Social Networks and the Informal Economy in Nigeria* (James Currey 2010), and *Globalisation, Economic Inclusion and African Workers: Making the Right Connections* (Routledge 2018), co-edited with Laura Mann and Maxim Bolt. Her current research interests include informal institutions, hybrid governance, religion and the informal economy, and youth unemployment and the gig economy in Africa.

Abubakar K. Monguno is Senior Lecturer and Head of the Geography Department at the University of Maiduguri, Nigeria. He holds a doctoral degree in Geography from Bayero University, Kano and teaches courses in Development Geography as well as Disaster Risk Management. He was formerly Deputy Director, Centre for Disaster Risk Management and Development Studies, University of Maiduguri. Dr Monguno was previously Chief Lecturer at Kashim Ibrahim College of Education, Maiduguri where he taught for nearly two decades. In addition to teaching, he engages in research activities, and has published widely in the area of development geography with particular reference to health, education, environment and conflict studies. Dr Monguno has provided consultancy services to a number of local and international organizations in the area of research and facilitation.

Abdul Raufu Mustapha was an Associate Professor in African Politics at the Oxford Department of International Development (ODID), University of Oxford, and the Kirk-Greene Fellow at St. Antony's College until his death in 2017. He studied Political Science at Ahmadu Bello University, Zaria and obtained a DPhil in Politics at St Peter's College, University of Oxford. He was the Principal Researcher in the Nigeria Research

Network and a member of the editorial advisory boards of the *Review of African Political Economy*, Sheffield, and *Premium Times*, Abuja. He was also the chair of the Board of Trustees of the Development Research and Projects Centre (dRPC), Kano. Dr Mustapha held previous academic positions at Bayero University, Kano and Ahmadu Bello University, Zaria. His areas of research interest were religion and politics in Nigeria, the politics of rural societies, the politics of democratization, and identity politics in Africa. His publications include the following edited volumes: *Gulliver's Troubles: Nigeria's Foreign Policy After the Cold War* (OUP 2008, with Adekeye Adebajo); *Turning Points in African Democracy* (James Currey 2009, with Lindsay Whitfield); *Conflicts and Security Governance in West Africa* (Malthouse & CLEEN Foundation 2013); *Sects & Social Disorder* (James Currey 2014) and *Creed & Grievance* (James Currey 2018, with David Ehrhardt).

Julie G. Sanda is Principal Research Fellow in the Centre for Strategic Research and Studies of the National Defence College, Abuja, Nigeria. A political science graduate of the University of Jos and Ahmadu Bello University, Zaria, she has published on the challenges of protecting civilians in armed conflict, Nigeria's role in global peacekeeping, as well as a co-edited volume with O. Ibeanu, *Women and Children in Conflict Situations: Conflict and Human Vulnerabilities in Nigeria* (Heinemann Educational Publishers, 2007). She is also Editor of the *Africa Peace Review* and her current research interests include peacekeeping and foreign policy, women in security, human rights and military operations.

M. Sani Umar is a Professor in the Department of History, Ahmadu Bello University in Zaria Nigeria. He has a PhD in History and Literature of Religion from Northwestern University. His research centres on religious violence and peace building, with a focus on understanding the roots of religious conflict and the dynamics of religious pluralism. Before joining Ahmadu Bello University in 2012, Umar was an Associate Professor at Northwestern University (Evanston, IL), and he previously taught at Lawrence University in Appleton, Wisconsin, and Arizona State University in Tempe, Arizona. He has held a Carnegie Scholars Fellowship as well as a Fellowship at the Wissenschaftskolleg zu Berlin, and was a Global Fellow at the International Institute, University of California, Los Angeles. In August 2007, Dr Umar was appointed Director of the Institute for Study of Islamic Thought in Africa (ISITA) at the Program of African Studies of Northwestern University. He is the author of *Islam and Colonialism: The Intellectual Responses of Muslims of Northern Nigeria* (Brill 2005), and numerous pieces in edited volumes and leading journals of Religious Studies, Islamic Studies and African Studies.

Ibrahim Umara is an Associate Professor of International Relations and former Head of the Department of Political Science, University of Maiduguri, Nigeria. He has published and contributed to many scholarly articles in both national and international journals and books. Ibrahim is the author of *National Interest and Foreign Policy options for Nigeria in the Central African Sub-region* (Joyce Publishers 2014). His recent research focuses on post-conflict rehabilitation and resettlement, deradicalization, internally displaced persons and the challenges of relocation and social cohesion, as well as trends of developmental regionalism in the Lake Chad region.

Zainab Usman is a development professional who works on governance, institutions and political economy of natural resources management, energy sector reforms, and service delivery, as well as South-South economic relations. She currently works at the World Bank in Washington DC at the Office of the Chief Economist of the Africa Region. She received her PhD from the University of Oxford in 2017 on the topic of 'The Political Economy of Economic Diversification in Nigeria'.

Glossary

achaba (Hausa)	nickname for motorcycle taxi
ahl al-Sunna	followers of the Prophet's way, a name some Salafi communities call themselves
Al-Gama'ah al-Islamiyya	an Egyptian radical Islamist movement (lit. the Islamic Group).
al-hafiz	title conferred after Qur'anic student has successfully memorized the Qur'an
alkali/joji (Hausa)	judge
almajiri (pl. *almajirai*)	from *al-muhajiroun* (Arabic) (lit.) 'emigrants'; Muslim pupil, usually male, who leaves home in search of Islamic knowledge under the guidance of a teacher
al-qisas	retaliation
ameera	female leader
Ansaru	moniker of *Jama'atu Anṣarul Muslimina fi Biladis Sudan* (Vanguard for the Aid of Muslims in Black Africa)
Ash'ariyya	theological school in Sunni Islam claiming reason must be subordinate to revelation
baraka	blessings, grace
boko (Hausa)	Western education (as opposed to traditional Qur'anic education using slates [*allo*])
Boko Haram	Western education is forbidden, moniker of *Jama'atul Ahlul Sunna li D'awati wal Jihad* (People Committed to the Propagation of the Prophet's Teaching and Jihad)
da'wa	proselytizing for Islam, good works, (lit.) call
Fatiha	the short first chapter of the Qur'an, used by Muslims as an essential element of ritual prayer

fiqh al-unf	Islamic legal discourses on violence
Hadith	traditions or sayings of the Prophet Muhammad, part of Muslim scriptures
halal	permissible
haram	forbidden
hijab	headscarf worn by Muslim women
Hisbah	'religious' police responsible for enforcing Sharia in some northern Nigerian States.
ijaza	certification of completing the study of a particular Islamic book
Ilmiyye	in the Ottoman Empire, the body of higher Muslim religious functionaries administering justice and teaching in religious colleges
imam	Islamic leadership position; leader of worship, mosque
Islamiyya	Islamic school modelled after modern government schools
isnad	accurate transmission of Islamic religious knowledge through a reliably authoritative chain of known experts
Izala	moniker of *Jama'atu Izalatul Bid'a wa Iqamat al-Sunna* (Society for for the Eradication of Innovation and the Reinstatement of Tradition)
jahiliyya	age of ignorance
jihad	struggle to conform to Muslim faith; holy war
Kala Kato (Hausa)	Islamic movement that rejects authority of all sacred books but the Qur'an
Kanawa (Hausa)	people who originate from the city of Kano
keke napep (Hausa)	motorized tricycle taxi
Khawarij (or Kharajite)	heretical Muslim sect that requires strict adherence to Muslim scriptures, and regards any deviation as apostasy punishable by death
kulle (Hausa)	wife seclusion
laïcité (French)	secularism
Mahdi	in Islam: redeemer, messiah
mai gida (Hausa)	head of household

Mai Tatsine or *Maitatsine* (Hausa)	violent fundamentalist Islamic movement in 1980s northern Nigeria, lit: one who curses
Maliki	one of the four major schools of Islamic jurisprudence within Sunni Islam
malam (pl. *malamai,* Hausa)	Islamic teacher or learned scholar
Maturidiyya	theological school in Sunni Islam that emphasizes revelation but allows rational inference where necessary
Mawlid	birthday of the Prophet Muhammad
mutunci (Hausa)	humanity, kindness
niqab	Muslim veil that conceals the entire face except for the eyes
okada	Nigerian nickname for motorcycle taxi (lit: the name of a local airline)
Qadi	Judge of a Sharia court
Qadiriyya	Sufi order popular among the northern Nigerian establishment
Salaf	pious predecessors, usually referring to first three generations of Muslims
Salafi	adherent of a branch of Sunni Islam that claims to emulate 'the pious predecessors'
Sarki (Hausa)	king, leader chief
shaheed/shahid	martyr
Sharia	legal system derived from Islamic principles
Shia, Shi'ite	Second largest Islamic sect that broke away from Sunni sect in the late 7th Century; in Nigeria, represented by the Islamic Movement in Nigeria led by Sheikh Ibrahim El-Zakzaki
Shura	a consultative or ruling council, (lit.) consultation
Sunna	body of Islamic law based on the words and acts of the Prophet Muhammad
takfir	excommunication – to declare a Muslim an apostate
talakawa (Hausa)	commoner
tarbiyya	training and disciplining of the soul
tariqa (pl. *turuq*; Hausa, darika)	'the path'; refers to an order or brotherhood within Sufism
Tijaniyya	Sufi order popular among commoners

	and commercial classes in northern Nigeria
tsangaya (Hausa)	traditional Qur'anic schools, adopted from Kanuri 'sangaya'
ulama (sing. *alim*)	community of Islamic scholars, (lit.) the learned ones
wa'azin	preaching, sermon
wahdatal-wujud	doctrine postulating that God and his creation are one, (lit.) the unity of Being
wazifa	Tijjani (Sufi) practice of recitation of a litany
'yan banga (Hausa)	thugs
'yan daba (Hausa)	gang members
Zakat	in Islam, obligatory giving of a share of one's wealth to the poor

Foreword

Writing a foreword to this collection of well-researched articles on Islamic radicalization in northern Nigeria was always going to be a difficult task. The range of authors, subjects and viewpoints is such that any attempt to capture a single dominant theme on which there is consensus would be presumptuous. And this is as it should be, given the complexity of this subject and the all-too-frequent tendency to over-simplify the phenomenon of Islamic radicalization.

Perhaps the best way to begin is, by way of tribute, to recollect my own relationship with my friend Professor Mustapha who passed away in 2017. Using our relationship as an entry point may help clarify my own approach to understanding radicalization. My admission to study Economics in the faculty of Arts and Social Sciences (FASS) at Ahmadu Bello University brought me into contact with Rauf and a few of his colleagues among the post-graduate students and graduate assistants, including Alkasum Abba, Sule Bello, Jibrin Ibrahim, Ayesha Imam, Altine Jafar, Sanusi Abubakar and George Kwanashie. Although Economics was considered the department of 'reactionaries' in the faculty, I spent most of my time with friends in political science, sociology and history. I soon found myself among a group of young undergraduates who took Rauf and his comrades as role models.

After my postgraduate Studies at ABU, I joined the academic staff as a graduate Assistant in the Economics department in the summer of 1983. Rauf and I briefly shared the same path as young academics committed to rigorous political economy and a materialist conception of history, but our paths diverged when Rauf went on to Oxford for his doctorate, while I left academia completely for a life in the banking industry. In 1991, I took a long break from banking to pursue a long-term interest in Islamic Studies at the University of Africa in Sudan, where I first studied Arabic before obtaining a second BA in Sharia and Islamic Studies in 1997. I returned to my banking career and ended up being appointed Governor of the Central Bank of Nigeria in 2009.

My background in political economy and Islamic law has shaped my reading of Muslim society. The influence of those early days remains strong, and I tend to be sympathetic to analyses that lay emphasis on material conditions. And this is the point here. I hold strongly to the view that many of the conflicts in the world – religious, ethnic, racial – tend to be caused, or at least inflamed, by grievances rooted in economics. Poverty, unemployment, marginalization and a general sense of being outsiders combine to bring together individuals who challenge the status quo, often violently. Sometimes this violence is properly directed at the real oppressors, while often it is misdirected at those who are 'not like us', those we define as the 'Other'. While vertical and horizontal inequalities are often the root cause of radicalization, the actual definition of the 'Other' is often not predictable in a straightforward manner, shaped as Gramsci has shown by the manipulation of ethnic over class identities, and as Foucault reveals by power relations that mould individual understanding.

The first point therefore is that I join Rauf and the contributors to this volume in the contention that any serious attempt at understanding Islamic radicalization in northern Nigeria cannot avoid discussion of material conditions – poverty, lack of opportunity, hopelessness, and economic inequality in general. Poverty is a relative phenomenon. Extreme inequalities among individuals or groups or regions breeds resentment that is much deeper and stronger than would exist in poor societies without extreme inequalities. So to understand radicalization in Nigeria we need to look at structural adjustment policies, de-industrialization and increased inequalities beginning from the 1980s. The neglect of agriculture and industry as the Nigerian State became a rentier State focused on the oil economy led to huge economic inequalities. The north, once the richest part of the country, became the poorest, compounded by high fertility rates, rapid demographic growth, desertification and climate change. Indeed, Christians in the north, especially in Plateau, Taraba and Southern Kaduna, have also become more polarized or 'radicalized' than Christians in Yorubaland where levels of poverty are far lower. By recognizing this fact we look for sources of radicalization in objective conditions of material existence rather than flawed understandings of Islam.

This brings me to the generally-held idea that 'radical Islam' or fundamentalist/Salafi ideology is something new and imported into northern Nigeria from the Gulf States. This is far from the truth. First of all, Salafi thought, while being literal and unaccommodating of contrary views, is not in itself violent. Several commentators work from a simplistic dichotomy between a 'pacifist' Sufi tradition that has deep roots in West Africa, and a 'radical' Salafi tradition which is foreign. But consider that Uthman Dan Fodio, the 19th century jihadist, was a Sufi of the Qadiriyya order. The success of his jihad lay largely in its ability to gather the support of a mass of the population who had faced marginalization, oppressive taxation and oppression from unjust leaders. His contemporary, Al-hajj Umar ibn Sa'id al-Futi Tal,[1] conqueror of the Bambara, was a Sufi Sheikh of the Tijaniyya order. Indeed the various Muslim Futa settlements of the Niger basin – Futa Bundu, Futa Jallon and Futa Toro – were established by radicalized Sufis. The presumption of pacifism among Sufis and violence among Salafis is largely unfounded. Indeed, in the case of Boko Haram, strong evidence suggests that the group has been openly opposed by Salafi scholars, and in fact Boko Haram most probably murdered prominent Salafi leaders like Jafar Adam in Kano and Sheikh Albani in Zaria.

Having said that, certain attributes in Salafi thought and terminology make it amenable to appropriation and instrumentalization in the process of classification of Muslims into orthodox and heterodox, rightly guided and deviant, and thus the construction of Self and Other as justification for action. The literalism, the intolerance, the very narrow definition of what is the 'straight path' (*al-sirat-al-mustaqim*) are all there to be appropriated in the service of political action, by Salafis and non-Salafis alike. Ibn Taimiyyah[2] himself used this Salafi heuristic in his othering of Sufis, Christians, Jews, philosophers and Shiites, etc. But to take one example, in spite of Ibn Taimiyya's reputation as a critic of Sufism, no one questions his sympathy and reverence for certain Sufi shiekhs like Abdulqadir Jilani,[3] and indeed there is a body of scholarship that suggests that he accepted the *khirqah* (a cloak signifying initiation into the Sufi path) and was in fact himself a devotee and member of the Qadiriyya order. Certainly, when one reads the works of the school of Ibn Taimiyya one wonders at the anti-Sufi label given to the school. His most famous student, Ibn al-qayyim al-Jawziyya, wrote a treatise, *Madarij al-Salikin*, which remains one of the greatest works of Sufism.

Muhammad Ibn Abdulwahhab, the founder of Wahhabism, also appropriated Salafi terminology and used it as a basis for his revolt. He was strongly opposed not just by mainstream Ottoman Sheikhs but by his own family. His own father disagreed with him, and there is significant literature left behind by his brother, Sulayman Ibn Abdulwahab, denouncing Wahhabism as deviance, and not consistent with Salafi doctrine. In the end Wahhabism was not so much established by its theological appeal but by a more political alliance between its adherents, the so called 'Brotherhood of those obedient to God' *(Ikhwan Man Ta'a Allah)* and the House of

1 An adventuring political leader, Islamic scholar of the Tijani order, and Toucouleur military commander from modern-day Senegal who spent time in the Bornu and Sokoto Caliphates, and returned home to found a brief empire in the mid-19th century encompassing much of what is now Guinea, Senegal, and Mali.

2 A 13th century Hanbali Muslim scholar and reformer, whose writings have been influential in the development of Wahhabism and contemporary Salafism.

3 A 12th century Muslim scholar and mystic who founded the Qadiriyya Sufi order.

Saud, an alliance that was backed by Christian Britain in its war against Muslim Turkey. To explain the rise of Wahhabism in simple theological terms without the geopolitical context of the post World War I world, would miss the point completely.

The Sahel is not without its own examples of the political use of Salafi doctrines. In the late 15th century, Askia Muhammad Al-Hajj[4] overthrew the reigning monarch Sunni Baru, son of the first Songhai king Sunni Ali, on the grounds that the Sunni dynasty kings were not faithful Muslims. Askia's questions to scholar Al-Maghili[5] and the scholar's answers provide a classic case of using 'Salafi' arguments to justify political action, as the Sunni dynasty was accused of innovation, syncretism but also oppression and injustice against the Muslim poor. Al-Maghili held religious views that would today be classified as Salafi.

The same arguments used by Askia to justify his coup were used by Uthman Dan Fodio to justify his jihad. In fact one very small but important pamphlet written by Uthman Dan Fodio, titled *Siraj al-Ikhwan*, was almost entirely a reproduction of Askia's questions and al-Maghili's answers. Clearly Uthman Dan Fodio, a Sufi, was not averse to basing his Jihad on Salafi premises. After his victory in the 1804 Jihad he adopted a much more accommodating and moderate view in works like *Najmul Ikhwan*. In this sense, when Boko Haram characterizes itself as *Jama'atu Ahlis Sunnah Lidda'awati wal-Jihad* (People Committed to the Propagation of the Prophet's teaching and Jihad), it is easy to see why some, especially Western scholars, interpret this as a continuation of a single radical theological chain from Askia Muhammad through Uthman Dan Fodio to Boko Haram and all the 'radical Salafis' in between.

But this is where the mistake is made. There is a certain failure to make a distinction between conjunction and causation. In the contemporary Sunni world many radical political movements claim Salafism. This is because Salafism provides a convenient heuristic for defining a narrow band of correct, orthodox or rightly guided Muslims on the one hand, and a wide range of heterodox, deviant, syncretist, apostate, heretical others who wrongly see themselves as Muslim. But this in my mind is where the association ends. Those who seek a religious justification for political or military action find in Salafism a convenient theological weapon that often conceals underlying political goals. While it is true that many

4 An emperor, military commander, and political reformer who seized control of the Songhai Empire in the late 15th century, expanding it into the largest empire in West African history.

5 A 15th century Muslim reformer from modern-day Algeria, Al-Maghili denounced the corrupt and unIslamic practices of West African rulers and called for the implementation of Sharia Law. He propagated the concept of mujaddid (cyclical Islamic renewal) and was an inspiration to the militant reformers and West African jihads of the 15th century onwards. He served as advisor to Muhammad Rumfa, Emir of Kano.

contemporary radical groups in Sunni Islam are Salafi, it is by no means true that the majority of Salafis are violent or radical. The majority of scholars of Salafi tendency condemn violence and bloodshed and radicalism and in fact frown upon any kind of rebellion against established authority. In this they mirror the views of the majority of Muslims of all sects and schools who view Islam as a religion of peace and justice. In any event, it is difficult to find any serious Salafi tract (or even Salafi-Jihadi tract) that recommends killing innocent people, suicide bombing or kidnapping of school girls. These are just criminal activities and have nothing to do with religion.

To my mind, this is the point missed by those who think radicalization is a product of Salafism. As this book shows, radicalization is caused by other factors in social conditions and then Salafism is appropriated as the legitimator for political action. We know from Vaclav Havel's reading of Karl Popper's Open Society for example, that when faced with insecurity and fear people tend to agglomerate into 'tribes' and see the world in terms of 'us' and 'them'. Emmanuel Sivan understands Ibn Taimiyya's radicalization in the context of the disintegrating late Abbasid Caliphate, under siege from the Christian crusaders in the West and Mongol hordes from the East. In such a situation, Salafism is a strong tool for defining and uniting a Muslim Ummah to fight external enemies.

This calls for reflection on a further source of popular insecurity and resentment in contemporary northern Nigeria. The very term 'Boko Haram' (western education is forbidden) is often attributed to the backwardness and xenophobia of members of the group. In dismissing this matter so superficially we are in danger of failing to address the underlying confrontation and contestation between an Islamic system of education and an imported colonial one.

For a Muslim, the Qur'an is the most sacred of texts. When we go to Qur'anic School we write the Qur'an on a tablet or writing board. We sit on the floor before our teacher. We are not allowed to touch the Qur'an without purification, we do not keep it on the ground or any unclean place. When we finish learning what was written we wash off the ink and drink it for closeness to God. On completion of training to recite the entire Qur'an, we are treated to a 'Walima', a party celebrating this feat, and he who has memorized the Qur'an (a *haafidh*) has a special place in the eyes of Muslims. It is the highest honour. This is how a student of the Qur'an sees himself.

But how is he seen by the wider society? The children who spend years studying the Qur'an are classified as 'out-of-school'. Those who have learnt to read and write the whole Qur'an and even memorized it are classified as 'illiterate' because they do not read and write in the Latin alphabet. They are viewed as poor and disdained as itinerant beggars.

They are not mainstreamed into modern schools. If they were in an Arab country they would be 'literate', and with literacy in Arabic they can become doctors or engineers or computer scientists through educational mainstreaming. In Nigeria they can only teach the Qur'an or be part of what is now called a 'prayer economy' praying for rich politicians and merchants in return for cash. Beginning with British imperialism and continuing with the neo-colonial post-independence elite, there has been a systematic debasement of Qur'anic education, and marginalization and devaluation of Qur'anic scholars. The elite in Nigeria do not see how the system of inclusion constructed in the image of the West has excluded the majority of the northern Muslim population, deprived the masses of opportunity and created resentment against the political system.

Let me stress that I do not believe that every marginalized or poor Muslim is an extremist. However, I believe the point has been made that certain social and economic conditions are fertile ground for breeding violent movements – be they religious extremists or ethnic militia or just criminal gangs. All of these are present in contemporary northern Nigeria so locating the violence of Boko Haram in religious doctrines misses the point. The group in the short-term must be defeated militarily. But, as this book argues, a long term solution must look beyond military tactics to issues of governance, economic inequality, social exclusion and marginalization and perceived injustices. As we reflect on the rise of religious extremism, ethnic conflict and criminal violence in Nigeria, we must not forget that explanations for Boko Haram lie in the failures of the state, not in the nature of Islam.

It was the struggle for control of political power and resources among the Nigerian political elite that led to the emergence of a 'Sharia Movement' in northern Nigeria. Beginning with Zamfara State in 1999, twelve states in northern Nigeria adopted 'full implementation' of Sharia including its criminal code. But this was also accompanied by a general politicization of religion, intensifying the polarized construction of Muslim and Christian identities in the North. This process of identity construction has had two mutually reinforcing effects that contributed to the emergence of Boko Haram. At the level of ideas, the sharp construction of an orthodox Muslim identity and the Othering of Muslims and non-Muslims alike created the space for the thriving of radical and divisive discourses. At the level of economics, the diversion of resources away from development needs (education, health, agriculture and industry) to the religious sector (Hisbah, Pilgrimage, Preaching, etc.) led to a perverse process of deprivation and the commodification of piety within the northern Nigerian Muslim population. This is an area that merits further attention.

I look forward to learning more from the scholars that have contributed to this book, and hope I have added one more perspective to this rich debate.

I close with a prayer for my late friend, Rauf. May his soul rest in perfect peace. Ameen.

Muhammad Sanusi II, CON
Sarkin Kano

Preface & Acknowledgements

With over 25 books published on Nigeria's violent Islamic insurgency since 2014, one could be forgiven for asking whether we really need yet another book about Boko Haram. Fortunately, this book is not about Boko Haram itself, but about the political and economic pressures driving it and the social and institutional resources within Nigerian society capable of overcoming it. After a decade of failed initiatives to combat the insurgency, there is a pressing need to address pervasive misconceptions about the religious and social realities that gave rise to violent extremism in northern Nigeria, and to gain a better understanding of the forces available for reining it in. The contributors to this collection are seasoned Nigerian and Nigerianist scholars with considerable lived experience in northern Nigeria, and specialized knowledge of the themes on which they write, including the Nigerian military, the Borno factor, the community of Nigerian Islamic scholars, the politics of Niger Republic, women and youth in northern Nigeria, and the Nigerian informal economy. In the field of 'Boko Haram-ology', crowded by a few too many instant experts on Islam in Nigeria, the depth of academic as well as cultural and institutional experience that informs this collection should not be under-rated. Locating internal social and religious processes in the context of wider economic and political pressures, the chapters in this volume offer an inside perspective on how this terrible eruption of violence could happen, with a view to seeking more grounded approaches to resolving it.

This book began as a research project commissioned by the Office of the National Security Adviser in Nigeria to produce evidence-based research for the development of a 'soft approach' to counter-terrorism. Sometime in late 2013, Raufu Mustapha was contacted by the DfID-funded Nigeria Security and Reconciliation Programme (NSRP) about putting together a research programme on radicalization and counter-radicalization in northern Nigeria. In collaboration with Professor M. Sani Umar of Ahmadu Bello University in Zaria, a research team was assembled, drawing on the Oxford-based Nigeria Research Network which Raufu had built up around previous research projects on religion in northern Nigeria. An early version of that research was presented to the Office of the National Security Adviser in 2015, and has fed into the development of society-focused approaches in Nigeria's policies for countering violent extremism.

While this was the end of the project, it was just the beginning of the book. Using the initial fieldwork conducted at the height of the Boko Haram insurgency, Raufu embarked on the task of turning a policy-focused research report into a deeper analysis of Islamic radicalization and counter-radicalization. The objective was a book that would build on two preceding edited collections on religious conflict in northern Nigeria, both also published by James Currey. The first in the series, *Sects and Social Disorder* published in 2014, focuses on intra-religious conflict among Muslims in the period before Boko Haram. The second book, *Creed and Grievance* published in 2018, explores Muslim-Christian conflict in northern Nigeria. But the completion of this third book was interrupted by Raufu's unexpected illness and death in 2017. When I contacted Sani Umar about taking up the project a year later, other academic commitments had altered the equation, but all of the contributors rallied to the task, making time in overstretched academic and research lives to undertake extensive updating, revisions and where necessary additional field research. I am extremely grateful for their patience and support in completing this work.

Indeed, there are many to thank for bringing this book together. On behalf of Raufu and myself, I would like to express my gratitude to Dr Fatima Akilu, a former Director in the Office of the National Security Adviser and now Executive Director of the Neem Foundation, to Dr Ukoha Ukiwo formerly of the NSRP, who oversaw the original project, and to DfID for funding the core research. I am also grateful to Dr Yahaya Hashim and Dr Judith Walker of the Development Research and Projects Centre (dRPC), long-time friends and collaborators who organized the logistics of the project as well as contributing to the research themselves, and who extended their hospitality to me and to Raufu on multiple occasions during research periods in Kano and Abuja. Special thanks also go to our dear friends Judge Patricia Mahmoud and Alh. A.B. Mahmoud (SAN), and to Comrade Issa Aremu and the late Biodun Aremu, all of whom offered both Raufu and me a safe haven, wise advice and invaluable contacts during tense fieldwork in Kano, Kaduna and Abuja.

In the field, particular thanks are due to the many research assistants and organizations, too numerous to mention by name, who supported the risky field research that forms the core of this book, facilitating connections, translating, administering questionnaires and helping some of us to blend in in markets and public places. Particular thanks are owed to the even greater number of professionals, officials and ordinary people in the north who faced these threatening conditions on a daily basis but took the time to share their experiences with us. I am also grateful to those who read chapters and offered valuable suggestions, including David Keen, Murray Last, Kole Shettima and the volume's two reviewers. Sincere appreciation is also due to the Oxford Poverty and Human Development Initiative (OPHI), Queen Elizabeth House, Oxford University, for producing and retrieving the poverty graphs, to Chatham House and the University of Maiduguri for kindly providing detailed maps, to the Oxford Department of International Development for many kindnesses and for continuing to host the Nigerian Research Networks on their website, and to all who helped in the quest for a cover photo. I must also express my thanks to the publishers, particularly Jaqueline Mitchell and Lynn Taylor of James Currey, who revived a publishing commitment that had all but lapsed, and weathered delays and multiple versions of titles and cover photos to bring this book to press. Finally, I must thank our children, Asma'u and Seyi, and the wider Mustapha family, who have offered encouragement and prayers during the long process of reading, editing, writing and rewriting.

In the end, this book has been as much a labour of love as a work of scholarship. For me, it was an opportunity to help Raufu finish his crowning piece of research on religion and identity in Nigeria into which he had poured decades of accumulated knowledge and experience. It also allowed me to deepen my own understanding of how religion and inequality shape political and economic struggles in the part of Nigeria that was our home for many years. As I worked, the bitter-sweet process of gathering the files from Raufu's computer, sifting through his earlier work, reading over his handwritten field notes, and remembering myriad thoughtful conversations has made the writing feel like a chance to do one last thing together.

For Raufu, and for many of us, this book is also a clarion call for Nigeria. The rise of Boko Haram disturbed Raufu deeply, as a Nigerian and as a Muslim. He told me that it was the first thing that had ever shaken his faith in the ability of Nigeria to survive as a country. Confronting the tendency to blame one region or one religious group, this book argues for a whole-of-society approach to what is fundamentally a whole-of-society problem of regional inequality, elite corruption and military excesses. National and international economic and political recklessness have done untold damage to what still remains a formidable national fabric, fashioned from more than a century of interweaving religious and ethnic populations through trade, migration, production, education, professional service, intermarriage and political identity. As a Yoruba Muslim born in the south-east, trained in the north and buried in Ilorin, Raufu belonged to the whole of Nigeria, and he was acutely aware that what tears Nigeria apart, tears every Nigerian apart. Boko Haram has given Nigeria a glimpse into the abyss, but the complexity and resilience of Nigerian society still holds out the chance to step back from the brink.

Kate Meagher
Eid, 11 August 2019

List of Abbreviations

AFSF	Armed Forces Special Forces
AIN	Association Islamique du Niger
AOR	Area of Responsibility
APC	All Progressives Congress (Nigerian political party)
AQIM	Al-Qaeda in the Islamic Maghreb
BOYES	Borno State Youth Empowerment Scheme
CDS	Chief of Defence Staff
CJTF	Citizens Joint Task Force
CMS	Church Missionary Society
COIN	Counter-insurgency operations
DCMA	Directorate of Civil Military Affairs
DSS	Department of State Services
EEN	Eglise Evangélique du Niger (The Evangelical Church of Niger)
ICC	International Criminal Court
IDP	Internally displaced persons
IED	Improvized explosive device
IFRA	Institut français de recherche en Afrique (French Institute for Research in Africa)
IRA	Irish Republican Army
IS (ISIS)	Islamic State (Islamic State of Iraq and Syria)
ISO	Internal security operation
ISWAP	Islamic State West Africa Province (or Islamic State in West Africa)
JTF	Joint Task Force
LGA	Local Government Area
LRA	Lord's Resistance Army
MACA	Military Aid to Civil Authority
MACP	Military Aid to Civil Power
MCCC	Military Command and Control Centre
MIA	Missing in action
MNJTF	Multinational Joint Task Force
NAF	Nigeria Air Force
NPF	Nigeria Police Force

NSCDC	Nigerian Security and Civil Defence Corps
NTA	Nigerian Television Authority
ORBAT	Order of battle
STTEP	Specialized Tasks, Training, Equipment and Protection International Ltd
TRADOC	Training and Doctrine Command
UN	United Nations
UNDP	United Nations Development Programme
UNICEF	United Nations Children's Fund

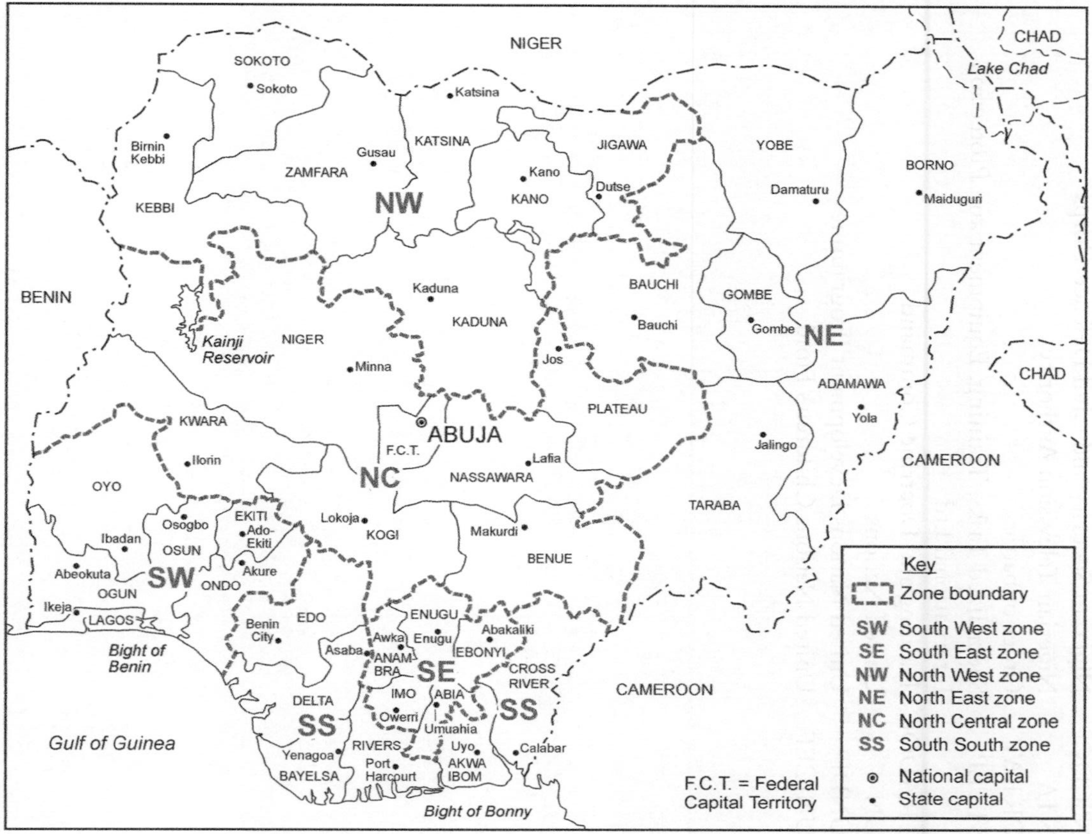

Map: Nigeria zones

(reproduced courtesy of Chatham House, The Royal Institute of International Affairs, London, from Africa Programme Research Paper 'Who Speaks for the North? Politics and Influence in Northern Nigeria', Leena Koni Hoffman, July 2014)

1

Introduction
Faith, society & Boko Haram

KATE MEAGHER & ABDUL RAUFU MUSTAPHA

Introduction

It is now a decade since the violent Islamic group popularly known as Boko Haram[1] launched its reign of terror in northern Nigeria. While Boko Haram's considerable territorial acquisitions in the North East have largely been recaptured, the insurgency still rages on. To date, Boko Haram has claimed more than 27,000 lives, displaced some 2 million people, and has cost the Nigerian economy an estimated $17 billion in infrastructural damage and output losses – not to mention the apocalyptic devastation it has wrought across vast swaths of north-eastern Nigeria, and the traumatized communities it has left behind (Munshi 2018a, 2018b; *Reuters* 2018; Thurston 2018; Masha et al. 2016). The group rose to international attention for the kidnapping of 276 school girls in the north-eastern town of Chibok, but Boko Haram is most infamous for its extreme brutality. In 2015, the Global Terrorism Index (2015, 2) declared Boko Haram 'the most deadly terrorist group in the world', and still classifies it among the four most violent terrorist groups (Global Terrorism Index 2018).

Emerging from a radical Salafist movement in the distant north-eastern Nigerian city of Maiduguri, Boko Haram was galvanized by a violent confrontation with the Nigerian State in July 2009 in which over 700 members died and their leader, Mohammed Yusuf, was killed in police custody. One year later, in July 2010, Boko Haram returned as a full-blown terrorist group under the choleric leadership of Abubakar Shekau. A shocked country witnessed this band of extremists evolve from hit-and-run operations such as suicide bombings, kidnapping and clan-

[1] Boko Haram is a Hausa term that translates as 'Western education is forbidden'. This is the popular and best-known epithet for the group, which calls itself *Jama'atul Ahlul Sunna li Da'wati wal Jihad* ('People Committed to the Propagation of the Prophet's Teachings and Jihad').

destine attacks on state buildings, into a complex insurgency deploying heavy weapons, armoured personnel carriers, technicals, and drones. By 2015, the insurgency had succeeded in capturing a territory the size of Belgium, and declared an independent Islamic caliphate in the north-eastern corner of Nigeria, as well as pledging allegiance to Al-Qaeda and later to Islamic State (Munshi 2018a; Thurston 2018).

Over the years, Boko Haram has proven as resilient as it is destructive. Following a concerted military offensive, President Muhammadu Buhari declared in December 2015 that Nigeria had 'technically won the war' against Boko Haram (BBC 2015). Unfortunately, this announcement proved premature. In 2018 alone, Boko Haram abducted over 300 people, including 110 school girls from the town of Dapchi in Adamawa State, and conducted scores of raids on towns and military bases in Borno State, leading to the death of some 1,200 people (*The Defense Post* 2018; Maclean and Alfa 2019; Human Rights Watch 2019, 1). Internal divisions, giving rise to the breakaway faction known as Islamic State West Africa Province (ISWAP) in 2016, have not caused the group to unravel. In fact, ISWAP seems to have given the group renewed energy for a spate of lethal attacks in the run-up to the 2019 Presidential elections (Munshi 2018a; Durmaz 2019). In January 2019, President Buhari once again assured supporters that Boko Haram had been 'fully decimated' (Maclean and Alfa 2019). Yet the insurgency continues to disrupt governance, livelihoods and food security across the north-east of Nigeria, as well as posing a nagging risk to security in neighbouring Niger, Chad and Cameroon (Thurston 2018, 291–2; Famine Early Warning Systems Network 2019).

But this tale of carnage is only one side of the story of Islamic extremism in Nigeria. The violence and chaos tend to obscure the more pervasive reality of religious co-existence and resistance to radicalization across the Muslim majority area of northern Nigeria. The sometimes erratic counter-insurgency and counter-radicalization initiatives of the Nigerian state rest on a deeper foundation of popular norms of religious tolerance, social cohesion, and resistance to extremism. These deep social foundations are not just a basis for generalized Islamic quiescence, but have given rise to numerous counter-radicalization initiatives from within northern Nigerian society – what Sanda (Chapter 5, this volume) refers to as a Polanyian 'double movement' in response to the ravages of violent radicalization. A growing number of political and social support movements have emerged around the conflict. These range from local organizations supporting youth education and widows' welfare to northern women's involvement in the Bring Back Our Girls movement, all operating alongside numerous northern Nigerian nurses, relief workers and journalists risking their lives in the fight against Islamic extremism (Usman, Taraboulsi and Hawaja, Chapter 7 this volume). There are also numerous stories of Muslims turning out to guard churches in the wake of Boko Haram bombings, in Kano, Kaduna and other northern Nigerian cities (Lodge 2014; Habib 2012).

In the heartland of Boko Haram, the Civilian Joint Task Force (CJTF) and other local groups, made up of men and women from the area, have played an essential role in the struggle against Boko Haram, many working without pay and without weapons to gather intelligence or conduct body searches in public places (Okeowo 2015; Collyer 2017; International Crisis Group 2017). Even the armed members often have only make-shift weapons. Serving as a less-than-ideal force in a desperate situation, the CJTF alongside local hunters and community vigilante groups have risked their lives to drive Boko Haram out of Maiduguri and other, less well-protected north-eastern towns such as Bama and Gubio. The vast majority in northern Nigeria are not attracted to the message or to the ranks of violent extremists. Religious attitude surveys by the Pew Foundation have shown that in 2014, 80 per cent of Nigerian Muslims had a negative view of Boko Haram (Pew Research Centre 2014). A subsequent survey in 2016 showed that such negative views of Boko Haram have increased to 94 per cent among Muslims, alongside 93 per cent among Christians (Pew Research Centre 2016).

In a context of pervasive resistance to radical extremism, how could northern Nigerian society have unravelled so violently? This book looks beyond the analysis of the Boko Haram insurgency to examine the wider social and political processes that explain why Boko Haram emerged when and where it did, and what levers exist within society to contain it. While the profusion of literature on Boko Haram has understandably been preoccupied with piecing together the details and causes of the insurgency (Mustapha 2014; Pérouse de Montclos 2014; Comolli 2015; Matfess 2017; Thurston 2018), or the motives and ideologies of Boko Haram fighters and supporters (Kassim and Nwankpa 2018; Thurston 2016; Mercy Corps 2016), this book focuses attention on the wider processes that explain how a diverse and economically dynamic West African society could have degenerated into violent extremism. Based on the detailed fieldwork by specialist Nigerian and Nigerianist scholars connecting the worst of Boko Haram violence to the wider realities of the present, the material presented here offers new insights into the drivers of Islamic extremism in Nigeria, with a view to charting more sustainable paths out of it.

With a view to confronting the realities of violent Islamic radicalization in northern Nigeria, this book will make three broad arguments. First, Islamic radicalization in Nigeria is not just about global terrorist ideologies or religious doctrine. It is a product of complex political and economic contradictions that arose in the interface of colonial legacies, market reforms, regional inequality and social protest. While foreign Islamic movements have played a limited role, Boko Haram is first and foremost a home-grown extremist movement and a political as much as a religious phenomenon. Serious responses to the Boko Haram insurgency require a Gestalt shift away from models of global terrorism toward alternative frameworks of Islamic populism, reflecting responses to extreme inequality and disaffection currently emerging in many other parts of the world (Hadiz 2018). Second, Islamic radicalization is not just about jihadis. Understanding Boko Haram must look beyond terrorist movements and the motivations of their members, to the wider societal processes and pressures that led to the rise of Boko Haram when and where it emerged. This involves a focus on societal counterforces as well as pathways, and calls for a comparative approach to explain why violent extremism erupted in north-eastern Nigeria rather than in surrounding Muslim majority areas which have remained relatively peaceful. Third, this book will argue that economic causes of Islamic radicalization are not just about individual poverty. Attendant dimensions of inequality, lack of opportunity, spiritual angst, and a thirst for alternative futures can transform regional material deprivation into violent revolutionary zeal, even among those who are not themselves poor.

This introductory chapter situates the book within wider discussions of Islamic extremism in Nigeria and in Africa more broadly, as well as laying out important background for the succeeding chapters. It will turn first to an examination of the concept of radicalization, and outline the distinctive approach to the issue taken by this book. A second section will highlight key historical pressures on northern Nigerian Muslim society. This will be followed by a third section on the role of Salafist ideologies in stimulating more extreme modes of religious expression and political engagement. A fourth section will focus on the role of poverty and inequality in intensifying a sense of grievance among northern Nigerian Muslims, especially in the North East, fostering new radical imaginaries. The exacerbating tendencies of the Nigerian state will be examined in the fifth section, particularly the state's role as an additional source of grievance and violence, and its endemic failure to contain extremist tendencies. A final section will present the structure of the volume.

Radicalization in Political and Social Context

Current thinking about Islamic radicalization tends to attribute religious violence to the nature of Islamic societies. Notions of the 'clash of civilizations', and assumptions about inherent tensions between Islam and modernity have encouraged the view that globalization and democratization trigger violent responses in Muslim populations (Huntingdon 1996). In the process, there has been a blurring of boundaries between religious and political action among Muslims, and between Islamic radicalization and Islamic terrorism (Borum 2011a, 2011b; Brown and Saeed 2015; Idrissa 2017b). Central to this book is a recognition that Islamic radicalization is a political rather than a religious phenomenon (Idrissa 2017b, vii; Mamdani 2005). Islamic radicalization involves the adoption of extreme views centred on the alignment of society and the state to strict Islamic practice through political action (Idrissa 2017b, vii). This process is not necessarily violent, and can operate through political pressure groups, educational networks, or electoral processes, as is evident in the activities of the Muslim Brotherhood in Egypt since the 1970s, or Salafist groups in Senegal and Niger (Hamzawy and Gebrowski 2010; Idrissa 2017b; Thurston 2009). For the purposes of this book, however, the term 'radicalization' will often be used as a shorthand for violent radicalization unless otherwise specified, since we are focusing on contexts that have already taken a violent turn.

In the context of terrorism, security studies specialist, Peter Neumann (2008, 4), defines radicalization as 'what goes on before the bomb goes off'. While this shifts attention from terrorist events to underlying causes, such definitions tend to focus unduly on individuals we suspect are likely to become involved in terrorism. This obscures the role of a wider spectrum of factors, including economic inequality or state-society tensions that may create the basis for radicalization without necessarily turning people into terrorists. Schmid (2013, iv) highlights the need to 'look for roots of radicalisation beyond this micro-level and include a focus on the meso-level – the radical milieu – and the macro-level – the radicalisation of public opinion and party politics – to gain a better understanding of the dynamic processes driving escalation'. In the process, the focus is shifted from the destructive behaviour of radicalized individuals, to the social damage that has already occurred before radicalization gathers pace. This wider lens into radicalization considers pre-existing social tensions, group-level deprivation and inequality, and political polarization, which lay the foundation for the radical reimagining of new pathways to justice and social dignity, and processes of othering that rationalize violent aggression (see Ehrhardt and Umar, Chapter 6 this volume; Schmid 2013; Moghaddam 2005).

This book will adopt a wide social and political perspective on Islamic radicalization in northern Nigeria, starting not from the motivations of jihadis, but from the society that produced them, and produced others who did not turn to violence. The dynamics of non-violent responses, from individuals and groups in the same milieu, and from those in nearby Muslim majority areas subject to similar influences, is equally important to understanding processes of radicalization and counter-radicalization. Why did violent Islamic radicalism erupt in northern Nigeria, while having virtually no purchase on Muslim majority areas in south-western

Nigeria (Soares 2009; Mustapha 2018)? Why did Boko Haram emerge in the peripheral Nigerian state of Borno, rather than in similarly poor and jobless centres of Salafist radicalism such as Kano, or in the even poorer and more marginalized Muslim region of central Niger just across the border?

Answering these questions requires a comparative approach alongside the macro-social and political lens, to highlight the specific features of other Muslim groups and countries subject to similar economic and political pressures, but capable of generating different, non-violent responses. As Idrissa (2017b) shows in his masterly book, *The Politics of Islam in the Sahel*, Burkina Faso, Senegal and Niger face similar conditions of poverty, high youth unemployment, and the penetration of radical Salafist ideologies to those prevailing in northern Nigeria. Yet these conditions have not sparked uncontrollable violence or serious challenges to the secular state. Indeed encounters with Islamic radicalism have so far failed to shake Senegal's 'Muslim social contract' based on stable democracy, tolerance and religious pluralism (Diouf 2013; Thurston 2009), while Islam in Burkina Faso continues to be characterized as a 'quiet' Islam (Otayek 1996; Gomez-Perez 2017; Idrissa 2017a). The ability of Niger to manage radicalizing forces from across its southern border is presented below in the contribution by Idrissa (this volume).

Recently, however, extremist violence in northern as well as southern Niger, and a rise in attacks by largely external jihadi groups along the northern border of Burkina Faso, is calling peaceful religious social contracts into question. Regional jihadi movements are seeking out a toehold in peaceful Muslim majority countries of the Sahel, in some cases developing fringe national Islamist cadres, while others co-opt local struggles against poverty and corruption in neglected regions (Ibrahim 2019; BBC 2019; *The Economist* 2 May 2019). Yet, as observed by Idrissa (personal communication 20 July 2019), in the heartlands of Niger and Burkina Faso, popular responses to Islamist pressures are leaning in the opposite direction. A surge of 'anti-jihadist nationalism' in Niger, and Muslim-led insistence on state secularism in Burkina Faso, are mobilizing local Muslim sensibilities against rather than in favour of fundamentalist Islam, perceived as an external attack on 'our' soldiers and sovereignty (see also Idrissa 2017b; Mueller 2016). Effective responses to extremist challenges in West Africa require a clearer understanding of the divergent responses of West African Muslim societies to violent radicalization, alongside greater attention to unbearable political and economic pressures and breaking points.

Similarly, the ongoing chaos of Boko Haram also raises new questions about the wider implications of Islamic extremism across Sub-Saharan Africa. Conventional characterizations of African Islam as peaceful and tolerant have been shaken in East as well as West Africa by the rise of less tolerant and more politically activist Salafist ideologies, and by ongoing Islamic insurgencies in other parts of the continent, most notably Somalia (Soares and Otayek 2007). With nine Muslim majority countries in West Africa, a further five in Eastern and Southern Africa, and significant Muslim populations in Benin, Cameroon, Côte d'Ivoire, Eritrea, Ethiopia, Ghana, Guinea Bissau, Kenya, Madagascar, Mauritius, Mozambique, Nigeria, South Sudan, Togo and Uganda, understanding the susceptibility of African societies to violent radicalization is of the essence (US Department of State 2018). By 2050, Sub-Saharan Africa is projected to have a larger share of the global Muslim population than the Middle East and North Africa combined (Desilver and Masci 2017). Comparative analysis provides a basis for more-informed assessment of the vulnerability and resilience of Muslim societies across Africa. Should attention to the risk of contagion from foreign jihadi groups give way to a stronger focus on internal threats of radical revolt in the face of unsustainable political and economic pressures, or a consideration of the factors that perpetuate peaceful political settlements in Muslim societies? Do differences in history and the nature of the state in various parts of Africa influence the ability of violent radicalism to take root? What kinds of historical and social tendencies enhance the resilience of the Muslim majority to extremist influences even in contexts of active radical uprisings?

In addition to considering how to avert violent radicalization, comparative approaches can also be helpful in assessing how to bring violent insurgencies to an end. Religious radicalization is not only about Islam, and has a long history outside as well as inside Africa. Chapter 10 by Umar and Ehrhardt examines divergent trajectories of religious insurgencies in Egypt, Uganda and Northern Ireland to assess the risk factors and outcomes that could be used to evaluate the endgame of the Boko Haram insurgency. A comparative approach to the Boko Haram insurgency contributes to a more nuanced understanding of the risks, resilience and resolution of violent radicalization in Africa and beyond. Using a comparative, 'whole-of-society' approach, this book casts new light on what the eruption of Boko Haram can tell us about the prospects and the limits of social cohesion and political stability in Islamic Africa, and what other religious insurgencies can tell us about the future trajectory of Boko Haram.

Historical Factors

Situating the rise of Boko Haram historically requires a gestalt shift from tracing histories of Islamic violence to tracing histories of violent political action and social protest in an Islamic society. Many current studies of

Boko Haram merge all religious conflict in northern Nigeria into a seamless jihadist tendency beginning from the jihad of Usman 'Dan Fodio, and running through the millenarian revolts of early colonialism, the Maitatsine riots of the 1980s, and religious clashes over the imposition of Sharia law from 1999. Virginia Comolli (2015, 42) refers to the 'almost cyclical nature of extremist Islamic group formation in northern Nigeria', while John Peel (2015) attributes the rise of Boko Haram to 'a jihadist tradition [that] has contributed to a pattern of endemic religious violence'. Even in the donor community, the UNDP's National Human Development Report 2018 (2018a, 15) on north-eastern Nigeria contends that 'the very emergence of Boko Haram reflects a long history of the militant type of the [*sic*] Islamic religion in northern Nigeria'.

What is missing from these historical reconstructions is a recognition of the political character of what is viewed as religious violence, embedded not in norms of religious extremism, but in wider norms of justice, political manoeuvring and social protest expressed in the institutional lexicon of an Islamic society. Islamization in the region dates back centuries, since the 11th century in the Kanuri-dominated region of what is now north-eastern Nigeria, and from the 15th century in the Hausa-Fulani majority regions of the north west. As Idrissa (2017b, 196) points out, by the mid-19th century the area that is now northern Nigeria was the most Islamized part of the West African Sudan. In other parts of Islamic West Africa, the penetration of Islamic norms and institutional systems into local identities was more uneven in pre-colonial times. In northern Nigeria, however, Islam was embedded in the pre-colonial states and societies of the Sokoto and Bornu Caliphates, both in cultural norms and in highly developed institutional systems of Islamic law, education, taxation, trade, record-keeping and active linkages with the wider Islamic world (Mustapha 2014; Meagher 2018).

After the colonial conquest in 1904, Islamic institutions of governance and education were preserved under the policies of indirect rule. This shielded the colony of Northern Nigeria from Christian missionary influence and Western education and maintained the Sharia court system. Just before Nigerian independence, oriental law specialist J.N.D. Anderson (1957) noted that there was nowhere outside Arabia that Islamic law was more pervasive than in Northern Nigeria. This underpinned a shared allegiance across Northern Nigeria to Islamic institutions of governance, and a common resentment against what Wakili (2009, 2) refers to as 'British tampering with the application of Sharia through the so-called colonial reforms of the judiciary', matched by a similar resentment against Western educational norms that denigrated the educational systems and extensive Arabic literacy of northern Nigerian scholars and government functionaries (Wakili 2009; Mohammed 2018; Mustapha and Gamawa 2018).

With the advent of decolonization, northern Nigeria was marked by educational, social and economic disadvantages. At independence, the north constituted some 30 per cent of the population, but had less than 10 per cent of primary school enrolment and only 2.5 per cent of secondary school enrolment, and southern Nigerians dominated most government institutions (Sanusi 2007, 181; Mustapha 2018, 20). A 'Northernization' process (see Kwanashie 2002) was implemented to build a northern united front against a perceived threat of domination from better-educated southern Nigerians. At the same time, legal and constitutional reforms of the post-independence state continued to bowdlerize Sharia law, removing criminal law from the jurisdiction of Sharia courts, and subordinating Sharia courts to Western courts of appeal at the federal level, stoking a sense of bitterness among many northerners (Mustapha and Gamawa 2018; Mohammed 2018; Wakili 2009).

The relevance of this history is twofold. First, northern Nigeria's 'reversal of fortunes' was not about the triumph of 'good' over 'bad' institutions (Acemoglu et al. 2002; Archibong 2018). It was the uprooting of northern Nigeria from the Islamic geopolitical sphere, and its incorporation into an institutionally divergent Western sphere, not the poor quality of its institutions, that translated into economic disadvantage in modern times. This nurtured a pervasive sense of resentment and marginalization among northern Nigerians in the face of competitive disadvantages relative to southern Nigerians, whose longer encounter with Western education and government institutions gave them a considerable edge in the struggle for jobs, resources and official positions. Second, this history highlights the fusion of Islamic identity with ethnic and political identity among the Hausa-Fulani and Kanuri ethnic groups after centuries of embeddedness in increasingly Islamic state systems (Sanusi 2007). In this context, Islam is not just a form of religious expression in northern Nigeria; it is a central idiom of identity and political expression, particularly among those with little Western education.

This historical context opens the way for a more politically informed understanding of Islamic extremism in northern Nigeria, in particular the recognition that not all Islamic violence is the same (Mustapha 2014, 200). Far from representing an embedded tradition of jihadism, Islamic violence in northern Nigeria is simply political violence in a largely Muslim society, expressing a range of different political meanings from revolution to elite struggles over power to inarticulate social protest. Casting these as an embedded tradition of Islamic violence makes no more sense than linking together the anti-monarchist French Revolution, the more monarchist July Revolution of 1830 and the populist '*gilet jaune*' movement as reflecting a continuous French tradition of 'secular violence'.

Notions of embedded jihadism also conceal important shifts in the nature of Islamic violence in recent decades: the shift from inter-religious or sectarian clashes and struggles over control of the state instigated by Muslim political and scholarly elites, to the rise of violent popular protests led by youth, migrants and the poor since 1980. While the Maitatsine riots of the early 1980s expressed the fury of the poor and marginalized though indiscriminate violence against society and symbols of modernization, clashes involving radical educated youth linked to the Nigerian Shi'ite movement called for direct violence against the state for its corruption and failure to respond to the needs of the people. What is most disturbing about these increasingly furious modes of social protest is not their Islamic character, but the entry of random violence against fellow Muslims and violence targeted at the state into the northern Nigerian lexicon of political violence. Conversely, recognizing the objectives and social origins of Islamic violence clarifies why certain segments of society become involved, while failing to mobilize the bulk of northern Nigerian society.

The Role of Salafism

In contrast to those who see Boko Haram as a product of embedded traditions of Islamic violence, others link violent radicalization in Nigeria to the intrusion of more radical Islamic ideologies from Iran and Saudi Arabia into the pacifist, tolerant terrain of West African Islam (Lubeck 2011; Soares and Otayek 2007). There is a general recognition that links with global jihadi groups were not significant in the radicalization of Boko Haram. While there is some evidence of a few recruits training with Al Shabaab and AQIM (Al-Qaeda in the Islamic Maghreb), and claims of membership in Al-Qaeda and ISIS, these are largely viewed as desirable accessories to Boko Haram's terrorist image, while bringing in little in the way of resources, weapons or ideological formation (Comolli 2015; Thurston 2018). Attention has focused instead on conservative Salafi ideologies that have filtered into Nigeria from students and scholars studying in Saudi Arabia, and Saudi outreach to spread Salafist doctrines (Thurston 2016, 62). While belonging to the same Sunni fold as traditional Sufi and other mainstream forms of West African Islam, contemporary Salafism represents a more fundamentalist strain of Sunni Islam that blends literal interpretations of Islamic scripture with a rejection of Islamic legal schools, and a focus on purity of Islamic practice and creed as set down in the Qur'an and Hadith (Thurston 2016, 62). Modern day Salafism is strongly opposed to Sufism and other African deviations from original Islamic practice.

The role of Salafism in the rise of Boko Haram is contentious. While Boko Haram is widely recognized as an extreme form of Salafism, modern

Salafi ideologies have played an active role in the northern Nigerian Islamic scene for over half a century without leading to terrorism (Mustapha 2014; Woodward et al. 2013; Thurston 2016). The popular religious movement, *Jama'atu Izalatul Bidi'a wa Iqamat al-Sunna* (Society for the Eradication of Innovation and the Reinstatement of Tradition), widely known as Izala, promotes a Wahhabi variant of Salafism (which retains adherence to Islamic legal traditions) and has been a major force in northern Nigeria since the late 1970s (Thurston 2016, 61; Umar 1993). Many contemporary Salafists reject all Islamic legal schools, adopting the name *Ahl al-Sunna* to distinguish themselves from Izala (Thurston 2016, 66, 93; Lubeck 2011). Neither of these movements has been associated with terrorism.

Yet, the radicalizing potential of Salafism remains a subject of debate. Thurston's (2016, 241) illuminating book, *Salafism in Nigeria*, challenges the idea of Salafism as inherently radicalizing, arguing that it is a socially engaged religious ideology, not a form of extremism. He points out that it was the non-radical tendencies of Salafism that made it appealing to Saudi rulers in the first place as they confronted Islamist challenges in the 1990s. Prominent Nigerian Salafis were active critics of Boko Haram and 'rejected the idea of revolt against Muslim rulers and anathemizing and killing Muslim civilians' (ibid., 62). Thurston and others also note the modernizing, rational individualist, socially progressive aspects of Salafism (Kane 2003; Soares and Otayek 2007, 19; Umar 1993). Nigerian Salafi activists combine Western and Islamic subjects in Islamiyya schools, promoting education and encouraging Muslim engagement in government service. Salafism also actively supports the education and public role of women, as discussed in the chapter by Usman et al. (this volume). The pro-education and pro-state stance of Salafis runs counter to the main tenets of Boko Haram.

In the process, Salafism offers an 'alternative modernity' that has allowed the less advantaged to navigate the environment of institutional disadvantage and neo-liberal market reforms. Particularly among members of the struggling commercial and middle classes, or migrants from lowly backgrounds, Salafi ideologies have offered new channels of survival and social mobility (Meagher 2009; Kane 2003; Thurston 2016). Austere Salafi practices liberated the less advantaged from costly marriage and other ceremonial expenditures, while new Salafi credentials of Islamic learning opened alternative avenues into the northern establishment. For such people, Salafism provided a modern, competitive 'conception of religion that is socially and ethically compatible with the neo-liberal economy' (Soares and Otayek 2007, 19). Thurston (2016, 2018, 13) argues that violent radicalization was a deviation from Salafi teachings in a context of 'backroom deals, impunity and state violence', exacerbated by exposure to foreign jihadi texts.

Conversely, Idrissa (2017b, vii) and Woodward et al. (2013, 64) contend that, except as a source of personal religious guidance, Salafism is inherently political and inherently radicalizing in the West African context, owing to its confrontational approach to the established religious and political orthodoxy. 'Salafi radicalism … is a political ideology … which, just like conservatism, liberalism and socialism, takes its meaning from temporal or secular struggles for the control of state power, not from a religious quest for eternal truths and for the adoration of God'. While Salafism may have been quietist in Saudi Arabia and other countries with Islamic systems of governance, it became a radicalizing influence when transplanted into a religiously diverse society with a secular state. As Lubeck (2011, 246) points out, problems are created 'when scriptural legal movements travel through global networks and are applied by reformers living in large complex societies, like those of northern Nigeria'.

Salafism did not import violent extremism into Nigeria, but it inflamed existing religious and political tensions. Excesses among ardent Salafi activists, such as intolerance against other Muslim sects as well as Christians, and aggressive struggles to control mosques, educational institutions and state bureaucracies, introduced an alarming climate of violence well before the rise of Boko Haram. What Thurston (2016, 157) describes as Salafi efforts to promote religious 'debate', involved vitriolic public preaching styles in a religiously polarized and volatile environment (Kane 2003; Mustapha 2014; Umar 1993). An erosion of civility in religious debate was matched by aggressive action by Salafi activists against members of other sects to drive them from mosques, or forcefully disrupt their efforts to engage in non-Salafi Muslim rituals such as Maulid or *wazifa* (Mustapha 2014; Kane 2003; Mustapha 2015). Salafi capture of key positions in a number of higher education institutions in Kano, Kaduna and Katsina, and a growing presence in state bureaucracies, involved political aggression accompanied by efforts to suppress other forms of Islamic practice by denying permits for Sufi or Shi'ite events or preventing them from preaching (Mustapha 2015; Umar 1993). Casey (2008) notes the use of violence in enforcing Sharia-mandated norms of dress and behaviour, largely inflicted on migrants, women and Christians through such actions as smashing consignments of beer, burning drinking places and attacking women deemed inappropriately dressed.

Efforts to 'bring politics back in' (Thurston 2018, 302) to the understanding of Boko Haram require a closer look at those on the losing side of Salafi reformism in Nigeria. While Salafism provided valuable support for spiritual and social welfare needs as well as channels to social mobility for many struggling with the pressures of corruption and economic reforms, it subjected others to yet another form of physical and structural violence. Blaming the turn to violent radicalization on external links to jihadi doctrines or Khawarij heresies ignores the role of the Salafist turn in stoking social violence from within Nigeria. Salafism was not a source of Islamic extremism, but it became an important catalyst in the northern Nigerian context, as detailed in a number of contributions in this book (see Umar, Meagher and Hassan, and Monguno and Umara).

Poverty, Inequality and Radical Imaginaries

The contention that poverty is not an important factor in the rise of Boko Haram is surprisingly widespread. In an interview with the *Sunday Trust* (Abbah and Odunlami 2013), Alhaji Tanimu Turaki, Minister of Special Duties and Chairman of the Presidential Committee for Dialogue with Boko Haram, argued that in contrast to the importance of economic grievances in the Niger Delta insurgency, Boko Haram insurgents hinged their agitation on 'ideology based first on rejecting Western education and anything that comes with it ... There is nothing economic about their agitation.' Similarly, prominent personalities such as Nobel Laureate Wole Soyinka and former Nigerian President Jonathan, and a number of major books and studies on Boko Haram dismiss the notion of poverty as a central cause of violent radicalization in northern Nigeria. While some claim that poverty is not causally significant because the membership of Boko Haram was not restricted to the poor (Comolli 2015; Mercy Corps 2016), others contend that many of the poor did not join Boko Haram (Thurston 2018, 31), or that poverty was not mentioned in Boko Haram discourse (Kassim and Nwankpa 2018, 4).

This book challenges the assertion that poverty is not central to violent Islamic radicalization in Nigeria. It argues that poverty is not just about individual deprivation, but involves a sense of group marginalization amid pervasive economic exclusion and economic inequality (Sanusi 2007; Mustapha 2014; Meagher 2015; Pérouse de Montclos 2014). Similarly, it is not just radical discourse, but poverty and a sense of economic injustice that gives popular resonance to violent religious ideologies. A focus on macro-economic patterns of poverty and inequality across Nigeria, and on social contexts of deprivation, grievance and imagined futures, provide a very different picture of the role of poverty in Islamic radicalization.

Macro-economic data on regional patterns of poverty and deprivation in Nigeria tend to support the contention that poverty is an important driver of radicalization. Table 1.1 shows patterns of poverty, education and literacy across the six geopolitical zones of Nigeria in 2010, the year that Boko Haram began its reign of terror. Even before the insurgency began to take its toll, absolute poverty levels in the Muslim majority states of the North East and the North West averaged 70 per cent, 40 per cent

Table 1.1 Indicators of socio-economic deprivation in Nigeria by zone, 2010

Zone	Absolute poverty	No schooling	Adult literacy	Unemployment
North East	69.0	63.7	23.0	31.9
North West	70.0	63.8	21.6	28.8
North Central	59.5	36.8	47.0	28.8
South East	58.7	14.4	81.8	19.6
South West	49.8	17.2	79.8	11.4
South South	55.9	10.7	77.1	24.6

(Source: NPC DHS Education Data Survey 2010; NBS Poverty Profile 2010; NBS Annual Socio-Economic Report 2011)

higher than in the South West zone (NBS 2010, 5). Levels of adult literacy hovered around 80 per cent in the three of southern zones of Nigeria, while averaging barely 22 per cent in the two zones of the far north. An alarming 64 per cent of the population in the far north had no Western education, compared to less than 15 per cent of people across the three southern zones (National Population Commission 2011, 13, 16). Unemployment figures for the states of the North East and North West stood at 30 per cent, while those of the southern zones averaged only 18 per cent. While the North West appears marginally poorer than the North East epicentre of Islamic extremism, illiteracy and unemployment were higher in the North East at the onset of the Boko Haram insurgency.

A recent study by Belinda Archibong (2018, 333) using longitudinal Demographic and Health Survey (DHS) data from 2003–2013, shows that the North East has suffered from the highest levels of deprivation of all of Nigeria's geopolitical zones in access to infrastructure, sanitation, power and water. More recent data paints an even more dismal picture. The UNDP's (2018a, 24) *National Human Development Report for North-Eastern Nigeria* highlights the stark contrast between the Human Development Index (HDI) in northern and southern Nigeria. The HDI for the high-performing South West zone, home of the Lagos miracle, is .536 which is higher than the national average. By contrast, the HDI for the North East zone is .378, and .348 for the North West. To put this in perspective, the HDI for Lagos State in the South West is comparable to that of India, while the HDI for Borno and Yobe States in the North East is lower than Afghanistan (UNDP 2018b).

Deeper analysis of poverty data offers a more detailed story about why Boko Haram emerged where it did. If poverty is an important factor, why has violent insurgency gripped northern Nigeria, while having relatively little purchase in Niger Republic just across Nigeria's northern border. Niger is a Muslim majority country facing much more serious levels of poverty than Nigeria. Niger is one of the poorest countries in the world, ranking second to last (187 out of 188) in the 2016 UN Human Development Index, while Nigeria ranked 152 out of 188 countries in the same year (UNDP 2018b). If poverty were the key driver of radicalization, one would expect Niger to be even more susceptible to radicalization than northern Nigeria. Closer attention to patterns of poverty in the region, and their relationship with regional inequalities casts additional light on the issue.

A closer examination of patterns of poverty draws on a data set from the Oxford Poverty and Human Development Initiative (OPHI), using DHS data for 2014.[2] OPHI's multi-poverty index (MPI) identifies the *prevalence* of poverty (the percentage of the population that is poor) and the *intensity* of poverty (how many of the 10 indicators of poverty are applicable) across the 36 states of Nigeria, and the seven regions of Niger. The poverty situation in Nigeria is shown in Figure 1.1, which illustrates that the distribution of poverty in Nigeria is highly uneven. Lagos State in south-western Nigeria shows a comparatively low prevalence and low intensity of poverty, while Bauchi State in the North East shows a very high prevalence and high intensity of poverty. This is a stark image of regional inequality across Nigeria, with the states of the North East and North West clustered at the highest incidence and highest intensity of poverty, while the states of the South West are all clustered around much lower poverty indicators. The North East states of Bauchi and Yobe show the worst levels of combined prevalence and intensity of poverty.

Figure 1.2 shows that Niger suffers from a very high prevalence and intensity of poverty across all of its regions. Most of Niger's population is clustered at the very high end of the prevalence and intensity spectrum, showing that over 90 per cent of the population are intensely poor. While poverty is high in Niger, it is also widely shared across all regions and ethno-regional groups, indicating low levels of horizontal inequalities. In Nigeria, by contrast, the prevalence and intensity of poverty is generally lower than in Niger Republic, but group inequalities across the various states and ethno-regional groups are extremely high. In particular, group inequalities between the heavily Christian states in the south of the country and the Muslim majority states of the far north are stark, stoking a long-standing sense of marginalization and grievance in the north. How poverty is distributed within and across regions and identity groups constitutes an important mechanism through which it feeds into grievances and radicalization. Regional feelings of deprivation in northern Nigeria are overlaid and further politicized by ethnic polarization around control of

[2] OPHI's Multidimensional Poverty Index (MPI) measures three dimensions of poverty (education, health, and standard of living) based on ten indicators (years of schooling, school attendance, child mortality, nutrition, access to electricity, sanitation, water, floor type, cooking fuel, and assets) based on DHS data.

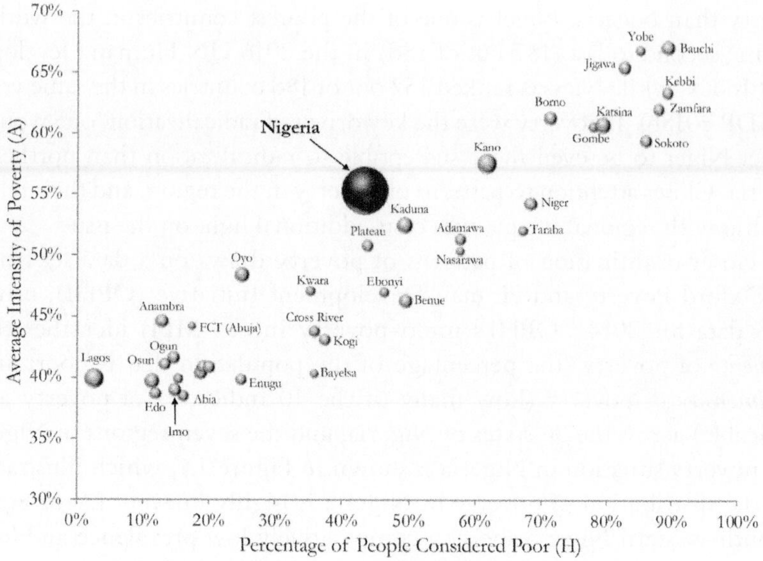

Figure 1.1 Nigeria – prevalence and intensity of poverty
(Source: Oxford Poverty and Human Development Initiative)

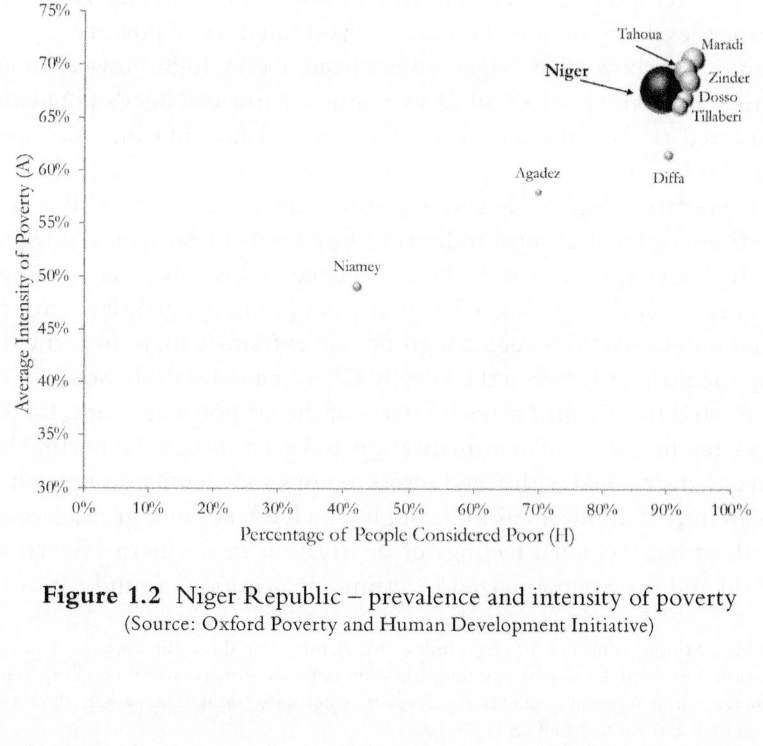

Figure 1.2 Niger Republic – prevalence and intensity of poverty
(Source: Oxford Poverty and Human Development Initiative)

the Nigerian state, which pits the Hausa-Fulani and Kanuri in the north against the Yoruba in the South West, and the Igbo in the South East.

Elsewhere, Mustapha (2015) uses OPHI data to show that the highest levels of within-state inequality are found in Borno and Yobe in the North East, along with Jigawa, Kano, and Katsina in the North West. Conversely, inequality within regions is much lower in the parts of Niger located along the Nigerian border, except for the region of Maradi. These poverty data lay useful groundwork for addressing two key questions about the emergence of Boko Haram: Why in Borno? and why not in Niger? The chapters by Monguno and Umara, and by Idrissa take these questions further to examine the historical and political factors that account for the intensity of poverty and disaffection in Borno, and the constraints on radicalization in Niger. These two chapters provide a richly detailed account of the social and political geography of radicalization in ways that look beyond ethnic and religious stereotypes to the institutional and environmental factors that shape dysfunctional as well as constructive responses to poverty and inequality.

But understanding the link between poverty and Islamic extremism requires attention to macro-social as well as macro-economic perspectives. While Salafism opened up new channels for those who were able to engage with the requirements of Islamic modernity, it left many behind (Meagher 2015). Within the vast informal economies of northern Nigeria, many faced the shattering realization in the years after the adoption of Sharia law that little had changed. For many ordinary northern Muslims, Sharia was seen as the restoration of a proper system of justice, freed from the disruptions of colonialism and the corrupt post-independence state. But Sharia implementation became entangled in the realities of cliental systems and indigeneity politics, delivering jobs and justice for those with the right status and connections, while violently excluding 'marginal Muslims' – migrants, and poor women and youth who found themselves unable to compete in the 'alternative modernity' created by Salafi reforms (Casey 2008, 82). Meagher and Hassan (Chapter 9 this volume) examine how Salafism and structural adjustment are reshaping the informal economy for those left behind, creating intensifying economic pressures, resentment and disaffection among those squeezed out of access even to basic informal livelihoods. Likewise, Monguno and Umara (Chapter 3 this volume) show how environmental stress, migration and ethnic rivalry in Borno State shaped the rise of Boko Haram.

In examining experiences of poverty and exclusion, it is important to note that the pathway to violent extremism is not always paved with rage. Some commentators highlight the vulnerability of youth to engaging in radical movements on the basis of a search for camaraderie, adventure or a quest for alternative futures, as Murray Last highlights in Chapter 8 on

Hausa youth (see also Apard 2015; Mercy Corps 2016, 14; Schmid 2013, 4). While denouncing the failures of Western education, democracy and the state, Mohammed Yusuf also offered a more positive message of personal dignity, self-worth and religious purpose for those left behind by the pressures of economic and Sharia reforms (Meagher 2015). As Apard (2015, 68) explains, disaffected Muslim youth may not be looking for money or venting their fury so much as seeking visions of a better future:

> The youth who make up the ranks of Boko Haram are not only attracted by the promise of a regular salary, or the gift of a Chinese-made motorcycle … they are also enticed by adventure, one symbolized by jihad, its myths, and its promises. Where many people see only desperate, extremely radicalized youth, we also see an exalted momentum comparable to that seen in revolutionary movements throughout history. Boko Haram's words are vehicles for an imagined, fantasized jihadist ideal.

The fact that these visions are based on scriptural and factual distortions is irrelevant to their mobilizing power, as recent populist mobilization in the Western world has shown. Severe and demoralizing forms of economic exclusion can create new macro-political dynamics that transcend poverty, while still having poverty at their root.

Governance failures

This brings us to the role of the state. Understanding how the Nigerian state can be part of the solution requires a clearer assessment of how it is part of the problem. The chapters in this book explore how neglect, corruption and eroded state capacity combine with violent political brinksmanship and human rights abuses to provoke and to perpetuate violent extremism. Endemic corruption and state violence not only fuel outrage, but exacerbate conditions of poverty and inequality that are key drivers of radicalization. The effective use of public resources is routinely disrupted by a parade of political godfathers, touts, electoral thugs, political entrepreneurs and ethnic as well as religious mobilization, even under President Buhari who has a reputation for honesty (Maclean and Egbejule 2019). A recent Oxfam report (2017, 5) on inequality in Nigeria observes: 'Public resource management is subject to elite capture, corruption and rent-seeking, and as such contributes to reproducing inequality … The shares of government budget allocation to education, health and social protection are among the lowest in the region.' The Oxfam report notes that Nigeria allots barely 40 per cent of the combined budgetary share allocated by Ghana to education, health and social protection.

There is increasing awareness of the ways in which Boko Haram is becoming embedded in the electoral cycle, and creating new dynamics of violence and corruption (Munshi 2018a; Mustapha 2014, 204; Thurston 2018, 230). In the 2015 and 2019 elections, Boko Haram intensified attacks before elections and influenced the credibility of candidates; but it has also become a feature of political resource mobilization and military corruption. In the early 2000s, the military budget was less than 3 per cent of overall government expenditure but increased to an average of 7.2 per cent of government spending 2009–2014 (International Crisis Group 2016). High levels of military spending have persisted through 2018, fluctuating between 6 and 21 per cent of the budget, with surges in defence spending in the run-up to elections (Ndujihe 2018; Olufemi 2015). The former National Security Adviser, Sambo Dasuki was charged with stealing $2 billion from funds allocated to fight the insurgency, while former President Obasanjo has accused the Jonathan administration of turning Boko Haram into 'an ATM machine for making money out of the treasury' (Adeniyi 2017; Collyer 2017; Thurston 2018, 214). As Sanda's contribution (Chapter 5 this volume) shows, defence funding is being diverted at the top while soldiers on the ground fighting Boko Haram lack appropriate supplies and equipment, a problem that continued to haunt the current administration in the run-up to the 2019 election (Ibrahim 2018). Over time, the Boko Haram insurgency has blurred the boundaries between security funding, electoral finance, and political and military corruption. Indeed, a motorized rickshaw driver in Borno State claimed: 'I don't truly believe they want this to end. They are profiting too much from it, there is a lot of money still to be made' (Tucker and Mohammed 2018, 10).

The Nigerian government's lack of effective regulation of religious activity is not only about corruption, but also relates to problems of state capacity (Mustapha 2015). The federal structure of the Nigerian state limits the capacity of the centre to discipline the sub-national states. In the context of intense competition over oil resources, and a polarized religious structure in which Christians and Muslims each make up just under 50 per cent of the population, the centre is a contested terrain where the relationship between the central government and elected governors can work at cross purposes. In was in this context that 12 northern states responded to the democratic opening of 1999 and the election of a Christian president to institute 'full' Sharia law within their jurisdictions. At the local government level as well, cuts in funding and constant processes of restructuring have undermined the capacity to monitor constituencies and prevent potentially undesirable developments from taking root within their jurisdictions (Wunsch and Olowu 1996; Mustapha 2015).

This points to a deeper problem of the relations between religion and the state. The Nigerian Constitution does not mandate secularism per se, but forbids the adoption of a state religion (Federal Republic of Nigeria, 1999, para. 10). The state professes neutrality in religious matters, and attempts to maintain a balance in its relationship to the two main religions, reflecting what Wakili (2009, 10) refers to as 'the national consensus that Nigeria is not a secular but a multi-religious country'. Unfortunately, efforts at religious neutrality have degenerated into a recipe for inter-religious competition (Mustapha 2014, 209). The demographic balance of Muslims and Christians, and the overlaps between religion, ethnicity and regionalism have contributed to highly polarized and competitive relations between the two faiths, drawing religion into competitive struggles over state power.

On paper, Nigeria has rules for regulating religious activities both at the federal and state levels. But these are often toothless in the face of lack of resources and an increasingly volatile religious culture. In the early 1980s, Islamic preaching was controlled by a government board, but these regulatory arrangements have largely atrophied (Umar 1993, 172). State-level bureaux of Islamic affairs have also lost their capacity to carry out regulatory responsibilities for monitoring Islamic school curricula, quality of instruction, and the political orientation of the burgeoning number of Islamic schools (Mustapha 2015). As a result, the state's capacity to intervene in local religious activities – either through carrots or sticks – is low in Nigeria. Instead of regulating religious activities and keeping destabilizing radical voices under control, many Nigerian institutions are being fought over and captured by these very religious forces. Idrissa's contribution (this volume) on Niger's ability to resist violent radicalization reveals how alternative forms of institutional organization can prevent violence from taking root.

The weak response of the Nigerian state to provocative and violent trends in religious preaching, and the weak and inconsistent response to the rise of Boko Haram are only part of the problem. In addition to the failure of the state to control religious violence, poor coordination and excesses within the military have exacerbated it (Matfess 2017; Thurston 2018; Comolli 2015). A number of chapters in this volume examine the various ways in which the state has intensified rather than assuaged the drivers of radicalization, through inadequate regulation of religious activity (Umar), unnecessary disruption of livelihoods (Meagher and Hassan), excessive violence (Monguno and Umara; Ehrhardt and Umar) and other forms of indiscipline (Usman et al.). In particular, Julie Sanda (Chapter 5 this volume) explores the role of the Nigerian security forces in perpetuating as well as countering the insurgency, creating a vicious cycle that undermines trust in the security forces, hampers the effectiveness of counter-insurgency activities and drives vulnerable civilians into the arms of Boko Haram.

Structure of the volume

This book explores the various dimensions of radicalization and the counter-radicalizing actors, institutions and conditions that contribute to understanding and to resolving the scourge of violent Islamic radicalization in Nigeria. In contrast to other books on the subject, the research presented here embeds the violent religious realities of Boko Haram in a wider understanding of the historical grievances, political vulnerabilities, geographical pressure points, Islamic diversity and institutional resilience of northern Nigerian society. The chapters are organized in three parts. The first examines the macro-social context of radicalization, focusing on the religious, environmental, geographical and security milieu in which Boko Haram emerged and operated. The second part focuses on the micro-social relations that inform the activities of northern Nigerians who join and do not join Boko Haram. Attention will focus on those most susceptible to radicalization: women, youth and the poor. The concluding part examines possible trajectories and policies for resolving the Boko Haram crisis through an analysis of endgames in radical religious insurgencies, and new policy perspectives arising from a serious engagement with wider social realities.

Part One begins with a chapter by Islamic history specialist, Sani Umar on Islamic scholars, the '*ulama*'. Umar examines their historical emergence in West Africa, their varied intellectual streams, and their training systems and social role in northern Nigeria. The magisterial historical sweep of the analysis lays the foundation for an incisive account of the rise of new Wahhabi-Salafi sects within Nigeria, their disruptive engagement with modernity and electronic media, and their problematic as well as their potentially stabilizing effect on scholarly discourse and public engagement.

An understanding of the positive as well as negative roles of Islamic scholars is followed by two chapters on the specific geography of Boko Haram. The chapter by Monguno and Umara explores the question: 'Why in Borno?' Both active academics in the University of Maiduguri, Monguno and Umara are living through as well as researching the effects of Boko Haram. They detail the patterns of insurgency across Borno State and within specific areas of the capital city, Maiduguri, and go on to examine the historical, environmental, ethnic, economic and religious factors that have shaped the unfolding of the insurgency within the state. The chapter deftly weaves together issues such as the extreme deprivation of migrant communities in Maiduguri, the drying up of Lake Chad, Muslim-Christian tensions in the south of the state, and pathways of recruitment and resistance within Borno State, providing a lucid analysis of how Boko Haram has reconfigured Borno, and how Borno has reconfigured Boko Haram.

The treatment of the Borno question is followed by Chapter 4, on the inverse question: 'Why not in Niger?' Here Rahmane Idrissa, a prominent Nigerien political scientist, provides an illuminating account of why Boko Haram has largely failed to spread its violent mobilization into neighbouring Niger Republic. The chapter begins with an itinerary of the ethnic, political and religious similarities and linkages between northern Nigeria and the bordering territory of central Niger. Despite a Nigerian saying, 'when Nigeria has a cold, Niger coughs', Idrissa details the various religious, demographic and political dimensions of Niger's resilience to violent radicalization, reducing the effect of Boko Haram to a sobering but containable frisson of radical activity (Masquelier 2009, 30). Focusing on the regions of Maradi and Diffa, the two regions of Niger most closely linked to northern Nigeria, Idrissa traces their distinctive dynamics of vulnerability and resilience, before situating the resistance to radicalization in the wider political context of the Nigerien state.

Chapter 5, by Julie Sanda, examines the role of the Nigerian security forces in the containment and continuation of Boko Haram. A seasoned practitioner and research specialist in peace and security issues in the National Defence College of Nigeria, Julie Sanda takes a sober view of the capacities and limitations of the Nigerian security services in counter-insurgency operations. While maintaining a critical perspective, Sanda advances the debate beyond the standard condemnation of human rights abuses to an examination of the complex security challenges of fighting Boko Haram and the problems of training, coordination and corruption that compromise effective engagement in asymmetric warfare. The chapter goes on to examine the rise of the unofficial Civilian Joint Task Force (CJTF), and its implications for peace and security in north-eastern Nigeria.

Part Two, on micro-social relations begins with an analysis of pathways into and around Boko Haram. This chapter is a product of collaborative research by Sani Umar and Nigeria specialist, David Ehrhardt working with an interviewer based in the Boko Haram heartland of Maiduguri. Interviews trace the characteristics and motivations of Boko Haram members as well as the experiences of friends and relatives who did not join the group. Rather than elaborating case histories, the chapter analyses the profiles, pathways and barriers to radicalization to develop an understanding of more effective modes of intervention and counter-radicalization. The analysis adds to existing perspectives on pathways to radicalization by attending to issues of social resistance as well as conduits, taking serious account of the positive as well as negative motivations for joining, and identifying shifts in motivations during the course of the insurgency.

The three succeeding chapters explore the social context of radicalization from the perspective of three key vulnerable groups: northern Nigerian women, Hausa youth and informal economy operators in urban northern Nigeria. Chapter 7, on the role of women, is a collaborative engagement by three Muslim woman scholars: Zainab Usman, scholar and development practitioner from northern Nigeria; Sherine El Taraboulsi-McCarthy, a specialist on conflict and development in the Middle East and North Africa region; and seasoned social activist, Islamic preacher, and head of a Muslim women's peace NGO, Khadija Gambo Hawaja. This chapter examines the varied ways in which women have been involved in Boko Haram, as victims, as perpetrators and as forces for counter-radicalization. Brushing past the culturalist assumptions of endemic misogyny that underpin current accounts of women's involvement in Boko Haram, this chapter explores the sources of vulnerability, as well as the space for gender struggles within northern Nigerian Islam. It also considers the new challenges and opportunities created by the growing influence of more fundamentalist Salafi ideologies and practices filtering into Nigeria from the Middle East. These developments lead into an analysis of the pathways and motives of women's involvement in Boko Haram, and the role of women as forces for counter-insurgency.

Chapter 8, on Hausa youth, by the venerable anthropologist of Nigerian Hausa society, Murray Last, draws on decades of deep field experience living and researching in rural Hausa communities. While Boko Haram emerged from the Kanuri ethnic group, Hausa youth constituted one of the key sources of foot soldiers for Boko Haram, and a critical social terrain for assessing the prospects for rapid expansion of the insurgency across northern Nigeria. Last draws us into the world of rural Hausa youth to examine the context of values, experiences, pressures and aspirations that lead poor youth to migrate to the city and seek out a livelihood and new social milieu. He traces the interaction of Hausa social foundations with urban poverty, adventure, fortuitous connections and dubious company as young Hausa migrants try to find a place for themselves in the city, and shows how inexperience, loneliness and youthful exuberance can be as important a source of risk factors for joining Boko Haram as economic grievance or ideological radicalization.

The informal economy constitutes a further important terrain of radicalizing pressures in northern Nigeria. In the final chapter in this section, Nigerian informal economy specialist, Kate Meagher joins forces with Islamic Studies professor, Ibrahim Haruna Hassan to examine how economic pressures within the informal economy in the northern Nigerian cities of Kano and Kaduna shape the vulnerability to Islamic radicalization. Focusing on eight informal activities, designed to capture a cross-section of gender, economic, educational and age categories, Meagher and Hassan reveal the new pressures and struggles emerging in the northern Nigerian informal economy, revolving around business ownership, indigeneity and the domination of profitable informal activities. They show how the increase in educated entrants into the informal economy and the rise of Salafism have contributed to intensifying marginalization and disaffection among poor migrants, apprenticeship-trained workers, and educated informal actors in lowly informal activities. The severe disruption of marginal livelihoods by heavy-handed security operations combined with economic and religious pressures, creating a tinderbox for radicalization among those excluded from decent informal livelihoods.

Finally, Part Three considers ways forward after a decade of Boko Haram violence. In Chapter 10, a comparative analysis by Sani Umar and David Ehrhardt uses an analysis of past religious insurgencies in and outside Africa to explore possible endgames for the Boko Haram insurgency. The chapter examines the factors that shape a range of possible outcomes: insurgent victory, government victory, negotiated settlement, and debilitating stalemate. These ideal types are used to analyse the trajectories of three religious insurgencies in Egypt, Uganda and Northern Ireland. Typological features derived from these insurgencies are used to plot the trajectory of Boko Haram, to assess probable endgame scenarios, and to consider how to move emerging trajectories in more productive directions.

Part Three and the book conclude with a brief chapter on rethinking prevailing policy approaches. Drawing on policy insights from all of the contributors, this chapter examines what a politically grounded, whole-of-society approach can contribute to the development of a more effective counter-radicalization policy. Rather than tinkering with standard counter-radicalization policy packages, recommendations centre on more-innovative approaches that look beyond security concerns to social needs, and beyond costly donor-led measures to accessible civil-society and community-led initiatives. Equally important is an emphasis on coherent, state-led institutional reform of the security services and of religious and educational activities oriented to rebuilding faith in government and restoring faith in society.

Bibliography

Abbah, T. and Odunlami, T., 2013 'Day We Wept While on Dialogue Assignment – Chairman, Presidential Committee', *Sunday Trust*, 8 December, https://allafrica.com/stories/201312091471.html, accessed 14 August 2019.

Acemoglu, D., Johnson, S. and Robinson, J.A., 2002. 'Reversal of Fortune: Geography and Institutions in the Making of the Modern World Income Distribution', *The Quarterly Journal of Economics* 117 (4), 1231–94.

Adeniyi, O., 2017, *Against the Run of Play: How an Incumbent President was Defeated in Nigeria*, Lagos: Kachifo.

Anderson, J.N.D., 1957, 'Law and Custom in Muslim Areas in Africa: Recent Development in Nigeria', Paris: Institut International des Civilizations Differentes.

Archibong, B., 2018, 'Historical Origins of Persistent Inequality in Nigeria', *Oxford Development Studies* 46 (3), 325–47.

Apard, Élodie, 2015, 'The Words of Boko Haram', *Afrique contemporaine* 3 (255), 41–69.

BBC, 2015, 'Nigeria Boko Haram: Militants "Technically Defeated" – Buhari', 24 December, www.bbc.co.uk/news/world-africa-35173618, accessed 5 December 2018.

BBC, 2019, 'Burkina Faso's War against Militant Islamists', 30 May, www.bbc.co.uk/news/world-africa-39279050, accessed 17 July 2019.

Borum, R., 2011a, 'Radicalization into Violent Extremism I: A Review of Social Science Theories', *Journal of Strategic Security* 4 (4), 7–35.

—— 2011b, 'Radicalization and Involvement in Terrorism Radicalization into Violent Extremism II: A Review of Conceptual Models and Empirical Research', *Journal of Strategic Security* 4 (4), 37–61.

Botha, A. and Abdile, M., 2017, 'Reality Versus Perception: Toward Understanding Boko Haram in Nigeria', *Studies in Conflict & Terrorism* 42 (5), 493–519.

Brown, K.E. and Saeed, T., 2015, 'Radicalization and Counterradicalization at British Universities: Muslim Encounters and Alternatives', *Ethnic and Racial Studies* 38 (11), 1952–68.

Casey, C., 2008, '"Marginal Muslims": Politics and the Perceptual Bounds of Islamic Authenticity in Northern Nigeria', *Africa Today* 54 (3), 67–92.Collyer, R., 2017, 'Meet Aisha, a Former Antelope Hunter who now Tracks Boko Haram', *The Guardian*, 8 February, www.theguardian.com/world/2017/feb/08/antelope-hunter-boko-haram-nigeria, accessed 4 April 2019.

Comolli, V., 2015, *Boko Haram: Nigeria's Islamist Insurgency*, London: Hurst.Desilver, D. and Masci, D., 2017, 'World's Muslim Population More Widespread than You Might Think', FactTank: Research in Numbers, Pew Research Centre. www.pewresearch.org/fact-tank/2017/01/31/worlds-muslim-population-more-widespread-than-you-might-think, accessed 8 April 2019.

Diouf, M. (ed.), 2013, *Tolerance, Democracy, and Sufis in Senegal*, New York: Columbia University Press.

Durmaz, M., 2019, 'Making Sense of Boko Haram's Comeback in Nigeria', *TRT World*, 9 January, www.trtworld.com/magazine/making-sense-of-boko-harams-comeback-in-nigeria-23210, accessed 19 May 2019.Famine Early Warning Systems Network, 2019, 'Intense Insurgent Attacks in Northeast Nigeria Lead to Increased Displacement and Food Needs', *Nigeria Food Security Outlook*, February to September, http://fews.net/sites/default/files/documents/reports/NIGERIA_FSO_2019_02_final.pdf, accessed 18 February 2019.

Federal Republic of Nigeria, 1999, Constitution of the Federal Republic of Nigeria, 1999 (No. 24 of 1999), *Official Gazette*, Extraordinary, 1999-05-05 86 (27), A855–1104.Global Terrorism Index, 2015, 'Measuring and Understanding the Impact of Terrorism', Institute for Economics and Peace, http://economicsandpeace.org/wp-content/uploads/2015/11/Global-Terrorism-Index-2015.pdf, accessed 28 April 2019.

——2018, 'Measuring the Impact of Terrorism', Institute for Economics and Peace, http://

visionofhumanity.org/app/uploads/2018/12/Global-Terrorism-Index-2018-1.pdf, accessed 28 April 2019.

Gomez-Perez, M., 2017, '"Political" Islam in Senegal and Burkina Faso: Contrasting Approaches to Mobilization since the 1990s', *Mediterranean Politics* 22 (1), 176–95.

Habib, H., 2012, 'Hisbah Men Guard Christian Worshipers in Kano', *Daily Trust*, 15 January, www.dailytrust.com.ng/hisbah-men-guard-christian-worshipers-in-kano.html, accessed 5 January 2013.Hadiz, V.R., 2018, 'Imagine All the People? Mobilising Islamic Populism for Right-Wing Politics in Indonesia', *Journal of Contemporary Asia* 48 (4), 566–83.

Hamzawy, A. and Gebrowski, S., 2010, 'From Violence to Moderation: Al-Jama'a al-Islamiya and al-Jihad', Paper 20, April, Carnegie Middle East Centre, Carnegie Endowment for International Peace, Washington, DC.

Human Rights Watch, 2019, 'Nigeria: Events of 2018', World Report, www.hrw.org/world-report/2019/country-chapters/nigeria, accessed 28 April 2019.

Huntingdon, S., 1996, *The Clash of Civilizations and the New World Order*, New York: Simon and Schuster.

Ibrahim, J., 2018, 'Telling Ourselves the Truth About the Boko Haram Insurgency', *Premium Times*, 21 December, https://opinion.premiumtimesng.com/2018/12/21/telling-ourselves-the-truth-about-the-boko-haram-insurgency-by-jibrin-ibrahim, accessed 27 April 2019.

—— 2019, 'Security and Development Challenges in the Sahel', *Premium Times*, 28 June, https://opinion.premiumtimesng.com/2019/06/28/security-and-developme nt-challenges-in-the-sahel-by-jibrin-ibrahim, accessed 17 July 2019.

Idrissa, A., 2017a, 'Genealogies of a Non-Political Islam in the Sahel: The Burkina Case', Working Paper 23, Adaptation and Creativity in Africa, German Research Foundation, Bonn.

—— 2017b, *The Politics of Islam in the Sahel: Between Persuasion and Violence*, New York: Routledge.

International Crisis Group, 2016, 'Nigeria: The Challenge of Military Reform', Report 237, 6 June, www.crisisgroup.org/africa/west-africa/nigeria/nigeria-challeng e-military-reform, accessed 23 April 2019.

—— 2017, 'Watchmen of Lake Chad: Vigilante Groups Fighting Boko Haram', Report 244, 23 February, www.crisisgroup.org/africa/west-africa/nigeria/244-watchmen-la ke-chad-vigilante-groups-fighting-boko-haram, accessed 28 April 2019.

Kane, O., 2003, *Muslim Modernity in Postcolonial Nigeria: A Study of the Society for the Removal of Innovation and Reinstatement of Tradition*, Leiden: Brill.

Kassim, A. and Nwankpa, M., 2018, *The Boko Haram Reader: From Nigerian Preachers to the Islamic State*, Oxford University Press.

Kwanashie, G.A., 2002, *The Making of the North in Nigeria 1900–1965*, Kaduna: Arewa House.

Lodge, C., 2014, 'Nigeria: 200 Young Muslims Protect Christians from Attack', *Christianity Today*, 29 December, www.christiantoday.com/article/nigeria-20 0-young-muslims-protect-christians-from-attack/45069.htm, accessed 13 April 2019.

Lubeck, P.M., 2011, 'Nigeria: Mapping the Sharia Restorationist Movement', in R.W. Hefner (ed.), *Sharia Politics: Islamic Law and Society in the Modern World*, Bloomington: University of Indiana Press.

Maclean, R. and Alfa, I., 2019, 'They Say Boko Haram is Gone. One Mother's Terror Tells Another Story…', *The Guardian*, 2 February, www.theguardian.com/world/2019/feb/02/election-nigeria-boko-haram-refugees, accessed 5 March 2019.

Maclean, R. and Egbejule, E., 2019, 'Nigeria Election: "Mr Honesty" Tainted by Failure to Tackle Corruption', *The Guardian*, 11 February, www.theguardian.com/world/2019/feb/11/nigeria-election-mr-honesty-muhammadu-buhari-tainted -by-failure-to-tackle-corruption, accessed 30 March 2019.

Mamdani, M., 2005, *Good Muslim, Bad Muslim: America, the Cold War, and the Roots of Terror*, New York: Random House.

Masha, M., Vunobolki, M., Ibrahim, M.A., Gana, B. et al., 2017, *North-East Nigeria – Recovery and Peace Building Assessment: Synthesis Report*, Washington, DC: World Bank Group, http://documents.worldbank.org/curated/en/542971497576633512/Synthesis-report

Masquelier, A., 2009, *Women and Islamic Revival in a West African Town*, Bloomington: Indiana University Press.

Matfess, H., 2017, *Women and the War on Boko Haram: Wives, Weapons, Witnesses*, London: Zed Books.

Meagher, K., 2009, 'Trading on Faith: Religious Movements and Informal Economic Governance in Nigeria', *The Journal of Modern African Studies* 47 (3), 397–423.

—— 2015, 'Leaving No One Behind? Informal Economies, Economic Inclusion and Islamic Extremism in Nigeria', *Journal of International Development* 27 (6), 835–55.

—— 2018, 'Taxing times: Taxation, Divided Societies and the Informal Economy in Northern Nigeria', *The Journal of Development Studies* 54 (1), 1–17.

Mercy Corps, 2016, 'Motivations and Empty Promises: Voices of Former Boko Haram Combatants and Nigerian Youth', www.mercycorps.org/sites/default/files/Motivations%20and%20Empty%20Promises_Mercy%20Corps_Full%20Report.pdf, accessed 29 March 2019.

Moghaddam, F.M., 2005, 'The Staircase to Terrorism: A Psychological Exploration', *American Psychologist* 60 (2), 161–9.

Mohammed, K. 2018, 'The History of Boko Haram', in A. Carl Levan and P. Ukata (eds), *The Oxford Handbook of Nigerian Politics*, Oxford University Press, 583–604.

Mueller, L., 2016, 'Religious Violence and Democracy in Niger', *African Conflict and Peace Building Review* 6 (1), 89–104.

Munshi, N., 2018a, 'Death of Nigerian Soldiers Puts Pressure on President', *Financial Times*, 25 November, www.ft.com/content/75374ffe-f02f-11e8-ae55-df4bf40f9d0d, accessed 11 December 2018.

Munshi, N., 2018b, 'Under Fire: Why Nigeria is Struggling to Defeat Boko Haram', *Financial Times*, 6 December, www.ft.com/content/62928c8e-f7b8-11e8-8b7c-6fa24bd5409c, accessed 14 December 2018.

Mustapha, A.R. (ed.), 2014, *Sects & Social Disorder: Muslim Identities & Conflict in Northern Nigeria*, Woodbridge: James Currey.

—— 2015, 'Violent Radicalization: Northern Nigeria in the Light of the Experience of Southern Niger Republic', in A.R. Mustapha and Muhammad Sani Umar (eds), *On Radicalisation: Counter-Radicalisation, and De-Radicalisation in Northern Nigeria*, National Security Adviser, Federal Republic of Nigeria, 234–74.

—— 2018, 'Religious Encounters in Northern Nigeria', in A.R. Mustapha and D. Ehrhardt (eds), *Creed & Grievance: Muslim-Christian Relations & Conflict Resolution in Northern Nigeria*, Woodbridge: James Currey.

Mustapha, A.R. and Ehrhardt, D. (eds), 2018, *Creed & Grievance: Muslim-Christian Relations & Conflict Resolution in Northern Nigeria*, Woodbridge: James Currey.

Mustapha, A.R. and Gamawa, A., 2018, 'Challenges of Legal Pluralism: Sharia Law and its Aftermath', in A.R. Mustapha and D. Ehrhardt (eds), *Creed & Grievance: Muslim-Christian Relations & Conflict Resolution in Northern Nigeria*, Woodbridge: James Currey, 139–64.

NBS (National Bureau of Statistics), 2010, *Nigeria Poverty Profile*, 2010 Report, Nigeria.

Ndujihe, C., 2018, 'Security: FG Spends N6trn on Defence in 7 Years', *Vanguard*, 29 July, www.vanguardngr.com/2018/07/security-fg-spends-n6trn-on-defence-in-11-years, accessed 12 April 2019.

Neumann, P.R., 2008, 'Introduction', in 'Perspectives on Radicalisation and Political Violence', Papers from the First International Conference on Radicalisation and Political Violence, 17–18 January, London: International Centre for the Study of Radicalisation and Political Violence, www.nonviolent-conflict.org/wp-content/uploads/2016/11/Perspectives-on-Radicalisation-Political-Violence.pdf, accessed 30 August 2019.

Okeowo, A., 2015, 'The Women Fighting Boko Haram', *The New Yorker*, 22 December, www.newyorker.com/news/news-desk/the-women-fighting-boko-haram, accessed 16 April 2019.

Olufemi, J., 2015, 'Nigeria Spends N4.62 Trillion on National Security in 5 Years, Yet Widespread Insecurity Remains', *Premium Times*, 18 June, www.premiumtimesng.com/news/headlines/185285-nigeria-spends-n4-62-trillion-on-national-security-in-5-years-yet-widespread-insecurity-remains.html, accessed 12 April 2019.

Otayek, R., 1996, 'L'islam et la révolution au Burkina Faso: mobilisation politique et reconstruction identitaire', *Social Compass* 43 (2): 233–47.

Oxfam, 2017, 'Inequality in Nigeria: Exploring the Drivers', www-cdn.oxfam.org/s3fs-public/file_attachments/cr-inequality-in-nigeria-170517-en.pdf, accessed 29 April 2019.

Peel, J.D.Y., 2015, *Christianity, Islam, and Orisa Religion*, Oakland: University of California Press.

Pérouse de Montclos, M.-A. (ed.), 2014, *Boko Haram: Islamism, Politics, Security and the State in Nigeria*, African Studies Centre, University of Leiden.

Pew Research Centre, 2014, 'Global Attitudes and Trends: Concerns about Islamic Extremism on the Rise in Middle East', 1 July, www.pewresearch.org/global/2014/07/01/concerns-about-islamic-extremism-on-the-rise-in-middle-east, accessed 15 December 2018.—— 2016, 'Global Attitudes and Trends', 14 November, www.pewglobal.org/2016/11/14/nigerians-bullish-on-the-economy, accessed 15 March 2019.

Reuters, 2018, 'Islamic Militants Kill Up To 30 Nigerian Soldiers in Attack on Base', *The Guardian*, 2 September, www.theguardian.com/world/2018/sep/02/islamist-militants-kill-up-to-30-nigerian-soldiers-in-attack-on-base, accessed 18 February 2019. Sanusi, S.L., 2007, 'Politics and Shari'a in Northern Nigeria', in Benjamin F. Soares and René Otayek (eds), *Islam and Muslim Politics in Africa*, New York: Palgrave Macmillan, 177–88.

Schmid, A.P., 2013, 'Radicalisation, De-Radicalisation, Counter-Radicalisation: A Conceptual Discussion and Literature Review', ICCT Research Paper, International Center for Counter-Terrorism, The Hague.

Soares, B., 2009, 'An Islamic Social Movement in Contemporary West Africa: NASFAT of Nigeria', in S. Ellis and I. van Kessel (eds), *Movers and Shakers: Social Movements in Africa*, Leiden: Brill, 178–96.

Soares, B., and Otayek, R., 2007, *Islam and Muslim Politics in Africa*, New York: Palgrave Macmillan.

The Defense Post, 2018, 'Nigeria Army Masses in Monguno, Moves to Clear Boko Haram from Baga', 31 December, https://thedefensepost.com/2018/12/31/nigeria-army-deploys-monguno-baga-boko-haram-iswa, accessed 20 March 2019.

The Economist, 2019, 'The West's New Front against Jihadism is in the Sahel', 2 May, www.economist.com/middle-east-and-africa/2019/05/02/the-wests-new-front-against-jihadism-is-in-the-sahel, accessed 17 July 2019.

Thurston, A., 2009, 'Why is Militant Islam a Weak Phenomenon in Senegal?' Working Paper 09-005, Institute for the Study of Islamic Thought in Africa (ISITA), Buffett Center, Northwestern University, Evanston, IL.

—— 2016, *Salafism in Nigeria: Islam, Preaching, and Politics*, The International African Library vol. 52, Cambridge University Press.

—— 2018, *Boko Haram: The History of an African Jihadist Movement*, Princeton, NJ: Princeton University Press.

Tucker, D. and Mohammed, J.A., 2018, 'Through Our Eyes: People's Perspectives on Building Peace in Northeast Nigeria', Policy Paper, April, Conciliation Resources and The Kukah Centre, Abuja.

Udo, B., 2018, 'Nigeria's Excess Crude Account Depletes 73% in Three Weeks', *Premium Times*, 11 Feb. www.premiumtimesng.com/news/headlines/302071-nigerias-excess-crude-account-depletes-73-in-three-weeks.html, accessed 16 February 2019.

Umar, M.S., 1993, 'Changing Islamic Identity in Nigeria from 1960s to the 1980s: From Sufism to Anti-Sufism', in L. Brenner (ed.), *Muslim Identity and Social Change in Sub-Saharan Africa*, Bloomington: Indiana University Press, 154–78.

UNDP, 2018a, 'National Human Development Report 2018: Achieving Human Development in North East Nigeria', Human Development Report Office, United Nations Development Programme, Abuja.

—— 2018b, 'Human Development Report 2018, Human Development Indices and Indicators', Human Development Report Office, United Nations Development Programme, Abuja.

US Department of State, 2018, 'International Religious Freedom Report of 2017', Bureau of Democracy, Human Rights and Labor, Washington, DC.Wakili, H., 2009, 'Islam and the Political Arena in Nigeria: The Ulama and the 2007 Elections', Institute for the Study of Islamic Thought in Africa (ISITA), Northwestern University, Evanston, IL.

Woodward, M., Umar, M.S., Rohmaniyah, I. and Yahya, M., 2013, 'Salafi Violence and Sufi Tolerance? Rethinking Conventional Wisdom', *Perspectives on Terrorism* 7 (6), 58–89.

Wunsch, J.S., and Olowu, D., 1996, 'Regime Transformation from Below: Decentralization, Local Governance, and Democratic Reform in Nigeria', *Studies in Comparative International Development* 31 (4), 66–82.

Part One

The Macro-Social Context

2

The roles of the *Ulama* in radicalization & counter-radicalization

M. SANI UMAR

Introduction

This chapter focuses on the religious dimensions of radicalization. More specifically, the chapter explores the roles of Muslim scholars known collectively as *ulama* – the plural of the Arabic term *alim,* which means the learned. The basic argument presented here is that the *ulama* can play active roles in promoting radicalization as well as counter-radicalization and deradicalization through the multiple roles they have historically played in Muslim societies. Over the last four decades, *some* Nigerian *ulama* have contributed to radicalization via four different but related mechanisms. First, they have created a *climate of opinion* in which individuals and social movements with radical tendencies have found in the discourses of the *ulama* the Islamic legitimation for their radical dispositions. Second, *some ulama* have also contributed to radicalization by *creating division and raising tension* among Muslims through polemical exchanges on religious beliefs and practices as well as social and political issues. Third, *some ulama* have contributed to radicalization through *constructions of Muslim victimhood,* often articulated in far-fetched conspiracy theories that provoke resentment and urge Muslims to react against the supposed conspirators. Fourth, *some ulama* have contributed to radicalization by *ridiculing and demonizing* their perceived enemies, including fellow Muslims who do not share their views. Demonization of the Other can provide a justification for *physical violence.*[1]

But it is important to offer some caveats. The *ulama* are not a monolithic entity but a heterogeneous group with many significant differences that will be highlighted in the following pages. The majority of the *ulama*

[1] For a comparative analysis of the contribution of *ulama* to radicalization in different contexts, see Bachar et al. (2006).

have *not* contributed to radicalization – indeed they can serve as important sources of counter-radicalization. The expression '*some ulama*' has been repeated above to underscore the need to examine the specific factors that lead to radicalization. There is diversity in the motives, modes of operation, intensity and frequency in contributions of the individual *ulama* towards radicalization. Furthermore, the *ulama* are not the sole creators of radicalization in Nigeria. Other social groups, especially religious extremists, ethnic chauvinists, politicians, and journalists have also played their own parts. Despite the focus on the *ulama*, this chapter will be attentive to the interactions among the several factors that have collectively contributed to radicalization in Nigeria.

Beginning with a brief discussion on methodology, the chapter examines definitions of the *ulama* and their educational formation and multiple roles in Muslim societies. It then examines the specific ways through which the *ulama* have contributed to radicalization, as well as highlighting conditions that made it possible for some *ulama* to radicalize their followers. The chapter concludes by shedding light on the possible roles of the *ulama* in counter-radicalization and deradicalization, thereby providing the basis of identifying policy options.

Methodology

The sermons, lessons, lectures, debates and speeches of selected *ulama* were collected in the course of field research in Kano, Kaduna and Jos in April–May 2014, when the Boko Haram insurgency was in full swing. Recorded in audio cassettes and compact discs, as well as digital video discs, these materials provide excellent data on what different members of the *ulama* say in normal settings, including sermons delivered at Friday noon prayers, preaching events, weddings, Islamic festivals, commentaries on the Qur'an during Ramadan, questions and answers on religious and non-religious issues, celebration of the Prophet Muhammad's birthday, debates staged to live audiences, admonition to voters during electoral seasons, etc. Some of the recordings provide important background information, including dates, venues, occasions, and sponsors of the recorded events. Starting from the 1980s to the present, such recordings have become very popular media of religious debate and discourse among Nigerian Muslims.

The themes in these recordings vary widely. They include religious exhortation, gender roles and family issues, rebuttals and rejoinders to other *ulama*, as well as commentaries on social, economic and political concerns. Other important themes are religious authority and leadership, polemical exchanges and conflictual interactions among different

Islamic groups as each seeks to attract followers, prevent defection from their ranks, and defend their theological convictions and the validity of their worship, among other things. Evidence from the field research indicates that recorded discourses of the *ulama* in the millions are bought and sold across Nigeria in specialty studios and kiosks, main markets, major mosques, and on the street by hawkers making quick sales in traffic hold-ups. Both the contexts and contents as well as the mass production and wide dissemination of the recorded materials provide ample data to study the roles of the *ulama* in natural settings, and without the constraints and self-censorship that are likely to occur in one-on-one interviews.

Using the method of discourse analysis, the materials are scrutinized to illuminate not only the theological issues in contention but also the important social, cultural, economic and political issues at stake. The recorded discourses of the *ulama* come with 'meta-data', such as dates, occasions and sponsors of the recorded sermons, adding meaning to content through explicit attention to the contexts in which discourses are articulated, communicated, received, challenged and defended, often in polemical exchanges. Equally important, discourse analysis directs attention not only to the purported meanings of discourses but also to their internal composition, including oratorical skills, techniques of performative speech, and devices of rhetorical persuasion. The dialogic between the contents of discourses and the realities they seek to signify are not simply referential or one-sided; rather the contents of discourses and their ostensible referents are mutually constitutive. Thus, the radicalizing discourses of the *ulama* can produce the realities of radicalism, while these realities can be echoed back into the discourses that have helped to produce them. By juxtaposing contents and contexts, and connecting discourses with their practical consequences, the technique of discourse analysis yields rich insights that could not be achieved through the mere focus on texts and their purported meanings.

The ulama and their roles in Muslim societies

Historically, *ulama* have played complex roles in Islamic societies. The multiple roles of the *ulama* individually and collectively rest upon their expertise in educational, legal, administrative, cultural, literary, intellectual and religious/spiritual domains. To grapple with the problems of defining the *ulama* and their multiple functions in the history of Islamic societies, Stephen Humphreys finds it easier to start *via negativa* by observing that the *ulama* 'are neither a socio-economic class, nor a clearly defined status group, nor a hereditary caste, nor a legal estate, nor a profession'. He then highlights the relevant social contexts within which *ulama* have been historically located:

> They appear in our texts as semi-literate village imams [prayer leaders] and erudite qadis [judges], as rabble-rousers and privy counsellors to kings, as spiritual directors and cynical politicians. Some are scions of wealthy and influential families; others are impoverished immigrants from remote villages. Some are landowners, some are salaried professors or bureaucrats, and some are merchants or humble artisans. The great majority are men, but there are a number of notable women in their ranks as well. In short, they seem to cut across every possible classification of groups within Islamic society, playing a multiplicity of political, social, and cultural roles. But in spite of this ambiguity, they are plainly a crucial element in Islamic society – the one group which in fact makes it 'Islamic' rather than something else – and wherever we turn we encounter them. (Humphreys 1991, 187)

Definitions of the *ulama* tend to echo the same key features even though some authors may emphasize different features as more important in defining them. First and foremost, the *ulama* are defined by their Islamic religious scholarship. Second, the *ulama* are the ones who construct Muslim individual and collective religious identities by articulating the norms, beliefs and practices that constitute Islam, using an array of interpretive strategies and legal traditions to determine the specific and enforceable rules of Islamic law. They also play an equally important role in judicial, educational and political institutions of Muslim societies. Third, the composition of *ulama* as an indispensable group in Islamic societies is characterized not only by their social diversity, but also by the incredible diversity of their religious worldviews.

It is worth emphasizing is that there is no official body that confers the title of '*alim*' on any individual. Instead, a Muslim becomes recognized as an *alim*, based on his (and sometimes her) achievement in learning and piety. At first, the title is often conferred by the person's own small circle of disciples. As the reputation for learning and piety grows, more disciples are attracted, thereby gaining more recognition that will eventually lead to other learned scholars acknowledging the person concerned as one of the *ulama*. Such recognition may lead to political appointment into various offices of state, including judge of Islamic law, public notary, vizier, prayer leader, etc. Of course such political appointments do not make an *alim*; they merely acknowledge and honour prior accomplishments of the appointee. While still a student (or disciple), there are traditions of ceremonially recognizing important scholarly milestones such as successfully completing memorization of the Qur'an, which confers the title of *al-hafiz* (or its synonyms in different communities). When a disciple completes the study of a particular text, his teacher may grant him an *ijaza,* a certificate of successful completion, which may also include permission to teach the same text to others. But neither memorizing the Qur'an nor receiving an *ijaza* transforms a disciple into a scholar. There is no formal mechanism of officially becoming an *alim*, which enables space for a self-starter to anoint himself as a scholar. The collegial body of the *ulama* can do little more than refuse to recognize the self-starter as one of them – a point explored in more detail below because of its important implications for radicalization among contemporary Nigerian *ulama*.

Even a sketchy overview of Islamic history reveals the incredible diversity of models of interface between the *ulama* and the other segments in Islamic societies, including the ruling elites (caliphs, sultans, princes, viziers, military commanders, regional governors, etc.). On the one end of the spectrum, we find in the Ottoman Empire the highly bureaucratic order of the Ilmiyye, an agency of the Ottoman state, which began in the reign of Sultan Mehemmed II (1451–81), and eventually became a 'thoroughgoing and highly elaborated *cursus honorum* of learned offices' headed by the *shaykh al-islām* (Gilliot et al. 2012). The holder of this office oversees numerous lower ranks of paid *ulama* recruited through regular procedures of appointment, and with clear schedules of responsibilities and jurisdiction over territorial districts or specialized sectors in society such as the army, markets, trades and crafts (ibid.). The Ilmiyye was a thoroughly organized bureaucracy through which the *ulama* were integrated into the state apparatus of the Ottoman Empire. On the other end of the spectrum, we find the unique case of Chinese Muslims, among whom the term '*ulama*' did not appear in 'Chinese Islamic works until the beginning of the 20th century'. Clearly, the *ulama* must have had the barest minimum of roles in this context, making sharper the contrast with the elaborate system of the Ottoman Ilmiyye.

In between the two ends of the spectrum found in the Ottoman Empire and the Muslim communities in China, relations between the *ulama* and ruling authorities have taken numerous forms that also changed over time and from one place to another, as amply demonstrated by many scholars (see Berkey 1992, 13–14; Arjomand 1999; Cohen 1970; Gilbert 1980; Petry 1981). Since space will not permit detailed examination of the historical evolution of the multiple roles of the *ulama* in general, it will suffice here to provide the following sketch of the historical evolution of the multiple roles of the *ulama* in the areas of present-day Nigeria. This sketch concentrates on demonstrating the quietist historical predisposition of the *ulama* as the necessary background for understanding the modern changes that have led some *ulama* to become agents of radicalization in contemporary Nigeria. Key changes in the professional formation and the modern career paths open to contemporary *ulama* began during the colonial era and continued to the present.

Islamic education and intellectual traditions in pre-colonial West Africa

In the earliest phases of Islamic history in West Africa, beginning from the eleventh century, the religion was brought by merchants and clerics, and was seen as complementing rather than replacing the existing religious beliefs and practices, thus laying the historical origins of a quietist stance among the *ulama*. Over time, this quietism became even more entrenched by the initial emphasis on the spiritual and ritual aspects of Islam rather than giving prominence to the political aspects, such as establishing a Muslim theocracy governed by Islamic law. Of course, the political aspects did become quite significant in due course.

Levtzion (1994) observes that there was a recurrent dynamic of accommodation and tension between *ulama* and ruling elites across West Africa. While *ulama* advocated Islamization of both social and political orders, ruling elites preferred to retain the original template of accommodating Islamic social and political norms within the pre-existing African social and political orders. Levtzion argued that this tension itself rests upon a division of labour between *ulama* and political rulers. While viewed as spiritual rather than political, *ulama* can still serve in many political roles such as arbiters and conciliators in conflict, envoys and peacemakers, and they may even be part of the electoral council charged with electing a new ruler when the need arises. Clearly, *ulama* wielded political influence on rulers that gave them vested interest in preserving the status quo rather than agitating for radical change. The influence of *ulama* on rulers was further enhanced by the widespread belief in their efficacious invocation of the divine power of Allah in favour of a client. Even non-Muslim rulers often sought the services of the *ulama*. Rendering such services provided the first openings for the *ulama* to introduce Islamic political norms into the otherwise non-Islamic polities in an 'evolutionary process of mutual adjustment between chiefs and Muslims' (Levtzion 1994, 338). Eventually, this process may result in converting the non-Muslim chief, but not necessarily the entire political system, which often continued to function according to both Islamic and non-Islamic political norms.

Historically, however, the political role of the *ulama* has followed two contrasting traditions in West Africa. The accommodationist tendency described above is termed the Suwarian tradition, named after Al-Hajj Salim Suware, a 13th century Islamic scholar from the area of the central region of modern Mali (Wilks 2012, 96ff). His scholarly career and legacy have been historically linked to the disintegration of the old Malian empire, and his greatest influence has been among Dyula (Juula) traders who often lived as a minority among various groups of non-Muslims. Launay observes that under these historical conditions, the tradition of Islamic learning founded by Suware 'stressed the religious co-existence of these two categories, Muslims and unbelievers', as well as emphasizing 'the separation of religion and politics', which became widespread in 'the southern fringes of the Manding trade network' (Launay 1996, 80).

The Maghilian tradition, named after the 15th century scholar from present-day Algeria, Abd al-Karim al-Maghili, represents the opposite tendency of seeking to install more purely Islamic political norms and institutions, including the application of Sharia, thereby bringing the *ulama* into their prominent judicial and legal roles (Batra¯n 1973). Al-Maghili visited several Muslim communities in West Africa, wrote treatises on how to rule in accordance with Islamic law, and served as a *qadi,* judge of Islamic law.[2] Al-Maghili wrote a treatise on how Muslim rulers should prevent their subjects from undertaking Islamically forbidden practices, which was specifically addressed by name to Abu Abdullahi Muhammad b. Ya'qub (i.e. Muhammad Rumfa) Sultan of Kano (*c.* 1463–99), and another treatise on Islamic government titled *Ta'rif fima yajib 'ala 'l-muluk*, which is now regarded as Kano's first Islamic constitution (Bivar and Hiskett 1962, 107). Both the Suwarian tradition of Islamic learning and its apolitical aspects, and the Maghilian tradition and its political activism were transmitted across the communities of West Africa (Idrissa 2018).

Beginning from the seventeenth century, the *ulama* influenced by the Maghilian tradition began proactively to seek changes in the political status quo by demanding strict adherence to Islamic norms, including the application of Islamic law. Thus began the series of jihads that raged across West Africa, including the jihad of Usman 'dan Fodio that led to the establishment of the Sokoto Caliphate in the areas of present-day northern Nigeria (Last 1967). The era of West African jihads ended at the beginning of the 20th century when European powers toppled all the Islamic theocracies established by the activist *ulama* (a vast literature includes Curtin 1971; Robinson 1985; Gomez 1993; Hanson 1996). The legacies of the Islamic theocracies have, however, continued to inspire contemporary *ulama* towards social and political activism, thereby demonstrating a historical and even nationalist dimension to contemporary Islamic radicalization.

[2] The most notable among al-Maghili's writings that remained influential in West Africa are his written responses to the questions of Al-Hajj Askia Muhammad, the ruler of Songhai empire from 1443 to 1538, translated into English with annotation and commentary by John O. Hunwick, *Sharia in Songhay* (1985).

In the pre-colonial era, becoming an *alim* took many years of training and apprenticeship in a master-disciple relationship that provided not only religious knowledge, but also spiritual insight, moral character, charisma and access to divine power. It also entails life-long loyalty of the disciple to the master. Equally important is the indispensable role of the master as the conveyor and guarantor of learning and piety, especially because in the ancient traditions of Islamic learning there is a deeply entrenched distrust of disembodied knowledge contained in the written corpus. The agency of the master is believed to be imperative for safeguarding orthodox Islamic tenets, and averting heretical doctrines. This collegial validation of Islamic knowledge had its origins in the rudimentary nature of the Arabic alphabet in the first centuries of Islam. The absence of diacritics and vowels made the early Arabic alphabet more of a set of mnemonic symbols that makes it exceedingly difficult to ascertain the correct reading of any written Arabic text without the guidance of an expert. Because the Qur'an was originally transmitted orally, coupled with the necessity of its correct ritual recitation in devotion, it was virtually impossible to satisfy the ritual requirement of correct recitation of the early copies of the Qur'an written in the rudimentary Arabic alphabet. To this day, the correct recitation of the Qur'an still requires oral instruction by a competent expert, who must have been similarly instructed by another expert, going back all the way to the recognized reciters who were taught by the Prophet Muhammad. The accurate transmission through a reliably authoritative chain of known experts is called *isnad*. It is such a basic axiom in the epistemology of Islamic learning that knowledge transmitted in other ways is, at best, suspect, if not totally invalid.[3] This point is supremely important: without the collegial validation of Islamic knowledge that *isnad* provides, idiosyncratic understandings of Islamic tenets that depart radically from the received traditions cannot be controlled.

It took centuries to develop the many features of this classical tradition of learning in which the *ulama* were historically trained, including the close association with the traditional political authorities that made the *ulama* integral members of the establishment, and therefore, a veritable force for counter-radicalization (see Bobboyi 1993). Yet, it is equally important to recognize the presence of the counter-current in the educational formation of the *ulama* that emphasized distance from political authorities. The jihad of Usman 'dan Fodio that led to the establishment of the Sokoto Caliphate in present-day northern Nigeria was part of the wider West African regional development of radicalized *ulama* seizing power to establish Islamic theocracies. Based on its own *isnad* such as the Maghilian tradition, this counter-current could lead to radical activism.

[3] For an insightful analysis of the centrality of *isnad* in traditions of Islamic learning, see William A. Graham, 'Traditionalism in Islam: An Essay in Interpretation'.

But the Maghilian tradition can also lead *ulama* to keep away from political authorities altogether to focus on Islamic piety. Rather than pursuing revolutionary politics, they turn to what could be termed 'private practice' of teaching and ministering to the social, economic, ritual and spiritual needs of their disciples. A focus on private practice is justified not only by the division between quietist and political traditions of Islam, but also by the division between public and private orientations within political traditions, which also tended to confine the *ulama* to spiritual pursuits.

Islamic education in colonial Nigeria

Both the political activism and quietism of the *ulama* were affected by the imposition of British colonialism in Nigeria at the turn of the 20th century. Among the major consequences of British colonialism are the transformation in the professional formation of the *ulama* as well as shifts in their multiple roles. The establishment of the Northern Provinces Law School in Kano in 1932, later renamed the School for Arabic Studies in 1946, began to introduce fundamentally different orientations in the professional training of the *ulama*. In contrast to the master-disciple model that formed the bedrock of the pre-colonial traditions of Islamic learning with its strong counter-radical potential, the new form of Islamic learning was modelled after the modern government school system introduced by the British. Since its establishment, the School for Arabic Studies has remained the template for dozens of similar Islamic schools subsequently established all over the northern parts of the country (Umar 2003). Comparable transformations of Islamic learning among Yoruba Muslims in the south-western parts of the country were led not by the British colonial authorities but by Muslim civic associations that emerged in the colonial era. The most prominent are: the Anwar-ul Islam Movement of Nigeria that began in 1916 as the Ahmadiyya Movement in Nigeria;[4] the Ansar-ud-Deen Society of Nigeria established in 1923 (Reichmuth 1993, 1996; Gbadamosi 1978), and the Nawair-ud-deen Society of Nigeria that merged two different societies to become one in 1939.[5] The *ulama* trained in these schools are in many respects recognizably different from the *ulama* trained in the older master-disciple traditions of Islamic learning.

In contrast to the already discussed pre-colonial traditions of Islamic learning, especially the historical patterns of interactions with political authorities and strong potential of *isnad* to inhibit radicalization, these then-new traditions of Islamic learning carry greater potential for radicalization. First, the new Islamic schools in which new generations of

[4] See: www.anwarulislam.com/beginning.asp, accessed 28 July 2014.

[5] http://nawair-ud-deen-society.com/about.html, accessed 28 July 2014.

ulama received their professional training are based on the technical transmission of Islamic religious knowledge embodied in the written corpus of Islamic classics rather than in the received collective expertise of the *ulama* – a very radical departure from the traditional emphasis on the centrality of *isnad* and the strong expectation of disciples' loyalty to their masters. Instead of the collegial validation provided through *isnad* and represented in certificates issued by the individual master attesting to the disciple's successful completion of a particular text, the new tradition of Islamic learning depends on the institutional validation provided by the new Islamic schools established or licensed by the authority of the modern state and represented in the certificate issued formally by the school attesting to the successful completion of an approved course of study. This circumvents the supreme importance of the disciple's life-long loyalty to the master, articulated in traditional aphorisms such as 'the disciple should be like a corpse at the hand of the person giving it ritual bath', and 'a disciple without a master will have Satan for his master'.[6] Nothing resembling such absolute loyalty is inculcated in the new traditions of Islamic learning. While graduates of the new Islamic schools respect their teachers, they are under no obligation to maintain life-long loyalty to their teachers or even to their alma maters. A disciple's absolute loyalty to the master is accompanied by deference that restrains intellectual dissent from the views of the master, creating a mechanism of moderation. Critical and independent thought are not totally absent in the older tradition of Islamic learning, as articulated in the aphorism that the truth deserves greater loyalty than the master. Yet, both are not particularly encouraged, and are in fact, rare.

Modelled after the modern government school system, the new Islamic schools foster the modern norms of critical thought and individual autonomy through the sort of institutional practices at schools called the silent curriculum (see Snyder 1973; Giroux and Purpel 1983). Additionally, these norms are also expected and valued in the careers in modern state bureaucracies available to the *ulama* trained in the new Islamic schools. Modernists like to valorise critical thought and individual autonomy as liberalizing catalysts. But there are unacknowledged modern authoritarian tendencies deeply rooted in the modern valuation of efficiency, technical precision, and rational calculation. These are expected to ascertain the optimal allocation of resources, including time and effort, for achieving greater and better outcomes of any endeavour. Once ascertained, the optimum trumps everything

[6] For elaborate articulation of the ethos undergirding the older tradition of Islamic learning, see al-Nu'man ibn Ibrahim Az-Zarnūjī (d. 1223), *Ta'līm al-Muta'allim-Ṭarīq at-Ta'-allum*, translated into English as *Instruction of the Student: The Method of Learning* by G. E. von Grunebaum and Theodora M. Abel (1947).

else, thereby creating a basis for what could be termed the modern authoritarianism of the optimum. Imbibed intellectually in the new Islamic schools and habitually internalized in the course of modern careers, the tyranny of modern norms, especially the relentless drive for the optimum, can easily combine to lead graduates of the new Islamic schools towards radical tendencies, largely non-violent, often in subtle ways that are not easy to discern.

For example, the origins of contemporary Islamic radicalism in Nigeria are located in the modern careers of Sheikh Abubakar Mahmud Gumi, who passed away in 1992, and his prominent disciple, Sheikh Isma'il Idris, who died in 2000. Both were educated in the School of Arabic Studies, the premier modern Islamic school. Gumi began his modern career in the early 1950s as teacher in Maru Teachers' College, where he was a colleague of Malam Aminu Kano, the doyen of radical Muslim politicians of then-Northern Nigeria. Gumi never studied in Saudi Arabia, but he was posted to Nigeria's Hajj Mission in Jeddah, Saudi Arabia, giving him ample opportunity to strengthen his existing Salafist convictions, particularly as he accompanied Sir Alhaji Ahmadu Bello, the Premier of Northern Nigeria and the Sardauna of Sokoto, on his many travels to Saudi Arabia, serving as his Arabic translator. Sheikh Gumi was also closely associated with Alhaji Ahmadu Bello's modernization policies, including the modern reform of Islamic law that led to Gumi's appointment as a Khadi of the Northern Nigerian Sharia Court of Appeal in 1962. A year later, he was promoted to head the court as the Grand Khadi, the position he held until he retired in 1976 (Umar 1993).

Even more important than his career in government was Gumi's preaching career using modern mass media. Gumi's preaching career in Kaduna while working closely with Alhaji Ahmad Bello started at the Sultan Bello Mosque, located next to the official residence of Alhaji Ahmadu Bello in Kaduna. As the imam of the mosque, Gumi's congregation included not only the Premier of Northern Nigeria, but also his ministers, advisers, and top ranking government functionaries, for whom Gumi's modernism must have resonated well. In addition to leading the prayers and giving sermons, Gumi also gave Islamic lessons through Hausa interpretations and commentaries on important Islamic texts, as well as Hausa commentary on the Qur'an during the annual fasting in the month of Ramadan. When Gumi's sermons and lessons began to be aired on Radio Television Kaduna (RTK), his audience was significantly enlarged to include the millions of listeners and viewers of RTK. Similarly, Sheikh Gumi wrote regularly in the Hausa-language weekly newspaper, *Gaskiya Ta Fī Kwabo*, thus adding another group to his audiences. Sheikh Gumi used the modern mass media to popularize his radical religious views against the Sufi orders to which the majority of northern

Nigerian Muslims belong, although he limited a full-blown critique of Sufism until after the death of Ahmadu Bello in 1966.[7]

The mass following that Gumi generated became organized into the *Jama'atu Izalatil Bid'a wa Iqamat al-Sunna* (Society for the Eradication of Innovation and the Reinstatement of Tradition, often referred to by its acronym JIBWIS, or simply Izala). Although Sheikh Gumi was the inspiration, it was his disciple, Malam Isma'il Idris, who formally founded Izala in 1978 (Loimeier 1997; Kane 2003; Ben Amara 2011). After graduating from the School for Arabic Studies in 1973, and on the advice of Sheikh Gumi, Malam Isma'il Idris' joined the Nigerian army as an imam. I have elsewhere examined the connection between the radicalism of Izala and its modernism (Umar 2001). The following analysis on the contribution of the *ulama* to radicalization provides an update, and explores the developments that have ended Izala's monopoly of Islamic radicalism in Nigeria.

Climate of opinion

The radio broadcasting of Gumi's ideas for Islamic reform began the process of the popularization of Islamic discourses. Starting in the 1960s, Gumi was the only speaker in the Islamic programs aired by RTK. Given his already developed Salafi orientation, his Hausa interpretations of Islamic texts, including commentary on the Qur'an during the fasting month of Ramadan, were radical departures from the established Islamic traditions prevalent in Nigeria. The millions of radio listeners and television viewers gave Gumi a vast audience for his radical criticisms against the prevailing Sufi beliefs and practices of the Tijaniyya and Qadiriyya – the two dominant Sufi orders with substantial following among Nigerian Muslims. In 1976, RTK was renamed Radio Kaduna, and in 1978, the federal government took ownership of Radio Kaduna and made it a branch of the Federal Radio Corporation of Nigeria (FRCN).[8] For many years, Sufi leaders have been demanding air-time on Radio Kaduna so that they could also present their views and respond to Gumi's criticisms. The transformation of Radio Kaduna into a branch of FRCN made it easier for Sufi leaders to achieve their goal of obtaining air-time. Shaykh Dahiru Usman Bauchi, a prominent leader of the Tijaniyya and very

[7] For details on the life history of Shaikh Abubakar Gumi and the development of his ideas, see M.A. Sanusi Gumbi, *Tarihin Shaikh Abubakar Mahmud Gumi* (published without bibliographical data), and *Tarihin Wa'azin Shaikh Abubakar Mahmud Gumi* (1988). See also Sheikh Abubakar Gumi's autobiography, *Where I Stand* with Ismaila Abubakar Tsiga (1992); and Andrea Brigaglia, 'The Radio Kaduna Tafsîr (1978–1992) and the Construction of Public Images of Muslim Scholars in the Nigerian Media' (2007).

[8] See 'Takaitaccen Tarihin Kafa Gidan Radiyo Kaduna' (Brief History of Radio Kaduna Station) at www.radionigeriakaduna.net/x/?page_id=8, accessed 28 July 2014.

vocal critic of Gumi, began to feature in the Islamic programs aired by FRCN.

More changes in the media landscape, including the commercialization of the FRCN and the introduction of private radio and television stations, have steadily led to more and more broadcasts of Islamic programs from the perspectives of different Muslim individuals and groups. It is now possible for individuals and organizations, including anonymous sponsors, to purchase air-time to broadcast their own views. In particular, during the fasting month of Ramadan, many radio and television stations alter their regularly scheduled programs to allow for more time to broadcast sponsored commentaries on the Qur'an from all kinds of perspectives. The air waves are now inundated with Islamic religious broadcasts from divergent doctrinal viewpoints.

Another track of the media-induced saturation of Islam in the public sphere is the use of what I call portable media, namely: audio and video cassettes, CDs/DVDs, media cards, cell phones, email, social media and the internet. Again, the use of these portable media can be traced to the initial recording of Gumi's religious lectures and commentaries on audio and video cassettes from the late 1960s. Following its establishment in 1978, Izala began to record the sermons, lectures, and speeches of hundreds of its *ulama*. These recordings are then mass-produced for sale not only to Izala followers but also to any interested buyer. As in the case of the radio broadcasts, the Sufi orders severely criticized in the cassette and video recordings of Izala discourses were left with no option but to resort to the same media. Apart from wholesalers in sections of markets in Kano and Kaduna – the major distribution hubs – there are many street hawkers struggling to make quick sales in traffic hold-ups in the big cities of northern Nigeria. In most of the production studios, distribution networks, and marketing outlets, recorded Islamic discourses, popular Hausa films, pirated copies of foreign films are bought and sold side-by-side, although some people specialize in one or the other. Many people are commercially involved in the recording and editing of these Islamic discourses, as well as their mass production, distribution and marketing. The growth of this industry since the 1990s has been facilitated not only by the policies of liberalizing communication and broadcasting, but also by the increasing availability of affordable technologies, including computers, cds/dvds, digital cameras, cell phones and access to the internet. Reliable statistics are not available, but observations from field research suggest that millions of copies are bought and sold in Nigeria and in all the Hausa-speaking communities across West Africa and other regions of the world.

The net effects of the burgeoning mass production and marketing of recorded Islamic sermons and discourses has been the saturation not only of the airwaves, but also of the homes and streets of even the remotest village in the country. The integration of the production of these recordings into the Kannywood Hausa film industry illustrates paradoxically the depth of the Islamic saturation of diverse sectors of life as evidenced in subtle and sometimes overt presence of Islam in Hausa films. Kannywood film scripts are sometimes adapted from the Qur'an. Even when scripts are not explicitly adapted from the Qur'an, the dominant narrative structure in Hausa films articulate the Islamic values of the Hausa culture, reflecting the many ways through which the rising tide of Islamic sermons and discourses have influenced the media landscape as well as the private and the public spheres. As documented in the chapter by Meagher and Hassan (this volume), Kannywood producers are put under considerable social and political pressure to make film plots more Islamic, under threat of bans or Islamic declarations that the industry is haram.

Malam Kabir Gombe, one the most prolific among Izala preachers, recounts proudly that the extensive reach of Izala can be seen in diverse places and forms across the country. He contends that Izala's struggles over the years have achieved a lot, to the extent that there are Izala followers in every Muslim home in Nigeria, despite the tremendous and brutal opposition of the Sufis and their supporters that included arrest, harassment, detention and disruption of Izala preaching events. He states that traditional rulers have also joined the ranks of Izala supporters, adding that even the Sultan of Sokoto emphasized that Shehu Usman waged his jihad to establish the Sunna, the main reason for the existence of Izala. Of course, the Sultan is not a follower of Izala, and as such could not have meant what Malam Kabir Gombe has in mind. The extensive spread of Izala influence has reached even the universities, where, according to Malam Kabir, only unsuccessful students could be found supporting Sufi orders.[9] Clearly, Malam Kabir Gombe is over-stating the extent of Izala's spread, but the relevant point to note here is that some of the *ulama* are very conscious of the importance of the size of their audience.

As social and political institutions, private homes, cultural norms, and aesthetic and artistic imagination have become saturated with the contentious religious discourses articulated by the *ulama*, a climate of opinion has emerged in which some individuals and groups could find justification for radicalism in the discourses of the *ulama*. The evolution of the saturation that began in the 1960s and continued to spread far and wide illustrates the changing nature of radicalization. It began with the simple increase in Muslims' shared-awareness of beliefs and practices that Muslims should uphold and observe. Then came the observable growth in public expressions and displays of those beliefs and practices, as evidenced by the proliferation of mosques. The saturation reached its zenith in the vigorous

9 Malam Kabiru Gombe, *Saki Shehu, Kama Ubangijin Shehu* (Leave the Sufi Mentor, and Hold onto the Creator of the Sufi Mentor).

contestations over the authenticity of Islamic beliefs and practices, as well as the authority Muslim preachers can invoke to recruit followers to their own interpretations of Islam. The numerous cases of acrimonious disputes and violent conflicts over control of mosques direct our attention to another arena in which the *ulama* contribute to radicalization, namely: the sectarian division and tension rising from fierce competition among the *ulama* for influence and followers.

Divisions and tensions

As already noted, the saturation of Islamic discourses was characterized by the rival conceptions and interpretations of Islamic tenets that began with Gumi's criticisms of the Tijaniyya and Qadiriyya, and those criticisms inspired the formation of Izala in 1978. The bitter sectarian conflict that has been raging between Izala and the Sufi orders has been amply documented in many studies that have also illuminated not only the religious polemics involved but also their social and political dimensions and consequences (Kane 2003; Loimeier 1997; Ben Amara 2011; Hiskett 1980). Other sources of sectarian division also existed between competing factions within both the Sufi orders and Izala. However, conflict between Sufis and Salafis prompted reconciliation between the Qadiriyya and the Tijaniyya as they joined forces to battle Gumi and Izala during from the 1970s, though since the 2000s now appears to be falling apart.[10]

Similarly, sectarian polemics over doctrines, and squabbles over leadership during the 1980s divided Izala in the two factions known as Izala A based in Jos and Izala B based in Kaduna. Finally, the 1990s saw the emergence of a younger generation who abandoned formal affiliation with Izala while still continuing to uphold Salafist beliefs. Boko Haram emerged from the ranks of this younger generation (Thurston 2013; Anonymous 2012). Again, there are detailed studies of the internal factionalization within Izala (see Ben Amara 2011). But there are two important features of the internal factionalization within both Izala and the Sufi orders that have contributed to radicalization but have not been sufficiently addressed in the existing literature.

A first mechanism that connects factionalization to radicalization is fragmentation *within* major religious sects. Faction leaders define their factions through distinctive beliefs and practices that depart significantly

[10] For example, see the evolving story about the accusation of the leader of the Sokoto branch of the Qadiriyya Youth (Shababul Kadiriya) that Sheik Dahiru Bauchi has impugned Shehu Usman 'dan Fodio by unfavourably comparing the influence of Shehu Usman 'dan Fodio as less than that of al-Shaykh Ibrahim Niasse. But Sheikh Dahiru Bauchi responded by denying that he had ever impugned Shehu Usman 'dan Fodio, and that he respects 'dan Fodio and his descendants. See the Hausa language weekly newspaper, *Aminiya* 25–31 July 2014, 9.

from the parent religious organizations they are breaking away from, or by more radical reformulations of the same beliefs and practices held by the parent organizations. In recent years, an emerging Tijaniyya faction known as 'Yan Hakika has defined itself by the radical reformulation of the Tijaniyya version of the Sufi doctrine known as *wahdatal-wujud* (unity of being/existence), which was also in contention in an earlier split within the sect. The historically contentious doctrine of *wahdatal-wujud* holds that there is no difference between Almighty Allah and His creation because the latter is a mere manifestation of the former. While deemed blasphemous by those who argue that no one can associate themselves with Allah, this doctrine is taken to the other extreme by 'Yan Hakika, who claim a closeness to Allah in which they are no longer bound by Muslim rules such as fasting, praying five times a day and other constraints. Another example of internal factionalization leading to religious radicalization is what one author calls 'ultra Salafism', which characterizes the doctrines of Mohammed Yusuf, the late leader of Boko Haram. Yusuf built his mass following on the radical view that any institution not ordained by Allah, including modern secular education and indeed all Western state institutions, are religiously forbidden to Muslims (Anonymous 2012). As internal factionalization divides religious groups, factional leaders may come up with more radical discourses as a strategy of recruiting followers and branding their faction. While 'Yan Hakika represent a form of internal factionalization viewed as morally dangerous, Boko Haram reveals an internal radicalization of belief that poses the danger of violence.

A second under-researched mechanism of radicalization in Nigeria emerges from the consequences of contestation between rather than within major sects. In contrast to the radicalization from internal factionalization, the sectarian divide between Izala and the Sufi orders has created a radicalization of the Sufi orders in subtle as well as flamboyant ways. Among the subtle ways are the increasing adoption of the Salafi scripturalism that encourages literal readings of the Qur'an and the sayings of the Prophet Muhammad. Salafi scriptural fundamentalism also entails the view that beliefs and practices can enjoy Islamic legitimacy only if they can be supported with quotation from the Qur'an and the sayings of the Prophet Muhammad. In contrast, the vast majority of non-Salafi Muslims approach Qur'an as a text requiring careful reading and learned interpretation before its injunctions can be properly understood. Prominent Sufi thinkers have found verses of the Qur'an and traditions of the Prophet Muhammad that support their beliefs and practices, and draw on a body of theological and legal scholarship. But equally important, Sufi thinkers have also grounded the Islamic validity of their beliefs and practices in non-scriptural bases, including mystical encounters with God, or with the Prophet Muhammad. For example, Sheikh Ahmad al-Tijani, the founder of the Tijaniyya, stated that he obtained the litany of his Sufi order in a live encounter with the Prophet Muhammad, who also guaranteed the superiority of the Tijaniyya and the salvation of its adherents. In response to Izala's vigorous criticisms articulated in the language of Salafi scripturalism, prominent Sufi leaders contend that there are Qur'anic bases of Sufi beliefs and practices, declaring Chapter 18 of the Qur'an as the chapter of Sufis and their followers. While this Sufi recourse to Salafi demands for scriptural proofs is evidence of radicalization of Sufi practice through interactive effects, other examples of Sufi radicalization are clearly and unmistakably the outcome of the confrontation with the Salafis.

For example, the celebration the Prophet Muhammad's birthday (*mawlid*) used to be observed annually by Sufis with modest festivities. But in response to Izala's criticism, Sufi orders have greatly intensified the observance of *mawlid*. Decoration of streets with flags and images of leaders of the Sufi orders, including giant posters on billboards illuminated with neon lights at night, have made it impossible not to notice that a major community festival is being observed. While the Prophet's birthday was previously celebrated for two nights only, contemporary celebrations last for more than a month, with posters and flags mounted weeks ahead of the actual birthday, and kept in place for many more weeks after the event. Also newly introduced is the 'national' observance of the *mawild* in major public arenas in one of the state capitals, which is video-recorded, mass-produced and marketed. Whereas only the birthday of the Prophet Muhammad used to be observed, nowadays, the birthdays of many saints of the Sufi orders are also celebrated in similarly elaborate fashion.

From the Izala perspective, these additions to the celebration of the *mawlid* are indicative of how the Sufi orders continuously add to their religion the heretical innovations (*bid'a*) that Izala has dedicated itself to eradicating. But, for the followers of the Sufi orders, Izala's continuing opposition to their elaborate celebration of the *mawlid* is clear proof of Izala's disrespect for the Prophet Muhammad and the Sufi saints. In a sense, the more elaborate celebration of *mawlid,* including that of the saints, seems to be motivated by spite against Izala, as much as by adoration of the Prophet Muhammad and the Sufi saints. Clearly, the unintended consequence of Izala's initial criticism against celebration of *mawlid* has been the amplification of that very practice, thus demonstrating the radicalization of the Sufi orders as an unintended consequence of the interactive effects.

Another illustration of the impact of interactive effects and unintended consequences can be seen in the evolution of the Shi'ite-oriented Islamic Movement in Nigeria led by Sheikh Yaqub El-Zakzaki since the late 1970s, not only in its opposition to the state, but also in its sectarian difference from the Sunni majority of Nigerian Muslims. Originating within the ranks of the Muslim Students' Society and thoroughly influenced by the Iranian revolution with its Shia ideology, El-Zakzaki's movement was initially characterized by its militant activism for the establishment of an Islamic state in Nigeria through the Iranian type of Islamic revolution. 'Islam Only' was the slogan that simply but powerfully proclaimed and popularized their radicalism, while their signature tactic for instigating the Islamic revolution in Nigeria were street demonstrations that often ended in violence when police attempted to control the demonstrations. Hundreds of lives have been lost, and leaders and members have been detained and imprisoned on several occasions. Another important tactic has been the use of *al-Mizan*, the weekly Hausa newspaper published by the Islamic Movement in Nigeria, to stir Muslims into the revolutionary action that will establish the Islamic state in Nigeria.

However, El-Zakzaki's agitation for the Islamic revolution was subsequently captured by political forces. A clear indication that the radicalism of the Islamic Movement in Nigeria had lost its revolutionary edge came in 1999–2000 when Governor Ahmed Sani of Zamfara State started the restoration of full Sharia law that rapidly spread to 12 other northern states. Muslims of various inclinations heralded Governor Ahmed Sani as an Islamic hero who has courageously championed the re-assertion of Islam into Nigerian politics (Ostien 2007, especially volumes II–IV). But El-Zakzaki was sceptical that this development would lead to the kind of Islamic state in Nigeria for which he has been actively working. He observed that the Islamic purification of society is the first order of business, and that the capture of political power is meaningful only when it is aimed at protecting the Islamically purified social order that has already been put in place. He added that the wisdom behind the penalties of Islamic law is to 'protect a pure society from being polluted'. El-Zakzaki holds that if Sharia law is applied outside the context of 'an Islamic government in an Islamic environment', it will become 'an instrument with which to punish poor people' (*Vanguard* 15 April 2000). Of course, El-Zakzaki and his Islamic Movement in Nigeria still affirm their Islamic activism but more in pious discourses and festivals, including several annual celebrations of the Shia heroes and solidarity with Muslims' political struggles in many parts of the world, especially the Palestine-Israel conflict. In the 2014 street demonstration in solidarity with the Palestinian struggle, more than 20 people lost their lives when soldiers opened fire on the demonstrators in Zaria for reasons that have remained in dispute. A more catastrophic encounter occurred a year later, leaving over three hundred followers of El-Zakzaki dead, according to official figures, and over one thousand dead according his followers. Clearly, the evolution of El-Zakzaki's Islamic Movement in Nigeria demonstrates the dynamic nature of radical movements, and the potential for radicalization to emerge from tensions with the state as well as relations between Muslim sects. Recent violent conflict involving the

Shia indicates that, when the state captures the form of radical movements while failing to deliver on ideals of justice and purity, the potential for violence lurks beneath the surface.

Both the climate of opinion that allows some individuals to find the religious support for their radical tendencies, and the radicalizing pressures created by factional bidding wars arise from internal dynamics within the *ulama* and the Muslim community at large. Other pathways to radicalization are rooted in the external dynamics of relations with non-Muslims. In this context, *ulama* articulate discourses that construct Muslims' victimhood in their relations with non-Muslims, while at the same time ridiculing and demonizing others, including Muslims who do not share such views. These discourses are capable of radicalizing some individuals and groups even to the extent of violent confrontation with the Other.

Construction of Muslims' victimhood

A popular theme in the discourses of the *ulama* is the articulation of Muslims' victimhood. Examples include denial of the right of Muslim women to wear what is deemed to be the proper Islamic dress in schools and working places, disrespecting Islamic sentiments and symbols, and obstructing Muslims' equal access to governmental positions and services. Proclaiming conspiracy theories is one major rhetorical strategy of articulating Muslims' victimhood. These conspiracies range widely from the simplest to the more elaborately conceived and camouflaged. Governor Murtala Nyako's claim that the Boko Haram insurgency was a genocide organized and executed by the Federal Government of Nigeria under President Goodluck Jonathan is a logical extension of the more widespread view that Boko Haram is sponsored by some prominent Christians in Nigeria and Islamophobes from abroad with the intent of damaging the image of Islam, humiliating Muslims, and killing them (Nyako 2014). Such conspiracy theories, a common theme in the discourses of Muslims' victimhood, indicate a need for Muslims to resist their victimization, and to seek revenge against their enemies who plot, execute or support these outrageous conspiracies.

The various constructions of Muslims' victimhood should be understood in the larger context of what I term 'the politics of ethnic and religious balancing' in Nigeria. There is a widespread expectation that the distribution of political power, appointments to governmental offices and political positions, provision of services and facilities, as well as the allocation of economic resources should be done in an even-handed and fair manner. Apart from its constitutional expression in the doctrine of federal character and the establishment of the Federal Character Commission, the politics of ethno-religious balancing is also deeply entrenched in the patterns of elite alliances in Nigerian politics. Arguably, the politics of ethno-religious balancing is the bedrock of both the stability and instability in Nigerian politics. When it works well, the politics of ethno-religious balancing ensures stability by promoting inclusion, a sense of belonging, fairness and equity. When it works badly, it leads to instability by fostering intense competition, resentment, and a sense of disenfranchisement, exclusion and marginalization. These negative dimensions of the politics of ethno-religious balancing provide the context for understanding radicalization through the discourses of *ulama* that articulate Muslim victimhood.

Sometimes Muslim victimhood is articulated in a sectarian fashion that ridicules Muslims who belong to a rival group for their failure to see the supposedly self-evident victimization of Muslims, or the underlying conspiracies. Muslim elites and politicians are also criticized for failing to upholding the interests and dignity of Muslims in Nigeria. These discourses tend to escalate from insipid accusations of naivety and negligence through the more insidious ridicule and demonization, and the discursive violence of *takfir* that excommunicates Muslims from the Islamic fold. The climax of this escalation can be seen in Boko Haram's extreme use of *takfir*, culminating in targeted assassinations of some *ulama*, emirs, Muslim community leaders, politicians and ordinary Muslims, because Boko Haram considers them traitors to Islam (see Zenn and Pieri 2017).

The late Muhammad Auwal Albani's elaborate opposition to polio vaccination provides a telling illustration of the construction of Muslim victimhood. On 13 January 2013, Albani organized a public event at his Dar al-Hadith al-Salafiya in Zaria for the purpose of expressing what he termed 'our Salafi stand on vaccinations of all types, not only polio vaccination, for which the Federal Government of Nigeria accepted the contract from World Health Organization'.[11] In his opening remarks, Albani states that he organized 'this gathering of the community, including journalists, *ulama*, experts and stakeholders in health matters in order to inform the Nigerian Muslims and the whole world at large about the bad stand taken by the federal and state governments, especially those in the north, to impose on Muslims the vaccinations against alleged diseases'. This remark alludes to both Muslim victims of unwanted inoculation campaigns, and the conspiracies behind those campaigns.

Albani invited a professor of pharmaceutical sciences and a professor of law, both from Ahmadu Bello University, as guest speakers. In introducing the guest speakers, Albani explains that the wisdom of inviting

[11] Muhammad Auwal Adam Albani Zaria, 'Polio: Cuta ko Kariay' (Polio [Vaccination]: Infection or Provention?) DVD recording by Sauturijjalisunna.

experts is 'to hear directly from those stakeholders in health matters who are the most knowledgeable. They are the ones entrusted by God with this entire business'. The professor of pharmaceutical sciences was to address scientific questions about the nature of polio and polio vaccinations. Albani also observed that there are legal aspects to the controversies about polio vaccination because of the harassments to compel people to be vaccinated, threatening them with arrest, detention, confiscation of properties, expulsion from towns, etc. For these reasons, the professor of law was invited to address the legal questions: Under Islamic law does government enjoy the power to do these things? Does English law (i.e. English Common Law) empower the government do these things? Does customary law permit these things?

Two key points sum up the contentions of the professor of pharmaceutical sciences in a lecture that lasted for over two hours. The first point is that God Almighty created two types of people: immuno-efficient people who can endure infections, and immuno-deficient people who are vulnerable to infections. It is for God to decide whether immuno-deficient people are exposed to the polio virus and become ill. By forcefully administering the polio vaccine on everyone, people without immunity will be exposed and become infected, and that is why polio vaccination lacks any benefit. The second point is that rather than the ineffective and potentially harmful vaccination, overcoming malnutrition is the more effective protection against viral infection. Exposing children to viral infection owing to the poverty and malnutrition inflicted upon them is an injustice. Given that poverty and malnutrition are considerably higher in northern Nigeria where Muslims predominate, it is an injustice targeted at Muslims. Given that scientific research has demonstrated that polio vaccination is more harmful than beneficial, its imposition on Muslims is the result of a Western conspiracy.

Turning to the legal issues, the professor of law indicated that there is no basis in Islamic law or in Nigeria's Constitution for the Federal Government of Nigeria to impose polio vaccination on Nigerians. Dwelling at length on the Western conspiracies to control and dominate Muslims, the imposition of polio vaccination on Muslims is presented as an example of the elaborately planned and systematically executed conspiracies that have been so relentless in pursuing their goal that they tolerate no opposition. Even the few courageous Westerners who voiced any opposition have been ruthlessly eliminated.

By marshalling the authority of scientific research and university professors, Albani fortifies the conviction in the conspiratorial construction of Muslim victimhood. For him, this approach indicates the sophistication of his generation of modern *ulama*, who are better prepared to confront the enormous challenges of the domestic and international conspiracies against Muslims.[12] Albani's elaborate articulation of Muslims' victimhood via the authority of university professors proclaims implicitly not only the imperative for Muslim solidarity but also the urgent need for action.

Another construction of Muslim victimhood is more explicit in its appeal for the urgent need to resist forcefully the conspiracies against Muslims. Malam Abubakar Gero Aragungu, a popular Izala preacher, delivered a lecture after the nomination of Dr Goodluck Jonathan as the People's Democratic Party (PDP)'s presidential candidate in the 2011 general elections. Malam Abubakar Gero began by reminding his audience that Nigerian Muslims were observing a three-day mourning period because of the calamity that had befallen them. He lamented that 'in the land of 'dan Fodio and Sheikh Gumi, Muslims have been defeated in an electoral contest even though Muslims constitute 75% of the population'.[13] Malam Gero claimed that, while President Yar Adu'a was sick, acting President Jonathan invited 'the biggest infidels in the persons of George Bush, Tony Blair and Condoleezza Rice' to the Presidential Villa. For Malam Gero, the visits of these Western leaders indicate the role of Western powers in the conspiracy of appointing the erstwhile Muslim Governor of Kaduna State, Alhaji Namadi Sambo, as vice-president so that his Christian deputy governor, Mr Patrick Yakowa, would take power in Kaduna State. As a result, Muslims forfeited control of the sensitive governorship of Kaduna State that has been central to Muslim influence in Nigerian politics.

According to Malam Gero, Muslims are obligated to vote for a fellow Muslim even if he belongs to another sect. He quotes Qur'anic verses (3:119) commanding Muslims to unite in solidarity against the unbelievers, whose words proclaim contentment with Muslims but their hearts conceal their enmity (9:8); hence Muslims should not vote for non-Muslims (68:35). Emphatically, Malam Gero insists that he is not articulating his personal opinion but the express commandment of God. He castigates the Muslim delegates to the PDP convention who voted for the 'infidel candidate' as acting contrary to God's commandment. He exposes the enormity of this political negligence by juxtaposing it with horrendous situations of Muslims in Plateau State, where 'the spilled blood of innocent Muslims had not yet dried on the ground'. Speaking with great emotion, Malam Gero charges that these remiss Muslim delegates are 'hypocrites of Usman 'dan Fodio'. He appeals to God to curse 'whoever casts his ballot for the infidel'.[14]

12 Muhammad Auwal Adam al-Bany Zaria, 'W.H.O. [Cibiyar Lafiya ta Duniyya] Taji Tsoro' (The World Health Organization is Afraid), DVD recording by Sautu Rijalissuna.

13 Malam Abubakar Gero, 'Nigeria ta Fara Hayaki' (Nigerian Has Begun to Smoke', DVD recording dated 15 January 2011.

14 Ibid.

Malam Gero's contention that his political views enjoy divine mandate represents a powerful discursive strategy that insinuates that Muslims who hold different political opinions are disobeying God. Invoking the deplorable atrocities against innocent Muslims, Malam Gero's construction of Muslim victimhood carries the clarion call to resistance if not vengeance. Also pointing in the same direction are the discourses of the *ulama* that ridicule and demonize other Muslims as well as non-Muslims.

Ridiculing difference and demonizing the Other

Acceptance of difference and diversity has been historically the dominant trend in Islamic societies across the globe. The Sunni-Shia divide, which originated in political differences, is common knowledge, so also the existence of seven different schools of Islamic law, four accepted as valid by Sunni Muslims, and three different schools recognized by the Shia Muslims. The Ash'ariyya and Maturidiyya have been the accepted theological streams within Sunni Islam, with further sub-divisions within both. In contrast to the traditionalist orientation of these Sunni theological groups, a rationalist theological orientation is associated with the Mu'tazila and the Shia. There are also the dozens of Sufi orders that reflect the historical and contemporary diversity within the mystical orientations among Muslims. In addition to the empirical existence of these overlapping and divergent differences in Islamic history and contemporary societies, there are also doctrinal foundations for the acceptance of difference and diversity in the Islamic traditions. Qur'an 49:13 states: 'Mankind! We [i.e. God] have created you male and female, and have made you nations and tribes that you may know one another'. Similarly, a tradition of the Prophet Muhammad states that the existence of differences among Muslims is a sign of Allah's mercy. Given these historical, sociological and theological bases of the acceptance of difference and diversity in Islam, it is a radical departure for any individual or group to claim exclusive ownership of the validity of one and only one interpretation or conception of Islam. The problem here is not internal fragmentation, but intolerance of difference within Islam.

As with any tradition, there are limits to the Islamic acceptance of difference and diversity. Therefore, it should not be surprising that there have also been counter-currents in Islamic theology, history and contemporary Muslim societies seeking to restrict the boundaries of Islamically acceptable difference and diversity. For example, Qur'an 3:105 commands: 'And do not be like the ones who became divided and differed after the clear proofs had come to them. And those will have a great punishment'. A tradition of the Prophet Muhammad states that Muslims will be divided into 73 sects but only one will achieve salvation. Yet, emphases in Islamic intellectual traditions remain firmly on acceptance of difference and diversity even while not denying the imperative for unity. This point is elegantly expressed in a saying attributed to Imam Muhammad ibn Idris al-Shafi'i (d. 820), credited with founding the field of Islamic legal theory, and one of the four Sunni schools of Islamic law. Al-Shafi'i is said to have stated that 'our school of interpreting Islamic law is correct but could be wrong, while the other schools of interpretation are wrong but could be right'. In other words, no one interpretation of Islam should exclusively enjoy absolute validity. Consequently, the discourses of Nigerian *ulama* that reject the validity of difference and diversity are radical departures from the mainstream of Islamic traditions.

As already pointed out, Nigerian Muslims have been historically divided into sects and sub-sects, and their differences have sometimes led to tension that contribute to radicalization. The key mechanisms of divisions and tensions leading to radicalization are the discourses of the Nigerian *ulama* that ridicule doctrinal differences, reject social diversity, and demonize other Muslims. Vehemence, animosity and indecorous rhetoric are the characteristics of the discourses that challenge the Islamic identities of other Muslims and question the validity of their worship. These rancorous discourses pose an existential threat in the here and now against Muslims with different opinions, and jeopardize their salvation in the hereafter. In Islamic law, a Muslim who becomes an apostate should be given three days to revert to Islam, and should be executed if he fails to do so. Thus the stakes are very high, and can lead to violence among zealots.

In contemporary Nigeria, the opening salvo in the war of words can be traced to Sheikh Gumi's severe criticisms of Sufi orders as religious systems totally outside of Islam. In his *al-aqidah al-sahiha* published in 1972, Gumi charged that followers of Sufi orders hold beliefs and practices contrary to Islam, thereby effectively declaring them apostates for which they could legitimately be killed. It is, therefore, not surprising that the Sufi leaders responded in kind by also excommunicating Gumi (Umar 1999). The following analysis demonstrates the more recent trends in the continuing saga of mutual excommunications between followers of Gumi and those of the Sufi orders.

Responding to Izala's scripturalist rhetoric of following only the Qur'an and the traditions of the Prophet Muhammad, Sheikh Dahiru Bauchi has repeatedly stated that the truly learned scholars of Islam have recognized his mastery of the Qur'an and its interpretation. In contrast, he describes Sheikh Gumi as 'the ignorant among the *ulama* but the learned among the ignorant' since Gumi failed to recognize what Sheikh Dahiru Bauchi believes to be the indisputable Qur'anic foundations of Sufism. In a recorded lecture titled the *Evil of Izala*,[15] Sheikh Dahiru Bauchi accused Sheikh Gumi not only of being ignorant of the true teachings of Islam, but also of being deceitful, a liar and an opportunist. According to Dahiru Bauchi, when Gumi used to work with the Sardauna of Sokoto in the early 1960s, he concentrated his objections on the Tijaniyya, and refrained from attacking the Qadiriyya because of its association with the legacy of Shehu Usman 'dan Fodio, with which the Sardauna of Sokoto strongly identified himself. But after the Sardauna of Sokoto passed away, Gumi began to condemn the Qadiriyya as worse than the Tijaniyya.

In another lecture, Sheikh Dahiru Bauchi continues with his exposé of the dubious character of Sheikh Gumi and his followers. He ridicules Sheikh Gumi's reported remarks that casting a vote in elections is more important than observing the five daily prayers, and also the reported claim that Gumi urged his followers to vote for a Christian rather than followers of the Sufi orders. For Sheikh Dahiru Bauchi, these opinions are egregious examples of Sheikh Gumi's utter lack of understanding the basic teachings of the Qur'an, which says absolutely nothing about modern voting and elections. Therefore, Sheikh Dahiru Bauchi emphasizes that it is his own personal opinion but not a commandment of God that followers of the Tijaniyya should vote for a Christian rather than an Izala candidate. And since the Qur'an says nothing about elections, he would only say that voting for Izala shows poor judgement but does not make a Tijaniyya follower an infidel. In fact, Sheikh Dahiru approaches the grave issue of *takfir* quite delicately. He points out that Izala has repeatedly accused Tijaniyya followers of *takfir*. Rather than accusing Izala of the same, he just said that Tijanis are Muslims while Izala members follow their own religion, implying Tijanis do not recognize Izala as fellow Muslims. Sheikh Dahiru Bauchi raised the stakes in the polemical exchanges by holding Sheikh Gumi as the source of all the evil (*shari*) in Nigeria. He supported this extreme contention with a tradition of the Prophet Muhammad, which says: 'Whoever is the enemy of a saint, he is the enemy of God'. He interprets this by claiming that the rampant murder of innocent people and bomb explosions in the country are the result of God's anger because of Izala's insults of the Prophet Muhammad and the Sufi saints.[16] Following on an earlier tradition of comparative tolerance, this kind of demonization demonstrates the radicalization of the Sufi orders resulting from the interactive effects of the increasingly rancorous competition between the *ulama* of Izala and those of the Tijaniyya. Izala's responses are no less vehement in their demonization of the Tijaniyya.

15 Shaykh Dahiru Usman Bauchi, 'Sharrin Izala' undated CD Audio-recording by Abul Inyas Production, Jos.

16 Sheikh Dahiru Bauchi, 'Ba Mu Hada Kai da Izala Ba,' undated Audio-recording by Inyas Islamic Studio, Kaduna.

In an apparent repost to Sheikh Dahiru Bauchi's repeated claims that reputable Islamic scholars have recognized his mastery of the Qur'an, Sheikh Sani Yahaya Jingir, successor to Sheikh Isma'il Idris and current chairman of Izala's national council of *ulama*, contends that mere mastery of the Qur'an is not sufficient to make one a pious Muslim. It is imperative that the Qur'an is recited in the name of Allah alone. In particular, Sheikh Jingir states that followers of Sufi orders who read the Qur'an but violate its sanctity by claiming that their distinctive mystical litanies are equal to, or better than, the Qur'an should not be considered Muslims. He contends that by insulting the Qur'an in this way, a person becomes an infidel who will roast in hell-fire forever – if he dies without recanting. He claims that there are people who do all kinds of magical practices with the Qur'an, such as reciting Qur'an Chapter 37 naked – a practice most Muslims will consider sacrilegious – in the mistaken belief that these practices are efficacious.[17]

Hurling charges of such repulsive practices against each other, these discourses of demonization put their opponents outside the pale of decency, which is often the first step in discursive violence that could incite their listeners to physical violence. Yet, the transition from the discursive violence of demonization to physical violence is not automatic; it requires triggers and linkages as can be discerned from the evolution of the discourses of Boko Haram.

The path to violent radicalization

While the development of Boko Haram was in part a product of the bidding war of exclusivity, invective and victimhood unleashed by the vitriolic struggles between Salafi and Sufi scholars, there were important differences in their use of Salafist discourses which served to tip the sect into violent extremism. One key difference was that the founder of Boko Haram, Mohammed Yusuf, extended the charge of apostasy from other sects to engagement with the Nigerian secular state itself. A common theme in the early discourses of Boko Haram has been that they recognize only the power of God and no other source of power, including that of the Nigerian state. Where mainstream Salafists focused on capturing and Islamizing the state, Boko Haram saw obedience to a secular state as idolatry and was intent on destroying it. Since the outbreak of the current phase of the insurgency in 2010, the discourses of Boko Haram have escalated from inciting violence against agents of the Nigerian state and against critics of Boko Haram's ultra-Salafist teachings, to the current

17 Sheikh Muhammad Sani Yahaya Jingir, 'Wa'azin Kasa na 2011 a Maiduguri,' undated audio recording by Akidatus Sahiha Sunnah Cassette, Jos.

situation of the indiscriminate violence against innocent Muslims and non-Muslims who do not subscribe to Boko Haram's radical precepts.

The discourses of Boko Haram are solidly grounded in Salafi/Wahhabi scriptural literalism, but with a jihadi twist. Shifts to extremist ideology are evident in Yusuf's book, *Manhaj Da'awatina*, as well as hundreds of his recorded sermons and lectures. They are also evident in the numerous statements released by Abubakar Shekau after succeeding Mohammed Yusuf as the leader of Boko Haram, as amply documented in the substantial literature produced by several scholars analysing the complex discourses of Boko Haram (Ibrahim 2019; Zenn and Pieri 2017; Thurston 2016; Mohammed 2014; Eveslage 2013; Anonymous 2012). Some scholars have drawn attention to the jihadist turn in Yusuf's teachings, emphasizing doctrinal linkages to foreign jihadi scholars such as Abu Muhammad Al Maqdisi (Thurston 2016). Yet understanding how the discourse of Boko Haram led to violent radicalization goes beyond a focus on theology. The assumption that the key to Yusuf's mobilizing power was in the theological content of his discourse tends to overlook other dimensions of his discursive appeal. As this chapter has shown, other discursive mechanisms were required to make these jihadi discourses credible and even attractive to thousands of followers in what has historically been a tolerant Islamic environment. In addition to his doctrines, Yusuf's capacity for violent mobilization relied on his extreme use of many of the discursive mechanisms identified above: auto-interpretation of the Qur'an, more polemical preaching styles, and the extension of Islamic interpretation into a wide range of contemporary debates.

The Salafi rejection of Islamic legal schools and traditions of theological interpretation eliminated important sources of discipline on the interpretation of scriptures, with the unintended consequence of opening space for self-taught preachers, or 'auto-didacts'. In a recorded debate with one of his critics, Mohammed Yusuf explained that he never attended any formal school, indicating that he was largely self-taught. Anecdotal evidence suggests that he experimented with different Islamic groups, including the Shia who overtly rejected the authority of the Nigerian state, before settling with the prominent Salafi leader, the late Sheikh Ja'far Adam, who publicly repudiated Yusuf and his views before he was assassinated in 2007. Independent use of Salafi techniques of interpretation and disregard for the authority of their teachers allowed Yusuf and other Boko Haram leaders to regard themselves as *ulama* and behave accordingly, despite a lack of formal theological education, expressing religious views in which they depart radically from other *ulama*.

In addition to claiming religious authority for idiosyncratic interpretations of the scriptures, Yusuf also took the engaging and vitriolic Salafi preaching styles to new levels. Yusuf was known for his particularly engaging oratory skills, making use of the more direct and egalitarian style of religious discourse introduced by Salafis to recruit followers to his doctrines (ibid., 104). He also drew extensively on the Salafi practice of connecting his teachings to wider local issues, such as politics or moral debates. Initially used to combat the portrayal of Salafism as an Arab import, this technique allowed Yusuf to make his preaching more relevant to the lives of a neglected and disenfranchised constituency. But it also accentuated the portrayal of Muslim victimhood, as is evident in a number of his sermons (Kassim and Nwankpa 2018). The combination of unmoderated teachings and these other discursive strategies was, as we have seen, explosive.

Conclusion

Despite their religious centrality in northern Nigerian society, the intensely competitive context of the struggle for followers and influence has fragmented the authority of the *ulama*, allowing self-starters, trouble-makers, and autodidacts to banalize the importance of *ulama* as religious authorities. Worse still, in stark contrast to the rampant poverty amid their followers, the growing affluence and ostentation of some members of the *ulama* expose an unholy alliance with the powerful and the wealthy, under which the *ulama* appear ready and willing to lend legitimacy for ill-gotten wealth and abuses of power. Clearly, the *ulama* can squander their moral authority and social influence when they fail to live up to the expectations attached to their exalted status, laying the basis for radical and potentially violent new religious messages.

While the *ulama* are capable of inciting and promoting radicalization; they can also play crucial roles in counter-radicalization. The biggest asset of the vast majority of the *ulama* is their religious learning, based on long religious traditions of scriptural interpretation and Islamic legal schools, through which they construct Islamic identities, norms, beliefs and practices.

While the reputation of the *ulama* has suffered in recent years, they still wield considerable influence. They are deeply rooted in their communities in ways that allow them to articulate community concerns in a language that is locally resonant. Pictures give visibility to the mammoth crowds that attend religious events to listen to *ulama*, often creating huge traffic jams in cities and towns for hours or even days. Loyalty to the *ulama* is also visible in the giant posters with images of revered *ulama* displayed in living rooms, entrances to private houses and vehicles, and in public spaces. Most Nigerian Muslims, and most of the *ulama*, are not affiliated to radical groups, creating considerable space for counter-radical messages and community engagement to address issues of uncertainty, neglect and disaffection that may lead to radicalization.

From the perspective of the *ulama*, it is vital to prioritize the challenging of radical worldviews through counter-radical discourses, supported with empirical evidence. Not all Muslims are persuaded by the seductive appeal of conspiracy theories; this fact provides a window to begin challenging the narratives used to construct Muslims victimhood. The discourses of ridiculing difference and demonizing the Other may be easier to challenge, if only because such discourses are alienating and abhorrent, and can be exposed as contrary to Islamic tolerance of difference and respect for human dignity. In addition, the potential of caustic rhetoric and demonization to lead to violence should be highlighted. The centrality of mass and portable media in creating a climate of opinion favourable to radicalization must also be squarely confronted. Arguably, without mass electronic media, acceleration of radicalizing discourses would not have been as destructive as they have been, nor would they have spread as far and as quickly. Effective strategies of controlling the role of mass media in spreading radicalization are essential. Borrowing from the media success of the adversary, saturation of the mass media with counter-radical messages is one clear option, but such messages should be developed in consultation with respected *ulama* across affected areas. Appropriate regulation of radicalizing discourses is another valuable option, including the enforcement of existing laws against incitement to violence and threat to public order. But none of these discursive and ideological solutions can be effective without addressing the explicitly stated grievances of radicalized groups and individuals, as well as those who share similar conditions without succumbing to violent radicalization, to ensure that the seeds of extremist teaching do not fall on receptive soil.

Bibliography

Anonymous, 2012, 'The Popular Discourses of Salafi Radicalism and Salafi Counter-radicalism in Nigeria: A Case Study of Boko Haram', *Journal of Religion in Africa* 42 (2), 118–44.

Arjomand, Said A., 1999, 'The Law, Agency, and Policy in Medieval Islamic Society: Development of the Institutions of Learning from the Tenth to the Fifteenth Century', *Comparative Studies in Society and History* 41 (2), 263–93.

Az-Zarnūjī, al-Nu'man ibn Ibrahim, 1947, *Ta'līm al-Muta'allim-Ṭarīq at-Ta'-allum,* translated into English as *Instruction of the Student: The Method of Learning* by G. E. von Grunebaum and Theodora M. Abel, New York: King's Crown Press.

Bachar, S., Bar, S., Machtiger, R. and Minzili, Y., 2006, 'Establishment Ulama and Radicalism in Egypt, Saudi Arabia, and Jordan', Hudson Institute Research Monographs on the Muslim World, Series 1 (4), December, 1–48.

Batrān, A.A., 1973, 'A Contribution to the Biography of Shaikh Muḥammad Ibn

'Abd-Al-Karīm Ibn Muḥammad ('Umar-A 'Mar) Al-Maghīlī, Al-Tilimsānī', *The Journal of African History* 14 (3) 381–94.

Ben Amara, R., 2011, 'The Izala Movement in Nigeria: Its Split, Relationship to Sufis, and Perception of Sharia Re-Implementation', PhD Dissertation, University of Bayreuth.

Berkey, J., 1992. *The Transmission of Knowledge in Medieval Cairo: A Social History of Islamic Education*, Princeton, NJ: Princeton University Press, 1992.

Bivar, A.D.H. and Hiskett, M., 1962, 'The Arabic Literature of Nigeria to 1804: A Provisional Account', *Bulletin of the School of Oriental and African Studies* 25 (1), 104–48.

Bobboyi, H., 1993, 'Relations of Borno Ulama with the Sayfawa Rulers: The Role of the *Mahrams*', *Sudanic Africa* iv, 175–204.

Brigaglia, A., 2007, 'The Radio Kaduna Tafsîr (1978–1992) and the Construction of Public Images of Muslim Scholars in the Nigerian Media', *Journal of Islamic Studies* 27 (1), 173–210.

Cohen, H., 1970, 'Traditionists in the Classical Period', *Journal of the Economic and Social History of the Orient* 13 (1), 16–61.

Curtin, P., 1971, 'Jihad in West Africa: Early Phases and Inter-Relations in Mauritania and Senegal', *The Journal of African History* 12 (1), 11–24.

Eveslage, B.S., 2013, 'Clarifying Boko Haram's Transnational Intentions, Using Content Analysis of Public Statements in 2012', *Perspectives on Terrorism* 7 (5), 47–76.

Gbadamosi, T.G.O., 1978, *The Growth of Islam among the Yoruba 1841–1908*, London: Longman.

Gilbert, J.E., 1980, 'Institutionalization of Muslim Scholarship and Professionalization of the Ulama in Medieval Damascus', *Studia Islamica* 52, 105–34.

Gilliot, C., Repp, R.C., Nizami, K.A., Hooker, M.B., Lin, C.-K. and Hunwick, J.O., 2012, 'Ulamā', in P. Bearman, Th. Bianquis, C.E. Bosworth, E. van Donzel and W.P. Heinrichs, *Encyclopaedia of Islam*, 2nd edition, http://dx.doi.org/10.1163/1573-3912_islam_COM_1278, accessed 12 September 2019.

Giroux, H. and Purpel, D. (eds), 1983, *The Hidden Curriculum and Moral Education*, Berkeley, CA: McCutchan Publishing Corporation.

Gomez, M.A., 1993, *Pragmatism in the Age of Jihad: the Precolonial State of Bundu*, Cambridge, UK: Cambridge University Press.

Graham, W.A., 1993, 'Traditionalism in Islam: An Essay in Interpretation', *The Journal of Interdisciplinary History* 23 (3), 495–522.

Gumi, A. with Tsiga, I.A., 1992, *Where I Stand*, Ibadan: Spectrum Books.

Hanson, J., 1996, *Migration, Jihad, and Muslim Authority in West Africa*, Bloomington, IN: Indiana University Press.

Hiskett, M., 1980, 'The Community of Grace and its Opponents', *African Language Studies* XVII, 89–140.

—— 1992, *The Sword of Truth: The Life and Times of the Shehu Usuman dan 'Fodio*, Evanston, IL: Northwestern University Press.

Humphreys, S., 1991, *Islamic History: A Framework for Inquiry*, Princeton, NJ: Princeton University Press.

Hunwick, J.O., 1985, *Sharia in Songhay*, Oxford: Oxford University Press.

Ibrahim, M., 2019, 'In Search of a Plausible Theory to Explain the Boko Haram Phenomenon: Analysis of Intellectual Discourses on Insurgency and Violent Extremism in Nigeria', The Centre for Contemporary Islam, University of Cape Town, South Africa, Occasional Papers 2, March, 24–35.

Idrissa, R., 2018, *The Politics of Islam in the Sahel: Between Persuasion and Violence*. Routledge.

Kassim, A. and Nwankpa, M., 2018, *The Boko Haram Reader: From Nigerian Preachers to the Islamic State*, Oxford: Oxford University Press.

Kane, O., 2003, *Muslim Modernity in Postcolonial Nigeria: A Study of the Society for the Removal of Innovation and Reinstatement of Tradition*, Leiden: Brill.

Last, M., 1967, *The Sokoto Caliphate*, London: Humanities Press.

Launay, R., 1996, *Beyond the Stream: Islam and Society in a West African Town*, Berkeley, CA: University of California Press.

Levtzion, N., 1994, *Islam in West Africa: Religion, Society and Politics to 1800*, Variorum Collected Studies Series, Brookfield, VT: Ashgate.

Loimeier, R., 1997, *Islamic Reform and Political Change in Northern Nigeria*, Evanston, IL: Northwestern University Press.

Mohammed, K., 2014, 'The Message and Methods of Boko Haram', in *Boko Haram: Islamism, Politics, Security, and the State in Nigeria*, M.-A. Pérouse de Montclos (ed.), Leiden: African Studies Centre, 9–32.

Nyako, M.H., 2014, 'On On-Going Full-Fledged Genocide in "Northern Nigeria": A Memo to the Northern Governors' Forum by His Excellency, V/Admiral Murtala H. Nyako (rtd.), CFR, GCON, Executive Governor Adamawa State, April 16, 2014', http://globalvillageextra.com/a-memo-to-the-northern-governors-forum-by-his-excellency-vadmiral-murtala-h-nyako-rtd-cfr-gcon-executive-governor-adamawa-state, accessed 8 May 2014.

Ostien, P., 2007, *Sharia Implementation in Northern Nigeria, 1999–2006: A Sourcebook*, Ibadan: Spectrum Books.

Petry, C., 1981, *The Civilian Elite of Cairo in the Later Middle Ages*, Princeton, NJ: Princeton University Press.

Reichmuth, S., 1993, 'Islamic Learning and its Interaction with Western Education in Ilorin, Nigeria', in *Muslim Identity and Social Change in Sub-Saharan Africa*, Louis Brenner (ed.), Indianapolis, IN: Indiana University Press, 179–97.

—— 1996, 'Education and the Growth of Religious Associations among Yoruba Muslims: The Ansar-Ud-Deen Society of Nigeria', *Journal of Religion in Africa* 26 (4), 365–405.

Robinson, David, 1993, *The Holy War of Umar Tal*, Oxford: Clarendon Press.

Sanusi Gumbi, M.A., 1988, *Tarihin Wa'azin Shaikh Abubakar Mahmud Gumi*, Kaduna.

Snyder, B.R., 1973, *The Hidden Curriculum*, Cambridge, MA: The MIT Press.

Thurston, A., 2013, 'Managing Ruptures, Telling Histories: Northern Nigerian Muslim Intellectuals and Arab Universities, 1900–2007', PhD dissertation, Northwestern University.

Thurston, A., 2016, 'The Disease is Unbelief: Boko Haram's Religious and Political Worldview', The Brookings Project on U.S. Relations with the Islamic World, Analysis Paper 22, January, Center for Middle East Policy at Brookings, Washington, DC.

Umar, M.S., 1993, 'Changing Islamic Identity in Nigeria from the 1960s to the 1980s: From Sufism to Anti-Sufism', in *Muslim Identity and Social Change in Sub-Saharan Africa*, Louis Brenner (ed.), Indianapolis, IN: Indiana University Press, 154–78.

—— 1999, 'Sufism and its Opponents in Nigeria: The Doctrinal and Intellectual Aspects', in *Islamic Mysticism Contested: Thirteen Centuries of Controversy and Polemics*, Frederick de Jong and Bernd Redtke (eds), Leiden: Brill, 357–85.

—— 2001, 'Education and Islamic Trends in Northern Nigeria: 1970–1990s', *Africa Today* 48 (2), 127–50.

—— 2003, 'Profiles of New Islamic Schools', *The Maghreb Review* 28 (1–2), 146–69.

Vanguard, 2000, 'Interview: My Grouse with the Amputation in Zamfara – Zakzaky', 15 April.

Wilks, I., 2012, 'The Juula and the Expansion of Islam into the Forest', in Levtzion and Pouwels (eds), *The History of Islam in Africa*, Athens, OH: Ohio University Press.

Zenn, J. and Pieri, Z., 2017, 'How much Takfir is too much Takfir? The Evolution of Boko Haram's Factionalization', *Journal for Deradicalization* 11 (3), 281–308.

3

Why in Borno?
The history, geography & sociology of Islamic radicalization

ABUBAKAR K. MONGUNO & IBRAHIM UMARA

Introduction

Since the return to civil rule in 1999 and especially since 2002, Nigeria has suffered from extreme insecurity owing to escalating communal clashes, electoral violence and religious crises – the most serious of which is the Islamic insurgent group known as Boko Haram whose anti-establishment campaign commenced in 2002. The American-based Council on Foreign Relations document that, since 2011, some 60,000 people were killed in Nigeria from various causes, with Boko Haram as the most significant source of violent deaths (Council on Foreign Relations 2019). Borno State is viewed as the most insecure of Nigeria's 36 states. Between November and December 2018 alone more than 200 people were killed by Boko Haram in Borno (Ogundipe 2018; *The Defense Post* 2018). From its origins in Borno State, the Boko Haram insurgency has threatened the security of the Nigerian state and the Lake Chad region, turning this remote North East state into a central focus of national as well as global attention. Amid the ongoing mayhem, many have wondered why this violent Islamic insurgency has emerged in the comparatively quiet state of Borno. For many people, the question 'why in Borno?' is important to explain the disproportionate effect of this remote insurgency on the stability of the Nigerian state.

The effect of the insurgency on Borno's social and economic activities has been devastating as loss of lives and abductions continue without an end in sight. Of the three Nigerian states previously placed under emergency rule – Borno, Adamawa and Yobe – Borno State has recorded the highest number of displaced persons, reaching over 1.5 million out of some 2 million displaced across all affected states (International Office for Migration, 2018). Many of the displaced are refugees in neighbouring

Chad, Cameroun and Niger. This disturbing trend is a radical departure from Borno's peaceful past. Few imagined that Borno would spark a crisis of this magnitude, or suffer such devastating effects. In fact, the security situation of the state at the moment is so overwhelming that even Nigeria's security officials appear helpless. We approach the search for explanations through historical, geographical and social science perspectives. Uncovering the contribution of these various factors will guide our understanding of radicalization, as well as how best to approach deradicalization and counter-radicalization efforts.

This chapter examines how various parts of Borno State have been affected by Boko Haram attacks and associated fatalities, as well as exploring the underlying reasons for these occurrences. In the first part, a brief background and methodology is presented. The second section looks at patterns of insurgency across the state, including in Maiduguri, the state capital. This will be followed by contextual explanations of the observed patterns of insurgency where the role of history, religious, ethnic and environmental issues are discussed. In the fourth section, social paths of radicalization are explored, while the fifth section concludes.

Borno State: Background

Borno State is currently the largest of the 36 states of Nigeria with an area of 69,435 square kilometres. It is the relic of the historically much larger Kanem-Borno Empire that covered many parts of present day Nigeria, Cameroun, Chad, Niger and some of Libya (Wakil 2009, 13). Kanuri is the language of the majority of the Borno population, who are bound together by a common cultural heritage linking the people of 'Nigerian' Borno as it exists today and their kith and kin in neighbouring countries (Tijani 1989, 81). But Borno also hosts a sizeable number of other ethnic groups who have coexisted peacefully with the Kanuri for centuries. Prominent among these are the Babur/Bura, Marghi, Glavda, Mandara, Shuwa Arab, Gamergu and Kibaku among others. Seibert (2000) has documented at least 30 different languages that are spoken in Borno State. However, it is worthy of note that the dominance of the Kanuri language and culture over these ethnic groups in the past has led to the assimilation of many individuals, especially from the Marghi and Gamergu, who have been 'Kanurized'. While Islam has been the dominant religion of the people of Borno and is significant in their daily lives, Christianity is also numerically significant in southern Borno especially on the Biu Plateau among the Bura, and the southern foothills among the Kibaku in Chibok. There are also pockets of Christians on the Gwoza Hills around Ngoshe, Ashigashiya and Attagara, near the border with Cameroun. Small numbers of followers of African religions are still found in the Gwoza Hills though intense proselytization by both Islam and Christianity (especially Islam) has succeeded in shaping the beliefs of many hilltop dwellers of Gwoza. The three emirates of Bama, Dikwa and Gwoza, together comprising five present-day Local Government Areas (LGAs), were previously under the trusteeship of the United Nations until the referendum of 1961 that brought them into Nigeria.

The early presence and acceptance of missionaries in southern Borno brought Christianity and secular education, accounting for the large disparity in educational attainment between the southern and other parts of the state, where Islamic systems of education prevail. Educational disparities are reflected in higher levels of development in southern relative to central Borno (except Maiduguri) and the northern part of the state in particular. Borno indigenes from the south form the bulk of the workforce at the state and federal levels, present in all sectors but especially in education and health. Conversely, Borno South continues to play a secondary role politically due largely to the numerical strength of the Kanuri that constitute the majority in the north and central parts, including Maiduguri. The colonial legacy of indirect rule has ensured that even the traditional institutions in some parts of the south such as Chibok and Damboa are under Borno Emirate Council which until very recently appointed Kanuri district heads.

In terms of party affiliation, the state has usually been led by the opposition rather than the ruling party at the federal level. Many citizens of Borno State believe this has partly accounted for the low level of infrastructural development compared with relatively younger states like Bauchi and Gombe that have always belonged to the same political party as the federal government. This view is supported by a recent quantitative study showing that among northern Nigerian states belonging to centralized states in pre-colonial times, oppositional politics was 'punished by underinvestment in access to these [federal] services with resulting unequal outcomes persisting till today' (Archibong 2018, 335). Downie (2015, 72) succinctly described the six states of the North East zone of Nigeria as the nation's political backwater, due to years of neglect by the central government which stifled opposition strongholds. Concomitantly, the states of the North East are among the states with the poorest development indicators, including poverty, education and other public services. Borno State became politically aligned to the federal government for the first time in 2015 when the All Progressives Congress (APC) won the presidential elections that brought President Muhammadu Buhari to power. Modest successes recorded in counter-insurgency operations by the military are generally perceived to have resulted from this alignment.

Methodology

This study was carried out based on quantitative and qualitative research conducted between April 2014 and February 2019, as well as drawing on the accumulated academic and local knowledge of the researchers who continue to live and work in Maiduguri. Mapping of fatalities covering the whole period of the insurgency was accompanied by two months of fieldwork, conducted largely in Maiduguri, between April and June 2014 at the height of the insurgency. Fieldwork involved 40 key informant interviews held with a wide range of people including Islamic scholars, academics, opinion leaders, people displaced by the insurgency, and friends/relations of insurgents. Data generated covered a range of areas – historical, life histories of known insurgents, areas affected by the insurgency and reasons behind their differing scales as well as factors involved including gender and ethnic dimensions. Snowball sampling was used owing to the sensitivity of the research, which necessitated extra caution to ensure the personal safety of the researchers, including recording some interviews as anonymous. This may introduce some measure of bias but, overall, offers useful insights into perspectives on the insurgency from within. Data on number of attacks and persons killed were based on media reports (print and electronic), and it should be borne in mind that many of the attacks may not have been reported (Terab 2014, 7), prompting studies by the Institut Français de Recherche en Afrique (French Institute for Research in Africa) on 'invisible violence' to trace unreported cases of violence in parts of Borno, Yobe and Kano States.

Records of the attacks attributed to Boko Haram within the period July 2009 to December 2018 were summarized and mapped according to LGA. The mapping took into account only two main factors, i.e. frequency of attack in any given LGA and total number of persons killed (including military, civilians and insurgents themselves). These two variables were separately mapped. For Maiduguri, the state capital, which constituted the epicentre of the conflict from 2009 to 2013, the views of the respondents interviewed on the levels of perceived insecurity within the different wards of the city were solicited and tabulated. Respondents were asked to rank the levels of insecurity in the 12 wards designated by the military Joint Task Force (JTF). These were the wards in which a 48-hour curfew was imposed by the JTF in May 2013. It is the sum of these ranks that was used in tabulating and mapping the perceived risk of living in certain parts of the city. Mapping perceived risk required considerable local knowledge because some of the names of the places used as hideouts for the insurgents were not administrative wards but names given by the locals for such neighbourhoods.

Patterns of insurgency

SPATIAL PATTERN OF INSURGENCY IN BORNO

While Borno State suffered the worst from the Boko Haram insurgency, there are spatial differences in the pattern of insurgents' attacks across the state. Figures 3.1 and 3.2 show the pattern of attacks by insurgents and number of persons killed respectively during the nine years from 2009 to 2018. Nearly all LGAs are impacted but the worst-affected areas are in Borno Central (Maiduguri, Konduga and Bama LGAs) and the northern part of Borno South (Gwoza and Damboa LGAs). In Borno North, the three contiguous LGAs of Abadam, Mobbar and Kukawa suffered high to moderate attacks. Overall, while Borno South is relatively less affected, the two LGAs of Gwoza and Damboa distinctively standout as areas with very high rates of attacks comparable to those in Borno Central. The same is true for Kukawa in Borno North.

In terms of the numbers of deaths, Maiduguri recorded the highest number of deaths, followed by Bama and Konduga (all in Borno Central). Gwoza recorded the highest number of deaths in Borno South. High casualty levels for Maiduguri are due to the high number of deaths recorded in the July 2009 uprising during which Mohammed Yusuf was killed, and the attack on Giwa barracks on 14 March 2014, as well as the targeting of the city in numerous bombings, which claimed thousands of lives. Apart from Damboa and Gwoza, there are fewer casualties in Borno South compared with the central and northern parts. Two LGAs in the south (Kwayakusar and Bayo) that were never attacked show no fatalities.

Table 3.1 shows the fatalities and the average number of persons killed in the attacks, by LGA. It may be observed that the fatality level is highest in the LGAs of Mobbar, Nganzai, Abadam, Kukawa and Monguno (in Borno North). These LGAs are closer to Lake Chad and now form the territory of the breakaway Islamic State in West Africa (ISWAP) headed by Abu Musab Al-Barnawy, son of the slain Boko Haram leader Mohammed Yusuf. The implication of this is that, although attacks and number of deaths are high in locations like Maiduguri, Bama and Gwoza, locations in northern Borno are more deadly as higher casualties are recorded with fewer attacks. For instance, in Mobbar an average of 56 fatalities are recorded in each attack compared with 25 in Maiduguri. The patterns of attacks and fatalities are mapped in Figures 3.1 and 3.2, respectively.

Exploring the reasons that explain the pattern described above is crucial to the formulation of effective counter-insurgency measures. In the first place, Maiduguri has the highest level of attacks because it is the epicentre of the crisis that has attracted a large number of insurgents over the years in addition to those who were recruited from within the

Table 3.1 Boko Haram attack severity ranking in Borno State, 2009–18

S/No.	LGA	No. of attacks	Fatality	Average fatality per attack	Rank
1	Mobbar	18	1,002	56	1
2	Nganzai	10	474	47	2
3	Kukawa	44	2,005	46	3
4	Abadam	30	1,212	40	4
5	Monguno	23	848	37	5
6	Ngala	38	1,381	36	6
7	Dikwa	23	737	32	7
8	Konduga	93	2,868	31	8
9	Jere	36	1,097	30	9
10	Kala/Balge	21	610	29	10
11	Bama	136	3,845	28	11
12	Kaga	28	790	28	11
13	Maiduguri Metropolitan	299	7,501	25	13
14	Damboa	88	2,140	24	14
15	Gwoza	158	3,406	22	15
16	Askira/Uba	35	746	21	16
17	Chibok	30	588	20	17
18	Marte	17	327	19	18
19	Mafa	37	645	17	19
20	Shani	4	63	16	20
21	Biu	42	525	13	21
22	Guzamala	10	126	13	21
23	Hawul	21	274	13	21
24	Magumeri	9	117	13	21
25	Gubio	10	122	12	25
26	Bayo	0	0	0	26
27	Kwayakusar	0	0	0	26
Total		**1,260**	**33,449**		

(Source: Computed based on IFRA database)

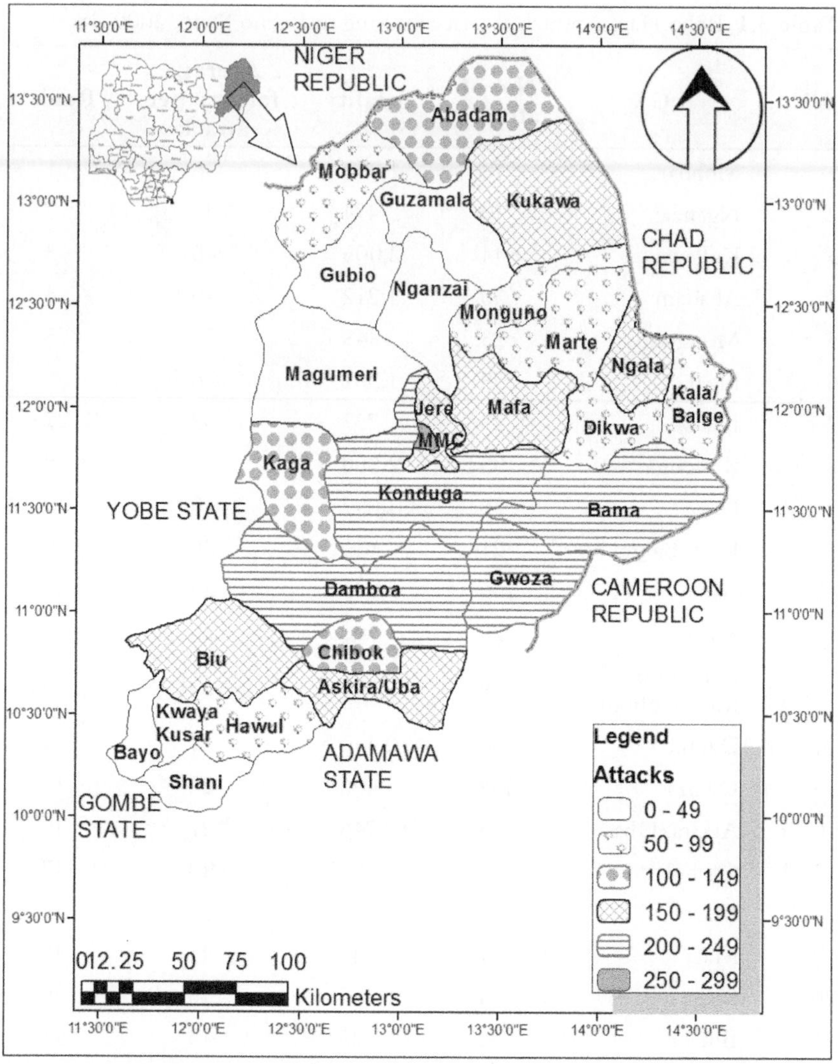

Figure 3.1 Number of attacks by Boko Haram July 2009 to December 2018
(Source: Based on data from IFRA's Nigeria Watch database, 2018)

city. The dislodgement of insurgents from the city in June 2013 led to their dispersal to the rural parts of Borno State. It is most probable that the division of Boko Haram into smaller cells was also maintained in the rural areas for operational efficiency. After the dislodgement from Maiduguri, in a video message vowing to recapture the city, Abubakar Shekau ordered the killing of Maiduguri residents. Since then, Boko Haram has targeted killing residents of Maiduguri along roads leading to the city.

Geographical factors played an important role in the movement of the insurgency into other parts of the state, specifically Bama, Konduga,

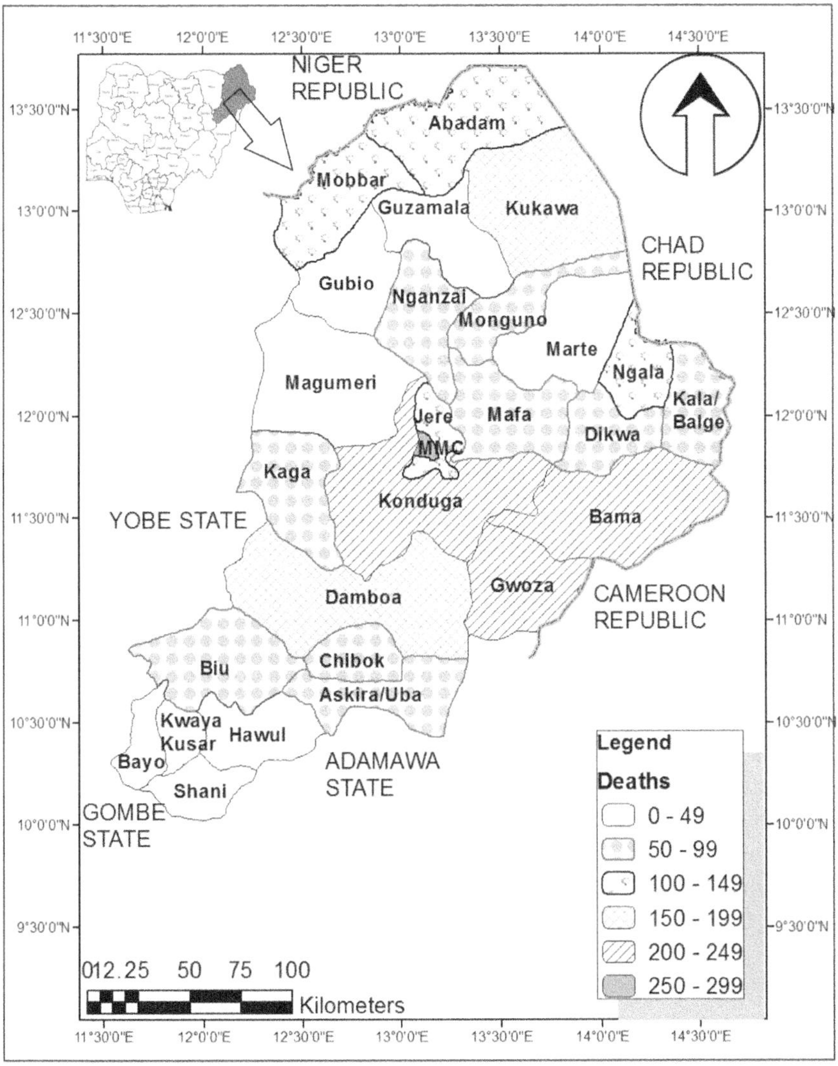

Figure 3.2 Number of deaths recorded 2009–18
(Source: Based on data from IFRA's Nigeria Watch database, 2018)

Damboa, Gwoza, Kukawa and Marte. The difficult terrain provided by these environments, especially the Sambisa forest and the area around Lake Chad, presented logistical barriers to counter-insurgency measures. The Sambisa forest was gazetted as a Game Reserve by Borno State Government in 1981. It covers an area of about 520 sq. km (128,500 acres) cutting across three LGAs of the state. These are Konduga, Gwoza and Damboa.[1] The greatest part of the forest lies in Konduga and Gwoza. The forest is more dense than the surrounding savannah grassland, and facilitates free

1 Interview with Assistant Director, Chad Basin National Park, Maiduguri 12 June 2014.

circulation of wildlife along an extensive east-west corridor that stretches into Cameroun via the Chingurmi Park in Bama LGA.

Although not part of the Sambisa forest, areas to the west as far as Gujba in Yobe State are also well forested. This entire forest belt has given refuge to Boko Haram insurgents whose cells occupied the different sections of the forest. Settlements especially of the Mulgwai and Maffa ethnic groups within the forest were later displaced when the activities of the insurgents became pronounced. Many of the youths from these communities later became recruits (discussed below). The high rate of insurgency in Konduga, Gwoza, Bama and Damboa LGAs can be seen from this perspective. Villages and the headquarters of these LGAs have suffered multiple attacks from Boko Haram including many unreported ones. It should be noted that these areas had very little history of insurgency prior to the entry of Boko Haram into the Sambisa forest.

Additionally Bama and Gwoza have other predisposing factors. The contiguity of these LGAs with the Camerounian border facilitates attacks on Nigerian villages and swift movement into Cameroun for safety. This must have prompted Cameroun to carry out counter-insurgency operations along her borders. Gwoza LGA has an additional peculiarity: its location in the Mandara hills, bestriding Nigeria and Cameroun, which presents further logistical difficulties for counter-insurgency operations. This has made the military reluctant to go after the insurgents, who have repeatedly attacked nearly all hilltop settlements of Gwoza LGA.[2]

With the exception of Monguno, which has a military barracks, LGAs adjoining Lake Chad have suffered more attacks and casualties compared with other LGAs in the northern part of the state. These include Kukawa (where Baga is located), Marte and Ngala which have experienced several attacks due to bad terrain. These LGAs have many settlements on Lake Chad that have become safe grounds for the insurgents and their activities, away from the Nigerian security forces in the interior. Insurgents often attack villages by looting, killing and sometimes abducting victims for use as recruits or sex slaves, thus crippling economic and social activities on the lake and in other settlements in the hinterland of these LGAs. A respondent displaced from Marte LGA reported that in one of such raid on 6 July 2014 the wife and four teenage children of the headmaster of Kirenowa Central Primary School in Marte were abducted by Boko Haram and taken to one of the settlements on the lake.[3] This mode of operation is similar to the Boko Haram cells in the Sambisa forest in the sense that they attack

2 Interview with anonymous respondent (displaced from Ngoshe village of Gwoza LGA, 58 years 3 June 2014). This respondent reported that Boko Haram has taken full control of some communities such as Ashigashiya to the extent that local disputes including matrimonial issues are arbitrated by the group.

3 Interview with anonymous displaced person, 49 years, Maiduguri, 10 July 2014.

their targets and swiftly move to their off-shore lake settlements for cover. Through these geographical shifts, Boko Haram has evolved from being a largely urban conflict into a threat to the whole of Borno State and to the Lake Chad Basin countries, putting it on the radar of global security threats, now heightened by nominal links with the Islamic State.

INSURGENCY PATTERNS WITHIN MAIDUGURI

Having examined patterns of insurgency at the state level, we will turn to a closer look at local patterns of the insurgency focusing on patterns of attack within Maiduguri. This reveals a great deal about the conditions that gave rise to Boko Haram. Table 3.2 shows the ranking of respondents' perceived risk of living within the different residential areas of Maiduguri which is used as a proxy for the scale of insurgency at the city level. The term residential area is used here to distinguish it from the conventional administrative wards because some of the neighbourhoods cover more than one ward while others form only a part, complicating the task of mapping.

Bulabulin Ngarannam, in the northern part of Maiduguri, was Boko Haram's major stronghold until June 2013 when they were finally chased out, and was perceived by respondents to be the most dangerous of all neighbourhoods. The area had bunkers for hiding kidnapped victims including women while also providing cover for the insurgents. The ranking pattern indicates a distance decay effect from the epicentre of the violence i.e. a decrease in risk with increasing distance away from Bulabulin Ngarannam. Most of the affected areas in the table are located in the central and northern parts of Maiduguri, similar to patterns of insurgency at the state level. Gwange ward in the southern part of Maiduguri, was perceived to rank higher in risk than some residential areas located nearer the epicentre of Boko Haram in the northern part of Maiduguri, such as Kumshe. This geographical risk pattern corresponds to socio-economic factors: Gwange is largely inhabited by the urban poor while Kumshe is inhabited by the middle class. Even though the first seven wards in rank are contiguous and predominantly inhabited by low-income residents the links between poverty and insurgency are neither simple nor direct. What is also clear from the table is that the last three wards in rank i.e. Custom, Goni Kachallari and Ruwan Zafi are mixed communities having especially a good number of the Shuwa-Arab ethnic group whose representation in the insurgency is minimal.

While these specific aspects are important for understanding the immediate issues surrounding the insurgency, it is equally relevant to explore broader historical and social contexts. It is the combination of the two that account for present-day activities of Borno.

Table 3.2 Respondents' ranking of high risk residential areas in Maiduguri (n=20)

Name of ward	Sum of ranks	Rank
Bulabulin Ngarannam	66	1
Kawar Maila	79	2
Bayan Quarters	89	3
Zajiri	123	4
Abbaganaram	130	5
Galadima	152	6
Old Maiduguri	155	7
Gwange	159	8
Kumshe	164	9
Lamisula	166	10
Custom	179	11
Goni Kachallari	190	12
Ruwan Zafi	193	13

(Source: Field data, 2014)

Contextualizing insurgency in Borno

THE ROLE OF HISTORY

Historical context provides rich evidence for understanding the society in which Boko Haram emerged. A good starting point is the common belief among many Borno elders that calamities befall the region cyclically every 100 years (Garba 2014, 15). This has been widely repeated in explaining the current insurgency by respected personalities of Borno and commonly believed by ordinary people.[4] The invasion of Borno during the Fulani jihad of Shehu Usman dan Fodio at the beginning of the 19th century, and the conquest by Rabeh Fadl-Allah about a century later, are often mentioned. Rabeh's invasion and rule of Borno (1893–1900) was one of the most turbulent times in the history of Borno. Rabeh, a Mahdist slave dealer from Sudan, made several attacks on Borno during which Kukawa, Borno's former capital, was destroyed and the Shehu of Borno was forced to flee to Maganna about 15 km (9 miles) south-west of Geidam in present Yobe State. Rabeh, described as a 'ruthless' leader (Connah 1981; Hallam 1993), ruled for seven years before he was killed by the French in 1900.

[4] Governor Kashim Shettima of Borno State has repeatedly made such statements publicly with reassurances that Borno has always overcome such calamities.

Parallels with Boko Haram are drawn in the popular imagination because Rabeh's attack on Borno came at a time when its leadership was weak and decadent. Commenting on the excesses of the court of Shehu Garbai, who ruled Borno before Rabeh's conquest, Kyari Tijani (1993) quoted the German explorer Barth as saying, 'the best of these mighty men cares more for the silver ornaments of his numerous wives than for the welfare of his people'.

Rabeh invaded Borno at a time of leadership crisis, specifically of decadence in the avowed values of piety, justice and religiosity demonstrated by earlier Sayfawa rulers of Borno. As in Rabeh's time, frustration with the corruption of local leaders was a key motivation for Boko Haram's attack on the Nigerian state, representing an attempt to impose Sharia law after the Borno State governor reneged on promises to adopt Sharia through the existing state system. As in past cycles of calamity, the Boko Haram insurgency was viewed as a rebellion against poor governance and failure to address the needs of the majority of Nigerians living in want (Sergie and Johnson 2014).The period between 2003 and 2011 is generally perceived by many in Borno State as the worst in terms of governance since its creation in 1976. Although Izala and Salafist scholars mobilized superior theological arguments in debates with Yusuf on the justification for participating in government, such intellectualism failed to change the course of the Boko Haram movement in the face of widespread disenchantment with a government that people considered to be corrupt and insensitive (Mohammed 2014, 48; Kassim and Nwankpa 2017, 11–26).

More recently, the Maitatsine rebellion in the 1980s led to the loss of hundreds of lives in Maiduguri. Similar attacks were recorded in Kano, Gombe and Yola but the casualties were much lower than in Maiduguri. Here as well, there are interesting parallels with Boko Haram. Both were sectarian rebellions against the state and popular among sections of the poor. Both groups recognized only their members as true Muslims such that the killing of other Muslims (and non-Muslims too) was permitted and worthy of reward from God. It is however interesting to note that despite these similarities, Maitatsine are still present in Maiduguri but have not been active or involved in the current insurgency. Maitatsine has rather confined itself to the practice of its rituals without being violent (Alkali et al. 2012).

Equally important to understanding the rise of Boko Haram is the secular education system that came with colonial rule, which has relegated to the backwaters the traditional *tsangaya* system of education in Borno. The secular education system was thought to undermine traditional values as it is perceived to glorify Western values, including Christianity. Even though schools were opened in Maiduguri as early as 1917, attendance was minimal due to stiff opposition by the *ulama*. Even though the longstanding resistance to Western education was not through violence as is the case today (Mohammed 2014), it influences a large population whose voice is strong in the current insurgency.

BOKO HARAM AS KHAWARIJITES

Historical occurrences outside Borno can also be helpful in comprehending the motives of the insurgency. The history of Islam is replete with sectarianism dating back to the period after the death of the Prophet Muhammad. Khawarij (Arabic: rebels) are the earliest sect that split off from the Islamic community during the reign of Caliph Ali ibn Abi Talib (r. 656–661). The sect adopted extreme doctrines, including a radical approach to *takfir* – declaring other Muslims to be non-believers – and significant deviations from strict Muslim observance was punished by death. Only those who shared the Kharijite views were considered true Muslims. Kharijites were known for their literal interpretation of the Qur'an, while indulgence in luxury and worldly pleasures was shunned.

According to many scholars, Khawarij tendencies are exemplified by Boko Haram and similar Islamic organizations such as Al-Qaeda and the Islamic State of Iraq and Syria (ISIS) (Garba 2014). These organizations are also known for their radical views about Islam and hence their attack on Western targets and symbols. Several debates took place between Boko Haram's leader Mohammed Yusuf and Salafist scholars like the late Sheikh Jaafar Adam and Sheikh Ibrahim Pantami over the legality of Muslims' quest for secular education. After the Boko Haram insurgency broke out in Maiduguri, the term Khawarij was used to describe Boko Haram and put in the public domain by scholars such as Sheikhs Bashir Mustapha Gwange, Abubakar Kachallah and Ibrahim Ngomari through radio programmes aired by the federal government-owned Peace FM and state government-owned Borno Radio. Since Boko Haram is widely recognized as an extreme form of Salafism, the association of the sect with the Khawarij heresy served to differentiate Boko Haram from mainstream Salafi scholars, who were keen to resist association of Salafism with extremism (Mustapha 2014; Thurston 2018). For this reason, Boko Haram's affiliation with the Sunni in its preferred name, *Jama'atul Ahlul Sunna li Da'wati wal Jihad* (People Committed to the Propagation of the Prophet's Teachings and Jihad), has been strongly resisted by Salafi scholars. Sheikhs Ja'afar Adam, Abubakar Kachallah, Bashir Mustapha and Ibrahim Ngomari were all Salafist scholars critical of Boko Haram. With the exception of Sheikh Abubakar Kachalla, all were later killed in acts widely attributed to Boko Haram.

ENVIRONMENT AND RADICALIZATION

The link between environmental stress and conflict has long been established by researchers (Homer-Dixon 1999; Kameri-Mbote 2005/2006, 12). Conflict, according to Homer-Dixon, is often the result of scarcity of environmental resources exacerbated by other factors like inequality, migration and the functioning of social institutions that act collectively to produce violence. These environmental factors are well demonstrated in the current insurgency in Borno. Vast portions of the entire north and central parts of the state suffer from the twin problems of drought and desertification. The phenomenon of 'cyclic and recurring' droughts has in fact been well documented in context of a larger Sudano-Sahel region that includes the northern and central parts of the Borno State (Thambyahpillay 1979). The harsh environmental conditions set in motion a southward migration of people from as far as southern Niger Republic into northern Nigeria including Maiduguri (Mortimore 1989). Maiduguri ranks 13th in the urbanization index in Nigeria, constituting the most urbanized state of the North East (National Population Commission 1998). Nearly a third of Borno's population live in Maiduguri (Waziri 2009). The city grew in size from 54,646 in 1953 (Ekanem 1972) to 740,123 in 2006, with an annual growth rate of 12 per cent (National Population Commission, 2010), acting as a central port of call for many of these environmental refugees who later settled permanently.

Interviews conducted by local population scientists indicate that the droughts of the early 1960s and 1970s gave rise to rapid in-migration of people from the northern part of Borno who settled in Zajiri and Bulabulin Ngarannam villages near Maiduguri. These areas are now suburbs in the northern parts of the city,[5] and later became notorious for insurgency (see Table 3.2). Yet, how could ordinary environmental refugees turn into insurgents? An initial factor relates to the fact that the people of northern Borno are particularly resistant to Western medicine and secular education in favour of the traditional systems, making this area educationally the most backward in the state. One informant disclosed that even in time of peace some LGAs of the north did not have more than five functional primary schools, and even these suffered from high attrition and dropout rates to enable children to help with animal rearing and domestic chores. A more shocking disclosure was that in the 1990s some politicians openly canvassed for votes by promising not to pressure parents to send their children to school.

While these attitudes were not absent from Maiduguri, the establishment of two new northern suburbs populated by migrants from northern

[5] Interview with Dr Muhammad Waziri, population geographer, University of Maiduguri, June 2013.

Borno represented a particularly concentrated cultural zone dominated by poverty and resistance to Western institutions. The combination of poor education and government neglect in terms of services combined to produce inequality between these individuals/communities and their relatively 'better-off' peers in other parts of Maiduguri. The message that egalitarian Sharia would replace the injustices suffered at the hands of the state as preached by Mohammed Yusuf tapped into a deep well of socio-historical as well as economic disaffection, offering a message that inspired followers and that many saw as worth dying for.

Lake Chad, the meeting point of several ethnic groups in the region for centuries, has been nature's greatest gift to Borno, providing sustenance and livelihoods. The relationship between man and his environment in the area around the lake has over the years been that of stress and opportunity (see Connah 1981, 244). Nigeria's portion of the lake (also shared by Chad, Niger and Cameroun) lies entirely within Borno State. But this vital resource has come under serious threat from climate change. While the lake's volume has been known to fluctuate historically, since the 1960s its surface area has reduced dramatically by 95 per cent from 25,000 sq. km (almost 10,000 sq. miles) in 1963 to less than 1,350 sq. km (520 sq. miles) at present, mainly attributable to drought and climate-related reduction in water flow from the rivers that feed the lake (Odada et al. 2006). The combined effect of these changes has over the years had a telling impact on Borno State in the form of severe loss of livelihoods and occasional inter-ethnic conflicts over water use. As the largest source of freshwater fish in Nigeria, the lake offers livelihoods to thousands of artisanal fishers and farmers, as well as associated livelihoods such as trading, transportation, boat making, etc. The importance of the lake to the communities it serves is underscored by de Graaf et al. (2014, 15).

> The majority of rural households participate in the fisheries of the Lake Chad on a seasonal and part-time basis. Throughout the year, local populations are alternately or simultaneously fishers, farmers and herders, and each part of land is potentially a fishing ground, a grazing area and a cultured field of arable crops, depending on the flood cycle. Therefore, depending on the flood cycle and income earning opportunities they will switch to fishing, agriculture or cattle raising and vice versa.

It has been estimated that the total population of the entire Lake Chad basin area is 37 million (UNEP 2004), two-thirds of whom live in the Nigerian portion of the lake. The effect of the receding lake on local livelihoods has been severe. In the 1970s the annual production of the entire lake ranged from 130,000–140,000 tonnes but this has dropped to an average of 84,030 tonnes between 1986 and 2013 (de Graaf et al. 2014). Suleiman (2013) reported that within a span of 20 years as much as 50 per cent of the lake's fish productivity may have been lost. Nigeria's annual fish catch currently accounts for 38 per cent of the total volume of fish caught from the lake, amounting to 45,854 tonnes. This is valued at US $106 million (£86.57 million as at August 2019), contributing about 0.03 per cent to Nigeria's GDP through export, while a sizeable quantity of fish from Chad, Niger, and Cameroun are also traded in Nigeria due to high demand. An informant who has been engaged in the marketing of fish at Baga fish market in Maiduguri also observed a noticeable decline in the quantity of fish brought from Lake Chad. When he started trading 25 years ago, an individual could bring as much as 100 cartons each market day. Today people hardly bring more than 20 cartons each.[6] Developments in Nigeria's portion of the Lake give further insights into how the drying up of the lake is related to the Boko Haram insurgency.

The main local population engaged in fishing on the lake has been the Buduma, the majority of whom live in the Chadian portion of the lake with extensive links to their kin in Nigeria. Over time, Hausa fishers – mostly migrants from Zamfara State – overwhelmed the Buduma numerically. With the receding of the lake, competition intensified between these groups for the lake's dwindling fish resources, leaving the Buduma economically marginalized in their own territory. The coming of Boko Haram to the lake settlements in pursuit of 'God's work' (Kanuri: *cida Alaye*; Hausa: *aikin Allah*) saw massive enlistment of Buduma youth into its fold, while there was much less engagement from the Hausa population. It became fairly easy to tell within each fishing island or community where Boko Haram members could be found. Enlisted Buduma youths thereafter terrorized all other groups around them, taking over the fishing and grazing lands in over 20 fishing islands.[7] *Ga kudi, ga lada* (Hausa: there is money, and there is God's blessing) became a popular dictum among the Buduma youths, justifying participation in the insurgency. It is worth observing that all ethnic groups previously lived peacefully together on the lake when resources were sufficient.

The loss of livelihood was not restricted to fishing alone, but farming as well. The South Chad Irrigation Project (SCIP), with its headquarter in New Marte (northern Borno), is one of West Africa's largest irrigation projects. The project provided thousands of jobs at its peak in 1983 (during which only a third of the total area was cultivated). It was later abandoned due to the drying up of the lake. Many of the farmers displaced

[6] Interview with Malam Yahaya Ibrahim, fish trader, 50 years, Baga road fish market, Maiduguri, 1 June 2014.
[7] Anonymous informant, 23 years, Hausa from Mari village, Lake Chad.

by the collapse of the irrigation project moved to the lakeshore to take up residual farming, but most of them ended up as migrants to Maiduguri and beyond, since the area is too dry for rain-fed agriculture. Attempts by the federal and state governments to resuscitate the scheme in 2012 were abandoned when the wheat fields came under the control of Boko Haram insurgents before the first harvest. With neither fishing grounds nor farmlands, thousands of villagers have been driven toward Maiduguri in search of livelihoods, contributing to rising social and economic pressures in migrant neighbourhoods.

EXTERNAL LINKAGES

Bordered by three countries, Niger, Chad and Cameroun, Borno State has a high level of cross-border movements of persons and goods. The 650 km (400 miles) of international borders around the state are porous and poorly manned. In the past there has been mutual understanding between local inhabitants and migrants from neighbouring countries, due to the prolonged civil war in Chad and ecological problems in Niger. Many migrants from these countries, while maintaining their links back home, have been integrated into Borno society, making a considerable contribution to the socio-economic development of the state (Bolori 2009). However, the porousness of the borders has made it difficult to bring the Boko Haram insurgency under control. Policing Borno's borders is an uphill task for Nigerian security officials, making cross-border movement of insurgents, small arms and other light weapons comparatively easy. Corruption on the part of officials has further compromised efforts to arrest the situation.

The role of external influence and foreign insurgents especially in the Boko Haram uprising remains a topic of debate. Mohammed (2018) traced the history of Boko Haram to Ali Mohammed, a Nigerian student in Sudan during the 1990s who was radicalized in Saudi Arabia, and is alleged to have taught Yusuf. During the Boko Haram violence in July 2009 in Maiduguri, residents living in the worst-affected areas noticed the involvement of Tuareg people (most probably from Niger) in the fighting.[8] Involvement of foreign nationals in religious conflicts is not new in Nigeria. Isa Abba (1993) argues that as many as 20 per cent of those arrested in the Maitatsine religious uprising in the 1980s in Kano were from Niger Republic. Nigerians have also crossed the border to train as insurgents. Even before the rise of Boko Haram, there was alleged involvement of Nigerians from Maiduguri in religious conflicts outside

[8] Anonymous respondent, 47 years, who resided at Galadima ward at time of the crisis reported seeing the presence of Tuaregs with arms fighting for Boko Haram on Monday 28 July 2009.

Nigeria, suggesting that external links with insurgents outside Nigeria is not a recent development.[9]

The leadership of Boko Haram has declared links with insurgents elsewhere in the Muslim world, and there is some evidence of limited international collaboration with international jihadi groups. Leading players in Boko Haram, Abubakar Shekau and Mamman Nur, have allegedly received training in Somalia (Mustapha 2014; Comolli 2015). There is also evidence that a small number of fighters were trained by Al-Qaeda in the Islamic Maghreb (AQIM) (Comolli 2015; Thurston 2018, 163ff.). The decision of Boko Haram to affiliate with the Islamic State in 2015 suggested loyalties to global jihadi movements, but was largely a vain attempt to attract international support following territorial losses suffered at the hands of the Nigerian military (Thurston 2016, 24). However, Islamic State has officially recognized the breakaway Boko Haram faction, Islamic State West Africa Province (ISWAP). Ethnic affinity among border communities also facilitates the insurgency. On either side of these borders lies not only the dominant Kanuri ethnic group noted for their heavy participation in Boko Haram but also smaller ethnic groups like the Buduma, Shuwa Arab and Mandara (see Idrissa, Chapter 4 this volume).

INTER-FAITH RELATIONS

Until the 1990s there have been cordial relations, even if mutually exclusive, between Islam and Christianity in Borno. Adherents of both religions have maintained their distinctive characteristics and identities devoid of rancour especially in inter-personal relations and the observance of rituals. Doctrinal differences within Islam were also present but less acrimonious. Both religions engage in proselytization. Of all the Nigerian ethnic groups, the Kanuri, probably due to their long history of contact with Islam, have remained most averse to Christian proselytization. So strong is this resistance that a freed Kanuri slave, Ali Aisami, living in Sierra Leone in *c.* 1871, was unwilling to accept Christianity and Westernization from the Church Missionary Society (CMS), unlike his companions such as Samuel Ajayi Crowther. The CMS declined a subsequent request by Rev. S.W. Koelle to visit to Borno, claiming: 'A proposal of Koelle to visit Borno for completing his Kanuri research was turned down by his mission superiors as they saw other regions more rewarding for evangelisation' (Benton 1916, 60 as cited in Geider 1997, 167).

To date, the Kanuri behave much like Aisami and take pride in their Muslim identity, which has both historical and sociological signifi-

[9] An anonymous respondent told the story of two youths from his neighbourhood in Maiduguri who went to fight for the Islamic Salvation Front in 1994 in Algeria. These youths were later also to partake in the 2009 insurgency that killed hundreds of people in Maiduguri.

cance. Since the 1990s, however, there has been growing polarization of Muslim-Christian relations in the state. Two related developments illustrate this growing unease among the Kanuri. The first was the circulation of a document entitled 'Harvesting the Kanuris', allegedly written by a Christian missionary and published in the 1990s, which spelt out strategies to deal with Kanuri resistance to conversion through penetration of Kanuri norms and values. There was also an alleged plan by the former military administration of Colonel Augustine Aniebo in 1998 for the introduction of Christian Religious Knowledge in the curriculum of public primary schools in the state. These attempts were vigorously resisted through mass circulation of the documents and sermons in mosques. Attempts have also been made to translate the Bible into Kanuri and broadcast Christian messages in Kanuri using a radio station based in Niger Republic, all of which have added to increasingly tense inter-faith relations in Borno. Ongoing resistance to Christian penetration may also be seen in the cumbersome procedure for acquiring land titles for building churches. The point must however be made that while Kanuri *ulama* (together with the Hausa/Fulani) also vigorously pursued the conversion of the pagan communities in the Gwoza Hills, they have jealously resisted proselytizing missions of Christians in Kanuri areas and elsewhere in Borno.

Ethnic and social dimensions of radicalization

An intriguing aspect of the current insurgency is the ethnic dimension it has assumed. Borno State, and the Kanuri in particular, have been important players in the insurgency – prominent in the leadership as well as in the 'rank and file' of Boko Haram (see Umar and Ehrhardt, Chapter 6 this volume). Thus the overbearing influence of the previously peaceful Kanuri in the present insurgency needs to be explained, especially in light of their dislike of military and related professions over the years, which has led some in Nigeria to characterize them as docile or lazy. Understanding the rise of Boko Haram in Borno requires a deeper look at how Islamic identities have been inflected through underlying ethnic and social issues

The Kanuri claim to be descendants of Saif Zhi Yazan who migrated from Yemen, and were Islamized centuries before other parts of northern Nigeria. One informant, a local traditional ruler, claimed that the Kanuri belong to the *tubawul awwal* – a term referring to the group of people who heard and believed in the coming of the Prophet Muhammad (SAW) even before the coming of Islam.[10] Although the Kanuri had the earliest contact with Islam in present-day Nigeria, they

[10] Anonymous respondent, traditional ruler, 51 years, Maiduguri 20 June 2014.

are nonetheless not regarded as good Muslims by the Hausa, hence their Hausa nickname *Larabawan bidi'a* (Arabs through innovation). This perception predates the Salafi incursion into Borno's religious terrain, which began in the late 1970s, significantly challenging the traditional Sufi and non-aligned Muslim orientation of Borno society, at the instigation of numerous young Salafi scholars. The key message of the Salafi is that sound Islamic knowledge and rituals devoid of innovations is what makes a good Muslim, and not any claim to a long Islamic pedigree. Some scholars interpret the ethnic dimensions of Boko Haram insurgency as a Kanuri attempt to reclaim the lost glory of their Islamic kingdom of Kanem-Borno (Pieri and Zenn 2017).

One respondent noted that, in their quest for Qur'anic education, large numbers of Hausa children are brought to Maiduguri and dumped in Bulumkuttu ward on the outskirts of the town, often unaccompanied by parents or guardians. Many of these children later become a source of social problems, living with virtually no parental care, and acquiring awkward social values including extreme views about Islam from uncertified scholars. Our informant has observed and written two memos (in 2001 and 2004) to the Borno State Government for action, but his concerns were downplayed. This also coincided with the Salafist invasion of Borno's religious landscape (two-thirds of the insurgents' life histories examined for this research provide evidence of affiliation with Salafism). Yet, despite constituting social problems fewer Hausa youths are represented in the insurgency than Kanuri.

There is overwhelming evidence to demonstrate that the outstanding Kanuri presence in the insurgency has been by supported by other ethnic groups within the state, especially the Gwoza Hill tribes of the south.[11] The radicalization of Gwoza youths has been described by Higazi (2015). Youths from the Gwoza Hills, particularly Dgwhede who migrated to Maiduguri for work, were recruited into Boko Haram, and these youths helped to radicalize their kinsmen back home. One of our respondents believes many of the arrests and executions of insurgents indicated a significant presence of Gwoza people over other ethnic groups of Borno apart from the Kanuri. The appeal of Boko Haram to Gwoza youths was, according to the respondent, a feature of over zealousness, many of them being recent converts to Islam, which in Borno means that their families have been Muslims for only two generations or less. Many young Gwoza people were seen to be eager to advance the cause of Islam, often identifying with Salafi doctrine so that their recruitment as foot soldiers in the insurgency also became fairly easy.

[11] Apart from the equally high rate of insurgency in Gwoza LGA, Gwozari (a neighbourhood in Maiduguri) whose residents are mostly from the Gwoza LGA were also notorious for participation in the insurgency before Boko Haram was chased out of Maiduguri in June 2013.

Beyond these various issues, social issues may also have contributed to the high rate of insurgency in Borno cutting across all ethnic groups. Poverty and high birth rates have posed considerable problems for parenting in the state such that children at tender ages are seen fending for themselves and sometimes even providing sustenance for their families as well. Teenagers become independent, and are often exposed to all manner of religious preaching and manipulation (Abbah and Idris 2014). The implication is that parental control over such children becomes compromised so that their decisions to belong to a particular group, including insurgent groups, suffer from a lack of parental guidance (see Last, Chapter 8 this volume).

Social strategies of recruitment

JOINING BOKO HARAM

The mechanisms of Boko Haram recruitment may have a bearing on socio-cultural, economic and environmental circumstances that surround the life of individual members. For this reason, some basic information gleaned from life histories of ten Boko Haram members are discussed here. The objective is to offer a social rather than a statistical understanding of how the people of Borno were drawn into Boko Haram, to complement more statistical approaches (see Umar and Ehrhardt, Chapter 6 this volume). On average, members were young (20–30 years), generally though not exclusively Kanuri, and of poor economic backgrounds. A good number of them had low levels of education, lived in the inner city area of Maiduguri and were born to large families, mostly polygamous. Nearly half (four out of ten) of the insurgents had lost their fathers during childhood and were brought up by their mothers or by relatives.

A profile of vulnerability suggests the importance of a 'slippery slope' or 'grooming' mechanism in the Boko Haram recruitment strategies, whereby individuals are gradually exposed to violence through a slow and steady path that moves them from being mere sympathisers to becoming part of a terrorist organization (McCauley and Moskalenko 2008). Initially (possibly beginning from 2002), the charismatic spiritual head of Boko Haram, Mohammed Yusuf, started by preaching a radical form of Islam in Maiduguri and major towns within Borno. Yusuf identified young students who mastered the Qur'an from the traditional *tsangaya* schools and organized a recitation competition for them with fantastic prizes for winners, followed by the teaching of radical lessons by Yusuf. Indeed, Yusuf was described as a 'gifted demagogue and persuasive debater' (Mohammed 2014, 19). Many people who knew Mohammed Yusuf well, including Christians, often make reference to his charismatic style of preaching with which he attracted followers. This was confirmed by an anonymous Igbo welder (44 years) who helped in the maintenance of Yusuf's mosque Markas Ibn Taymiyya before the 2009 rebellion. He confessed that Yusuf would convince almost anyone listening to him at that time, whether Christian or Muslim, because he knew so much of the way government was run (including security matters). The Igbo man confessed that he almost became a Boko Haram member himself because the sect was not violent at that time. The students, who became radicalized gradually, went back to their traditional schools filled with radical ideas, and many rebelled against their teachers, parents and the communities to which they belonged by becoming students and die-hard supporters of Yusuf.[12]

Yusuf later progressed to offering economic benefits to members in the form of start-up capital to establish petty businesses. Three main sectors – transportation, retailing and agriculture – were Yusuf's main preoccupation. Motorcycles and cars were given to youths on hire-purchase, attracting very small daily returns (N200 for motorcycles and N500 for taxi cabs). Petty retail businesses in hawking perfumes, sale of dates and Islamic materials like audio compact discs (CDs) and video DVDs as well as medicines, were also encouraged and supported by Yusuf. Hundreds of Boko Haram members who have become bona fide members also worked on the large parcels of land belonging to Yusuf during the rainy season. The produce was used to feed indigent members, including men, women and children. Youths numbering 300–500 worked voluntarily on the many parcels of land that belonged to the Mohammed Yusuf, a practice that was a common feature of Islamic training in West Africa. In this way the entire Boko Haram membership acted like a small commune, being almost entirely independent of government for their needs. Needless to say, all beneficiaries (some of whom also brought in new members) went for spiritual training in Yusuf's mosque which he called *Markaz Ibn Taimiyya* – popularly called Markaz in Maiduguri – where radical Islamic ideas were propagated.

It was through this process that membership of Boko Haram swelled, affecting many homes in Maiduguri. Estimating the membership strength of Boko Haram at that time is difficult but a respondent who lived close to Markaz quoted as many as 5,000 active and passive members in 2009.[13] While some suggest that Yusuf's sources of wealth included external

[12] An example of this rebellion may be seen in the narrative given by one of our respondents, Kanuri, 40 years: a young member of Boko Haram embarrassed his uncle (a local *malam*) who was about to lead a funeral prayer for his deceased brother (also father to the Boko Haram member). Dissatisfied with the arrangement mobilized, the youth and his fellow Boko Haram members took the corpse away and called on Mohammed Yusuf to lead the funeral prayer while other mourners simply looked on.

[13] Anonymous respondent, Kanuri, 45 years, Maiduguri.

funding from Al-Qaeda and related organizations, others highlight more obvious internal sources of funding such as Nigerian businessmen, links with the Borno State government, and his wealthy father-in-law, Alhaji Ba Fugu, a celebrated litigant, well known by the security agencies and the courts in Maiduguri for winning many high profile court cases (Comolli 2015; International Crisis Group, 2014; Thurston 2018).Yusuf also exploited the prevalent poor economic condition of his time effectively to garner support from his immediate community to fight a cause that attracted thousands of youths even after his death.

Social ties were also used as a recruitment strategy, bringing members into the groups through friends, relatives and marital relationships, and even children have become members. Some teenage boys followed their parents to Markas for routine lessons in the period before the 2009 'jihad'. Younger children of Boko Haram members learned hate messages against the Nigerian state and government workers from their parents and at Markas, where such messages were regularly propagated. Boko Haram members also enrolled their children in Boko Haram-approved schools only, owned by members. The Boko Haram ideology was taught to children in the schools together with other aspects of the religion as deemed appropriate by the group. A few such schools sprung up between 2007 and 2009 in Bulabulin and Bulumkutu neighbourhoods of Maiduguri, but the general public was suspicious of them, and they were treated the same way Izala schools were in the 1980s.

Widowhood also became strong inducement for women to become Boko Haram members. Women whose husbands were killed by the military often joined. Members are also known to facilitate marriages between fellow members and their siblings and relatives for the support of the group. Upon the 'martyrdom' of a member, marriages are quickly arranged with other Boko Haram members for the widow(s) of the 'martyr(s)', and before they remarry, the welfare of such women and children becomes the responsibility of the group through regular cash flows and hand-outs to families. Women have also played the role of preachers through which radicalization at the household level took place surreptitiously. Through a slow but steady process of preaching, female Boko Haram members handed down anti-establishment and hate messages to other women in their homes while also calling on them to shun worldly desires by living pious and ordinary lives. Donations for the sake of Allah became priorities in order to sustain the movement. Through this process many women have been known to sell off their personal possessions and donate to the cause of Boko Haram.

A drive for martyrdom also played an important role in radicalization. In the case of Boko Haram, this connects to the strategy of suicide bombing used by the group where the motivation of bombers is martyrdom.

Members hold the belief that they are rewarded by God if they kill or are killed and that their victims also go to heaven if they are righteous, and to hell if they are infidels (Abbah and Idris 2014). The power of martyrdom can be seen in the case of women's views of their husbands killed during insurgencies. Wives of Boko Haram members often take pride in the death of their husbands whom they believe are *shaheed* or martyrs.

The mechanism of 'condensation' also played a role in recruitment, especially in the period between 2011 and 2013. This is a mechanism by which a group with little support draws support from the surrounding population largely because of the excessive and often illegal use of force by the state against it (McCauley and Moskalenko 2008). The extra-judicial killing by police of the Boko Haram leader, Mohammed Yusuf, and the global condemnation of this action marked a key phase in this process. Later Boko Haram used the tactic of deliberately provoking the military Joint Task Force (JTF) in Maiduguri who in turn often retaliated by indiscriminate shooting and damaging of property (Idris 2012). This action led to very poor civil-military relations in Maiduguri to the extent that many Maiduguri residents of Maiduguri preferred to remain with Boko Haram rather than assisting the military. Unfortunately this was interpreted by the JTF to mean the community's acceptance and collusion with Boko Haram, which further heightened the insecurity.

Mass radicalization also requires the stimulation of hatred and instilling of the value of martyrdom (McCauley and Moskalenko 2008). In the context of killing, abduction and damage to property, relations between Boko Haram members and their surrounding community have hardened. After being driven out of Maiduguri, the new leader of Boko Haram, Abubakar Shekau, specifically declared that the blood of the people of Maiduguri was lawful and that they all deserved to be killed. In one of his statements he declared: 'the person from Maiduguri, my job is to kill. I will kill, kill, kill and kill. Let me be questioned by God in the hereafter' (widely circulated Boko Haram propaganda video).

This was later widened to affect the rural areas as well such that a clear line between 'us and them' was drawn. Boko Haram's targets are now all persons who are non-members, including women and children. It is interesting to reflect on how the scope of hate widened to this level. Boko Haram's main targets were initially the security personnel but this was later widened to include politicians, Christians, traditional rulers and, much later, government workers. But equally true is the feeling of the average person in Borno that all members of Boko Haram deserve to be killed so that hate in this case is two sided.

Other modes of recruitment emerged that had less to do with radicalization and instilling loyalty to Boko Haram than other forms of inducement. The relocation of Boko Haram to the rural areas which had enjoyed peace until June 2013 saw the birth of a new recruitment strategy: conscription. In addition to the use of money to attract poor youths from the villages across the state, many more youths were conscripted to maintain a reasonable number of followers so as to carry on with 'God's work', in Boko Haram's parlance. This mechanism was observed by residents of Jakana, Mainok and Beni Sheikh villages along the Maiduguri to Damaturu road who suffered several attacks from Boko Haram. Youths from these villages believed to have been either 'bought' or conscripted led the attacks on their villages by openly identifying persons to be killed, properties to be looted or even assisting in razing the village completely. The teenager Baba Goni was conscripted into Boko Haram when the group attacked his community in Damboa LGA when he was 13 years old, spending two years with them in the Sambisa forest (Jones 2014). The use of economic inducements also persisted alongside conscription, and may be seen in the case of Boko Haram's incursion into Bauchi State in the villages around Balmo Forest where youths were offered motorcycles and N50,000 cash rewards to join Boko Haram. Previously, preaching sessions conducted in these villages had been sufficient to win local support (Mukhtar et al. 2014).

Children of non-Boko Haram members were lured and recruited as couriers of deadly weapons. Such children transported guns and IEDs to designated points for use by Boko Haram. In other instances they were given cash rewards to burn down schools and other public facilities. On 23 June 2013 for instance, a teenager was shown on the Nigeria Television Authority (NTA) *Maiduguri News* caught in the act of burning classrooms in Gwange Primary school. It was reported that he received N5,000 as inducement. There were also instances of abduction and indoctrination of children by Boko Haram. Scores of children were conscripted and indoctrinated by Boko Haram to perform domestic chores, surveillance and attacks. As many as 1,861 teenage boys and girls are associated with armed groups in the three states under emergency rule (Watchlist 2017).

Many observers in Borno also believe that Boko Haram has used fetishism in both recruitment and control of its membership (Mohammed 2014; Garba 2014; Last 2012). This belief was reported by Mortimore (1989) in other forms of Islamic radicalization elsewhere. Also when Bulabulin Ngarannam, a Boko Haram stronghold in Maiduguri, was attacked in June 2013, it was claimed that jerry cans containing human blood and remains of human parts were recovered from the bunkers used as hideouts by Boko Haram. More research is needed to understand the specific role of juju and witchcraft as mechanisms of recruitment and control.

Conclusion

Borno State has been devastated by the decade-long Boko Haram insurgency. Many have wondered why Borno became the theatre of the insurgency given its comparatively peaceful past. A closer look at the pattern of attacks, ethno-religious tensions, and environmental pressures helps to answer this question. The central part of the state, especially Maiduguri, Bama and Konduga LGAs, have been the worst hit, along with the more religiously mixed areas of Damboa and Gwoza LGAs in the southern part of the state. While the central and southern parts of the state have endured a larger share of attacks, the deadliest attacks have been in the northern parts of the state around Lake Chad where conflict over water and fishing resources is acute. What is clear from such patterns is the complex ethno-religious and economic dimensions of the insurgency. In Maiduguri, the epicentre of the insurgency, violence was concentrated in neglected migrant neighbourhoods filled with poor, mostly Kanuri, settlers and environmental refugees from the north of the state. Gwoza youth, who are more recent Muslim converts from the religiously mixed areas of southern Borno, represent a second important feeder group for the insurgency. Buduma fishers around Lake Chad were a third group of active participants in the Boko Haram insurgency as they struggled to defend fishing livelihoods against better-capitalized Hausa migrants from other states. In all of these cases, the common factor for Boko Haram recruitment was not ethnicity, but disaffection among those on the losing end of struggles for basic services, jobs and resources for a decent livelihood. Poor migrants living in squalid conditions with strong traditional anti-Western worldviews, or disaffected youth in the Gwoza Hills or around Lake Chad, found succour in Mohammed Yusuf's extremist ideology that offered salvation by promoting religious purity over corruption, and called for the violent rejection of the failures of the Westernized state to attend to the needs of the people.

The emergence of Boko Haram in the Kanuri heartland of Borno is not an indication of an embedded propensity to Islamic radicalization among the Kanuri. Most Kanuri people are opposed to Boko Haram; the greater proportion of its victims in the state are Kanuri (including the Shehu of Borno who barely escaped being killed in 2014), and the Kanuri dominate the Civilian Joint Task Force (CJTF) that has assisted the military in fighting Boko Haram. While the Kanuri resist conversion to other religions, the *ulama* of Borno have historically been neither radical nor violent in their missionary activities. This has been adequately documented by Kalli Gazali (2005) who chronicled Kanuri *ulama* contribution in Nupe and Yoruba lands. The Boko Haram conflict is not a product of local social or religious values, but of the dysfunctional effects of extreme environmental and economic stresses amid political indifference and social neglect. Despite the fluidity of borders around Borno State, the influence of Salafi doctrines from Saudi Arabia, and limited international linkages to jihadi groups (Mohammed 2018), Boko Haram is a home-grown northern Nigerian insurgency, but not an intrinsically Kanuri insurgency. Far from being driven by the concerns or resources of international actors, Boko Haram emerged from the most disaffected parts of society across several ethnic groups, and made use of frustration, loyalty, manipulation and coercion to draw in those around it.

Bibliography

Archibong, B. 2018, 'Historical Origins of Persistent Inequality in Nigeria', *Oxford Development Studies* 46 (3), 325–47.

Abba, I.A., 1993, 'The Niger Factor in the Implementation of Kano's Policy on Almajirai', in A.I. Asiwaju and B.M. Barkindo (eds), *Nigeria-Niger Trans-Border Cooperation.* Lagos: Malthouse, 390–96.

Abbah, T. and Idris, H., 2014, 'It will be a Disaster to Impose a Military Ruler in Borno – Gov. Kashim Shettima', *Sunday Trust,* 4 May, 7.

Alkali, M.N., Monguno, A.K. and Mustafa, B.S., 2012, 'An Overview of Islamic Actors in Northeastern Nigeria', Nigeria Research Network Background Working Paper 2, Oxford, www.qeh.ox.ac.uk/research/research-networks/nrn/nrn-wp, accessed 2 July 2014.

Benton, P.A., 1916, 'A Bornu Almanac for the Year A.D. 1916', Jos, reproduced in P.A. Benton, 1968, *The Languages and Peoples of Bornu*, Vol. 2, London: Frank Cass.

Bolori, A.S., 2009, 'Political Crisis in Chad and Migration into Maiduguri and Jere Local Government Areas of Borno State in Nigeria', research report submitted to the Research Committee, University of Maiduguri.

Comolli, V., 2015, *Boko Haram: Nigeria's Islamist Insurgency*, Oxford University Press.

Connah, G., 1981, *Three Thousand Years in Africa: Man and his Environment in the Lake Chad Region of Nigeria*, London: Cambridge University Press.

Council on Foreign Relations, 2019, *Nigeria Security Tracker: Mapping Violence in Nigeria*, www.cfr.org/nigeria/nigeria-security-tracker/p29483, accessed 3 January 2019.

de Graaf, G., Nouhou, Y., Diyaware, M.Y., Rimadoum, A. and Mahaman, A., 2014, 'Regional Fisheries Report: Lake Chad', Lake Chad Rural Development Programme (PRODEBALT).

Downie, R., 2015, 'Collective Insecurity in the Sahel: Fighting Terror with Good Governance', *Georgetown Journal of International Affairs* 26 (1), 70–78.

Ekanem, I.I., 1972, *The 1963 Nigerian Census: A Critical Appraisal*, Benin City: Ethiope.

Homer-Dixon, T.F., 1999, *Environment, Scarcity and Violence*, Princeton, NJ: Princeton University Press.

Garba, A. 2014, 'Religious Beliefs and Rituals among Bornoans and the Emergence of Insurgency in the Lake Chad Basin', paper presented at the Mega Tchad Association Conference, Tilburg University, Netherlands 24–27 September.

Gazali, K.A.Y., 2005, *The Kanuri in Diaspora: The Contributions of Ulama of Kanem-Borno to Islamic Education in Nupe and Yorubalands*, Lagos: CSS Bookshops.

Geider, T., 1997, 'The Universe of Kanuri Oral Literature', in N. Cyffer and T. Geider, (eds), *Advances in Kanuri Scholarship.* Frankfurt: Rudiger Koppe Verlag.

Hallam, W.K.R., 1993, 'Rabih: His Place in History', *Borno Museum Society Newsletter* 15/16, 5–22.

Higazi, A., 2015, 'Mobilisation Into and Against Boko Haram in North-East Nigeria', in M. Cahen, M.E. Pommerolle and K. Tall (eds), *Collective Mobilisations in Africa: Contestation, Resistance, Revolt*, Leiden: Brill.

Idris, H., 2012, 'JTF Destroyed N187m Property in Maiduguri', *Daily Trust*, 23 October.

International Crisis Group, 2014, 'Curbing Violence in Nigeria II: The Boko Haram Insurgency', Africa Report 216.

—— 2016, 'Nigeria: Women and the Boko Haram Insurgency', Africa Report 242.

International Office for Migration 2018, 'Nigeria: Displacement Tracking Matrix (DTM) Round 25', October.

Jones, B., 2014, 'Boko Haram Life as told by Baba Goni', *Daily Trust*, 19 May, 3.

Kameri-Mbote, P. 2005/06,'Environment and Conflict Linkages in the Great Lakes Region', IELRC working paper, International Environmental Law Research Centre, Geneva.

Kassim, A. and Nwankpa, M., 2018, *The Boko Haram Reader: From Nigerian Preachers to the Islamic State*, London: Hurst and Company.

McCauley, C. and Moskalenko, S., 2008, 'Mechanisms of Political Radicalization: Pathways Toward Terrorism', *Terrorism and Political Violence* 20 (3), 415–33.

Mohammed, K. 2014, 'The Message and Methods of Boko Haram', in M.-A. Pérouse de Montclos (ed.), *Boko Haram: Islamism, Politics, Security and the State in Nigeria*, African Studies Centre, University of Leiden, 33–62.

Mohammed, K., 2018, 'The Origins of Boko Haram', in A.C. LeVan and P. Ukata (eds), *The Oxford Handbook of Nigerian Politics*, Oxford University Press, 583–604.

Mortimore, M., 1989, *Adapting to Drought: Farmers, Famines and Desertification in West Africa*, London: Cambridge University Press.

Mukhtar, A., Anako, A. and Mohammed, A., 2014, 'Boko Haram Opens New Frontier in Bauchi, Jigawa', *Daily Trust*, 19 May.

Mustapha, A.R., 2014, 'Understanding Boko Haram', in A.R. Mustapha (ed.), *Sects & Social Disorder: Muslim Identities & Conflict in Northern Nigeria*, Woodbridge: James Currey, 147–98.

National Population Commission, 1998, *Analytical Report of the 1991 Census at the National Level*, Abuja: NPC.

—— 2010, *Population Distribution by Sex, State, LGA & Senatorial District*, Abuja: NPC.

Odada, E.O., Oyebande, L. and Oguntola, J.A., 2006, 'Lake Chad: Experience and Lessons Learned Brief', www.worldlakes.org/uploads/06_Lake_Chad_27February2006.pdf, accessed 30 April 2014.

Ogundipe, S., 2018, 'Metele Boko Haram Attack: Soldiers' Death Toll Rises to 118; Over 150 Missing', *Premium Times*, 24 November, www.premiumtimesng.com/news/headlines/297343-metele-boko-haram-attack-soldiers-death-toll-rises-to-118-over-150-missing.html, accessed 3 May 2019.

Olugbode, M. and Iroegbu, S., 2013, 'JTF: Boko Haram Leader, Abubakar Shekau, is Dead', *This Day*, www.thisdaylive.com/articles/jtf-boko-haram-leader-abubakar-sshekau-is-dead/156754, accessed 16 February 2014.

Pieri, Z.P. and Zenn, J., 2016, 'The Boko Haram Paradox: Ethnicity, Religion and Historical Memory in the Pursuit of a Caliphate', *African Security* 9 (1), 66–88, http://dx.doi.org/10.1080/19392206.2016.1132906, accessed 8 December 2018.

Seibert, U. 2000, 'Languages of Borno State', www.uiowa.edu/intlinet/unijos/nigonnet/nlp/borno.htm, accessed 20 June 2011.

Sergie, M.A. and Johnson, T., 2014, 'Boko Haram', www.files.ethz.ch/isn/180698/Nigeria's%20Boko%20Haram%20and%20Ansaru%20.pdf, accessed 25 June 2014.

Suleiman, S., 2013, 'Before Lake Chad Disappears', www.nigeriaintel.com/2013/03/04/before-lake-chad-disappears, accessed 22 June 2014.

Terab, A., 2014, '80% of Boko Haram attacks unreported', *Leadership*, 8 July.

Thambyahpillay, G.G.R., 1979, 'Climate Change: The Contemporary Understanding', Maiduguri: Inaugural Lecture No. 3, University of Maiduguri.

Thurston, A., 2015, *Salafism in Nigeria: Islam, Preaching, and Politics*, Cambridge University Press.

—— 2016, 'The Disease is Unbelief: Boko Haram's Religious and Political Worldview', The Brookings Project on U.S. Relations with the Islamic World, Analysis Paper 22, January, Center for Middle East Policy at Brookings, Washington, DC.

—— 2018, *Boko Haram: The History of an African Jihadist Movement*, Princeton University Press.

Tijani, K., 1989, 'The Kanuri Factor in the Nigeria – Niger Border' in A.I. Asiwaju and B.M. Barkindo (eds), *The Nigeria–Niger Transborder Co-operation*, Lagos: Malthouse.

—— 1993, 'Borno, Rabih and the Challenge and Response of History', *Borno Museum Society Newsletter* 15/16.

The Defense Post, 2018, 'Nigeria Army Masses in Monguno, Moves to Clear Boko Haram from Baga', 31 December, https://thedefensepost.com/2018/12/31/nigeria-army-deploys-monguno-baga-boko-haram-iswa, accessed 3 May 2019.

UNEP, 2004, 'Lake Chad Basin', GIWA Regional Assessment 43, United Nations Environment Programme, www.unep.org/dewa/giwa/publications/r43.asp, accessed 13 June 2014.

Wakil, B.G., 2009, 'Kanem-Borno Empire – A Historical Introduction to the Geography of Borno', in M. Waziri, A. Kagu and A.K. Monguno (eds), *Issues in the Geography of Borno State*, Kano: Adamu Joji, 14–19.

Watchlist, 2017, '"Who Will Care for Us?" Grave Violations against Children in North-east Nigeria', https://watchlist.org/wp-content/uploads/2111-Watchlist-Nigeria_LR.pdf, accessed 30 November 2014.

Waziri, M., 2009, 'The Geography of Borno: An Overview', in M. Waziri, A. Kagu and A.K. Monguno (eds), *Issues in the Geography of Borno State*, Kano: Adamu Joji, 6–13.

4

'Boko Halal'
Limits to radicalization in southern Niger Republic

RAHMANE IDRISSA

Introduction

Southern Niger and northern Nigeria are the two main parts of the Central Sudan, an area of West Africa that extends roughly from the Mossi Plateau to Lake Chad, and in which populations share much in common in terms of culture, language, economic interactions, political history and social relations. Despite the national border cutting through it, separating Nigeriens from Nigerians, the Central Sudan remains a coherent unit in which networks of all manner of exchanges and contacts maintain, as of old, an apparently seamless web of human relationships. In a very tangible sense, as we will see in this chapter, southern Niger is only the northern fringe of northern Nigeria, especially owing to the dominance of Hausa language and culture, and of the Islamic religion. Given this general context, one would expect the current violent crisis in northern Nigeria to have a direct impact on southern Niger and indeed, to result in copycat actions there, since it is highly likely that radical ideas and sentiments originating in parts of northern Nigeria are broadcast throughout the Central Sudan. So far, however, and despite a small number of incidents, Niger remains largely unscathed. Even the incidents just mentioned occurred either in isolated areas in the far-eastern Diffa region, or in connection with the Malian and Libyan, rather than the northern Nigerian, crises.[1] It is thus particularly interesting to study contexts in southern Niger that might illuminate the relative but very real calm experienced there. Why has religio-political radicalism been so muffled in southern Niger compared to northern Nigeria? What specificities in the Nigerien context would explain that ideas and sentiments that result in violence and mayhem in

1 See Idrissa 2014a.

northern Nigeria seem to lose their teeth in Niger? To respond to these and related questions, I will focus on two Nigerien regions that share a border with Nigeria: Diffa and Maradi – creating a lens into the factors underpinning the contrast between the two countries.

Northern Nigeria is bordered by five of Niger's eight administrative regions, belonging to all four larger geopolitical sections of the country. These are, from west to east, Dosso (west), Tahoua (north), Maradi and Zinder (central), and Diffa (east). While also describing the overall Nigerien context, I have focused on Diffa and Maradi for a number of obvious reasons. Diffa borders the state of Borno, the epicentre of the current crisis in northern Nigeria, and it is the only Nigerien region where the presence of elements close to the *Jama'atul Ahlul Sunna li Da'wati wal Jihad* – popularly known as 'Boko Haram' – has been ascertained at an early stage of the movement's existence. Maradi is important for a trajectory that turned it from Niger's least Islamized major town to its most Islamized, in an evolution driven essentially by the *Jama'atu Izalatil Bid'a wa Iqamat al-Sunna* (Society for the Eradication of Innovation and the Reinstatement of Tradition), commonly referred to as Izala, from which Boko Haram emerged in Nigeria in the early 2000s. These two regions are presented in some more detail below.

The chapter is primarily based on three weeks of fieldwork in both regions, conducted in the summer of 2014, although further observation was made on their evolution since then, involving visits to Niger and newspaper reviews over the succeeding years. In the two study areas, leading clerics and some individuals belonging to the main religious groupings were extensively interviewed. In Maradi, besides the main Muslim groups, such groupings included also two Christian churches. Additionally, I have consulted various officials working in Niger's security system in both places as well as in the capital, Niamey. For obvious reasons, these persons have accepted to speak only on conditions of strict anonymity. Deskwork was conducted to collect socio-economic data and substantiate historical information. Findings were analysed in accordance with a theoretical framework that linked them to potential sources of radicalization of a social, political, economic, historical or ideological nature.

The administrative Maradi region borders the state of Katsina, and the city of Maradi itself is only 150 km away from the city of Katsina and about three hours away from Kano by car. Maradi along with these two Nigerian cities forms the KKM (Kano–Katsina–Maradi) economic corridor. The Diffa region borders Borno State, and the city centre of Diffa is just 4 km from the Komadugu River valley, which forms a natural boundary between Niger and Nigeria. Proximity with Nigeria is not just geographic. As part of the KKM corridor, Maradi has since the 1990s been playing the role of a dry harbour to Katsina and Kano within a trading scheme known informally as 'special transit'.[2] This involves trading companies based in Nigerian cities importing consumer goods through Niger's docks at the port of Cotonou (Benin) on the basis of partnerships with Maradi traders, and sanctioned by administrative facilities granted by Nigerien customs. Maradi is also the main port of entry of northern Nigerian financial capital into Niger. In this way, the city has become – commercially, but with other implications as well – a satellite of Katsina and Kano.

Similarly, and until the Boko Haram crisis, Diffa was an economic satellite of Maiduguri, with the Nigerian Naira being slightly more present in the markets than the local currency (CFA Franc) and the region being isolated from the larger Nigerien economy by distance and poor transport infrastructure. The bulk of the Kanuri in particular live in numerous villages and small towns close to the Nigerian border. Diffa and Maradi – and to a lesser extent, Zinder and Konni – are thus the closest points of contact between Niger and Nigeria, on the Niger side of the border.

The main finding of research conducted in these regions is that there is incipient violent extremism in Diffa, while the situation in Maradi seems less worrisome – although ideological factors of radicalization, for instance, are clearly present. The variation may be explained by the different relations that each of these places has with Nigeria, as well as by structural dissimilarities between the two cities themselves.

This chapter begins by outlining the religio-political landscapes of Diffa and Maradi, stressing in particular elements that point to actual or potential violent radicalization and establishing the analytical significance of the structural differences between the two places (in terms of social, political and economic parameters). I also highlight the general context of the two regions within Niger and in relation to Nigeria. Against this background, I then examine the historical, social, political, economic and ideological factors that characterize the phenomenon of religio-political radicalization in Niger through the prisms of Diffa and Maradi. Finally, I place these case studies within a broader contextualization of national-level factors that account for differences in the impact of radicalizing religious influences in Niger relative to Nigeria – followed by some concluding thoughts.

Diffa and Maradi in context

Diffa is, arguably, Niger's most marginal region. With a territory of 157,000 sq. km (larger than Benin Republic), it has a population of less than 600,000 – about 3.5 per cent of the total population of Niger – 58 per

2 The name refers to the facilitation offered by the state of Niger, to distinguish it from other transit trade in the country.

cent of whom are Kanuri, followed by 27 per cent Fulani and 7 per cent Tubu, with smaller minorities of Hausa and Arabs. Located at 1,360 km from the capital Niamey, the town of Diffa is the remotest major administrative centre of the country. The region's population is very young, but within the Nigerien average: about 50 per cent are less than 15 years of age (national average being 49.2 per cent). Given the stark lack of economic opportunities in the region, the working age population is a very mobile fringe, not easily captured in demographic records. It is well known that large numbers of especially young men migrate temporarily or semi-permanently to Nigeria. The administrative divisions also reveal that Diffa's economy is slightly dominated by pastoral activities: there are 885 *tribus* (the administrative sub-unit for nomadic or semi-nomadic herders) to 821 villages (farmers and fishermen).

The important point here is that the villages are chiefly Kanuri while the pastoral 'nomadic groupings' (in administrative terms) are Fulani, Tubu and Arab. Until recently, the main security issue in the area had to do with fractious relations between the pastoral groups, while the Kanuri villages were considered peaceful and law-abiding. The security situation began to deteriorate in the early 1990s, when groups of Chadian Tubu, fleeing ethnic repression at the hands of the Deby regime in Chad, settled in the area with large amounts of weapons. The refugees were eventually resettled outside of the region, in Gouré (a district in the neighbouring *département* of Zinder), but they left behind much of their weaponry. These circulated especially among the pastoral groups and helped in the development of the mid-1990s unrest known as the Tubu rebellion. Because the insurgency involved acts of banditry against other groups – in a context of natural resource conflicts – the Fulani and the Arabs formed vigilante posses, secretly helped by the army. After the end of the rebellion in 1998, many former combatants especially from the Tubu and Fulani groups turned to armed robbery and market raiding. In the overwhelmingly rural context of Diffa region, targets of such crime are mostly traders, peddlers and travellers (especially market-goers) plying the numerous tracks between village markets. This situation is especially characteristic of the eastern sections of the region, specifically the *départements* of Diffa and Nguigmi, rather than that of Maïné Soroa (another *département* of Diffa region, in its western section).[3]

All of this is significant in order to better interpret the situation in a region where, since the late 1990s, violent death has become, if not

[3] This description is based on interviews with people in Diffa – ordinary people and security workers – and research in the Nigerien press. I do not know of any academic study that documents this earlier context of insecurity in some detail, although some NGO reports offer valuable information. See also Small Arms Survey's report on Niger, at www.smallarms-survey.org/fileadmin/docs/D-Book-series/book-01-Armed-and-Aimless/SAS-Armed-Aimless-Part-2-11-Niger.pdf, accessed 27 July 2019.

commonplace, at least unexceptional. Before the Boko Haram crisis, the killings were the doing of marauders, mostly in the eastern districts of the region, closer to Chad. In more recent times, local witnesses have attributed several incidents – some of them leading to violent deaths – to groups affiliated with Boko Haram, as we shall see below.

In contrast to Diffa, Maradi is a region very much central to Niger. Diffa is a region of minorities: its main ethnic group, the Kanuri, are only 4.4 per cent of the total population of the country, while the Hausa – Maradi's main ethnic group – form, at 53 per cent, the country's largest ethnic group. Despite a smaller territory (41,796 sq. km), Maradi is much more populated, with 4,160,231. In fact, it is the most densely populated region in Niger, boasting the highest birth rate in a country that has one of the highest population growth rates in the world (3.9 per cent). It is also the region of Niger with the youngest population (55 per cent are younger than 15 years), and the highest incidence of poverty and illiteracy (see Table 4.1). Demography is clearly a vital variable in this picture, which, however, says little about the fact that, after Niamey, the city of Maradi itself is the most economically vibrant town in Niger to the extent that it is sometimes dubbed (not quite deservedly) the country's 'economic capital'. The city combines a culture of commerce with proximity to Nigeria to produce a bustling market economy, further enhanced by the strong presence of the state that comes with being the capital of a region which has eight *départements*, 47 *communes* (of which nine are urban) and a public university. Financial capital in Maradi is however mostly commercial and speculative (on agricultural produce) and does not create many jobs. Unemployment is rampant and has created an underclass of mostly young people who live on *la débrouille* (ingenuity; scraping by) but generally migrate very little, internally or externally.[4]

Maradi does not have the kind of record of insecurity that characterizes Diffa. The region has a stronger articulation of state and 'customary' authorities, having been proclaimed a sultanate (of 'Katséna-Maradi') in 2010, with local traditional chiefs (*sarakuna*) playing an important role in local and civic politics. Such structures are much weaker in Diffa region, which, in pre-colonial times, was a largely ungoverned northern fringe of states centring on Borno and Lake Chad.

Diffa and Maradi present the same sociology as other Nigerien towns: a small class of 'modern' educated individuals working in the modern sector (public and private) and generally hailing from all regions of the country; a slightly larger local elite of notables, clerics and merchants; and the masses (*talakawa* in Hausa) who may engage in small-scale or informal economic activities, or work for the two other classes, or both.

[4] Grégoire's 1987 study on youth, employment and self-employment in the city remains largely relevant.

Table 4.1 Diffa and Maradi in comparison with other Nigerien regions, 2010–17

Region	Total popn	Popn <15 yrs	Urban	Rural	Poverty	Literacy
Agadez	556,447	46.5%	44.7%	55.3%	20.7%	-
Diffa	593,821	48.3%	14.8%	85.2%	34.0%	27.0%
Dosso	2,368,651	50.7%	9.0%	90.0%	52.9%	-
Maradi	4,160,231	54.5%	13.0%	87.0%	57.8%	29.5%
Niamey	1,164,680	42.2%	100.0%	0.0%	10.2%	-
Tahoua	3,839,457	52.7%	12.5%	87.5%	47.9%	30.4%
Tillabéri	2,954,817	48.9%	15.1%	84.9%	56.0%	25.1%
Zinder	4,132,321	53.4%	16.1%	83.9%	47.7%	-

(Source: Compiled from population estimates and measurements of 2010–17 by Institut National de la Statistique, Niger)

Note: The Région de Niamey is made up essentially of the city of Niamey. Statistics on poverty and literacy date back to 2011 except for literacy in Maradi, which dates back to 2017.

At any rate, the socio-economic determinants point in both cases to an entrenchment of poverty for the vast majority of the common people. In particular, the very young population, which is partly a result of better maternal-infant care, creates a high dependency ratio that translates into rural crisis – especially in Maradi – with acute poverty and social problems preventing households from planning for the future of their young. Levels of inequality, however, are moderate in contrast with the prevailing situation in Nigeria.

Like many African countries, Niger suffers from centrifugal pulls of ethnicity and political economy. With the exception of the Tuareg rebellions in the early 1990s and late 2000s, these have never reached a crisis point, however. They have been further mitigated by the politics of democratization (after 1991) and decentralization (after 1998).[5]

Niger was cobbled together in the early years of the 20th century from three pieces of French territorial possessions: the 'Cercle du Djerma' along the Niger River and Dallol valleys; the 'Territoire Militaire de Zinder' covering what is now central and eastern Niger; and the arid north, around the Azawak fossil valley, the Aïr mountains and the Djado plateau. Each of these geographical regions – 'west', 'east' and 'north' – became identified with its preponderant ethnic group: the west is a metaphor for the Zarma-Songhay, the east (or central and east) for the Hausa, and the north for the Tuareg. Moreover, as a grimly poor Sahelian country, Niger has had, from its earliest history, a population seeking economic relief in more alluring settings on the Gulf of Guinea and in North Africa. In this

[5] For further details, see Idrissa 2014.

way, and roughly speaking, the west was drawn by Ghana and, to a lesser extent, Côte d'Ivoire; the east by Nigeria; and the north by Algeria and Libya.

This general setup was politicized by issues in decolonization, especially when the retreating French Empire, wanting a pliant ruler in Niamey, stemmed the rise of the independent-minded Sawaba Party in a referendum in 1958 and organized the ascent of the Parti Progressiste Nigérien (PPN) instead.[6] This latter, partly owing to tactics from the Sawaba Party that aggressively excluded it from all eastern districts during its own time in power in 1957, had developed a much stronger power base in the 'west'. While the PPN was inclusive of elites from 'east' and 'north' at lower political echelons (party structures, cabinet and legislature), it firmly placed decision-making power in the hands of men from the 'west'. Its political bureau was exclusively 'western' and the three men at the helm of the state were one Zarma (President Diori) and two Songhay. This situation generated political resentment in the 'east', especially among the Hausa, who were the majority group in the country (53 per cent to the 21 per cent of the Zarma-Songhay). After the PPN was toppled in 1974, this resentment did not abate, since the rulers who next imposed themselves (Kountché, 1974–87 and Saibou, 1987–91) were both Zarma. Maradi and Diffa are both parts of the geopolitical 'east'.

If that particular situation never reached a boiling point, it is very likely due to the fact that the 'domination' of the 'west' did not carry with it a discriminatory agenda. It was chiefly a matter of symbolic perception where, as the popular language had it during that period, the 'west' had 'scored' three (presidents) against nil. Overall, policies of 'national unity' successfully placated elite groups from the 'east'. These policies were strongly sustained by other factors such as the prevalence of Islam as a cultural 'cement' throughout the country, as well as the commonality of Sahelian lifestyle across 'west' and 'east'. This is in marked contrast with the situation in Nigeria, where the challenge of 'national unity' involves much greater religious, cultural and ecological diversity.

With democratization and decentralization, the old geopolitics of west, east and north gradually underwent dramatic changes, and appear to be making less sense as each year passes. The strategies of the more successful political parties now transcend these divisions, and decentralization tends to concentrate regional identity at the level of the administrative region rather than ethnicity. In the older dispensation, both the executive rulers of districts (prefects and sub-prefects) and the mayors (then only in the principal towns of the country) were appointed by the central government, while the status of traditional chiefs lacked formality, and therefore legal autonomy. There were no local politics worth the name, a fact that

[6] See van Walraven 2013, for a meticulous narrative history of this episode.

strengthened the grip of the state, but also ethnic identification to larger, romanticized 'homelands', especially in the north. Decentralization maintained centralism while relaxing it sufficiently to allow the advent of local politics. Executive authorities (governors and prefects) are still appointed by the central government but, since the creation of multiple municipalities throughout the country, local affairs have been run by elected officials (mayors and councillors), and the status of traditional chiefs was thoroughly formalized by 2010. What emerged from this process is a local political stage dominated by three forces: the central government through the appointment of executive officials, local constituencies through the election of mayors and councils, and regional notables through a hierarchy of traditional chiefs – a kind of state-sponsored peerage. It is the centrist structure of the state which helps define Niger's specific security policy response in Diffa, through the appointment, until recently, of a high-ranking military officer as the governor of the region. This would have been impossible in a federal structure such as that of Nigeria, where the governor is elected.

In this new context, the positioning of regions relative to the 'national cake' is preponderantly determined by outcomes in local political processes and the importance of regional constituencies to national parties. It is obvious that Maradi is among Niger's leading regions, while Diffa is consigned to the bottom. The large population of Maradi region makes it a key electoral battleground, with attendant influence of its local elites. This explains to a great extent the operation of the 'special transit' arrangement mentioned earlier as well as significant infrastructural development in many parts of the region and in the city of Maradi itself. In contrast, while lightweight Diffa is the geographic source of Niger's new-found oil riches, the vaunted refinery that was built to supply part of national needs was 'given' to Zinder region – a much bigger voting constituency. The quiescence of Diffa was maybe purchased at the time by the fact that the man who made the decision – President Tandja – was himself a native of the Diffa region. However, the feeling of marginalization has probably intensified in Diffa as a result of this development.

Religio-political landscapes and the issue of violent radicalization

The 2012 population census indicated that Nigeriens are 99 per cent Muslim, the remaining 1 per cent being split between Christians and animists (INS-Niger 2015, 50). However, these figures are not sensitive to the nature of and the variation in the practice of religion, including between regions. In Niger – as in many African countries – animism is no longer the antagonist of the revealed religions it might have been in earlier eras. Although it has lost most of its organizing powers, the vast majority of adherents to the revealed religions continue to practice animism insofar as it continues to be the basis of many cultural and ritualistic traditions. Christianity appears to have strongholds especially in regions where animism has successfully preserved some of its past sway: in the Songhay and Gourmantché regions of western Niger, in the Arewa historical region around the town of Dogondoutchi, and – importantly for this chapter – in the Arna or Anna country, south of Maradi. It appears that Roman Catholicism is more important in the west, and Protestantism in the east (i.e. in Arewa and Maradi regions).

Most Nigeriens are Sunni Muslims. The basis of Nigerien Sunni Islam is known in the country as *Islam traditionnel* (French for 'traditional Islam') and is described as the simple practice of the Sunni creed without Sufi affiliations or any specific theological or doctrinal flourish. It is likely that, until very recently, this traditional Islam has been the dominant form of the religion in the country, especially since it was supported by the state-sponsored Association Islamique du Niger (AIN) – the Islamic Association of Niger – which is still viewed today as the backbone of the Nigerien idea of Islam.

Sufi organization has been historically important especially in eastern and northern Niger where, prior to colonization, the Senoussiyya and the Qadiriyya had developed strong bases in Adages and Zinder, and also in Say, in the western part of the country, under the influence of Sokoto and Gwandu. During the colonial era, the Tijaniyya gained pre-eminence among the Sufi groups across the land: this was in no small part due to the charismatic work of the Niassene branch of the Tijaniyya, based in Senegal, and active both in western and eastern Niger as well as in northern Nigeria.

The Izala current of Islam entered in Niger from Nigeria in the early 1980s essentially through Maradi. While this initially led to clashes with the established sects, Izala became mainstream in the 1990s, in a 'neo-liberal' ambiance of economic depression, burgeoning corruption and loss of state power. The initial resistance to Izala in the 1980s was supported by the state in view of its origins in Nigeria which, at the time, was still reeling from the violent '*Maitatsine*' insurgency that smouldered there at least until 1985. *Maitatsine*, however, never became a Nigerien problem, although its adherents exist in the country in very small numbers, being known especially under their pejorative name 'Kala Kato'.

Recent Islamic entrants onto the Nigerien religious scene include the Shia and the Ahmadiyya, both considered with particular suspicion especially by the leaders of traditional Islam and of Izala.

Against this general background, what is the situation in Diffa and Maradi?

DIFFA

In this section, I first describe briefly the religio-political landscape of Diffa as understood after fieldwork, and I analyse in particular evidence of what is termed here 'limited' or (in some sense) 'incipient' radicalization. I then examine the interplay of the various factors – historical, social, economic, political and ideological – that shape the situation in the region.

Islam dominates the religious landscape in Diffa, and Christianity is almost entirely absent. The main Islamic currents are those of traditional Islam, Izala and Tijaniyya; other currents are imperceptible, apart from Boko Haram, which emerged here in 2007 under names such as 'Talibans'[7] and 'Yusufiyya'. Boko Haram then went underground after the events of 2009 in Maiduguri that led to the killing of Mohammed Yusuf. These events were later echoed in Diffa, with several arrests of alleged members of the group, who were subsequently transferred to prisons in Niamey and the small town of Kollo, in the vicinity of the capital.

Ethnicity is a salient feature of the religious landscape in Diffa. While the Kanuri are the majority group, they are only 58 per cent of the regional population, meaning there are strong minorities. The Kanuri are not hegemonic, as indicated by the status of Hausa as the lingua franca in the area, and also by an ethnic pattern of doctrinal affiliations. In general, the Kanuri live in the southern section of the region (Manga and Lake Chad), and are therefore closer to Nigeria than other groups.

A consensus among those interviewed indicates that traditional Islam is dominant but rapidly losing ground. While the more common Hausa name of the adherents of traditional Islam is *Galgajiya* ('tradition') or *'Yan allo* ('Those with the slate'), their practice is also popularly called *Adinin sohi* ('the old folks' religion') or *Adine Ceriyaye* (the same, in Kanuri), stressing the impression that it is out of fashion with the region's growing young population. The leading clerics of traditional Islam are the religious advisers of the local chief and they also staff the local branch of AIN. Their role and influence are therefore bound up with that of local authorities, especially since, in the Nigerien administrative scheme, chiefs are (paid) agents of the state. As AIN representatives, these clerics play important social and official roles. Interviewed clerics said AIN has not so far spoken publicly about the Boko Haram situation, but they warn people against it through private advice (*nasiha*). Traditional Islam is therefore a force of social stability and political quiescence in Diffa. In this respect, the continuing decline of its influence may be interpreted, to some extent, as a sign of Salafization in parts of the population, a

7 In Nigeria, an early name for Boko Haram was 'Nigerian Taliban', rendered as 'Talibans' in Niger.

process which is a necessary, though not sufficient, condition of radicalization.

The strength of traditional Islam in Diffa is based on the old neighbourhood mosques and about 30 so-called Qur'anic schools (*cangaa* in Kanuri; *makarantan allo* in Hausa). Two of its leading clerics, Malam Awariet and Malam Ibrahim, control the two main Friday mosques in the vicinity of the palace of the local chief. It is a matter of tradition in these circles to send pupils who have finished learning to read the Qur'an, and want to become clerics, into Nigeria's Borno State for further training. This is especially the case for pupils of Kanuri ethnicity, given that Borno is predominantly Kanuri. Lately, this practice has led to students being exposed to the exciting new doctrines and radical conceptions brewing in Maiduguri, the cultural and economic capital of the Kanuri. It is mainly in this way that traditional Islam lost many younger adherents first to Izala, and then to Boko Haram, an extremist spin-off of Izala.

The declining influence of traditional Islam mostly benefits the Izala movement, a latecomer in Diffa. The movement became noticeable only in the 1990s and its prominence dates from the 2000s. Like in other Nigerien towns, Izala here are divided in two rival associations, the Kitab wa Sunna and the Ihiya wa Sunna. The division is more political than doctrinal. These groups run many small mosques besides two bigger ones, Oumar Ibn Afane, which is patronized mostly by Izala of Hausa and Fulani ethnicity as well as some members of the modern elite, and Abba Adji – named after a famed Kanuri cleric who died in Mecca – which is strongly Kanuri and oriented toward the Ihiya wa Sunna grouping. Incidentally, the Imam of Abba Adji mosque, Malam Boulama, was, at the time of this research, detained in Nigeria under allegations (false, according to his followers in Diffa) of a financial crime in relation to some traders there. The mostly Hausa-Fulani Kitab wa Sunna group is financially supported by a wealthy Fulani businessman, Elhaj Dayel.

From a doctrinal point of view, Izala is closer to traditional Islam, which may explain why it recruits most of its adherents from there. Both groups claim to be simply Sunni, in contrast with the Tijaniyya, which adds its liturgy to common Sunni rites and tenets. Izala asserts a firmer orthodoxy, as well as proselytizing zeal and organization. In future, Izala seems set to become the major Islamic sect in Diffa.

Izala does not play the same role of anchor of stability and quiescence as traditional Islam. For instance, by working with state and local authorities, the leading clerics of traditional Islam implicitly accept Niger's constitutional policy of *laïcité*, the practice of political secularism that formally excludes religion from the public sphere, notably by limiting religious education to Qur'anic schools and by stimulating adherence to secular programmes of social policy. In contrast, Izala groups promote advanced religious education in *makarantan islamiyya* (Islamiyya schools), and perceive government schools as rivals that hamper the progress of religion (Islamiyya schools were purely religious when they were first established in the 1990s, but have later converted into the secular-religious Franco-Arabic madrasa system promoted by the state). They move public debate in Diffa into suspicion against programmes of social policy, especially those funded and/or implemented by Western organizations (that is, most of them), perceived as Christian. A pronounced anti-*boko* (against Western-style education) orientation is certainly something that distinguishes Izala from other groups, and that places it on a subversive course against the contemporary Nigerien system. As a matter of fact, some of our Izala informants said that 'those who think that Boko Haram came out of an extremist wing of Izala are right'. The consensus, however, is that

> very early on, our great preachers had detected the threat that some extremists among us represented for Islam and the Muslims, and they issued warnings about them. From that moment, the latter decided to wage war on Izala by attacking our ulemas.

This informant was referring to events in Nigeria, including the assassination of prominent Izala preachers such as Sheikh Jaafar Adam.

Despite its subversive tendencies, Izala's methodology in Diffa has significant accommodating aspects. The principle of *da'wa* (proselytizing) implies patience, persuasion and organization, as well as the building up of positions of notables in the community to get one's voice heard far and wide. Because of this investment in social stability, Izala sides with other groups in Diffa in rejecting Boko Haram. Such positions will be further clarified when I present the situation in Maradi, where our informants had the opportunity to better articulate the opposition to Boko Haram.

Tijaniyya is a minority group in Diffa, important chiefly among the Fulani. They are sustained by the international organization of that Sufi order. Besides their two mosques in Sabon Carré and Festival neighbourhoods, they are currently erecting a grander one, with funding from wealthy Sufi traders. A high-ranking Tijani cleric from Kaolack (Senegal) led the ceremonial laying of the foundation for the mosque. It is possible that Tijaniyya has greater prominence in the rural areas; as we will see, such is the case in Maradi region, but it has not been ascertained in Diffa.

The general opinion in Diffa is vocal against Boko Haram, even if we take into account the selection bias of informants not associated with the movement. However, there is widespread agreement that the movement is present in Diffa town and region. The analysis of the informants' attitude suggests that some sociological and ethnic parameters affect their perspective.

Sociologically, it would seem that the message of the movement is well received among the *maajir* (the Kanuri word for 'theology students'; see Hausa *almajirai*) and also among some unemployed youth with little or no formal education. In the case of the latter, the economic factor would play a non-negligible role. A 20-year-old man in that category said that the movement is 'an easy opportunity to earn money, and if one dies, one goes to paradise'. More anecdotally, the message of the movement has also stimulated among primary and secondary school pupils a trend of refusing to attend classes by complaining of being 'compelled' to go to the 'infidels' school. While Izala has already spread such anti-*boko* ideas, the fact that children are expressing the same ideas appears to be something new and more related to the extremist views of Boko Haram. Indeed, it is reported that, despite surveillance from the security and defence forces to stamp out the Boko Haram message, the three principal preachers of the movement, the late Mohammed Yusuf, current leader Abubakar Shekau and Muhammad Nur, have a large audience (sympathetic or not) in the region.

Such currents of opinion are strongest among the Kanuri. Indeed, Boko Haram preachers would be much more 'eloquent' in Kanuri than in Hausa, and would also play on different, more ethnic feelings when using their mother tongue. Thus, Boko Haram militants (who would have seen action in Nigeria) and sympathisers would benefit from the fact that the movement's actions are viewed by some as a defence not only of Islam, but also of the Kanuri people. This kind of Kanuri nationalism would, however, be directed at situations in Nigeria (rather than Niger) and is related to the fact that Diffa region is heavily affected culturally, economically – and even politically – by Borno State.

Perhaps the best way to describe this situation is that there was incipient radicalization in the region going back to the emergence of Boko Haram affiliate groups in 2007; and that later turned into violence and a low intensity war as the Boko Haram insurgency grew in Nigeria. But by forcing Diffa militants and sympathisers to go underground, the events of July 2009 in Maiduguri hampered its maturation into the violent radicalism of the main Boko Haram group in Nigeria. Indeed, very few of the reported incidents in the region bear the movement's known trademarks. After 2012, defence and security forces in the region made dozens of arrests and there were early clashes between military patrols and armed gangs. At the time, many of these incidents were very likely related to the general situation in the region, where insecurity due to banditry had become something of a norm, as noted earlier. If arrests and clashes multiplied, it was, initially, as a statistical result of security reinforcement following the Borno conflagration, not because insecurity per se has increased: in fact, there was a perception at the local level that insecurity has actually decreased, due to the greater presence of defence and security forces.

Some incidents that then occurred are harder to interpret. Thus, shortly after our fieldwork in Diffa, a gang of ten motorcyclists claiming to be members of Boko Haram assassinated the chief and a prominent trader of Chetima Wango – a village south of Chetimari. They assembled the villagers and told them that they killed the two men because they were denouncing them to the authorities; they also warned eight other residents. Some of the young men were recognized as being from the village. In late 2013, in this same village, a woman was beheaded and her severed head placed on her back – a ritual characteristic of Boko Haram's grisly slayings. The assassins' claim to be Boko Haram members was not necessarily true. They might have been bandits exploiting the scary reputation of the movement for their own ends. But they might also have been telling the truth, and their action might have been related to the murder of the beheaded woman. It is also possible that they were both bandits and Boko Haram members. Precisely because of such confusion, the region fell into the grip of a Boko Haram scare, making it harder to evaluate the true extent of the movement's presence and actions there.

The presence of Boko Haram in Diffa region needs some elucidation. Is this just an echo of events in Borno State? Or are there local developments in Diffa pointing to a home-grown radicalization even if under the influence of the movement in Nigeria? Which factors are most prominent in this context?

Historically, Diffa region encompasses Manga, the arid region north of the Komadugu Yobe and territorially distinct from the Bornu Empire. Although independent of the old Bornu Empire, the people of Manga derived their livelihood from trading with their more prosperous southern neighbours. The confines separating Bornu from Manga coincide almost exactly with the modern border between Niger and Nigeria, and so, in this sense, colonization did not here break up a pre-colonial entity. More generally, the social and economic transformations introduced by the colonial process have been minimal here, and the ancient relations between Manga and Bornu are strikingly similar to the modern ones between Diffa and Borno. As in the past, the northern region is territorially independent from the southern entity, but economically dependent on it, establishing strong social and cultural ties based on that dependence.

In this way, Borno is the centre and Diffa the periphery, which means that influence tends to run from Borno to Diffa rather than the other way around. In the descriptions above, we have seen a key example of this, with the Diffa tradition of sending Qur'anic students out to Maiduguri and other Borno towns to complete their education. The historical factor implies therefore that developments in Diffa tend to echo at some level events in Borno.

The social and economic context is one of moderate inequality amid great poverty, chiefly due to the isolation of the region leading, in turn, to lifestyles not very differentiated by class. The small local elite, apart from some big traders, is not very wealthy. The region therefore lacks the kind of strident social contradictions found in regions with big cities, and some access to international markets such as Borno and Maiduguri. This more egalitarian social context is conducive to social stability, which may paradoxically have some disturbing implications in terms of radicalization. The relative social stability in Diffa makes for strong family and community ties, which have often been described by our informants as the factor that works in favour of protecting Boko Haram militants and sympathisers in the region, along with fear of reprisals. This is expressed in terms of a cultural trope: 'Kanuri don't betray their family'. This indicates a sturdy social cohesion that provides a convenient shelter for radicals, and may help them spread their message in the long run. Since 'family' extends to relatives in Nigeria, this means that help and protection are likely extended also to Nigerian militants. For this reason, Niger's defence and security forces at one point virtually suppressed the lawful movement of men – especially young men – between Diffa and Borno, with the consequence that the bulk of Diffa's trade went through the regions of Zinder and Maradi, causing marked price inflation in the Manga area of the region.

At the political level, there is a trans-ethnic consensus among the inhabitants of the region that Diffa is a marginalized area in Niger. This consensus is borne out by objective data as we have seen above. The marginalization is a function of the remoteness, isolation and small population of the region, not of repressive or discriminatory policies from the state. Still, this is resented in the region. The resentment is however greatly tempered by the fact that Diffa is a stronghold of the Mouvement National pour la Société de Développement (MNSD) party, which ruled Niger from 1999 to 2009. This single-party dominance was slightly fractured when MNSD split in 2009, and the breakaway party Loumana became a secondary political force in the region. The two parties cater for all ethnic groups in the region, taking into special account the fractious politics in the nomadic and semi-nomadic zones where groups compete for the creation, by the state, of *groupements nomades* – 'nomadic groupings', the nomadic chieftaincy administrative sub-divisions. It must be noted that both parties are now in the opposition, which may have negative repercussions on the political atmosphere in the region. On the religio-political scene, ethnic patterns remain prevalent and work against the coalescing of strong radical currents. Overall, this political factor does not seem to contribute much to radicalization in Diffa.

In this region as elsewhere in Niger, the Izala movement is the bearer of the ideology of Islamism that rejects the state's commitment to secularism, but two major configurations of politics in the area combine to limit the scope for the development of that ideology, and therefore its diversification into more extreme wings. These are the isolation of the region relative to the rest of Niger, and the fact that political developments here are strongly bound up with decision making at the centre, owing to the underlying centralism of the Nigerien system. As a peripheral region with minority populations, Diffa could hardly be the terrain of a driving ideological force in Niger, and the centrist Nigerien political system easily stifles local efforts at building autonomous ideologies – if any arise.

Thus, historical and social factors appear most important for radicalization in Diffa. They indicate that the phenomenon has taken form in the region as a result of its historical connections with Borno, and it eventually became a security problem because of the protection afforded to militants and radical ideologues by the social system especially in the Kanuri area of Manga. The economic, political and ideological factors appear less important in this specific context. Since the time of fieldwork, events have borne out this analysis. Diffa did not become a centre of the Boko Haram insurgency, but violence became entrenched, with militants able to secure assistance from the local population through a mix of terrorism and communal support.

MARADI

Unlike Diffa, Maradi region did not experience incipient radicalization, at least not in the violent Boko Haram form. The reasons for this shed further light on the situation in Diffa, but also raise some intriguing questions about the origins and nature of radicalization in this context. As in the previous section, I will first give a focused description of the religio-political landscape before delving into the issue of radicalization and ending with an analysis of a possible trajectory of radicalization in this region.

Maradi has one of the liveliest religious scenes in Niger. The three major Islamic sects – traditional Islam, Izala and Tijaniyya – are strongly implanted, in addition to three minority groups, the Shia, the Ahmadiyya and the Kala Kato (*Maitatsine*). The Roman Catholic Church has been present for decades and Maradi was recently made a bishopric. Many Protestant churches also exist in the city and region, with the Eglise Evangélique du Niger (EEN – the Evangelical Church of Niger) being the most important due to its rootedness in the local population. In fieldwork, only representatives from the major Islamic sects, the Catholic Church and EEN were interviewed, in part due to time constraints. Fieldwork also included interaction with traders in Islamic tracts and recordings, and people residing in the countryside. Some of the key features present in Diffa are also noticeable in Maradi, but they are modified by the size of the city, the political economy of the region, and the much greater ethnic homogeneity across the area.

Here, as in Diffa, traditional Islam derives much of its strength from ties with the 'palace' of the Sultan and from the state Islamic association (AIN). But the old practice has lost constituency, according to the famed and elderly Malam Mai Zaboura, first to the Tijaniyya (during the 1950s–1960s), and more recently to Izala. Many of Mai Zaboura's former students have become Izala in recent years, and traditional Islam seems nowadays to retain its influence chiefly among the clients of the old elite of the town.

The Tijaniyya sect appears here more important than in Diffa. Although it does not dominate religious life in the city itself, it is apparently predominant across the region, and especially in the dense tapestry of villages and small towns surrounding the regional capital – hence the insistence of Tijaniyya leaders that they are currently numerically more important than other sects in Maradi. The base of Tijaniyya is, at any rate, much wider than that of traditional Islam.

Both traditional Islam and Tijaniyya leaders entertain friendly relations with the Catholic bishopric and EEN. In the case of the leaders of traditional Islam, friendliness to Christians derives from a policy of tolerance willed by its main support – the state and palace – in the framework of *laïcité* and, more generally, a doctrinally laidback attitude that places social stability and political harmony above theological righteousness. Mai Zaboura expressed this point with particular clarity when he described the differences between the Sunni groups as a matter of politics rather than religious doctrine – meaning that Tijaniyya and Izala are driven by a kind of will to power. He added, 'they are more interested in forcing others to do what they want than in simply practicing their religion'. Thus, he reaffirmed the established view that traditional Islam is the simple practice of Islam without public fuss or a political agenda.

It is noteworthy, however, that in his criticism Mai Zaboura singled out Izala for the radical nature of their ambition, comparing them, on this score, to 'Satan': this is a reference to the pride which led Satan to refuse to bow to God's new creature – man – when God told him to do so. In the same way, Mai Zaboura said, conceited Izala refuse to acknowledge social and political authorities – 'established by God' – and are bent on subverting them out of extreme admiration for their own reasoning.

Among the Christian groups, the Roman Catholics are a minority. According to the curate of their church in town, there are about 500 of them in Maradi and its environs. Many of the Roman Catholics residing in the Maradi area are citizens of countries such as Benin, Togo and Cameroon. Established in the late 1960s, the EEN has a few thousand faithful. Both churches refrain from proselytizing. The Roman Catholic bishopric runs charitable and educational organizations that are mostly staffed with local Muslim personnel, a fact sometimes surprising to the local people, according to the head of its medical centre, a Muslim man from Zinder.

Together, the leading clerics of traditional Islam and Tijaniyya, the leadership of EEN and the Catholic bishopric constitute the camp of religious tolerance and political moderation in Maradi. They are all active in a religious dialogue committee established after a tense episode in town when angry Muslim youths threatened to destroy the headquarters of the Christian charity World Vision because they suspected a qualified Muslim driver lost a job competition to a Christian because of religious discrimination. Perceptions of insecurity and intolerance vary between the two Christian groups. The Catholic Church leaders stress that even though hostility toward Christians has risen in recent years, they do not feel threatened, mentioning easy access to the governor's office and a sense of safety derived from support found in their neighbourhood community. Residents of the community thwarted an attempted attack on the church during the 'Innocence of Muslims' YouTube video outrage of July 2012,[8] before security forces could be sent. At EEN, there is greater worry, especially in relation to recent events and Izala preaching that is sometimes venomous or derisive about Christians. Both churches agree that the greater threat in the future lies in the spread of anti-Christian ideas and feelings through Izala preaching. So far in vain, EEN has repeatedly called on the governor to monitor Izala for hate speech. As shown below, this concern is not limited to Christian groups.

While Tijaniyya and Izala are critical of *laïcité*, the Christian leaders believe it hardly exists in practice. The Catholic curate explains, for instance, that the bishopric has given up its right of access to state radio for a few minutes on Sundays because it was often curtailed in favour of Muslim events. In contrast, the criticism one Izala leader levelled against *laïcité* was illustrated by the fact that it might 'one day' be used by some *dan boko* (educated person) to require that the state rescind the new practice of paying the water and electricity bills of the grand mosques of the town, a privilege not extended to Christian religious houses.

Izala is arguably the most important Islamic sect in the city of Maradi itself. Although not necessarily numerically greater, in terms of influence,

[8] In July 2012, an anti-Islamic short film, *The Innocence of the Muslims*, produced by a Christian Copt residing in the United States, Nakoula Basseley Nakoula, was uploaded on YouTube, provoking a furore in many Muslim countries as well as protest rallies of Muslims in Western Europe and Australia.

Izala is unquestionably preponderant. As remarked in the case of Diffa, here too Izala gains recruits through its doctrinal closeness to traditional Islam. Even without formally embracing Izala by frequenting its mosques, attending its events and behaving in conformity with its codes of conduct, people still tend to imbibe some of its principles, due to the intense proselytizing organized by the *da'wa* system of the Izala groups (Ihiya wa Sunna and Kitab wa Sunna). Most importantly in this quintessentially commercial city, all of the big names in the Maradi business community are Izala followers – with only one known exception. Indeed, the earliest Izala association in Niger as a whole, the Association pour la Diffusion de l'Islam au Niger (ADINI), was created with the help and funding of Alhaj Rabé dan Tchadoua, a wealthy Maradi Izala ideologue. Through the efforts of dan Tchadoua and his friends, Maradi has become, by the mid-2000s, something like the Izala capital of Niger. It is in Maradi that another wealthy Izala ideologue, Siri Niéré, though a native of Kollo in western Niger, decided to build the grandest Izala mosque in the country. Apart from the numerous mosques, Izala has also inundated Maradi with the so-called Islamiyya schools, the most important of which follow the state-sanctioned format of the Franco-Arabic school (for more details on Franco-Arabic education, see the final section, 'Developments at the national level').

Izala differs from other groups in that they have a political agenda. Although, in interviews, their leadership said that 'Izala and Tijaniyya have the same notion of political governance (*shugabanci*)', the Tijaniyya do not currently have the oppositional language and practices that denote political ambition. Izala deplores the divisions among the Sunni Muslims as demonstrated in Maradi by the hostility between Izala and the Tijaniyya. That hostility runs deep, especially among the foot soldiers of both sects. The apparent conciliatory discourse, which I heard in an interview, referred to the tactical need to create a Sunni convergence against *laïcité*. Indeed,for Izala, there are three real enemies: secularist *'yan boko* (Western-educated people), the secular West and the Shia. The animus against *'yan boko* is limited by the fact that Izala recruits converts among them, labelling those who refuse to convert as mere stooges (*wakilai*) of the West. Hence Izala's veritable enemies are ultimately the West and the Shia. Malam Aboubacar dan Katsina, an Izala cleric, claims that there is geopolitical evidence of the 'fact' that the West and Shia are allied in a long-standing anti-Sunni plot. In part because of their perceived association with the West, Christians are also suspect, and Izala hardliners advise against befriending them, and even being friendly to them. This translates into real-life situations: the pastor of the EEN church in Maradi narrated an encounter in a bus when, after greeting and chatting with a man seated next to him, he pulled out his Bible for a bit of reading. The man then exclaimed: 'What! Are you a Christian?' and upon the pastor's positive answer, he cried that he did not know and that he regretted ever having shaken his hand and talking with him at all. According to the pastor, everyone in the bus immediately chided the man.

Given the sense that the West and the Christians are the enemy, aid from Western countries is a highly contentious issue for Izala. It is perceived to be either a form of spying, or at the very least something deeply humiliating, especially since Muslims in a poor country such as Niger are not free to choose the kind of aid they want to receive from 'infidels'. For Aboubacar dan Katsina, it would be much better if the United Nations should agree on a rule that only wealthy Muslim countries should provide international aid to poor Muslim countries.

With political ambitions pointing toward the establishment of an 'Islamic' form of governance, specific enemies to fight, a theory of history defining them as the victimized heroes of Sunni Islam – considered the only 'true' and unadulterated form of Islam – and a strategy for expansion through proselytizing, education and a code of conduct, Izala has many of the elements of a political ideology, with the potential for violent radicalization. Because of the size of Maradi, a city of about 210,000 inhabitants, and the wealth of the movement's key supporters, Izala is well structured, active and developed in the town. It has also gained some prominence in local politics through electioneering; its wealthy patrons have the means to influence voters and buy favours from the municipality. Izala in Maradi is also strongly defined by connections with its Nigerian counterparts in Katsina and Kano. While nearly all the religious audio-visual media shops (*discothèques*) in the city cater exclusively for an Izala audience, nearly all the materials sold in these shops come from Nigeria. The city's own Izala preachers, Aboubacar dan Katsina, Sani dan Toudou and a few others, are recorded and packaged on cheap-looking discs that are stacked in boxes below the counter, chiefly, it would seem, because they do not have the appealing covers of the Nigerian products.[9]

The mass consumption of Nigerian preaching tends to create a Nigerian frame of reference for Izala culture in Maradi, certainly more so than in Niamey, for instance, where the importance of the Zarma language has a limiting effect on this kind of Nigerian influence. This is compounded by the frequent visits of preachers from Kano and Katsina to Izala preaching events in town. There are four levels of these events: the *wa'azin unguwa* (neighbourhood sermon), the *wa'azin gari* (city sermon), the *wa'azin kasa* (national sermon) and the *wa'azin kasa da kasa* (international sermon). The latter level was set up essentially for events gathering preachers from Niger and Nigeria, but because of the proximity of Nigeria, Nigerian preachers may contribute to the lesser events too. Maradi preachers also participate

[9] Sounaye describes and analyses this trade in 'La "discothèque" islamique', 2011.

in similar events in Nigeria, as the town is part of a geography of Izala events and cooperation that ignores the national boundary. However, it is not one of the top cities in the region, and during an earlier piece of fieldwork (2007), an Izala cleric working at Moufida, the educational complex founded by Rabé dan Tchadoua, stated that the main objectives of the Izala community in Maradi are: first to gain autonomy relative to foreign centres (essentially meaning to be able to train the majority of Izala theology students in Maradi itself) and, second, to expand Izala in the countryside.[10]

For some key actors on the religio-political scene in Maradi, the relations the local Izala have developed with Nigerian congregations are too close for comfort. They are viewed with concern by police officials in Maradi, including the fact that they were encouraged by the mayor for electoral and business reasons. There is the notion that this trend risks importing 'Nigerian troubles' in the region, and one police official told me he has written reports alerting his hierarchy in Niamey to the 'danger.' Incidentally, the same reaction is observed from Tijaniyya practitioners, including in the countryside. An Izala man who resides in the small town of Madarounfa – a major Sufi centre in the region, located at a very short distance from Maradi – told me that people there reject his efforts at 'setting them on the right path' by claiming it is such behaviour that led to 'the troubles in Nigeria'. So, if Nigeria is something of a model, or at least a frame of reference for Izala, it is clearly an anti-model for opponents of Izala, essentially in view of the development of violent radicalism there.

There are other religious groups that the fieldwork did not directly cover, and which have a lesser impact on the religio-political scene in Maradi. These are principally the Shia, the Ahmadiyya and the 'Kala Kato'.

From what has been indirectly gathered about them, it appears that the Shia are a very small minority following the same policy of non-proselytizing as the main Christian groups, for similar reasons of public peace and protection of their minority status. The Ahmadiyya are also a very small minority, but one that is more active in courting the local population. They have a formal centre and engage in charity and mosque building across the region. During the 'Innocence of the Muslims' YouTube video outrage in summer 2012, the Ahmadiyya Centre sought to organize a peaceful demonstration in town in which it asked the Catholic Church – and possibly other Christian groups – to participate. The Christians declined. Ahmadiyya theology emphasizes actions conducive to peace and harmony among religious communities. They notably confine armed jihad to the status of only a defensive struggle against cases of extreme persecution and condemn seeing it as a method of propagation of the

[10] For further details, see Idrissa, 2009.

faith, which is Boko Haram's view of jihad. It is in this spirit that Maradi's Ahmadiyya Centre wanted to organize the multi-faith demonstration, but that was not how the Catholic leaders understood the initiative.

The Kala Kato – a group that believes that the Qur'an is the only valid basis of the faith, to the exclusion of the Hadiths and the Sunna, and that stems from the *Maitatsine* of Kano – is another unobtrusive minority concentrated in one of the poorer neighbourhoods of the town. They have the reputation of being an impenetrable community and are rumoured to hoard weaponry because they have the constant feeling of living under threat of attack. Obviously, this should be assessed just as a perception of the Kala Kato in Maradi.

Lastly, there are a number of missionary Protestant groups that are smaller than EEN, but nonetheless engage in proselytizing.

Does Boko Haram exist in Maradi? The general belief is that there is no Boko Haram in the region, or at least it is not known to exist there. Unlike in Diffa, indeed, no group claiming to be affiliated to the movement tried to organize there before 2009. Among all the groups reviewed above, only Izala may harbour some sympathy for Boko Haram's views, since they represent an extreme version of Izala principles and goals. The leading clerics of Izala, in Maradi as in Diffa, reject Boko Haram on account of its violence against Muslims. Aboubacar dan Katsina, in particular, put Boko Haram in the same league as Kala Kato (which used also to resort to large-scale indiscriminate violence in the early 1980s, in Nigeria). As such, he views Boko Haram as an inheritor of the spirit of Kharijism (*Khawarij*), although he thinks that Boko Haram belongs in the Sunni sphere, unlike Kala Kato. Kharijism – a now all-but-defunct doctrine – considered deadly violence against Muslims to be a key solution to the early divisions within the faith, following the civil war over succession to the Prophet that created the Sunni/Shia split. Izala, he contends, differs from Boko Haram in that it does not see violence against Muslims as legitimate and does not practice *takfir* or excommunication of non-conforming Muslims. Without delving into scholarly niceties, the foot soldiers of Izala sometimes agree with the logic of Boko Haram. One of them explained that calling people to embrace true faith through proselytizing is not enough, since many will refuse and, when doing so and persisting in their error, will also lead other people astray: in that case, it is lawful to fight and kill them.

It is to be noted that there has been, in the region, at least two cases of beheading that follow the gruesome Boko Haram ritual of slicing off the head and putting it on the back of the victim, and there might have been other instances. In each of these two cases, the offenders, because they had killed close relatives (in one case, the victim was the mother of the perpetrator), were deemed by the local courts to be suffering from mental problems. But in some cases, mental illness might just be a description of the results of Boko Haram's influence.

So it would seem that, although Boko Haram does not have in Maradi the comparatively stronger showing it has in Diffa, it certainly has sympathisers and may have led to acts of violence less obtrusive than the abductions and mass murders that make it to the news. A review of the potential factors of radicalization may give us a better handle on the matter.

Strangely enough, Maradi used to be – until the late 1980s – the least Islamized of Niger's principal towns. This is not an old centre of Islamic learning like nearby Zinder, which was the capital of a mid-size Bornu vassal state since the late eighteenth century. Maradi was a small northern establishment of the Hausa kingdom of Katsina which, in the seventeenth and early eighteenth centuries, dominated trade in the area. It is not clear whether what was no more than a village serving as a caravan station even bore the name Maradi at the time. Situated in the fertile drainage of the Sokoto and Rima valleys, the area was a bone of contention between Katsina and the Hausa kingdom of Gobir. In much of the eighteenth century, Gobir and Katsina were at war over hegemony in the Sokoto-Rima basin, with Gobir coming off generally on top by the 1770s. Some three decades later, however, the rivalry between the two Hausa kingdoms was superseded by the rising threat of the Fulani jihad of Usman 'dan Fodio and his followers. This paved the way for the foundation of Maradi.

After the defeat of Gobir and Katsina at the hands of Usman 'dan Fodio, the Korau ruling family of Katsina retreated in 1808 to Damagaram – the king himself committing suicide on the way north – where they received some assistance and were able to regroup. From there, they struck an alliance with the people of the area of Maradi in northern Katsina, who had remained faithful to the old Hausa belief system and rejected Islamic rule. With the help of these *Arna* (literally pagans), as they are called, the Korau seized northern Katsina and established at Maradi a *sansanin yaki* ('war camp') with the objective of recapturing their lost kingdom. Because of these circumstances, Maradi was born as a political entity with a strong anti-Islamic element in its ruling ideology. Islam as such was not rejected, however. Rather, Maradi kept the pre-Fulani-jihad pattern of associating Islam and Hausa animism in the governing rituals of state and society. On the other hand, the rulers of Maradi maintained the alliance with the *Arna*, who, while they remained resolutely hostile to any attempt at Islamization, were honoured in all major ceremonies of the rump Katsina kingdom. As time passed, the Fulani emirate of Katsina gave up the notion of conquering Maradi, and another fluke of history consecrated the cultural separation between northern (Maradi) and southern Katsina:

that is, the fact that the colonial border negotiated between the French and the British in the early 20th century unintentionally followed the separation line between the two Katsinas.[11] So, just as in the case of Diffa, the colonial border did not here divide a united political entity.

During the colonial period, the way Islam was conceived in old Maradi – laidback, supportive of the reigning civil order – became what is now known as 'traditional Islam'. Apart from the now-forgotten troubles caused by the introduction of Niassene Tijaniyya in the 1950s,[12] the general context that emerged from the Korau flight of 1808 and the later foundation of Maradi remained largely unchanged until the 1980s. Why and how did change come at that point?

Two sets of events strongly contribute to explain why Maradi went from being the least Islamized Nigerien city to the most Islamized in just two decades. One was rooted in the political economy of Niger, and the other in religious fermentation in Nigeria. Both sets of events should be understood against the underlying historical background of Maradi discussed above.

In the late colonial and early independence periods, Maradi had become a major economic centre in Niger. Perhaps building on the ancient Katsinawa acumen for commerce, the city had profited more than neighbouring Zinder from the development, in this entire area, of Niger's so-called 'groundnut basin'. The city's position at the gate of Nigeria also helped in the organizing of an import-export trade system where many local agricultural and pastoral products of the region were exported into the large markets at Katsina and Kano. By the early 1980s, Maradi was known as the 'economic capital' of Niger and boasted a vibrant class of wealthy business people known more for their acquisitiveness than for their piety. The business model on which this prosperity depended had a lot to do with the activism of the state. In its development plans, the government of Niger had created – or had prodded private investors to create – local industries. This led to modest but significant levels of salaried employment in the city, which, added to the larger consumer class of civil servants, buoyed markets already energized by the proximity of Nigeria. However, by the late 1970s, groundnuts had lost their international market value and, by the mid-1980s, International Monetary Fund-prescribed public retrenchment and austerity programmes were leading to the collapse of local markets. In that same period, Nigeria itself was becoming more stringent about border control – at one point expelling hundreds of thousands of

[11] For a fuller recent historical and theoretical analysis of this context, see Idrissa 2014b; Miles 1994, 2003.

[12] In the 1950s, from a base in Kano, Sheikh Ibrahim Niasse, the Tijaniyya reformist from Senegal, organized a reform movement with strong ideological accents that created tension and open conflicts with the established Tijaniyya and Qadiriyya in Hausaland.

Nigeriens and closing the border (1983–84). These events brought about the perfect storm that pushed Maradi downhill through the 1990s.

Meanwhile, in the late 1970s, the Izala movement had emerged, quickly gaining strength in northern Nigeria. It was introduced in Maradi at first by people on the lower rungs of the social ladder: petty traders, manual workers and such. As the crisis of the Maradi economy deepened, however, Izala attracted a growing and more diverse constituency and started in particular to draw in people higher up in the social pecking order, including the scions and heirs of wealthy merchants. Izala grew nationally in the 1990s, when its leadership could take advantage of the retreat of the state in the era of political liberalization and austerity to formally broaden the movement's constituency through associational life, and also to occupy some of the social space deserted by the enfeebled state. This was especially the case in Maradi, where the phenomenon of the Islamiyya schools – copied from Nigerian models – boomed in that period, taking aback state officials who, at first, called them 'pirate schools' because they challenged the official educational policy of secularism. In the context of the 1990s, which saw the collapse of Maradi's post-colonial order, these developments soon amounted to a historical game-changer. By the end of the decade, Izala had become the driving force for cultural change in the city, not insignificantly helped by the fact that most of the heirs of the ebullient self-made men who had dominated the 'economic capital' in the 1960s–80s period were now unsmiling Izala converts who would support the new Izala clerical class instead of the old traditional Islam *malamai* favoured by their fathers and uncles.

So in just two decades, under the spur of changes in political economy (structural adjustment, political liberalization) and religious culture (the emergence of Izala), Maradi had gone from being Niger's least Islamized major town to becoming its most vibrant religious (Islamic) centre. Local students of this process in fact explain the changeover precisely by the fact that Maradi was less Islamized than other places such as Zinder and Say for instance. In these other towns, the strength of the existing Islamic establishment worked as a major obstacle to the development of the late-comer Izala. Maradi was easier to take over, given in particular the state of disarray in which it found itself at the critical juncture of the late 1980s and early 1990s. I have expanded on this historical development because it clarifies all the other factors at play in Maradi – the social, the economic, the political and the ideological.

Thus, on the social and economic levels, Maradi eventually 'rebounded' in the 2000s, but in ways that yielded a different system from the one that prevailed before the crisis. The lifeline was now provided by the creation of the 'special transit' that transformed Maradi into northern Nigeria's dry harbour. The 'special transit' built on the old state-run transport system Organisation Commune Bénin-Niger (OCBN, the Benin-Niger Organization) set up in the 1960s to organize the export of groundnuts through the Beninese port of Cotonou, thus avoiding southern Nigerian ports during the Nigerian Civil War.[13] After the collapse of groundnut prices in the late 1970s, OCBN was maintained as an 'import-export' facility for Maradi merchants. In the 1990s, with the economic crisis, it was shut down, before being revived in the early 2000s under the name 'special transit' as earlier discussed in the Introduction. In this new economic context, trade and private investment are the order of the day, while the large state-based consumer class of the developmental era has withered. Petty salaried employment is now more ubiquitous but also flimsier. Maradi is less poor than in the 1990s, but also less equal than in the 1980s, something signalled in the cityscape by the multiplication of over-sized private residences and the preponderance of market interests. During fieldwork, I found out, for instance, that the mayor had ordered the destruction of the city's sole public park, a relic of the egalitarian ideals of the developmental state, to be replaced by a lucrative conference centre. Moreover, if the city itself is now a bustling centre of economic activities, it is partly at the expense of the rural areas, since commercial capital does not get invested in agricultural development but in speculation on agricultural production.

To understand how these developments play out in the issue of radicalization, it is useful to examine how they translate into the new political context of the region. There was a real possibility of violent radicalization in Maradi in the late 1990s. At that point, as we have seen, the old social and political order was in its final death throes, and there was no new working dispensation. The state was at its weakest, while still trying to maintain some of its traditional policy orientations – *laïcité* in particular – that infuriated the rising forces of religious opposition.[14] In neighbouring Nigeria, similar developments were tackled through the electoral response afforded by federalism: while the federal state remained bound by the constitutional separation of state and religion, individual states in the north blurred that line by reincorporating Sharia criminal law into their legal systems, thus defusing potential explosions of popular anger spurred by religious ideologues. In Niger, this type of 'solution' was not an option, and it is likely that the fact that it was applied in Kano and Katsina further frustrated the Maradian colleagues of apparently successful Nigerian ideologues. Thus, in November 2000, authorities in Maradi were unable to prevent riots that led to the

13 OCBN itself was a successor scheme to 'Opération Hirondelle' (Operation Swallow), a transit system put in place by the French in the 1950s because they were loath to be reliant on British (Nigerian) harbours.

14 See in particular Sounaye, 2010.

burning of the public park (alcohol was sold there, and music played) and the destruction of a number of churches. If the leaders of the riots were young Izala preachers, the perpetrators were not necessarily Izala: many were members of the drifting underclass of frustrated young men spawned by the city's economic crisis.

In the course of the 2000s, the political conditions for this sort of uncontrolled radicalism frayed. Without going so far as to incorporate Sharia law, the state relaxed the practice of *laïcité* (to the disgust of Christian groups, as we have seen). Economic stability was rebuilt through the 2000s on the basis of decentralization and the 'special transit'. Some of the local Izala star preachers, such as Malam Fallalou, the man behind the riots of November 2000, moved to wider fields of action, becoming fixtures of the preaching scene in Niamey and among Nigerien communities abroad. The state accommodated the Islamic educational demand spurred by Izala – which has now become mainstream – by ramping up its hitherto rather listless Franco-Arabic educational system. By the end of the decade, Izala had become so much part of the reigning order that it could no longer be a source of uncompromising radicalism, and this combined with the 'rebound' of Maradi to return the city to its erstwhile peace-loving affair with commerce and speculation.

Ideologically, it is often said that it is precisely the reaction to a similar deradicalization of Izala that led to the emergence of Boko Haram in Nigeria. If this has happened in Nigeria, why not, then, in Maradi, which seems to be so much a part of the same story?

In Maradi, Izala itself eliminated the very cultural context that had been favourable to its own emergence there. In the 1980s, as we have seen, Maradi had a laidback religious scene, which was easily penetrated and subverted by Izala. Today, however, the Shia and the Ahmadiyya are finding out that the local religious (Islamic) scene is much more organized and impervious, with the high street being occupied by Izala and Tijaniyya – the latter becoming better organized in reaction to Izala's incursion into what they thought was their turf. If peaceful, non-radical groups such as the Shia and Ahmadiyya are content to make small incremental gains in a strategically patient way, the solidity of the Izala-Tijaniyya dual hegemony may invite violent responses from more extremist groups. And as we have seen above, it is very likely that groups of people with radical views inspired by Boko Haram already exist in the region. In that case, and if the story of the rise of Izala is any lesson, another systemic crisis in Maradi could be the occasion for their springing into action. Barring such a circumstance – which may not recur for decades – it is hard to see how radical groups could make a breakthrough in the region.

Developments at the national level

Revisiting the conclusions drawn from the two case studies, I will here focus on a broad comparison between the two countries, looking in particular at elements that show why religio-political radicalism remains a dormant risk in Niger, in contrast to what obtains in Nigeria.

The ground for comparison between Niger and Nigeria is common ethnicity (Kanuri and Hausa in particular) and thus, potentially, common political and cultural identity, a fluidity of economic and social exchange, and the probability that what happens in Nigeria will also happen in Niger or vice versa. The difference in state-national identity and conditions then creates the key element of possible divergence between the two countries.

HISTORY

An initial paradox is that the commonalities between Niger and Nigeria really emerged during the colonial period and were strengthened by the two post-colonial entities. Historically, Manga (the Kanuri section of Diffa region) maintained its independence vis-à-vis the Bornu Empire (the Kanuri political entity that became Borno State). Similarly, northern Katsina (Maradi and its Katsina brethren in Tessaoua and the surrounding area) defined its political identity in opposition to southern Katsina that fell to the Fulani and their Islamic caliphate. The shifts introduced by the colonial regimes, such as the collapse of the trans-Saharan caravan trade which used to prop up the independence of the pre-colonial areas of what is now Niger, reinforced the links that existed between Manga and Bornu on the one hand and between the two halves of old Katsina on the other hand. Anti-imperialist ideas in the mid-20th century buttressed this with notions of ethnic and racial fraternity between people on each side of the border.

ECONOMIC AND POLITICAL STRUCTURES

The strengthening of these ties went on, however, against the background of key national differences at the levels of political and economic structures, as shown in Table 4.2.

These structural differences mean that prospects for social and political stability are brighter in Niger. While Nigeria is vastly wealthier than Niger, it has a population below the poverty line that is actually a few percentage points above Niger's, based on the World Bank's methodology. The consequences of this fact are particularly notable in the much higher level of inequality in Nigeria. Inequality translates more easily into political instability than poverty. Niger's Gross National Income

Table 4.2 Some structural differences between Niger and Nigeria

Indicator	Niger	Nigeria
Population	21.4 million	191 million
Poverty rate	44.1%	46%
Inequality	[32.0–36.4]	[45.5–49.9]
Urbanization	17.8%	49.8%
GDP	US $8.12 billion	US $375.8 billion

(Source: Data compiled from World Bank databases)

per capita is at only about US $400, while that of Nigeria soars at over $2,000, a striking indication of the maldistribution of wealth in the latter country. Urbanization, with its heightened competition, innovations, social contradictions and erosion of communal traditions, contribute also more to fermentation than the slower pace of rural life, which dominates the culture in Niger, even in the principal towns. Nigeriens are wont to say that their towns are only '*gros villages*' ('big villages'). That is certainly true of Maradi, and even more so of Diffa.

On the political level, the main difference is between Niger's centralism and Nigeria's federalism. Even with decentralization, the impetus of policy in Niger ultimately comes from the central government, especially since regions do not have real legislatures and the head of the regional executive (the governor) is appointed, not elected. Decentralization only gives to elective districts the power to regulate how they would meet the policy priorities decided in Niamey. Also, the *communes* are autonomous: thus, the other *communes* in Maradi region pursue policy priorities independently of what municipal authorities in Maradi itself have decided. In short, in order to achieve any structural political change, citizens in any Nigerien region need to go through Niamey. For instance, no region could have autonomously incorporated Sharia law in its administration as was done by the northern Nigerian states. And, as per the so-called republican principle of national unity, the central government does not make separate laws of such scope for regions. Beyond the elements mentioned in the concluding analysis of the case studies, this is an important explanation of why radical societal movements emerge more easily in Nigeria's states than in Niger's regions. In Niger, national politics count much more than regional politics, with the consequence that, in terms of religion-based reform, the push of the border regions (Maradi, Zinder and Diffa), influenced by developments in northern Nigeria, is generally counter-balanced by the pull of, or rather, the lack of interest from the influential riverine regions nearer the capital city (Tillabéri, Niamey and Dosso).

CHRISTIANITY

The Christian religion, which plays an important role in religio-political radicalism in Nigeria, where it has nearly the same demographic size as Islam and responds in kind to Muslim hostility, is almost irrelevant in Niger. As we have seen, it is all but absent from Diffa and it is a minority religion in Maradi, where it mostly refrains from competing on the religious scene. However, it is engaged in charity, and this may raise suspicion and resentment among Muslims in Maradi, especially among Izala adherents. In Diffa too, international aid – recently for the Nigerian refugees fleeing the Boko Haram war in Borno – raises similar suspicions, given the fact that, in the mind of most local Muslims, non-religiousness does not exist and therefore international 'Western' aid is really 'Christian' aid. Such angst does not have, however, the political acuteness and sensitivity of competition between Muslims and Christians that prevail in Nigeria's starkly polarized religious climate. That being said, Nigerian anti-Christian discourse – which really amounts to a form of Christianophobia – does cross into Niger, leading to attacks against a minority which does not present, here, the same threat that its co-religionists are perceived to present south of the border.

SECULARISM

Despite having a massively Islamic population, Niger, like other French-speaking countries, pursues a policy of political secularism (*laïcité*) which is perceived by Muslim ideologues as a policy of secularization, and thus the antagonist of their own Islamization project. In effect, this policy was assertive only in Niger's first decades of independence. Recent developments and events indicate, however, that Niger's *laïcité* has become more passive. I borrow these terms from Ahmet Kuru's concepts of assertive and passive secularism. According to Kuru's analysis, modern secular states have tended to practice two types of secularism: an assertive kind, which confines religion to a private sphere and bars it from having any significant influence on public order and the formation of citizenship; and a passive kind which, while maintaining a 'wall' between the state and religion, allows religion to be an influential force in the public sphere. Moreover, Kuru describes at least two types of assertive secularism. One, which has been long practised by France, is based on 'separation,' meaning that the state formally refrains from engaging religion. The other, historically developed by Turkey, rests on 'control' in that the state organizes religion in ways that formally enable its confinement into state-sanctioned roles. Niger's assertive secularism has been closer to the Turkish than to the French model, especially after 1974. In contrast, Nigeria practices a form of passive secularism.

What all kinds of assertive secularism have in common is that they have an openly transformative agenda in which religion should be removed as far as possible from public life and detached from the rights and obligations of citizens qua citizens. Nowhere is this issue more salient perhaps than in Niger's educational policy. In a 1917 volume, the colonial education theorist Georges Hardy advocated the creation of Franco-Arabic schools which would serve as bait to lure Muslim children in France's Islam-dominated colonies. Once in these schools, Hardy explained, the children would be acquainted with modern culture in its wondrous French form, and would thus gradually change into Frenchmen of sorts, endowed with the desired secular conceptions of political and social life. The work, aptly titled *Une Conquête morale* (*A Moral Conquest*), theorized attempts already made in 1911 at the madrasa of Timbuktu (French Sudan, now Mali). These ideas proved at first rather naïve, especially since the cash-strapped colonial governments did not make much effort to develop these Franco-Arabic schools, preferring to allocate funds to French schools, whose assimilationist benefits were more directly apparent. They were not forgotten however, at least not in Niger.

As soon as it approached independence, Niger set up a madrasa at Say (1958) and, after 1960, its newly independent state launched a full-blown programme of Franco-Arabic education in the country. The 1964 bill that organized that form of education enunciates motivations that are eerily reminiscent of Georges Hardy's arguments. Although less cynical, the bill does indicate that the state of Niger wished to attract students interested in religious knowledge, but that the Franco-Arabic schools' goal was to train them in ways that would render them useful to 'progress' and 'development', without mentioning religion. The curriculum of the schools emphasized religion only in the early grades: as the student would progress, secularization would increase, to the extent that religious studies would have a negligible mark at the final, high school examination, the *baccalauréat* (French equivalent of A Levels). The curriculum is clearly constructed to attract students with religious inclinations, or whose parents have religious inclinations, and then gradually set them on a more secular course, to the extent that when they reached the university, Franco-Arabic graduates would be indistinguishable from graduates from the French schools, apart from their (unobtrusive) mastery of Arabic. In part, this is justified by the fact that, as a secular state, the Nigerien state could not develop or fund religious schools. Moreover, religious education was not considered a component of national education, but of national security, and as such, an office in the Interior Ministry supervised it (a French legacy). This encouraged in private investors the preference of creating secular schools, while the mission schools of the Catholic Church also adopted a secular curriculum that allowed them to deliver state-sanctioned degrees.

Hence the astonishing fact that, until the 1990s, formal religious education did not exist in Niger beyond the Qur'anic schools (and with the exception of the Islamic University of Say, funded by the Organization of Islamic Cooperation). Nigeriens seeking further education in religious matters had to travel outside of Niger, many to Nigeria. This history also created a strong attachment to state secularism in Niger, but one that has been growing measurably weaker especially in the 2000s. With the growing Islamization of society first spurred by Izala, and now a mainstream concern, *laïcité* (assertive secularism as it were) has much altered in practice. The word itself became controversial in the 1990s and has been finally stamped out from the latest Nigerien constitution (2010), where it has been replaced with 'separation of state and religion', a phrase characteristic of passive secularism (and found in Nigeria's constitution). To be sure, there are remnants of *laïcité* in Niger's public order. For instance, in the educational sphere, a subtle compromise has been achieved between the state and the private investors who want to run religious, so-called Islamiyya schools, in response to a massive societal demand. The founders of such madrasas must adopt the Franco-Arabic form, including its secularizing curriculum, but they are free to develop religious extra-curricular courses and activities for their students, thereby maintaining the religious cachet of their institutions.

So secularism – *boko* as it were – still looms much larger in Nigerien state and politics than in northern Nigeria, something that ultimately prevented Niger's Islamist lobbies from achieving success similar to the one attained by their Nigerian counterparts in undermining the secular bases of governance in the 1990s and early 2000s. However, recent events point to the fact that such lobbies might be more successful going forward. Only some months after this study was completed, some violent events revealed just how frail Niger's policy of secularism might have become. On 7 January 2015, terrorist killers in Paris attacked the headquarters of satirical anti-clerical magazine *Charlie Hebdo* and murdered 12 people. As the French rallied in shock to mourn and show support to the victims, Niger's president Issoufou flew to Paris to take part in a massive demonstration there, on 11 January. In Niger, where *Charlie Hebdo* was known only for its abusive depictions of the Prophet Muhammad, the president's actions, and his adoption of the motto 'Je suis Charlie' ('I am Charlie') outraged the public. After the Friday prayer on 16 January, crowds of people in Zinder attacked the French Cultural Centre and the city's churches, which were torched. The next day, a demonstration planned in Niamey by people opposed to the president's 'Je suis Charlie' stance, as well as by members of the political opposition, was banned. As a result, riots broke out across the city, targeting bars, betting booths and Orange (a French telephone company) kiosks, as well as dozens of churches, which were torched and ransacked. Ten people died, the majority – but not all of them – Christians.

The riots can be read in terms of a failure of state secularism in the country, but Islamic riots are rare in Niger. The only ones to have occurred before 2015 happened in 2001 in Maradi and Niamey over the holding of an international fashion festival in Niamey, and in 2012 in Zinder over the outrage arising from the 'Innocence of the Muslims' YouTube video. The main difference, however, was the government's response. For instance, in 2001, it was highly repressive. Hundreds of people were arrested and detained for months, and dozens of Islamic associations were dissolved. The fashion festival went on as planned and the Prime Minister attended its opening and closing sessions. In 2015, large-scale arrests were also made, but people were detained only for a few weeks at most, despite the fact that the destruction had been more serious and had resulted in deaths. The government also appeared eager to 'appease' Muslim opinion and at the end of the day, on 16 January, a humbled President Issoufou appeared on television to ban *Charlie Hebdo* from Niger (the magazine had a tiny readership of mostly French expatriates who bought it in an exclusive shop in Niamey's city centre, and only a handful of Nigeriens had known about its existence before the events). Instead of blaming Muslims for the damage, he then accused the opposition parties of manipulating the masses and had several of their members arrested.

The 2015 riots confirm some of the conclusions of the study. The anti-Christian feeling detected in Maradi has emerged at the national level, and the importance of socio-economic factors has also been supported. In the regional case studies, I stressed that Maradi, which was an economic basket-case in the late 1990s to early 2000s, has become economically dynamic again and may not easily revert to radical action. Indeed, people in Maradi remained quiescent in the 2015 riots. On the other hand, Zinder, where the Charlie Hebdo riots started, has been in the limelight in Niger for its economic decline and the edginess of its burgeoning youth population. Social and 'political' riots have become something of a norm in the town through the 2000s, something unique in Niger.

The novel thing revealed by the riots, however, is that representative-democratic politics tend to undermine assertive secularism. There is no space for developing this argument here, although there is no lack of evidence stemming from developments in Niger since 1991, when politicians wooing voters started to consider issues important to Islamic groups – the Family Code for instance – to be hot potatoes. The constitutional and practical erosion of *laïcité* and its final eradication in the 2010 Constitution indicates that politicians have gradually bowed to the pressures of Islamic associations and leaders, and have allowed views based on Islam to become active components of Niger's public order. Although this evolution lacks the weight of formal rules and laws, it explains the feeling of insecurity of Christians, since the informal influence of Islamic views in state institutions would weaken the protections afforded by the state. States are complex objects, however, and the fate of Niger's tradition of state secularism cannot be determined in any simple and quick way. It is, for instance, my suspicion that, while *laïcité* has weakened in government, it remains quite robust in its traditional stronghold, the *magistrature* (judiciary). With these caveats in mind, one can still recognize that the necessity of pandering to the majority in a representative democracy opens the way to changes that might move Niger closer to some of the problems that passive secularism has nurtured in Nigeria.[15]

Yet, *laïcité* may not be the only bulwark against radicalization in Niger. Other dynamics of counter-radicalization within society have begun to surface since 2016 as terrorist violence takes its toll on the Nigerien military in the Lake Chad region and in parts of western Niger. 'Jihadist' violence is perceived as a problem created by foreigners, arising from developments that have their epicentre outside the country – in north-eastern Nigeria and north-eastern Mali. There is growing public outrage about the killing of 'our soldiers' in struggles against jihadis, leading to a public backlash among the Muslim majority against what is perceived as Islamic fundamentalism. In this new context, the message of Izala and other Salafi ideologues now has to battle the headwind of negative public opinion. The counter-radical shift is expressed in popular culture through folk music critical of Boko Haram (such as the song *Wata kungiya da a ce ce ma Boko Haram – A Group known as Boko Haram*); or from a new reticence to allow Islamic rituals – such as the reciting of the Fatiha (the opening verses of the Qu'ran) – at the beginning of official functions, reversing an earlier trend toward adopting an opening prayer in meetings.

These shifts in public sentiment are being reflected in regulatory shifts. In April 2019, the government adopted a law designed to reinforce state control of the 'religious sphere'. The law states – in a veiled reference to Nigeria and Mali – that 'to prevent the risk of mishaps (*dérives*) such as those that are seen in other countries, it is of overriding importance that the state endows itself with the means to control practices in the religious sphere'. A formal Salafi organization – the Association Nigérienne pour l'Appel et la Solidarité Islamique – protested the introduction of the law but could not muster public support against it. In Maradi, the chief cleric of the Sahaba mosque (a Salafi mosque), Oustaz Riyadin Ishaq, managed to mobilize a riot in the town's popular neighbourhoods, but was only able to do this by wildly misrepresenting the law as seeking to establish homosexual marriage in Niger – clearly because the actual contents of the

15 But see the analysis of Mueller (2016) which reaches slightly different conclusions on this score.

bill would not have provoked the level of anger he wished to stoke. When the bill was debated in the National Assembly, a deputy with Salafist leanings tried to invoke the *laïcité* principle to oppose the bill, arguing that the separation of state and religion means that the state should not try to control practices in the religious sphere. The irony is even greater given that Salafist pressures led to the removal of the term *laïcité* from the 2010 constitution. The argument did not succeed. Just a few years back, it would have been hard to imagine such a law being proposed, or a Salafi sympathiser referring to *laïcité* (of all things) to defend Islamic practices against state regulation.

Conclusion

So why did Boko Haram not emerge in Niger despite the cultural and religious similarities – indeed, continuities – between southern Niger and northern Nigeria? The study shows that this is not quite the right the question. Boko Haram is the violent, extremist manifestation of something else that did emerge in Niger, a form of non-violent Salafi radicalism which, using the theology of Izala as its legitimating religious anchor, sought, and still seeks, to 'Islamize' the government of Niger, following a distinctive understanding of what such Islamization entails. In Nigeria, this non-violent radicalism did achieve a modicum of success, through the so-called 'Sharia Implementation' process of the early 2000s, across the north, while Boko Haram took root essentially in the north-east. Mirroring this, in Niger, it is in the south-east (Diffa) that Boko Haram made some inroads as we have seen, creating a reign of violence there that is still worrying at the time of writing – while the centre-south was subjected to Izala enterprise. The real question then is, why the *limited* success of both Boko Haram and Izala in Niger relative to northern Nigeria?

Responses to this question lie in a Nigerien difference that ranges from the country's history to its religious landscape, specific socio-economic makeup, and political organization. We have seen that, despite the cultural continuities between Niger and northern Nigeria, there were significant historical differences from the religious point of view in the pre-colonial era. Northern Nigeria was the realm of the Sokoto Caliphate and the Bornu Empire – a devotional state – while southern Niger was the refuge of resentful – against Sokoto – Hausa dynasties and, in the far east, Kanuri and Mangari communities that kept some autonomy from Bornu. To a large extent, the religious rapprochement was, paradoxically, an effect of colonialism, and it took shape as an influence of northern Nigerian Islam over southern Niger. This influence was strong enough to spawn an Izala phenomenon in Niger, which imported in a country where Christianity was traditionally viewed as a non-threatening minority, the Muslim-Christian violence and hostility that has increasingly characterized Nigeria's polarized religious landscape since the 1970s. In Niger, given the minority status of Christianity, this rather led to episodes of violence against Christians, not to any Muslim-Christian riots. Both for Boko Haram and Izala, the ideological appeal – which makes an enemy of secularism and 'the West' – is key to radicalization. An ideological appeal is a broad factor that connects with heterogeneous motivations. In Diffa, I found that, at least at an initial stage, Boko Haram's appeal combined the ideological discourse against secularism with subjective familial and communal linkages. The economic marginalization of a region dependent on Nigeria's Borno State further reinforced this dynamic by the lure of economic compensation. Yet the entire dynamic has remained derivative, and centred around the Lake Chad section of Diffa region for geostrategic reasons: the ethnic support base of Boko Haram lives there, and the type of guerrilla warfare at which Boko Haram is adept is practicable there rather than in the arid expanses that make up much of the region. In Maradi, Izala developed in a congenial religious landscape and with the dual stimulus of economic downturn and democratization in the 1990s. But the Nigerien state's centralism and principled secularism, though weakened by decentralization (after 1998) and the 'Islamization' of society, preserved enough resilience through the period to check Izala's inroads in the public sphere. In a sense, Izala-inspired riots – besides reflecting the influence of Nigerian issues – express this relative failure. They tend to happen only in cities connected to northern Nigeria (Maradi and Zinder) and in Niamey (the capital city, the premier target of emigration from Maradi and Zinder) and they have never been turned into political capital to pressure governments into the reforms desired by Izala. As we have seen in Maradi, the latter remain suspicious and mistrustful of Niger's *'yan boko* ('secular-educated') whom they have been far less successful than their counterparts in northern Nigeria at bringing into their camp.

While, from the point of the view of the secularist, *laïcité* has unhappily lost ground to the 'Islamists', Islamic opponents of *laïcité* have less and less hope of displacing it. Indeed, in the intervening years, the radical ideology of Salafism that fuelled Izala activism and led to the Boko Haram insurgency has in fact lost a significant degree of its public appeal, as violence from both Boko Haram and jihadist groups operating from northern Mali has come to define it as an existential threat to Niger. This, in turn has revived the appeal of *laïcité* in the public sphere.

Given the foregoing, what course of action or policy would appear advisable in the Nigerian predicament, especially as compared to what *did not* happen in Niger? The apparent good luck of Niger has much to do with differences that make it rather difficult to engage in very specific policy recommendations for Nigeria based on what transpired in its northern neighbour. However, a number of policy *orientations* could take inspiration from the Nigerien experience. Niger's forte seems essentially to reside in the domains of national cohesion and educational policy, and the ways in which these factors are organized by a centralist state. While Nigeria's federal governance structure – and perhaps also its much larger and more heterogeneous population – are ill suited to policy making at the centre, this may not preclude the formation of consensus on a social policy that aims at bolstering national cohesion and favouring education with a strong secular accent. In fact, the two agendas are interconnected: in Nigeria, historical as well as current events have abundantly shown that religion divides the national consciousness. While freedom of religion may never be denied, only secular themes and agendas can unite all Nigerians in a shared vision of their country.

Secular themes and agendas do not arise spontaneously, or at least do not prevail unaided, and must be nurtured primarily in the nation's government school system,[16] in ways that should be both bold in their goals and sensitive to local situations. Similarly, elementary education with a secular accent must be expanded vigorously across the land, if strategically, i.e. by taking into account the potential for resistance, accommodation and goodwill. This recommendation does not address the current crisis, but the issues that lie at its ideational roots. While the crisis itself must be tackled – and the other chapters in this volume focus directly on this – it is bound to recur in another shape if actions are not taken at deeper cultural levels with longer-term effects. The Niger case shows that a social policy that puts a premium on the content of education in ways that promote national cohesion and secularism strongly contributes to providing balance and ideological resilience to even such a cash-strapped state and impoverished society. While the recommended policy does not entail a costly reform process – it can be fused into the existing educational organizations of the country – it does require political will and a broad support basis in communities across the land. But it is imperative. The popular moniker of the predicament stresses the required response: *boko halal*.

[16] But also through incentives to the private education system.

Bibliography

Grégoire, E., 1987, 'Emploi et travail non-salarié à Maradi (Niger)', *Cahier des Sciences Humaine* 23 (1), 35–47.

Idrissa, A., 2009, 'The Invention of Order: Republican Codes and Islamic Law in Niger', dissertation, University of Florida.

——2014a, 'In a Neighborhood on Fire: Security Governance in Niger', Sahel Research Group Paper 008, University of Florida.

—— 2014b, 'The Fish that Refuses to Die: Islam and the Government of the West African Sudan', in *Saharan Crossroads: Exploring Historical, Cultural and Artistic Linkages Between North and West Africa*, T.F. Deubel, S.M. Youngstedt and H. Tissieres (eds), Cambridge Scholars Publishing.

——2014, 'Security Sector Governance in Niger', in A.R. Mustapha (ed.), *Conflicts and Security Governance in West Africa*, Abuja: Malthouse and CLEEN Foundation, 57–78.

——2017, *The Politics of Islam in the Sahel. Between Persuasion and Violence*, London: Routledge.

INS-Niger (Institut National de la Statistique), 2015, 'Etat et structure de la population du Niger en 2012', RGPH, INS, Niamey.

Kuru, A.T., 2007, 'Passive and Assertive Secularism: Historical Conditions, Ideological Struggles, and State Policies toward Religion', *World Politics* 59 (4), 568–94.

Miles, W.F.S., 2003, 'Sharia as De-Africanization: Evidence from Hausaland', *Africa Today* 50 (1), 51–75.

—— 1994. *Hausaland Divided: Colonialism and Independence in Niger and Nigeria*, Ithaca, NY: Cornell University Press.

Mueller, L., 2016, 'Religious Violence and Democracy in Niger', *African Conflict and Peacebuilding Review* 6 (1), 89–104.

Sounaye, A., 2011, 'La "discothèque" islamique: CD et DVD au coeur de la réislamisation nigérienne', ethnographiques.org, 22.

——2010, *Muslim Critics of Secularism: Ulama and Democratization in Niger*, Saarbrücken: Lambert Academic Publishing.

van Walraven, K., 2013, *The Yearning for Relief: A History of the Sawaba Movement in Niger*, Leiden and Boston: Brill.

5

The effects of security measures on youth radicalization

JULIE G. SANDA

Introduction

A primary duty of the Nigerian state is to provide for the security of its citizens. The Constitution of the Federal Republic of Nigeria (1999 as amended) invests the responsibility for security in certain organs of the state, chiefly the police and the armed forces (military). The Nigeria Police Force is responsible for internal security, law and order while the primary roles assigned to the armed forces of Nigeria (AFN) are: to defend Nigeria from external aggression, protect its territorial integrity and secure its borders from violations. The armed forces may also be called upon to suppress insurrection and provide aid to civil authorities to restore order and perform other roles as the National Assembly may prescribe (Section 217 (2) a–d). The authority to offer assistance to civil authority or civil power is referred to in military doctrine as 'Military Aid to Civil Authority' (MACA) and 'Military Aid to Civil Power' (MACP), respectively.[1] When the military is deployed in an internal security operation (ISO), the goal is to put an end to violence and restore normalcy and law and order as quickly as possible so that the civil power, in this case the Nigeria Police Force, can resume its normal duties. The ability of the Nigerian military to perform these roles has been severely tested in its decade-long struggle against the extremist religious group, *Jama'atu Ahlul Sunna li Da'wati wal Jihad*, popularly referred to as Boko Haram. Not only has Boko Haram inflicted devastation on the Nigerian population, but fighting this brutal and complex insurgency has challenged the capacity and integrity of the Nigerian military, raising questions about

1 In the case of MACA the state deploys military assets not requiring arms to help with an emergency that the civil power is unable to cope with, such as a humanitarian disaster while in MACP the military is deployed against threats to internal security requiring the use of force.

whether it is becoming part of the problem rather than a key player in the solution.

In conformity with constitutional provisions and other relevant legal instruments, the Nigerian state has deployed the armed forces, comprising the Nigeria Army (NA), Nigeria Navy (NN) and Nigeria Air Force (NAF), in several conflict and crisis zones throughout the country. The military has been engaged in such operations in every state, including the federal capital, Abuja. These deployments are undertaken as single service operations, joint operations combining two or three services or even multi-agency operations. According to a former Chief of Defence Staff (CDS), 'the Joint Task Force system has been operating very well. It is not new to us; it is the way it is done all over the world, so it is not something that is peculiar to Nigeria' (cited in Omeje 2012, 22). Nigerians have become familiar with Joint Task Forces (JTF), including Operation Restore Hope (Niger Delta) and later Operation Pulo Shield (expanded to cover nine states), Operation Flush, Operation Restore Order (JTORO) (North East), Operation Safe Haven (Plateau and some parts of Kaduna and Bauchi) and Zaman Lafiya. More recent deployments include Operation Lafiya Dole (North East), Sharan Daji (North West), Python Dance (South East), Operation Crocodile Smile (Niger Delta and parts of Ogun) and Operation Awatse (South West), among several others. While the use of military task forces is not unusual, numerous security challenges across the country mean that the military is deployed in 32 of Nigeria's 36 states, posing problems of overstretched capacity, hasty recruitment, and inadequate training, and limiting effective surges in the fight against Boko Haram (International Crisis Group 2016, 16).

In many states the internal security operations are mounted with the police and other security agencies, as has been done in Operation Mesa to help deal with a range of violent criminal activities such as hostage-taking, trafficking in persons and cattle rustling. This underlines the importance of effective coordination among the various arms of the security services. The principal security agencies that operate alongside the military in such operations include the Nigeria Police Force, Dept of State Services, Defence Intelligence Agency, National Intelligence Agency, Nigeria Customs Service, Nigerian Immigration Service, Nigeria Prisons Service and the Nigerian Security and Civil Defence Corps (NSCDC). The specific composition of a task force depends on its mandate and Area of Responsibility (AOR). More recently international security cooperation has become more visible such as the Multinational Joint Task Force (MNJTF) initially set up in 1988 and now comprising Nigeria, Niger, Cameroon, Chad and Benin.

Government recourse to use of the military for internal security operations remains a contested option in Nigeria. The debate is not so much because there is no merit in that policy choice but that it is perceived as a first-line response rather than a last resort. Moreover, the consequences have at times left much to be desired, and the continued reliance on the military option seems to blur the utility of other options. While acknowledging that these military operations have achieved some successes, it is a fact that they have also inflicted damage on the civilian population, even if unintended. Such losses, which have been in terms of civilian casualties and destroyed property have sometimes gone beyond the bounds of collateral damage. The 17 January 2017 air raid that accidentally bombed the camps of internally displaced persons in Rann, Borno State killing over 200 persons including aid workers, is one such case in point (Haruna 2017). There have been allegations of human rights violations and reports of communities refusing to cooperate with the military or outrightly rejecting the deployment of soldiers. In Jos, women have staged protests against the Special Task Force (STF) in which they openly accuse the military of excesses and asked that they be withdrawn (Ajijah 2013). There have also been reports of a number of soldier suicides in what some have suggested could be manifestations of post-traumatic stress disorder (Ogundipe 2018). Over time the damage to the military goes beyond such isolated cases to create a general atmosphere of distrust and loss of confidence in the military. Looking through the lens of Hungtington's 'objective control' theory of civil-military relations, Ayo Sogunro (2019) opined that 'the Nigerian military lacks proper civilian control, professionalism and political autonomy' and that it has 'lost public trust'.[2]

These factors have hugely complicated engagement of the Nigerian military with the ruthless and cunning extremist group, Boko Haram. One of the deadliest terror groups in the world, Boko Haram has killed over 30,000 people in Nigeria and neighbouring countries since 2011 (*The Economist* 2017). Boko Haram has engaged in a succession of attacks on military and purely civilian targets; religious and traditional rulers, places of worship, markets, women, children and schools have not been spared as part of the campaign to expose the vulnerability of the populace even in the face of government security measures. The group introduced suicide bombing in 2011 as a key part of its operations and has used women and girls as suicide bombers since 2014 after the abduction of the Chibok girls.[3] Boko Haram now has the infamous record of being the terrorist group that has deployed the highest number of female suicide bombers. Between April 2011 and June 2017, 244 out of 434 suicide bombers deployed by the group have been female (*The Economist* 2017). Between June 2014 and

[2] In recent years military authorities have devoted considerable time and resources to regaining public confidence through dedicated departments of civil-military relations and human rights desks (see Nigerian Army website, February 2016).

[3] There is no evidence that the Chibok girls have been employed as suicide bombers.

February 2018 more than 1,200 people have been killed and nearly 3,000 injured in such attacks (Warner and Matfess 2017, 29–30).

The complex terms of engagement and prolonged stay of the military among the civilian population has been problematic, with allegations of unprofessional conduct against some personnel. Where military tactics appear overbearing or heavy handed, Boko Haram has seized the propaganda opportunity to its own advantage among the youth, hoping to attract some of them to its ranks. The youth constitute a group that already feels alienated from mainstream society and provide a pool of potential recruits. Scholars point out that extremists are made not born that way but that there are several entry points or pathways to radicalization (Onuoha 2014c; Bramadat 2011, 56). In a synopsis of the causes of terrorism a study found that retaliatory factors are among the complex of possible causes. The UN Special Rapporteur on drones, Ben Emmerson, on a visit to Pakistan in 2013, observed that the 'consequence of drone strikes has been to radicalize an entirely new generation' (Robertson 2013). Grievances against the state could therefore provide fodder for radicalization. As Scheinin (2005, 20) explains, 'repression, extra-judicial killings, excessive and heavy-handed security measures, torture in detention, abuses in prison, and indiscriminate arrest of innocent individuals' could create 'conditions conducive to' radicalization.

The aim of this inquiry is to investigate the extent to which security measures employed in the security strategy of the Nigerian state fosters an environment conducive to radicalization of youth.[4] It examines the extent to which the actions of the security agencies deployed by the state have served as a push factor for youth towards radicalization. The first section of this report identifies the specific security measures that have been employed in the North East, particularly Borno, to counter the violence perpetrated by Boko Haram. It then examines the effects of these security measures on youth radicalization, followed by a discussion of the implications of the emergence of the vigilante group known as the 'Civilian Joint Task Force' (CJTF). The concluding section offers policy recommendations and a suggestion for further research.

RESEARCH METHODS

The research methods comprised a desk review of relevant literature and a field study conducted in two locations, Abuja and Maiduguri. I conducted

[4] Nigeria's National Youth Policy recognizes that the definition of youth is dynamic depending on several factors including political, economic and socio-cultural realities and so, for the purpose of implementing the policy, adopts the statistical definition that regards 'all young males and females aged 18–35 years' as youth. It considers the UN definition of 18–24 years as 'too narrow', yet the latter approximates more closely to the global norm. This chapter uses the above official Nigerian definition in view of the policy implications of the study.

several face-to-face interviews between June and August 2014 with seven senior military officers and two academics in Abuja with the help of a research assistant. Further interviews were held with military and academic experts in January and February 2019. Interviews with security personnel and civilians sought their perspectives on the security measures employed and the extent to which the interface between civilians and the security personnel involved in the security operations has contributed to radicalization. Primary data was collected through face-to-face interviews and focus group discussions (FGDs) with civilian respondents in Maiduguri, Borno State, based on a questionnaire and interview guide. Interviews were conducted with members of CJTF and Borno Youth Forum to find out their views on security operations and the effects of these on members of the communities particularly youth. Some of its leaders were also interviewed.

The interviews and FGDs were carried out by a research assistant engaged from the community and based in Maiduguri to leverage his contacts with the target groups. The main objective of conducting the FGDs was to find out more about CJTF with a view to understanding its contributions to the security operations and counter-radicalization in communities in Borno State and elsewhere affected by Boko Haram. The interviews also sought insights into how Boko Haram recruits and radicalizes its members. Focus groups involved the leadership and operatives of CJTF at community levels since they are more directly involved with the issues, including some leaders at state level and women from CJTF. A few members of the Borno Youth Council, and a couple of community leaders were included in the two FGDs to get their own perspectives. In keeping with the principle of 'do no harm' it was made clear to respondents that no one would be identified in the research report, and that they were free to withdraw from the research if for any reason and at any point they thought their security was being compromised.

Security operations in the North East

The Nigerian state has employed a number of measures in countering violent extremism, specifically that manifested by Boko Haram. These measures have been both military (hard) and non-military (soft), in nature. They have included at various times policy, legislative and judicial instruments, deployment of military and other security assets including intelligence, third-party mediation, dialogue and negotiation, special education intervention (such as *almajiri* schools and Safe Schools Initiative[5]), percep-

[5] *Almajiri*: a disciple or someone who leaves his home in search of Qur'anic education. The Safe Schools Initiative (SSI) was launched in the wake of the Chibok school incident to protect

tion management and foreign military and diplomatic assistance (Onuoha 2014a; Bakut 2013; International Crisis Group 2014; Okereke 2012). On the whole, the most visible and consistent of the government approaches is an amalgam of war and criminal justice models of counter-terrorism in which the principal agents deployed by the state are military and intelligence units, police and the criminal justice system. The defensive and reconciliatory models noted by Pedahzur (2009) have enjoyed less public visibility. The war and criminal justice methods have tended to occupy centre stage, focusing on the elimination of terrorism by the use of force and punishing perpetrators through the judicial and penal system.

The criminal justice system has made some convictions using special courts set up for that purpose. The courts, set up in a military detention facility, sat over cases of 1,669 suspects in trials commencing in October 2017 and continuing in 2018. Despite thousands of detainees, only 13 suspects had previously been tried in the eight years since the insurgency began, with nine convictions secured (*Vanguard* 2017). While some experts agreed that the trials were largely fair, they expressed concern that suspects had been kept in detention for long periods before being prosecuted, and that during pre-trial processes, 'defence lawyers did not spend sufficient time with the suspects' (Adesomoju 2018). The trials were also criticized on grounds of 'failing to prioritize prosecution of those most responsible for the group's atrocities' and concentrating instead on those who provided 'material and non-violent support' (Human Rights Watch 2018). Moreover, many of the detention centres which are administered by the military owing largely to the lack of capacity in the police and corrections systems, are overcrowded and do not distinguish between combatants and non-combatants. According to Femi Falana, over 3,000 suspects were held in Giwa barracks without trial and in terrible conditions (Akosile 2018). The already congested prisons have been repeatedly attacked by Boko Haram as they seek to rescue their incarcerated members. The brazen Boko Haram attack to release some of their members in 2014 exposed the condition of the Giwa detention facility. Attempts have been made since then to improve both the facilities and the conditions of detention but rights activists insist there is still room for improvement.

MILITARY OPERATIONS IN DESPERATE CONDITIONS

The most prominent of the security measures in the North East zone (NE) have been the military deployments in Borno, Yobe and Adamawa

(contd) schools in the North East and so making it safe for children, especially girls, to return to school. It was a collaboration between the President Jonathan government, the UN Special Envoy for Global Education, Gordon Brown and a coalition of Nigerian business during the World Economic Forum on Africa (WEFA) held in Abuja in May 2014.

States. Since 2009 the military has operated under different arrangements: a hybrid operation, a task force code-named Operation Flush Out II; a joint military task force (JTF), 'Operation Restore Order' (JTORO) deployed in 2011; also, a new army division, the 7th Division (Div) became operational on 22 August 2013. The federal government also imposed emergency rule at various times between 2012 and 2014. Other major operations in NE since 2009 include 'Zaman Lafiya' (Let's live in peace), Operation Lafiya Dole (Peace by all means) and Last Hold. Operation Lafiya Dole was set up in July 2015, a few months into the new administration of President Muhammadu Buhari, specifically to counter terrorism and insurgency in NE. Its activities were later expanded with the insertion of specialized operations like, 'Crackdown', 'Gama Aiki' (Getting the job done) and 'Safe Corridor'. Gama Aiki, for instance, involved cooperation between the military and the Multinational Joint Task Force (MNJTF) to clear Boko Haram from the Chad and Niger border regions (Maliki and Mutum 2017) while Safe Corridor is the government's deradicalization, rehabilitation and reintegration programme (Alkassim, 2019). The actual tasks performed by the military include protection of key points and vulnerable points, checkpoints designed to control movement, long-distance patrols to seek out insurgents, arrests and detention, VIP (very important persons) protection, guard duties at military installations, cordon and search for seizing arms and suspects, and air strikes on Boko Haram bases. These tasks are now undertaken as part of the counter-terrorism and counter-insurgency operations that began in 2014. It is important to identify these tasks in order to show the circumstances in which excesses can or do occur.

The shortcomings of the Task Force (Operation Flush) became manifest in its handling of the July 2009 Boko Haram uprising that culminated in the death of its then leader, Yusuf, in police custody. The casualties from that raid have been put at 700–800 civilians. The approach used by the Task Force can be said to have backfired badly, since Boko Haram increased its violent campaigns and changed its tactics in the wake of that debacle, further stretching the capacities of the ill-equipped Task Force. The Task Force, comprising the Nigeria Army, Nigeria Air Force, Nigeria Police Force and other security elements had some degree of coordination between them though this did not eliminate areas of disagreement and controversy such as the killing of Yusuf in 2009. Yusuf was killed in police custody after the military had handed him over to the police as required by the rules governing internal security operations. According to a military source, that incident accounts for the disagreements that arose over matters of detention and arrest and may have influenced the decision to keep detainees in barracks, rather than handing them over to the police. Funding was also a problem area. It is not unusual for state governments to make contributions in both cash and kind in support of federal security agencies operating in the states; the contention among members of the Task Force was often about who would control the 'joint' purse.

When the Joint Task Force (JTF) deployed in 2011, it comprised the three military services – army, navy and air force, the police and the Department of State Services (DSS). The military component of JTF dominated the operation and also undertook police duties, particularly when the federal government declared a state of emergency in the three states of the North East zone. The JTF deployment had its own challenges. The composition of any such joint task force is determined by the operational environment, at least theoretically, so also its command and control. According to an army officer who had served in JTF, the navy had no business serving in Maiduguri. He did acknowledge that the military was faced with many operational challenges, chiefly force generation, wherein 'navy and air [force personnel] were assembled from different parts of the country and brought under command of people they didn't know', meaning they had not trained or served together previously. Moreover, in his view 'the navy and air force were not suitable for roles like [manning] checkpoints, long range patrols, cordon and search' and there was no training provided in-theatre to bring them up to speed. Countering claims from navy personnel that all military officers got the same training at point of entry, he argued that 'the operational environment was too severe to not get it right'. The army officer insisted that the introductory training received by its sister services did not suffice for a terrorist environment. On matters of command and control another source explained that with such a 'hybrid force' the situation was one akin to 'a Commander working with strangers'.

The operational problems encountered by JTF led to a strategic review by military authorities that resulted in the creation of the 7th Division which, as noted above, became operational on 22 August 2013, covering Adamawa, Borno and Yobe states, with headquarters in Maiduguri. It was created to enable the army to adopt 'a more agile and robust posture to meet the full spectrum of asymmetric warfare challenges' (Murdock 2013). This move was also expected to guarantee operational efficiency by routinizing operations as opposed to the task force approach. A division is solely an army formation and its operations are carried out by army personnel; other military assets play supporting roles as required with their own line of command. The Nigeria Air Force (NAF) whose operational base is in Yola, Adamawa State, carries out the air operations alongside the army. The navy also provides specially trained personnel (similar to the Navy Seals of the United States) for specific assignments. A military source agreed that the creation of the new division tackled the problem of force generation by tripling the size of the army component available in the operational area. But he also pointed out that the troops were 'haphazardly generated' as in the days of JTF, meaning that they were assembled from different units without having been trained or been in operations together. Given time, he expected that the haphazardness would give way to a more cohesive unit as the personnel train and deploy together.

Another source disagreed on the numbers, adding that the creation of the 7th Division was still inadequate to effectively counter the challenge posed by Boko Haram in the state, given its large landmass. The operations in the states of Adamawa and Yobe are covered by the 3rd Armoured Division with headquarters in Jos, Plateau State. Given the spread and concentration of militant attacks to these two states, some military sources suggested the creation of another division in Yobe. As realities of the threat posed by the insurgents became more manifest, the military has had to fully prepare for and is now engaged in specialized operations. The Nigerian military is now occupied with counter-insurgency operations (COIN) with varying degrees of success. As the insurgents vary their tactics so also the nature of military operations have had to adapt in order to cope, and the scope of actual operations keeps widening from the metropolis to cover more communities in the hinterland as they track the insurgents down to their hidden bases.

The federal government first declared a partial state of emergency in 15 Local Government Areas across four northern states (Plateau, Niger, Yobe and Borno) in January 2012 that ended six months later, to the relief of many residents who said it had affected their economic activities negatively (Ibrahim and Yaya 2012). Under a state of emergency, the military is empowered to arrest and detain longer than is normally provided for under the law, bail provisions are not applicable, and search without warrant is permissible, as are certain traffic violations in response to emergency. A rights activist, Shehu Sani, cautioned at the time that the state of emergency would neither stop nor reduce the violence. He rather saw it as 'a blank cheque for human rights violations by security agents' (quoted in Squires and Heaton 2012). Yet government declared another emergency in May 2013 covering the entire Borno State as well as Yobe and Adamawa States, those directly affected by the Boko Haram insurgency. This state of emergency was extended twice, ending eventually in 2014. In a national broadcast declaring the expanded state of emergency, the then-President Jonathan directed the Chief of Defence Staff to deploy more troops to the affected states for more effective internal security operations: 'These terrorists and insurgents seem determined to establish control and authority over parts of our beloved nation and to progressively overwhelm the rest of the country. In many places, they have destroyed the Nigerian flag and other symbols of state authority and in their place, hoisted strange flags suggesting the exercise of alternative sovereignty' (Jonathan 2013).

A senior official of the Borno State government was of the view that the measure did not succeed as attacks by the insurgents actually increased during the period of emergency, and he challenged government to find another military strategy other than extending emergency rule (Daniel 2014). Critics resist the wide latitude given to security agencies by emergency powers, particularly when direct political control is muzzled. Jonathan secured the support of the state governors who remained in their positions as political authorities. The Governor of Borno in a separate address called on the people of the state to cooperate with the 'strange rules' imposed by state of emergency (Audu 2013). Another problem that arose was that the proper detention facilities were not put in place to cater for the large number of those detained, many arrested indiscriminately. This may have been responsible for the overcrowding of whatever facilities existed in Giwa barracks which had about 3,800 detainees (according to a military source) prior to the Boko Haram invasion in March 2014. In a counter attack to regain control of the barracks, security forces allegedly tortured and killed unarmed recaptured detainees (Audu 2014; Amnesty International 2016).

Faced with the worsening security in NE and its implications for the presidential elections scheduled for early 2015, the government turned to another external partner for operational support. The United States had maintained its hard stance against the Nigerian government, citing a law that prohibits military training assistance and sales of arms that could be used by units or individuals against whom there was credible information on human rights violations. Yet the poorly equipped military faced repeated Boko Haram (BH) attacks, and one incident too many had been recorded of the military fleeing from BH and abandoning their equipment. The human rights record of the Nigerian military was a deciding factor in the refusal of the US to sell much needed arms and equipment for the fight against BH. The souring relations between the Nigerian government and the US on both military and economic fronts came to a head in late 2014. Following the continued refusal of the latter to sell military arms and equipment, the Nigerian authorities stopped a training programme of a battalion as part of a larger project of building more capacity for countering Boko Haram (Tukur 2014).

The government turned to another external source for help, this time a South African private military contractor – Specialised Tasks, Training, Equipment and Protection International Ltd (STTEP) – was contracted for three months by the Jonathan administration in January 2015. The mission of the group was initially to train special forces to rescue the Chibok girls but it later changed to include a combat role in view of the continued advances of Boko Haram fighters in 'unconventional mobile warfare' (Freeman 2015; Barlow 2018). Although government spokespersons would not admit the presence of the foreigners, the president referred to 'trainers and technicians' provided by two companies (Cropley and Lewis 2015). Reports put the number of mercenaries at 100–300. They are credited with helping the Nigerian military root out Boko Haram to the extent that the 2015 elections were not only held in NE but internally displaced persons were able to vote in those elections (Smith 2015). An unnamed senior government official was quoted as saying that the mercenaries were in 'the vanguard of the liberation' of several communities that had been under Boko Haram control, although the mercenaries did most of their fighting at night to avoid being seen (Nossiter 2015).

The use of special forces in NE actually commenced in 2014 as a special forces unit, now the Armed Forces Special Forces (AFSF), with elite military personnel from the army, navy and air force, trained in Nigerian special forces training institutions and a European country (Olatunji 2018). In 2017 they had further training in Pakistan in counter-terrorism and counter-insurgency (CT/COIN). The army chief enthused about their ability to fill in capacity gaps for the military given their special training in tactics (Olatunji 2018). However, a respondent explained that, while special forces may be able to hit their targets, the military and other security agencies simply do not have the numbers required to hold the ground, accounting for repeated military reversals.

OPERATIONAL PROBLEMS, CORRUPTION AND HUMAN RIGHTS ISSUES

Operation Zaman Lafiya, which replaced Restore Order in August 2013, was dogged by controversy. In 2014, military authorities charged and dismissed hundreds of soldiers and officers for a range of offences including refusal to comply with deployment orders (to fight Boko Haram), attempted murder and mutiny, among others (Ibeh 2014; Associated Press 2014; BBC 2014). Following court martial, many of them were dismissed and others sentenced to death, but their cases were reviewed in 2015 and the convictions were overturned. Shortly after coming to power, President Buhari replaced the failing operation with Operation Lafiya Dole, launched 16 July 2015. Buhari had based his campaign on three major pillars, – security, the economy and the fight against corruption – so expectations were high that the new leadership would deliver where previous ones had fallen short. President Buhari ordered that the military command centre move to the theatre of operation, Maiduguri, and a deadline of December 2015 was set for ending the insurgency (Nwabughiogu 2015). To that effect a Military Command and Control Centre (MCCC) was established in Maiduguri on

16 August 2015 with an alternate command centre in Yola, Adamawa State (*Nigerian Bulletin* 2015).

However, the new operation, like others before it, faced a number of problems. Regarding equipment, officers interviewed in 2014 agreed that the equipment in use, both personal kits and unit requirements, were not suitable for the operational environment. They said most of the equipment was procured long before, and could not deal with the new threat of asymmetric warfare and specifically terrorism. In other cases, even where the right kind of equipment was available, it was not up to the required scale. This was exacerbated by loss of armaments to the militants resulting from direct seizures, and equipment abandoned by fleeing troops. The issue of weapons and other equipment has remained a recurring challenge in counter-terrorism and counter-insurgency operations, in spite of the huge sums voted for arms procurement. In September 2014, just months before the 2015 elections, the National Assembly approved a loan of US $1 billion (about GBP £0.825 billion in August 2019) for the Jonathan administration to procure arms. In December 2017 the Buhari government got approval for another $1 billion from the excess crude account for the same purpose. The approval was mired in controversy as critics recalled that the funds approved in 2014 had become embroiled in corruption proceedings against the erstwhile National Security Adviser, accused of stealing over 2 billion US dollars (Agencies 2015). Allegations that these funds were diverted to electioneering purposes led officials of the Buhari government to provide extensive details on some of the procurements such as the US $593 million (GBP £489 million) worth of equipment from the United States that included 12 Super Tucano A-29 surveillance and attack planes valued at $490 million (£404 million) (Aliyu 2017).

The lack of appropriate doctrinal guidance and training also affected operations in the field. As one respondent explained, for a long time the military operated under an order of battle (ORBAT) for internal security operations which was 'unrealistic and required review', including a greater focus on equipment for counter-terrorism units and specialized training. As the respondent further explained, there are fundamental differences between the conventional warfare tactics with which Nigerian troops are more conversant and the new counter-insurgency operations they are 'learning as they go along'. In the view of a military source, the differences are not entirely appreciated by political authorities and some military leaders. He explained that tackling insurgencies often involved a long drawn-out engagement, not a rapid-response action. Boko Haram is able to employ hit-and-run tactics then disappear because its operations are very light on the ground and very mobile. The military on its part, is almost 'tied to the ground' with their heavy tanks and other armaments not suitable for fighting in populated areas.

Furthermore, cases of human rights abuses and violations by military personnel have been widely reported in the media as civilian populations in the operational areas have suffered losses in the course of the military campaigns from military personnel as well as insurgents. Criticisms of unprofessional conduct have been made against personnel, who have been accused of brutality, extra-judicial killings, rape, extortion, indiscriminate mass arrests and unlawful detention or detention under inhuman conditions, among others. According to Amnesty International (2018a), by April 2017, 4,900 detainees were being held in Giwa barracks, including some 200 children, and detention conditions were reported to be plagued by overcrowding, disease, dehydration and hunger. Some cases had been investigated and confirmed, and others refuted by the authorities. Military authorities have often had to answer to allegations of violations of both human rights law and international humanitarian law. Some have argued that the extreme conditions encountered by the military call for extreme measures, yet the state has an 'obligation to respect human rights while prosecuting efforts at national security'; this obligation is universal, having neither geographical nor cultural exemption (Olujinmi 2012, 124). This means all states and governments are obliged to follow the rule of law in respect of the fundamental rights of its citizens.

The government has acknowledged some of the difficulties associated with the operations in the North East. On detention facilities, for instance, towards the end of 2013 the erstwhile President approved that the sum of N1 billion be disbursed to upgrade detention facilities, particularly that of Giwa barracks which he said was of particular concern to the international community. On a number of occasions he acknowledged that abuses had been carried out by the military but also that some of the allegations levelled against the military were largely exaggerated, and yet others were actions of the insurgents wrongfully attributed to the military (Jonathan 2014). Human rights desks have also been set up to handle complaints or allegations of rights violations brought by the public against military personnel. In addition, some international organizations have been working with the military to improve detention facilities and procedures. Other efforts include 'strengthening the existing Rules of Engagement, Code of Conduct, empowering the DCMA [Directorate of Civil Military Affairs] ... establishment of Free Call Numbers' (Musa 2019), among others.

Yet allegations have not abated, and groups such as Human Rights Watch and Amnesty International, as well as local groups and media, continue to insist that the military must be held accountable for human rights violations. In August 2017, the federal government set up a Presidential Investigation Panel to review Compliance of the Armed Forces with Human Rights Obligations and Rules of Engagement. This move came after several reports and petitions had been filed against the military, including at the International Criminal Court (ICC). The panel was to investigate allegations against the military of human rights violations and non-compliance with rules of engagement in local conflicts and insurgency. However, a year after the panel's report was received, the government was yet to issue a White Paper on it. According to prominent human rights lawyer, Femi Falana, '[t]he panel confirmed grave human rights abuses by the military. Unfortunately, the government has not been able to release the report. Further, the government has not released the White Paper on the panel's findings' (*Vanguard* 2018). The military authorities on their part usually respond to allegations of abuses by refuting them or promising to investigate.

The military as an institution and the individual soldiers and their families have not gone unscathed. The military has experienced heavy losses and casualties such as personnel deaths, destruction of equipment and physical infrastructure such as barracks, as well as loss of equipment, arms and ammunition to Boko Haram fighters. Personnel deployed without being properly equipped or kitted have also been put in harm's way. There have been reports in the media, some confirmed by military authorities, of troops and even officers abandoning their duty posts and barracks, with some fleeing across the borders. Such incidents have been explained as a combination of two factors: soldiers fleeing to escape instant death at the hands of Boko Haram, or Boko Haram sympathisers within the military who mislead the soldiers into being ambushed, also abandoning their weapons and formations. These incidents have contributed to eroding the sense of security and confidence of affected communities in the military. Demoralization and reputational damage are challenging the re-professionalization of the military that has been underway since 1999.

Families of military personnel have also borne the brunt of inadequately planned and equipped deployments in many ways. For instance, many families still await closure on the loss of their loved ones when the remains are not returned, nor are they declared 'missing in action' (MIA). In either situation they are not given the honour due them as fallen soldiers. Ordinarily, soldiers who desert would bring humiliation on their families but that is not the case anymore as they find some sympathy among the populace. The psychological impact on troops and their families has also been negative and wives of soldiers have on occasion, publicly demonstrated against the posting of their husbands to battle theatres. Such action was of course roundly condemned by military authorities (Azubuike 2014).

Beyond the personal losses experienced by victims, civic life dies when the military is deployed for a long time in such operations that keep them in close proximity with the civilian populace (Vombatkere 2012). In Borno, as in other places that have been under a state of emergency, community life suffers in ways that are yet to be fully appreciated. In all these, a key question is about the extent to which security operations have contributed to the security of the populace or heightened their sense of insecurity in both real and perceived terms. The military has stepped up its engagement with the public in terms of information sharing and addressing grievances. For instance, military spokespersons have taken sole responsibility for public information which hitherto (until 2015) was a joint effort between civil and military agencies. Civil-military relations departments set up in each of the services have been engaging with civilians, communities and civil society organizations to enhance understanding and cooperation. Various training programmes are being undertaken under the auspices of foreign military assistance teams and national training institutions to foster interagency cooperation.

Security operations and youth radicalization in Borno

In examining the deployment of security measures as a response to the violent campaigns of Boko Haram, we sought to find out if and how the actions of security personnel have affected the youth – in particular whether their reported excesses served to swell the ranks of radicalized youth. The most significant finding in this regard is the effect of the extra-judicial killing of Mohammed Yusuf in police custody on youth in Maiduguri and surrounding villages. In the immediate aftermath of his death, the avenging of Yusuf's death became a rallying cry or, according to Sampson (2014, 67), a 'radicalizing opium'. From then on, attacks by Boko Haram on police and related targets such as prisons increased, the most brazen being the sacking of a police training school in Gwoza where five units were stationed at the time (*Sahara Reporters* 2014). Other operational difficulties and excesses have been recorded since 2009. Inadequate personnel, according to one respondent, has meant that troops have on occasion had to go on assignment with little supervision, leaving 'soldiers to supervise soldiers'. The implication of this is that they were able to commit abuses and 'get away with it'. In 2015, President Buhari ordered the relocation of commanders to the theatres of operation ostensibly to improve command and control. The effect of this decision on operational effectiveness is that command decisions can be made in-theatre, thereby speeding up communication, but the high turnover of commanders suggests that there could be other factors to be considered in determining the effectiveness of that order.

Another challenge posed by the Task Force was the poor collaboration with police which meant that military personnel conducted searches in residential areas of the affected communities without the other security agencies and without keeping search records. The other side of the story, as related by an officer interviewed in the course of this study, is that given the risky environment, non-combatant security elements have been reluctant to engage alongside the military. Some abuses common at checkpoints have included extortion, assault, and corporal punishment such as flogging and caning of civilians. Other recorded abuses are lack of respect for local customs when conducting searches, and arbitrary arrests and detention. An interviewee recounts that, prior to the first attack on Giwa barracks by Boko Haram, the military allegedly kept up to 4,000 suspects in makeshift detention centres – old warehouses that had been converted for that purpose. According to the informant, the majority of detainees were youth aged between 16 and 25. He alleges that anywhere an explosion or attack occurred, the security operatives would raid the place and round up youth they found in the vicinity and 'dump' them in Giwa barracks. In his view, whereas the raids may be justifiable, the conditions under which youth were detained were not. They were cramped in unsanitary conditions for indefinite periods, without adequate arrangement for their maintenance. There have also been allegations of rape and extra-judicial killings made against the military, many of which they have strenuously denied.

In the field we were unable to interview Boko Haram members but found some sketchy evidence linking the security measures to radicalization. A respondent in Maiduguri cited a few instances where male youth had ostensibly joined Boko Haram to avenge the deaths of family members and their own unwarranted ordeals in the hands of the military. Another interviewee said he knew of an imam who became a Boko Haram sympathiser when four of his sons (out of five) were allegedly killed in a military raid. His complaint was that Boko Haram had specific targets and did not engage in indiscriminate killings. A female member of CJTF said she knew of a boy who joined Boko Haram because his father was killed by a military operative.

Another respondent in Abuja who had been a member of the Presidential Dialogue Committee[6] said that, in the course of their assignment, they had visited prisons and other detention centres in Bauchi, Lagos and Abuja, among others, where suspected Boko Haram members were being held. Significantly, the respondent said that, although the question of security excesses as a push factor towards radicalization was not a direct concern of the committee in engaging with the detainees, they did ask if

[6] Full name: 'Presidential Committee on Dialogue and Peaceful Resolution of Security Challenges in the North', set up in April 2014 by President Jonathan on recommendation of the National Security Council. Its terms of reference included developing frameworks for granting amnesty, conducting disarmament, victims support and addressing the underlying causes of insurgencies (Abati 2013).

detainees knew why they were being detained. Quite a number of them said they did not even know why they were being detained since in their view, they had a right to freedom of association and some said they were engaged in a just cause. In the respondent's words:

> When asked why the organization to which they belonged had been killing people some of them replied they were only doing what was expected of them. The truth is that most of them are willing to confess, while some have gone metaphysical in the radicalization because of the kind of books and scriptures they read and their belief about Islam. Some are afraid to confess because they believe that God has given them the vision and will not forgive them if they didn't accomplish the vision.

Interestingly also, they met a Christian in one of the prisons.

> We came across a Christian converted to Islam because he thought that the [Boko Haram] revolution was against Nigeria, but he later discovered that it was not a revolution involving Nigeria but that he had joined a religious sect. He later re-converted to his former faith.

A 2016 study on perceptions and personal stories of children associated with Boko Haram in Borno, Yobe and Adamawa States sought to identify key pathways to radicalization. It was the perception of a government official that some boys joined because of perceived injustice over the way they or community and family members were treated by security forces (NSRP and UNICEF 2017, 9–13). An earlier study that sought to identify key drivers towards radicalization among youth in six northern states found that the 'alleged excesses of security forces [were] not a major driver of youth extremism'. Citing alleged abuses such as 'unlawful killings, dragnet arrests, extortion and intimidation by security forces' the study sought to know how these ranked, collectively, in turning youth towards extremism in view of 'claims by sections of the media, especially international media [that] have repeatedly mentioned that the excesses of the security forces are a critical factor in youth radicalisation' (Onuoha 2014b, 101, 2014c, 6). In a ranking of 16 drivers of radicalization, the finding in Borno was that actions of security agents towards religious groups ranked 15th and actions of security agents towards members of the public ranked 16th, with similar findings in Yobe State (CLEEN Foundation 2014, 32, 39).

It is worth noting that the survey results are drawn from perceptions of respondents; this implies that the results might be different if actual Boko Haram members or recruits were included in the survey. The UN

High Commissioner for Human Rights reported that, during her visit to Nigeria in March 2014, she met people who 'openly acknowledge human rights violations have been committed by the security forces, and these have served to alienate local communities, and created fertile ground for Boko Haram to cultivate new recruits' (OHCHR 2014). Her conclusions serve to buttress the point that even where radicalization cannot be directly traceable to indiscriminate and excessive actions of security forces, such actions where unchecked can be counter-productive, and with regard to this point, 'the Government is evidently aware'.

THE ROLE OF THE CIVILIAN JOINT TASK FORCE

Fear has also been a potent force in preventing affected communities from cooperating with the military. As a respondent in our study observed, each time the military inflicted serious damage on Boko Haram, the group would retaliate even harder to convince communities of their potential to 'punish' them if they did not join or at least sympathise with the Boko Haram 'cause'. Communities that did not support them paid dearly. Soft targets like places of worship (churches and mosques) and schools were repeatedly attacked in order to instil fear in communities. Military excesses compounded this situation of profound insecurity, placing local communities in impossible situations. It was in this context that some youth in Maiduguri decided to band together not to support Boko Haram, but to counter their actions. This confirms the premise that harmful forces of radicalization are not necessarily a sign of violent societies, but can in some cases call forth a counter-radicalizing Polanyian 'double movement' (Goodwin 2018) wherein actors, forces and conditions emerge from within society to inhibit its growth and spread. In mobilizing to restrict the incursions of the military into communities, the so-called Civilian Joint Task Force (CJTF) has emerged as a direct countervailing force to Boko Haram.

Since 2013, military operations, launched in Maiduguri as a major part of the overall strategy to curb Boko Haram activities, have been supported by civilian vigilantes and youth groups from various communities within the state. These civilian groups came together to form the Borno Youth for Peace and Justice Association. Originally called 'Yan Kato Da Gora the group later came to be known as the 'Civilian Joint Task Force' (CJTF). It was when they began to undertake joint security patrols with the military Joint Task Force (JTF) that the latter gave the organization the nickname 'Civilian JTF'. The vigilante group was founded in February 2013 by some youth in Hausari ward of Maiduguri with the major goal of total eradication of Boko Haram members from Borno State and the wider north-eastern region through collaboration with the military JTF and host communities. The initiators of CJTF were convinced that their knowledge of the environment and the people involved in perpetrating the insurgency in the region would be useful in countering Boko Haram. Their in-depth knowledge of the various areas in the state, Local Government Areas, villages, units and families fuelled their resolve to come together to form a youth volunteer force that would combat and eradicate the insurgency and restore peace in their region. To this end CJTF volunteered to synergize efforts with the military in carrying out security operations. They supported the military by providing intelligence and directing their movement in host communities especially in remote areas, as well as in house-to-house searches, mounting of road blocks, night vigilante guards and patrols, among others.

One respondent claimed that CJTF was a spontaneous reaction of members of local vigilante groups that felt they were being unduly targeted by soldiers through indiscriminate arrests and shootings. To protest and prove their innocence they decided to help fish out Boko Haram elements and sympathisers in their communities and hand them over to security agents. Another respondent argued that a major vigilante leader based in Bauchi was actually instrumental in bringing the groups together to support the military. According to this source, the man had helped the military on other occasions and had more than a cursory idea about the difficulties faced by the military in their operations. Be that as it may, CJTF has become a household name not only in Maiduguri but all over the country, not only for some of the successes it has recorded but also for its larger-than-life status.

Leaders of the group in a focus group discussion provided some details about the organization. The pioneer members of the Borno Youth for Peace and Justice Association were 42 in number but their total strength was about 26,000 and counting in 2014, and 'every day, youth are joining for self-defence' to help in 'apprehending the BH'. Their stated goals are 'to protect our community and expose whosoever is a member of BH'. At the initial stages they contacted each other mostly through cell phones and social media and held their first meeting in February 2013 in Borno State Nitel Building which served as the operational duty post of sector 04 of the former JTF. Members claimed that the association was registered as a non-governmental organization with the Corporate Affairs Commission, which gives it a legal status, although this has not been independently confirmed.

About 85 per cent of the members of CJTF are youth between the ages of 20–39 years spread across the 27 Local Government Areas in Borno State. Recruitment is done among volunteers who show 'commitment and sincerity of purpose' towards assisting the various vulnerable communities and the military in restoring peace to Borno State. According to their leader, members are also required to be 'of good behaviour and conduct in the society' to which end they have a code of conduct to which all members are expected to adhere. Although we were not shown any written document, the leader maintained that any member in breach faces the disciplinary committee. The Civilian JTF is headed by a Chairman, it also has a Vice Chairman, Secretary and Legal Adviser, and its headquarters are located in Maiduguri. It has an operational department and ten sector commands that mirror that of the military task force. At the local government level they have their own chairmen and secretaries, among other officials. They also have village and unit commands whose leaders are appointed by the overall executive body. It tasks its members to raise funds which they use to purchase locally sourced weapons and run the organization.

The successes recorded by CJTF have attracted substantial support from the Borno State government. In 2013 the government provided some operational vehicles (ten Toyota Hilux pick-ups) and financial support for their security operations. Furthermore, the state pledged to pay 1,500 of its members the sum of N15,000 (about GBP £34 or US $41 in August 2019) per month under the Borno State Youth Empowerment Scheme (BOYES) and provide some training to enable them to discharge their duties better. The government said it created the BOYES programme to provide a platform for training the youth volunteers and keeping them gainfully employed and regulated (Mshelizza 2013). At the launch of the programme, when the first set of 632 volunteers was trained, the state governor enthused about their exploits: 'These youth have demonstrated extraordinary courage and love for Borno State. They are soldiers who return from the war front and should be integrated into the larger society. We are training them to be conscious of the security situation around them' (*The Will* 2013). The group has since received more vehicles and money from the state government (Anonymous n.d.).

The first major achievement of the CJTF was in helping life in Maiduguri return to near normalcy after about three years of being under constant attacks by the insurgents. The group helped revive communities where hopes of living normal lives were almost lost due to constant attacks by Boko Haram. The fact that the volunteers came from within the communities meant that they knew those areas in a way security personnel could not know in only a short period of deployment. The first-hand information and other support they were able to provide have been invaluable in identifying Boko Haram members, fishing them out and handing them over to the authorities. They deploy in patrols in various areas of the metropolis and over time have spread out all over the state. The group's extensive engagement in security patrols in various areas within the region especially in remote villages, wards and streets have supported the overstretched military strategy and personnel. The existence of the group has further reduced the fear of many residents in communities, especially youths, who might have joined the ranks of Boko Haram out of fear or as a means of livelihood. In addition, CJTF has through its campaigns tried to educate and turn many young people in their communities against radicalizing ideologies and beliefs.

Although the group carries out its operations alongside the military, its members are aware of their limitations. For one thing, they are armed only with crude locally sourced weaponry such as cutlasses, machetes, bows and arrows and sticks and charms. Also, they do not have powers of arrest or detention, so when they identify or locate a suspect they hand the person over to the military JTF. There are occasions in which they have had to engage in battle with Boko Haram elements, leading to deaths on both sides. While CJTF has sometimes exceeded their mandate, they have also risked their lives to improve local security, and provided an alternative pathway for youth who may have been pulled towards joining the ranks of Boko Haram as a way out of poverty, insecurity and disaffection.

On 17 July 2013 President Jonathan called them 'new national heroes'. The military has also been highly appreciative of them: 'We support, we commend, and we appreciate the efforts of the Youth Vigilante Groups called Civilian JTF in Borno state', enthused Lt. Colonel Sagir Musa, then JTF spokesman in Maiduguri. These successes attracted more volunteer members to the group. The commendations they received have further encouraged more people, especially youth volunteers, to support and complement government security effort either as informants or 'civilian combatants'. A female member who said she joined because BH killed some of her relatives, clarified further that she 'did not join ... to take vengeance per se, but to fight the evil that is insurgency' (Abubakar 2016). The successes of CJTF are also unwittingly attested to by the hostility of Boko Haram, who threatened all-out war on youths in Maiduguri and Damaturu for helping the military (IRIN 2013). The governor of Borno State also expressed gratitude for their role in repelling Boko Haram in an attack that included plans to capture Maiduguri, saying, 'I have never been as proud of our youth as much as I am today' (Daniel 2015a).

Not everything about the Civilian JTF is salutary. Areas of concern about the group have centred principally around excesses in its mode of operation, recruiting minors as members, and abuses carried out by its members. Taking advantage of the 'larger-than-life' image, the group seems not to fully grasp the legal limits imposed on their operations. It has had to be reminded by the Borno State government itself that its main duty was 'to assist law enforcement agencies in their jobs of providing security ... This does not give them licence to take laws into their hands by harassing or arresting innocent members of the society.' The group had on occasion acted alone in setting up checkpoints, and conducting arrests and detention (*Vanguard* 2013). The military has also cautioned the Civilian JTF several times over such overzealousness. The latter has also made requests for firearms which have always been rebuffed. At the launch of a 'Police-Vigilante Youth Groups and Civil Society Organizations Monthly Meeting' in Maiduguri, the state police commissioner reminded them about the constitutional limits on their operations and advised them to seek police cover before proceeding on any mission that would endanger them (Daniel 2015b).

In some of the communities, members have complained about the activities of CJTF because of the humiliation, harassment and maltreatment they allegedly receive from the group. Women have also alleged rape and torture at the hands of CJTF (alongside the accusations directed at military personnel) (Taiwo-Obalonye 2018). Members of the group have been accused of torture, summary executions, sexual violence and exploitation of women and girls in IDP camps (UNSC 2017, 11). Several informants confirmed that videos of such abuses have been posted online. It is on such grounds that local and international human rights groups have been strident in their condemnation of the CJTF. One such group, Human Rights Monitor, bemoaned what it saw as a 'sad fact' that the military JTF was engaging youth whose background, political and religious affiliation they did not know. The group alleged that the military had 'apparently handed over part of their responsibilities' to youth who 'take up arms and weapons in an unregulated manner … dangerous to the rule of law' (Alli 2013). In a report released in 2018, Amnesty International reported: 'Scores of women … described how soldiers and Civilian JTF members commonly used force and threats to rape women and girls' in satellite camps' (Amnesty International 2018b), an allegation denied by the leadership of the group (Haruna 2018).

The Civilian JTF has also been accused of using children in its operations. In an interview for this study its members admitted to using community sources including children in gathering information and in support roles for some other operations. The UNSC investigation corroborated as much and explained that CJTF had recruited and used 228 children (209 boys and 19 girls), some as young as nine years. According to its report:

> Children were used mainly for intelligence-related purposes, search operations, night patrols and crowd control and to man guard posts. Some reportedly conducted arrests of suspected Boko Haram elements while others allegedly participated in combat during the initial emergence of the Civilian Joint Task Force. (UNSC 2017, 7)

Although the presence of CJTF has re-awakened the confidence of vulnerable communities in the region to defend themselves against Boko

Haram attacks, it has also provoked increased violent attacks against local communities, families and individuals suspected of collaborating with both military and Civilian JTF. Following advocacy by UNICEF, the leadership of CJTF cooperated in tackling the issue of children among its ranks (UNSC 2017,15). An Action Plan was signed by both parties in September 2017 (Abubakar 2018) and a year later, in October 2018, the group released 833 children and handed them over to UNICEF for reintegration. International protocols prohibit the recruitment and use of children, being anyone below the age of 18, by any armed force or group (Office of the Special Representative n.d.). The organization lacks professional security training and is poorly equipped to withstand the sophisticated arms used by Boko Haram and so has suffered heavy casualties in confrontations with the insurgents. Furthermore, the majority of CJTF members are not paid, which makes them more vulnerable to being drawn into criminal activities. The Borno State government has however claimed that the state governor has in the last six years approved operational vehicles, logistics, recruitment, training, payment of allowances, kitting and surveillance equipment to 'over 20,000 heroes, under the Civilian JTF that have given everything to the fight against Boko Haram' (Asadu 2019). The support also includes 'allocation of lands to own houses so as to encourage them and guarantee their future'. According to a government spokesperson, 'mischief makers ignore that back in 2013, it was Governor Shettima who drove the process of getting the Office of the National Security Adviser to approve the operational activities of the Civilian JTF and he has remained the only one funding all their operations including the coordination of their recruitment and deployments after clearance by the DSS [Department of State Services]'. Apart from those registered in the youth empowerment programme of the state government (BOYES), and some others who have been absorbed into the army having undergone proper screening and vetting and met the criteria for recruitment, there is no well-defined government programme or plan for the future of CJTF. Although it has graduates in its membership including its President, Lawan Jaffar, and its legal adviser, Jibril Tela Gunda, many of its members are local hunters, and illiterate unemployed youth who joined the organization as a means of security and livelihood, and have thereby acquired status in their communities. In addition, the recruitment and screening process into the organization, whose membership is based on volunteers, makes it more vulnerable and open to infiltration by Boko Haram militants and criminal elements. Indeed it has been alleged that former Boko Haram members have joined CJTF as a means of 'laundering' their status. Nevertheless, the commendations it has received have continued to endear them to many residents.

The emergence of CJTF can be best described as a counter-radicalization movement because of its mode of operation and the issues that led to its formation. Since the emergence of this vigilante group, it has been committed to the elimination of Boko Haram and its sponsors in the region. Its successes have made it a model for several states in the north of Nigeria. with internal security challenges such as Yobe, Adamawa and Zamfara, among others. In 2018, the government of Zamfara pledged N1.5 billion (£3.1 million or US $4.2 million) from the state's security vote to be dedicated to mobilizing 8,500 youths, who would also be required to undergo para-military training to prepare them for their new roles in fighting crime, intelligence gathering and dissemination (*Premium Times* 2018). The continued relevance and staying power of the Civilian JTF lies in its ability to contribute effectively to the security operations, the public endorsements they receive from high-ranking government and political authorities and the patronage/benefits they receive from the state. However, concerns about the future of members of the vigilante group remain unresolved and in the run up to the 2019 general elections these were heightened by the fact that the tenure of the state governor, under whom they had enjoyed unmitigated support and patronage, would end. The fear about the group losing legitimacy and support from government appears unfounded as the new governor, just few days into his administration, announced an increase in the allowances paid to CJTF members, and a donation of additional operational vehicles (Marama 2019). The question still remains about the sustainability of such a policy in the face of competing demands for state resources such as the huge burden of rehabilitation and reconstruction.

It would be remiss to conclude without addressing other pertinent questions that have arisen in the course of the study. First, why and how has the Boko Haram insurgency continued for so long, despite the deployment of enormous resources, periods of strong military successes, and the help of CJTF? Second, why does Boko Haram continue to pose a serious threat after nearly a decade, even though President Buhari declared them essentially defeated in December 2015? Moreover, for an administration that made the defeat of Boko Haram a cardinal pursuit, why does the group continue to inflict pain and destruction on Nigerians? In December of 2015 the military announced that Boko Haram had been technically defeated and several times in the two years following the army said they were degraded. In addition to the hit-and-run attacks of the group they have also inflicted major damage not only on the civilian population but also on the military itself. A few examples will underscore the point. An attack on a military base in Metele in 2018 left 23 soldiers dead according to military authorities, although media sources reported over 100 dead and over 153 missing (Munshi 2018). In the same year, over 19 attempts were made on military installations (ibid.). The question is why would a 'defeated' group be so intent on hitting military targets?

Analysts are of the view that the 2016 split of Boko Haram into two factions headed by Shekau and Mohammed Yusuf's son Abu Musab al-Barnawi explains the sustained campaign against military targets as the strategy of al-Barnawi's ISIS-linked group. The overall strategy of the military has been severely tested as is the state of its equipment holding, force strength and morale of troops – all issues that have persisted for as long as the insurgency has been on. However, operational successes recorded as a direct result of military operations include the reclaiming of territory from the insurgents, containing Boko Haram activities within the North East zone, a decline in numbers of female suicide bombers, and surrender and arrests of large numbers of operatives, among others. The challenge remains in sustaining these successes and taking them to a logical conclusion. There is also concern about what would constitute a logical conclusion or resolution, and how long it would take to arrive at one.

An insurgency is essentially a political struggle and its end must also be politically determined, and so any counter-insurgency would necessarily call for a whole-of-government and whole-of-society approach. The call of army chief, Buratai, to other stakeholders to do their part recognizes that a security approach alone would not end the insurgency. He called on 'other stakeholders – the political class and intelligence community – to take up the salient aspects of this war to the remaining ill-fated insurgents' (Olanrewaju 2017).

Conclusion and recommendations

The fight against the Boko Haram insurgency is no doubt problematic and challenging to both federal and state governments, host communities and the international community. The threat it poses to civilian populations and Nigeria's territorial integrity has warranted the deployment of the military and other security agencies in internal security operations in the north-eastern part of the country, specifically Borno, Yobe and Adamawa States. The deployments have recorded some success such as facilitating the return to normalcy in some communities, recapturing territory and communities taken over by Boko Haram and reducing suicide and other attacks on civilians. However, in the course of operations, the security agencies have inflicted varying degrees of collateral damage on civilians; and some of their personnel have engaged in unprofessional conduct on a number of occasions, thereby hurting the communities and people they were sent to protect. In the early phase of its operations particularly, the military engaged in populated areas in a manner that compromised the security of the communities and citizens. In that context, youth were a vulnerable part of the population as they constituted a major recruitment pool for Boko Haram and so were also of interest to security operatives. For this report we went to the field to examine the effect that the security measures, specifically the military operations employed by government, had on youth radicalization in Borno State. While we found that in the area of study the link between security actions and radicalization was not very significant, it did not diminish the allegations of abuse levelled against security personnel. We also found that the Civilian JTF formed in the wake of the military deployments turned out to be a counter-radicalizing factor in Borno, even if as an unintended consequence. Again, this development created its own challenges for security and protection of civilians.

In the light of these findings some recommendations have been identified. Adherence to rule of law presents a dilemma for states in finding the right balance when security of citizens and indeed the nation is severely threatened as is the case with the insurgency in north-eastern Nigeria. In countries like Australia, the United Kingdom and the United States, governments have gone to their parliaments to seek legislation more suited to the challenges of fighting terrorism. Similarly in Nigeria, the state could not prosecute suspects on grounds of terrorism when there was no law to that effect. After all 'where there is no law there is no transgression'. If security agencies need special conditions to tackle a 'special' situation, then government would be better served by seeking appropriate changes to the law, be it constitutional amendments or judicial rulings. To this end a more conscientious approach to the rule of law is required of the nation's security agencies. Upholding the rule of law also means that the relevant authorities should on the one hand endeavour to bring closure on the allegations made against security personnel, and on the other address the grievances of the military to enable them perform their duties with dignity. Moreover, as the extra-judicial killing of Yusuf has shown, the incidents of human rights violations by security forces, if unchecked, could serve as a trigger for revenge by aggrieved parties. A recurring difficulty in prosecuting suspected Boko Haram members is the paucity of evidence with which to build up cases, and the lack of transparency in pre-trial processes. Specialized training of military personnel in gathering and preserving evidence and for judicial officers in trying terrorism-related offences must be fast-tracked.

As long as violent threats to civilian security remain, the military will be called upon in one way or another. This could be in direct confrontation such as in an all-out war or to carry out specialized operations within and outside national borders such as in humanitarian intervention, counter-terrorism or counter-insurgency. In Nigeria, the military is currently engaged in countering insurgency being waged by violent extremists at a scale the country has not experienced before. The military undertakes periodic reviews of its doctrines, incorporating lessons learned and best practices in order to enable it to prepare and plan its operations more rationally and effectively. The plethora of assistance programmes being offered by different countries should be centrally 'filtered' and streamlined to ensure that they are aligned with national military doctrines before use. It would be appropriate to have the Training and Doctrine Command of the Army for example, process all offers of assistance for doctrinal coherence and standardization. Closely aligned to this is the need for continuous upgrading of specialized training curricula in light of dynamic security realities.

The need for an overarching national security policy cannot be over-emphasized. Policy provides vision and direction, in this case for national security. Its strength would lie in two areas: providing the framework for cooperation and collaboration, as the case may be, among actors or sectors since their roles and responsibilities are already defined in the laws setting them up; and providing the basis for a long-term and institutionalized approach to security as opposed to the ad hoc and reactive manner that has become the norm. The policy must place the citizen firmly at its core and the process of its formulation would also allow Nigerians to publicly engage in discourse about the kind of military they really want and not one foisted on them by circumstance. It is from this overarching security policy that different sectors would draw guidance to fashion sectoral policies or strategies according to their assigned roles. If, as the popular Nigerian cliché goes, 'security is everybody's business', then the policy would also spell out the citizen's place and responsibility in the business of security. There is not a one-size-fits-all approach to dealing with the severe challenges that Nigeria has experienced since 1999, particularly the challenge of domestic terrorism being experienced with the emergence of the Boko Haram-led insurgency.

The complexity of the situation calls for a multi-stakeholder consideration of both the problem and the solution. An amalgam of measures would serve the country better than one skewed militarily as is the case now. But the over-militarization is not the only challenge that would be addressed with a comprehensive approach; solutions that are being applied in silos and reactively would be integrated and routinized. It is still not clear how much and along what lines interaction takes place between different security actors on a regular basis. Another thing that is certain is that government does not employ all of its available assets. The problem of militarization applies not to the civil populace alone but is damaging to the military itself. Civil-military relations have suffered a setback as the military is gaining undue prominence if not pre-eminence in the national scheme of affairs. It is in the interest of Nigerians to protect their military and a sure way to do that is to confine it to clearly defined roles and minimize its use outside of those roles. Its deployment in internal security operations is statutory; however, its prolonged and continual engagement in these roles is risky. A military that is engaged in internal security operations, including election duty in all 36 states of the federation and the federal capital has become like an alternative police force.

So long as the Nigeria police remains the 'tag-along younger brother' of the Nigerian army, so long will the military continue to occupy the internal security space in a disproportionate manner. The primary responsibility for internal security lies with the police. For as long as that has not changed, so long does it remain an aberration for the military to be involved in tackling a wide array of criminal threats to security, including kidnapping, armed robbery, sabotage of critical infrastructure and containment of violent communal conflicts on a prolonged basis. The police force has been consistently maligned and 'underutilized' on the premise that it is overwhelmed by the security challenges and so has to stand aside for the military to normalize the situation. The security operations in Borno have been going on for a decade yet the end game is not obvious. As has been shown, counter-insurgency is not a short-term, rapid-response operation. It is important to have an integrated plan that would involve the police progressively resuming its policing duties as the military rolls back its activities while stabilizing the environment. The police must also take the command lead in law and order operations, and hold the purse for these activities. On a general level, the state must make concrete and actionable plans to reinvigorate the police in a comprehensive and sustainable manner. In this regard also, the police force must adopt a concept of policing that places citizens at its core and empowers the individual, community and the police itself; it must also be intelligence-driven. The community-based intelligence-led policing model brings the two components together (Matthew 2012, 78). Community policing is inherently participatory and so encourages ownership.

The Civilian Joint Task Force has shown the difference that community participation can make to any security operation. Just as important is its emergence as a counter-radicalizing agent in Borno State to the extent that it stood as an alternative at a time when youth were most vulnerable to recruitment by Boko Haram elements. The successes it recorded notwithstanding, the fact remains that it was an unusual model that is not sustainable as it stands currently. In addition to the difficulties arising from its organizational setup is the question of its legality. The Constitution places management of defence and security at the level of the federal government, yet the challenges to insecurity occur at state level. It is clear that security gaps exist at state and community levels and state governments have found creative ways of boosting security. In Borno for instance, the government 'adopted' the Civilian JTF, and local hunters. In states like Adamawa, Taraba, Benue and Zamfara, among others, local hunters and vigilantes also enjoy varying degrees of government or community patronage. The body needs to be re-organized under an appropriate regulatory framework if it is to be retained for the period of heightened insecurity. Issues of training, discipline, funding and accountability should be handled transparently. In the immediate term, the efforts of the Borno State government towards re-organizing the group and training its members must be continued until all members are trained. In the long term the group will have to be better regulated or disbanded altogether but the implications of doing so without a well-thought-out exit strategy and well-managed process could be disastrous. It is imperative for government to develop an effective and comprehensive policy for managing CJTF post-insurgency. This would entail a more nuanced understanding of the composition of the group and a resolution of the allegations of abuse levelled against some of its members. The fact that the model is being replicated in other states makes the resolution more urgent.

Finally, this study recommends further inquiry into the effect of prolonged military deployment on civic and community life in Borno State. There has been a tendency in Nigeria to leave communities and individuals to rely on their own initiatives and resilience mechanisms for coping with disrupted lives and livelihoods. There have been cases of compensation and other relief assistance by governments and their agencies, but these tend to be spontaneous and not comprehensive or evidence-based. The findings of such a study would help facilitate in-depth understanding of the situation as well as ascertaining the precise nature and nuances of intervention required in rebuilding community life and restoring healthy civil-military relations. This could also have implications for other parts of the country where there have been heavy and prolonged military deployments, such as Plateau State, where security agencies have been deployed in one form or the other since 2001. Other sites of concern in the north include Kaduna, Yobe and Adamawa, among others.

Bibliography

Abati, R., 2013, 'President Jonathan Sets Up Committees on Boko Haram and Other Security Challenges', *Sahara Reporters*, 17 April, http://saharareporters.com/2013/04/17/president-jonathan-sets-committees-boko-haram-and-other-security-challenges, accessed 10 September 2019.

Abubakar, S., 2016, 'Stories of Borno's Fierce, Female Civilian JTF Personnel',

Daily Trust, 8 October, www.dailytrust.com.ng/stories-of-bornos-fierce-female-civilian-jtf-personnel.html, accessed 4 February 2019.

Abubakar, U., 2018, 'Civilian JTF Disengages Underage Children', *Daily Trust*, 5 November, www.dailytrust.com.ng/civilian-jtf-disengages-underage-children.html, accessed 23 January 2019.

Adesomoju, A., 2018, 'Trial of Boko Haram Suspects: Lessons for Judiciary', *Punch*, 22 February, https://punchng.com/trial-of-boko-haram-suspects-lessons-for-judiciary, accessed 13 February 2019.

Agencies, 2015, 'Nigeria Orders Arrest of Ex-Adviser over $2bn Arms Deal', *Al Jazeera*, 18 November, www.aljazeera.com/news/2015/11/nigeria-orders-arrest-adviser-2bn-arms-deal-151118043340314.html, accessed 5 May 2019.

Ajijah, A., 2013, 'Women Protest in Jos against soldiers', *Premium Times*, 10 January, www.premiumtimesng.com/regional/nnorth-east/114658-women-protest-in-jos-against-soldiers.html, accessed 23 January 2019.

Akosile, A., 2018, 'Falana Decries Prolonged Detention of Terror Suspects in Giwa Barracks', *ThisdayLive*, 25 February, www.thisdaylive.com/index.php/2018/02/25/falana-decries-prolonged-detention-of-terror-suspects-in-giwa-barracks, accessed 13 February 2019.

Aliyu, A., 2017, 'Federal Government Justifies $1 Billion for Boko Haram', *Sahara Reporters*, 27 December, http://saharareporters.com/2017/12/27/federal-government-justifies-1-billion-boko-haram, accessed 15 April 2019.

Alkassim, B., 2019, 'Breaking Boko Haram with "Operation Safe Corridor"', *Leadership*, 7 March, https://leadership.ng/2019/03/07/breaking-boko-haram-with-operation-safe-corridor, accessed 29 April 2019.

Alli, Y., 2013, 'Boko Haram: Rights Group Protests Engagement of "Civilian JTF" in Borno', *The Nation*, 4 July 2013, http://thenationonlineng.net/boko-haram-rights-group-protests-engagement-of-civilian-jtf-in-borno, accessed 4 February 2019.

Amnesty International, 2016, 'Nigeria: No Justice for the 640 Men and Boys Slain by Military Following Giwa Barracks Attack Two Years Ago', 14 March, www.amnesty.org/en/press-releases/2016/03/nigeria-no-justice-for-the-640-men-and-boys-slain-by-military-following-giwa-barracks-attack-two-years-ago, accessed 23 January 2019.

—— 2018a, 'Nigeria 2017/18', www.amnesty.org/en/countries/africa/nigeria/report-nigeria.

—— 2018b, 'Nigeria: Starving Women Raped by Soldiers and Militia Who Claim to be Rescuing Them', 24 May, www.amnesty.org/en/latest/news/2018/05/nigeria-starving-women-raped-by-soldiers-and-militia-who-claim-to-be-rescuing-them, accessed 23 January 2019.

Anonymous, n.d., 'Brief History of the Borno Youth for Peace and Justice Association (Civilian JTF)' unpublished.

Asadu, Chinedu, 2019, 'Borno Gov is Sole Person Funding Civilian JTF, Says Spokesman', *The Cable*, 6 January, www.thecable.ng/borno-gov-only-person-providing-funds-for-civilian-jtf-says-spokesman, accessed 4 February 2019.

Associated Press, 2014, 'Nigerian Soldiers Fighting Boko Haram Sentenced to Death for Mutiny', *The Guardian*, 16 September, www.theguardian.com/world/2014/sep/16/nigerian-soldiers-boko-haram-sentenced-death-for-mutiny, accessed 13 February 2019.

Audu, O., 2013, 'Jonathan Acted Rightly in Declaring State of Emergency – Borno Governor', *Premium Times*, 15 May, www.premiumtimesng.com/news/134478-jonathan-acted-rightly-in-declaring-state-of-emergency-borno-governor.html, accessed 13 February 2019.

—— 2014, '207 Boko Haram Militants Killed in Maiduguri Attack, Says Civilian-JTF', *Premium Times*, 14 March, www. premiumtimesng.com/news/156763-207-boko-haram-militants-killed-maiduguri-attack-says-civilian-jtf.html, accessed 23 January 2019.

Azubuike, V., 2014 , '"I Will Chase Your Wives Out of Barracks" – Chief of Army Staff Warns Soldiers', *Daily Post*, 19 August, https://dailypost.ng/2014/08/19/will-chase-wives-barracks-chief-army-staff-warns-soldiers, accessed 13 February 2019.

Barlow, E., 2018, 'The Rise, Fall and Rise Again of Boko Haram', Business AM Live, 28 November 2018, www.businessamlive.com/the-rise-fall-and-rise-again-of-boko-haram, accessed 13 February 2019

Bakut T.B., 2013, 'Federal Government Responses to Insurgency in Northern Nigeria', Nigeria Stability and Reconciliation Programme (NSRP), Lessons Learned in Response to Violent Conflicts in Nigeria project.

BBC, 2014, 'Twelve Nigerian Soldiers Sentenced to Death for Mutiny', 16 September, www.bbc.com/news/world-africa-29216432, accessed 13 February 2019.

Bramadat, P., 2011, 'They Were Always Such Nice Boys: Religion, Radicalization and Securitization in Canada and Beyond', *Our Diverse Cities* 8 (Spring), http://canada.metropolis.net/pdfs/odc_bc_2011_e.pdf, accessed 27 March 2014.

CLEEN Foundation, 2014, 'Youths, Radicalisation and Affiliation with Insurgent Groups in Northern Nigeria', Monograph Series No. 20, Abuja.

Cropley, E. and Lewis, D., 2015, 'Nigeria Drafts in Foreign Mercenaries to Take on Boko Haram', Reuters, 12 March 2015, www.reuters.com/article/us-nigeria-violence-mercenaries/nigeria-drafts-in-foreign-mercenaries-to-take-on-boko-haram-idUSKBN0M81CN20150312, accessed 13 February 2019.

Daniel, 2013, 'Defence HQ Says Origin of Boko Haram "Sophisticated" Weapons Difficult to Trace', *Information Nigeria*, 16 July 16, www.informationng.com/2013/07/defence-hq-says-origin-of-boko-haram-sophisticated-weapons-difficult-to-trace.html, accessed 13 August 2014.

—— 2014, 'Declaration of Emergency Rule, A Failed Experiment – Borno Attorney General', *Information Nigeria*, 26 April, www.informationng.com/2014/04/declaration-of-emergency-rule-a-failed-experiment-borno-attorney-general.html, accessed 13 February 2019.

——2015a, 'Maiduguri Attack: Shettima hails Soldiers, Civilian-JTF', *Information Nigeria*, 2 February, http://informationng.com/2015/02/maiduguri-attack-shettima-hails-soldiers-civilian-jtf.html, accessed 4 February 2019.

—— 2015b, 'Civilian JTF Want Firearms to Fight Boko Haram', *Information Nigeria*, 8 November, http://informationng.com/2015/11/civilian-jtf-want-firearms-to-fight-boko-haram.html, accessed 4 February 2019.

Federal Republic of Nigeria, 2009, 'Second National Youth Policy Document of the Federal Republic of Nigeria', https://openaccess.leidenuniv.nl/bitstream/handle/1887/23853/ASC-075287668-3441-01.pdf, accessed 21 August 2019.

Freeman, C., 2015, 'South African Mercenaries' Secret War on Boko Haram', *The Telegraph*, 10 May, www.telegraph.co.uk/news/worldnews/africaandindianocean/nigeria/11596210/South-African-mercenaries-secret-war-on-Boko-Haram.html, accessed 13 February 2019.

Goodwin, G., 2018, 'Rethinking the Double Movement: Expanding the Frontiers of Polanyian Analysis in the Global South', *Development and Change* 49 (5), 1268–90, https://onlinelibrary.wiley.com/doi/full/10.1111/dech.12419, accessed 13 February 2019.

Haruna, A., 2017, '236 People Buried After IDP Camp Bombing by Nigerian Jet – Official', *Premium Times*, 23 January, www.premiumtimesng.com/news/headlines/221343-236-people-buried-idp-camp-bombing-nigerian-jet-official.html, accessed 13 February 2019.

—— 2008, 'Alleged IDPs Rape: Civilian JTF Reacts to Amnesty Report', *Premium Times*, 25 May, www.premiumtimesng.com/news/more-news/269773-alleged-idps-rape-civilian-jtf-reacts-to-amnesty-international-report.html, accessed 13 February 2019.

Human Rights Watch, 2018, 'Nigeria: Flawed Trials of Boko Haram Suspects Ensure Due Process, Victim Participation', 17 September 2018, www.hrw.org/news/2018/09/17/

nigeria-flawed-trials-boko-haram-suspects, accessed 13 February 2019.

Ibeh, N., 2014, 'Nigerian Military Sentences 54 Soldiers to Death for Mutiny', *Premium Times*, 17 December, www.premiumtimesng.com/news/headlines/173470-breaking-nigerian-military-sentences-54-soldiers-death-mutiny.html, accessed 13 February 2019.

Ibrahim, M., 2017, 'Osinbajo Orders Service Chiefs to Relocate to Maiduguri', *The Cable*, 27 July, www.thecable.ng/breaking-osinbajo-orders-buratai-relocate-maiduguri, accessed 13 February 2019.

Ibrahim, Y. and Yaya, H.G., 2012, 'Nigeria: Borno People Hail End of Emergency Rule', *Daily Trust*, 20 July, https://allafrica.com/stories/201207200285.html, accessed 23 January 2019.

International Crisis Group, 2014, 'Curbing Violence in Nigeria (II): The Boko Haram Insurgency', Africa Report No. 216, 3 April, Brussels.

International Crisis Group, 2016, 'Nigeria: The Challenge of Military Reform', Report No. 237, 6 June, www.crisisgroup.org/africa/west-africa/nigeria/nigeria-challenge-military-reform, accessed 5 May 2019.

IRIN (Integrated Regional Information Networks), 2013, 'Nigeria: School Attacks Spur Vigilante Groups', 27 June, http://allafrica.com/stories/201306271549.html, accessed 16 June 2014.

Iroegbu, S., 2013, 'Terrorism: Ihejirika Consults Top Army Commanders', *ThisDay*, 5 October, www.thisdaylive.com/articles/terrorism-ihejirika-consults-top-army-commanders/160746, accessed 16 June 2014.

ISS (Institute For Security Studies), 2013, 'Lessons from Nigeria: How not to Handle Radical Groups', *Polity*, 11 December, www.polity.org.za/article/lessons-from-nigeria-how-not-to-handle-radical-group-2013-12-11, accessed 27 March 2014

Jonathan, G.E., 2013, 'The Declaration of a State of Emergency in Borno, Yobe and Adamawa States in Order to Restore Public Order, Public Safety and Security in the Affected States of the Federation', 14 May.

—— 2014, 'Opening Address' at International Workshop, 'Civil-Military Cooperation for Effective Internal Security Operations', organized by the Office of the National Security Adviser (ONSA), at the National Defence College, Abuja, 23–25 October.

Maliki, A. and Mutum, R., 2017, 'How Nigerian Military Operations are Named' *Daily Trust*, 28 October www.dailytrust.com.ng/how-nigerian-military-operations-are-named.html, accessed 13 February 2019.

Marama, N., 2019, 'Boko Haram: Zulum Increases Civilian JTF Monthly Allowance', *Vanguard*, 6 June, www.vanguardngr.com/2019/06/boko-haram-zulum-increases-civilian-jtf-monthly-allowance, accessed 10 September 2019.

Matthew, O.O., 2012, 'Multi Agency Approach to Internal Security Operations in Nigeria', *The Triple S*, a publication of the SSS, October, 76–81.

Mshelizza, I.-G., 2013, 'Youth Volunteer Group Urged Not to Abuse Powers Given Them', *Nigerian Voice*, 28 November, www.thenigerianvoice.com/news/130042/youth-volunteer-group-urged-not-to-abuse-powers-gi.html, accessed 12 August 2014.

Munshi, N., 2018, 'Under Fire: Why Nigeria is Struggling to Defeat Boko Haram', *The Financial Times*, 6 December, www.ft.com/content/62928c8e-f7b8-11e8-8b7c-6fa24bd5409c, accessed 10 April 2019.

Musa, S,, 2019, 'Nigerian Army and Allegations of Human Rights Abuses', Nigeria Army Official Website, 21 February, www.army.mil.ng/nigerian-army-and-allegations-of-human-rights-abuses-by-colonel-sagir-musa, accessed 29 April 2019.

Murdock, H., 2013, 'Analysts: Information is "Warfare" in Nigeria', *VoA*, 8 October, www.voanews.com/africa/analysts-information-warfare-nigeria, accessed 11 September 2019.

Nigerian Bulletin, 2015, 'Buhari Effect: Nigerian Army Moves Base to Maiduguri', 8 June, www.nigerianbulletin.com/threads/buhari-effect-nigerian-army-moves-base-to-maiduguri.112785, accessed 23 January 2019.

Nossiter, A., 2015, 'Mercenaries Join Nigeria's Military Campaign against Boko Haram', *The New York Times*, 12 March 2015, www.nytimes.com/2015/03/13/world/africa/nigerias-fight-against-boko-haram-gets-help-from-south-african-mercenaries.html, accessed 13 February 2019.

NSRP and UNICEF, 2017, 'Perceptions and Experiences of Children Associated with Armed Groups in Northeast Nigeria', Research Report, www.nsrp-nigeria.org/wp-content/uploads/2017/03/Research-Report-Children-Associated-with-Armed-Groups.pdf, accessed 23 January 2019.

Nwabughiogu, L., 2015, 'Boko Haram, Insurgency'll End by December, Buhari Insists', *Vanguard*, 15 October, www.vanguardngr.com/2015/10/boko-haram-insurgency-ll-end-by-december-buhari-insists, accessed 13 February 2019.

Ogundipe, S., 2018, 'Nigerian Soldier Kills Colleague, Self in Another Suicide Rage', *Premium Times*, 24 September, www.premiumtimesng.com/news/headlines/286061-nigerian-soldier-kills-colleague-self-in-another-suicide-rage.html, accessed 23 January 2019.

OHCHR (UN Office of the High Commissioner for Human Rights), 2014, 'Opening Remarks by UN High Commissioner for Human Rights Navi Pillay' at a press conference during her mission to Nigeria, 14 March, http://reliefweb.int/report/nigeria/opening-remarks-un-high-commissioner-human-rights-navi-pillay-press-conference-during, accessed 12 November 2013.

Office of the Special Representative, n.d., 'Child Recruitment and Use', Office of the Special Representative of the Secretary-General for Children and Armed Conflict, official website, https://childrenandarmedconflict.un.org/six-grave-violations/child-soldiers, accessed 2 May 2019.

Okereke, C. N.-E., 2012, 'Containing Religious Extremism and Radicalisation in Nigeria, Perception Management and Deradicalisation of Islamists Explained', *African Journal for the Prevention and Combating of Terrorism* 3 (1), 237–52.

Olanrewaju, T., 2017, 'Why Boko Haram Insurgency Persists', *The Sun*, 10 December, www.sunnewsonline.com/why-boko-haram-insurgency-persists, accessed 10 April 2019.

Olatunji, O., 2018, 'Armed Forces Special Force: The Inside Story', *Daily Trust*, 15 December, www.dailytrust.com.ng/armed-forces-special-force-the-inside-story.html, accessed 13 February 2019.

Olujinmi, A., 2012, 'Striking the Balance between Human Rights and National Security in a Transforming Environment', in *The Triple S*, a publication of the SSS, October, 121–4.

Omeje, C., 2012, 'Focus on the Joint Task Forces: A Prologue', *Nigerian Defence Magazine*, Directorate of Defence Information, Defence Headquarters, Nigeria.

Onuoha, F.C., 2014a, 'Terrorism: The Case of the Boko Haram in Nigeria', lecture delivered to Participants of the National Defence College Course 22, 10 February, 25–33.

—— 2014b, 'Major Findings, Recommendations and Conclusion', in CLEEN Foundation, Youths, Radicalisation and Affiliation with Insurgent Groups in Northern Nigeria', Monograph Series No. 20, 98–106.

—— 2014c, 'Why Do Youth Join Boko Haram?' Special Report No. 348, June, United States Institute of Peace (www.usip.org).

Pedahzur, A., 2009, *The Israeli Secret Services and the Struggle against Terrorism*, New York: Columbia University Press.

Premium Times, 2018, 'Zamfara to Spend N1.5 Billion on Civilian JTF', *Premium Times*, 6 November, www.premiumtimesng.com/regional/nwest/294445-zamfara-to-spend-n1-5-billion-on-civilian-jtf.html, accessed 13 February 2019.

Punch, 2014, 'Soldiers Attack B'Haram Camp, Seize 700 Vehicles', 11 March, www.punchng.com/news/soldiers-attack-bharam-camp-seize-700-vehicles, accessed 13 August 2014.

Reinares, F., Alonso, R., Bjørgo, T., Della Porta, D. et al., 2008, 'Radicalisation Processes

Leading to Acts of Terrorism', a concise report prepared by the European Commission's Expert Group on Violent Radicalisation, https://rikcoolsaet.be/files/2008/12/expert-group-report-violent-radicalisation-final.pdf, accessed 16 June 2014.

Robertson, N., 2013, 'In Swat Valley, U.S. Drone Strikes Radicalizing a New Generation', *CNN*, 15 April, http://edition.cnn.com/2013/04/14/world/asia/pakistan-swat-valley-school, accessed 27 March 2014.

Sampson, I.T., 2014, 'State Responses to Domestic Terrorism in Nigeria: The Dilemma of Efficacy', *Nigerian Journal of International Studies* 39 (1/2), 45–74.

Scheinin, M., 2005, 'Protection of Human Rights and Fundamental Freedoms while Countering Terrorism', Report of the Special Rapporteur, United Nations Economic and Social Council, E/CN.4/2006/98, 28 December, http://daccess-dds-ny.un.org/doc/UNDOC/GEN/G05/168/84/PDF/G0516884.pdf, accessed 27 March 2014, www.europarl.europa.eu/meetdocs/2004_2009/documents/dv/un16082006_/un16082006_en.pdf, accessed 31 August 2019.

Smith, D., 2015, 'South Africa's Ageing White Mercenaries Who Helped Turn Tide on Boko Haram', *The Guardian*, 14 April, www. theguardian.com/world/2015/apr/14/south-africas-ageing-white-mercenaries-who-helped-turn-tide-on-boko-haram, accessed 23 January 2019.

Sogunro, A., 2019, 'The Case Against the Nigerian Military', *The Guardian*, 1 January www.google.com/amp/s/guardian.ng/features/the-case-against-the-nigerian-military/amp, accessed 28 January 2019.

Storm, L., 2009, 'The Persistence of Authoritarianism as a Source of Radicalization in North Africa', *International Affairs* (85) 5, 997–1013.

Squires, N. and Heaton, L., 2012, 'Nigeria's President Declares State of Emergency after Christmas Attacks' *The Telegraph*, 1 January, www.telegraph.co.uk/news/worldnews/africaandindianocean/nigeria/8987229/Nigerias-president-declares-state-of-emergency-after-Christmas-attacks.html, accessed 23 January 2019.

Taiwo-Obalonye, J., 2018, '…Soldiers, Civilian JTF Fathers of Our Children – Rape Victim', *The Sun* (Nigeria), 25 May, www.sunnewsonline.com/soldiers-civilian-jtf-fathers-of-our-children-rape-victim, accessed 23 January 2019.

The Economist, 2017, 'Why Boko Haram uses Female Suicide-Bombers', 23 October www.economist.com/the-economist-explains/2017/10/23/why-boko-haram-uses-female-suicide-bombers, accessed 23 January 2019.

The Will, 2013, 'Borno Partners NYSC, Trains 800 Civilian JTF Members', 26 September, https://thewillnigeria.com/news/borno-partners-nysc-trains-800-civilian-jtf-members, accessed 13 August 2014.

Tukur, S., 2013, 'Update: Jonathan Ignores Governors, Anglican Church, ACN, CPC, Others to Declare State of Emergency in Borno, Yobe, Adamawa', 14 May, www.premiumtimesng.com/news/134266-update-jonathan-ignores-governors-anglican-church-acn-cpc-others-to-declare-state-of-emergency-in-borno-yobe-adamawa.html, accessed 28 January 2019.

—— 2014, 'Nigeria Cancels U.S. Military Training as Relations between Both Nations Worsen' *Premium Times*, 1 December, www.premiumtimesng.com/news/headlines/172178-nigeria-cancels-u-s-military-training-relations-nations-worsen.html, accessed 13 February 2019.

United Nations, 2013, 'Promotion and Protection of Human Rights and Fundamental Freedoms while Countering Terrorism', Report of the Special Rapporteur to the General Assembly, United Nations A/68/389, 18 September, http://justsecurity.org/wp-content/uploads/2013/10/2013EmmersonSpecialRapporteurReportDrones.pdf, accessed 27 March 2014.

UNSC, 2017, 'Report of the Secretary-General on Children and Armed Conflict in Nigeria', United Nations Security Council S/2017/304 10 April, https://reliefweb.int/sites/reliefweb.int/files/resources/N1709682.pdf, accessed 23 January 2019.

Vanguard, 2013, 'Borno Cautions "Civilian JTF" Against Abuse of Power', 28 October, www.vanguardngr.com/2013/10/borno-cautions-civilian-jtf-abuse-power, accessed

23 January 2019.

Vanguard, 2017, 'FG Begins Mass Trials of Boko Haram Suspects', 9 October, www.vanguardngr.com/2017/10/fg-begins-mass-trials-boko-haram-suspects, accessed 13 February 2019.

Vanguard, 2018, 'Stop Targeting Amnesty, Falana tells Nigerian Army', 19 December, www.vanguardngr.com/2018/12/stop-targeting-amnesty-falana-tells-nigerian-army, accessed 4 February 2019.

Vombatkere, S.G., 2012, 'AFSPA: Who wants the Military for Internal Security?' *Indian Defence Review*, 4 December 2012, www.indiandefencereview.com/news/afspa-who-wants-the-military-fo-r-internal-security, accessed 9 September 2013.

Warner, J. and Matfess, H., 2017, 'Exploding Stereotypes: The Unexpected Operational and Demographic Characteristics of Boko Haram's Suicide Bombers', Combating Terrorism Center, West Point, NY.

Part Two

Micro-Social Relations

6

Pathways to radicalization
Learning from Boko Haram life histories

DAVID EHRHARDT & M. SANI UMAR

Introduction

In this chapter we seek to understand the process of radicalization by examining the life-histories of 59 (former) members of the Nigerian Islamic terrorist group widely known as 'Boko Haram'. Life histories offer more complex insights into the motives behind violent radicalization, rather than 'labouring in vain for simplistic answers to equally simplistic questions about root causes of radicalization and violence' (Horgan 2008). Attention to root causes of extremist violence remains important, but only where they are set in a richer social and policy context that reveals the interaction of causes to create paths into radicalization. Radicalization pathways are useful tools to combine root causes with a process-based analysis, channeling otherwise ordinary people into violent action. In this approach, root causes of radicalization are factors that either push people away from the non-violent 'mainstream' or pull them towards a violent organization.

Radicalization is most clearly analysed as a process that individuals go through, as they are pushed and pulled by root causes of radicalization triggered by a variety of historical contingencies, while others are hindered by barriers to violent action. Studying life histories of radicalized individuals has allowed us to identify some of the key causes and barriers in the pathways that Boko Haram members have taken and describe parts of the sequences in which these factors have pushed, pulled and hindered violent radicalization. Focusing on interacting causes plays an essential role in identifying suitable points of policy intervention. As Bjørgo (2005, 256) explains:

> Addressing factors that cause a recurring problem is usually preferable to dealing with symptoms and consequences … The approach requires,

however, that we can identify causes and mechanisms that are of such a nature that they are available for intervention and possible to change.

This chapter contributes to the growing body of empirical studies on the nature of Boko Haram membership and the radicalization paths that have led towards it (e.g. Onuoha 2014; Mercy Corps 2016; Botha and Abdile 2017; Ehrhardt 2019). Its contribution is empirical as well as theoretical, as it analyses the 59 narratives in the context of radicalization theory, and begins to formulate empirically driven models for Boko Haram's radicalization pathways. The chapter aims to complement existing contextually rich histories of the movement (Pérouse de Montclos 2014; Mustapha 2014; Comolli 2015; Smith 2015; Thurston 2017; Kendhammer and McCain 2018; Mustapha and Ehrhardt 2018). It does so mainly by describing and theorizing the micro-narratives of individual members' lives that, at the macro-level, have coalesced into one of the most world's most violent terrorist movements.

Theoretical perspective

In explaining violent radicalization, there is a tension between theories that focus on root causes and terrorist 'profiles', and those that analyse radicalization as a process. Root-cause theories and profiling approaches tend to search for generalizable and static explanatory variables for the incidence of violent radicalization, such as poverty, inequality, religious identification, mental instability or political marginalization. Among the significant contribution of studies on the root causes of violent radicalization is the widespread recognition that it is not useful to search for common causes of all cases. Instead, it is more fruitful to disaggregate causes so as to identify different causes operating at different levels in different ways, or different parts of a radicalization process, depending on the case.

One example of a nuanced root-cause analytical approach is Bjørgo (2005). In his introduction to a volume of 19 case studies, Bjørgo offers a framework for causation modified slightly from Crenshaw's (1981) approach: *structural causes* 'which affect people's lives in ways that they may or may not comprehend'; *facilitator causes* that 'make terrorism possible or attractive, without being prime movers'; *motivational causes* in the form of 'actual grievances that people experience at a personal level, motivating them to act'; and *triggering causes* that 'may be momentous or provocative events, a political calamity, an outrageous act committed by the enemy, or some other events that call for revenge or action' (Bjørgo 2005, 3–4).

Despite polemical caricatures by opponents, studies of the root causes of terrorism do recognize the complexities of social causation, as demonstrated in numerous studies (e.g. Davis and O'Mahony 2013; Victoroff, 2005). Yet critics of root-cause theories have argued for the need to focus on pathways that individuals follow in the process of radicalization. Such process-based theories focus on the sequence of steps that violent individuals and groups have gone through and tend to emphasize the variation between different cases and situations rather than universal causal mechanisms. The insights of process approaches can fruitfully be combined with those of the root-cause theorists by focusing on pathways of violent radicalization.

Horgan (2008) highlights this approach, arguing that specific individuals take different 'routes to, through and away from terrorism' (82). He reframes root causes as risk factors that can jointly but incrementally draw different individuals towards violent radicalism, keep them involved, or push them away from violence and eventually lead them to deradicalization. Horgan's risk factors include factors that 'push' people away from the mainstream, such as emotional vulnerability, perceived failure of all non-violent alternatives, or identification with victims of injustice. But they also include 'pull' factors of violent radicalism, such as rewards for joining a terrorist group, or social ties to friends and family members who are already radicalized into violence. Somewhat more elaborately, McCauley and Moskalenko (2008) articulate a model of three-level (individual, group and mass) pathways of radicalization toward violence.

In all pathways approaches, an obvious analytical implication of the dynamic understanding of radicalization as an incremental process is that different factors may be the driving force at different stages. It is, therefore, imperative to remain alert to combinations of and sequences of factors rather than exclusively focus on one factor only; incremental evolution requires analytical attention to the issues that are salient at different stages. One evocative conceptualization of the pathways approach is Moghaddam's (2005) 'staircase to terrorism', that leads from the ground floor of the mainstream to the fifth floor of violent radicalism.

For Moghaddam, individuals becoming radicalized reduce in numbers but become more committed to violence as they step up the stairs to the higher floors. On the ground floor, millions of people 'perceive injustice and feel relatively deprived', but most people will do nothing about it, while some individuals from the millions of 'the disgruntled population will climb to the first floor in search of solutions'. Continuing frustration at this level can push some individuals up to the second floor where their grievances may not be solved, thereby leading to more anger and frustration, and hence becoming more receptive to being 'influenced by leaders to displace their aggression onto an "enemy"'. On the third floor 'a gradual engagement with the morality of terrorist organizations' transforms some individuals to begin 'to see terrorism as a justified strategy', while the fourth floor sees individuals recruited into terrorist organizations and further transformed to accept categorization of 'the world more rigidly into "us-versus-them"'. The fifth floor, finally, is where 'specific individuals are selected and trained to sidestep inhibitory mechanisms that could prevent them from injuring and killing both others and themselves, and those selected are equipped and sent to carry out terrorist acts' (Moghaddam 2005). It is where Borum's (2011b) action pathways kick in, as:

> radicalization – the process of developing extremist ideologies and beliefs – needs to be distinguished from *action pathways* – the process of engaging in terrorism or violent extremist actions. Ideology and action are sometimes connected, but not always. Most people who harbour radical ideas and violent justifications do not engage in terrorism. (Borum 2011b, original emphasis)

There has been more theoretical discussion of violent radicalization that brings out further nuance, specific causal mechanisms, insights into the dynamics of the action pathways (e.g. Sykes and Matza 1957; Bandura 2004) as well as highlighting the different types of radicalized individuals and groups (e.g. Crone and Harrow 2011; Bartlett and Miller 2012; Nesser 2012). The contribution of this chapter will be to show how, in the case of Boko Haram, risk factors and barriers to radicalization have played out in different pathways of violent radicalization. This case study will generally underline the usefulness of the approach integrating both root causes (risk factors) and pathways. But it will also complicate the theory, for example by highlighting how the process of individual radicalization interacts in difficult ways with higher-level transformations of the radical organizations, and how the sequences of real-life radicalization belie the deceptively intuitive model of a uniform staircase.

Methods and limitations

This chapter draws on short life histories of Boko Haram members to identify risk factors and pathways of violent radicalization of Nigeria's notorious insurgency movement. Life histories were collected through 38 interviews conducted in Maiduguri and Bama in September–October 2014 with family members, friends and other people close to members of Boko Haram. Respondents were asked about Boko Haram members they know or knew very well. In total, the life histories of 59 Boko Haram members were collected, 27 of whom were still alive at the time of interviewing, while 32 were already deceased. Several of the Boko Haram members were part of the same family: this has been taken into account in the analysis.

Respondents were selected through personal contacts. Some of them were introduced by friends of the interviewer; some of them were members of the Civilian Joint Task Force (CJTF), a civil society vigilante group that assists in the identification and arrest of, and fight against Boko Haram. Others lived in the interviewer's neighbourhood and had knowledge of the members in those areas. A snowball sampling strategy was necessary because of the sensitivity and high risk of disclosing information on Boko Haram members, particularly in Borno State, requiring the interviewer to use known and trusted contacts. Owing to the risks to both interviewer and respondents, it is not possible to provide more specific details on how interviews were conducted.

Although the sample is reasonably large for a life-history analysis, it is too small and non-random to be representative of the entire Boko Haram membership. As a result, it cannot be interpreted as statistically representative of the entire Boko Haram population. It does, however, provide an accurate cross-section of the types of people who joined Boko Haram. To safeguard the identities of those involved, engagement with these life histories will not take the form of descriptive recounting of the lives of Boko Haram members. The analysis will focus instead on patterns, more specifically the profiles of participants and pathways to radicalization, with a view to distilling causal pressures and processes from the collection of life histories. To this end, the quantifiable data from the interviews has been coded and is presented numerically in the text; illustrative qualitative information is presented through quotations from the source material. Codes were used to indicate which life history is being referenced; e.g. LH56 denotes life history number 56. The chapter will proceed by discussing the profiles of the Boko Haram members as well as the barriers, push/pull factors and pathways that shaped their way into the violent insurgent movement.

Profiles of Boko Haram members

When it comes to 'terrorist profiling', a consistent empirical challenge is that different people join terrorist groups for different reasons; in other words, it is rare to find predictable and consistent patterns in the background characteristics of violent radicals (Horgan 2008). This general diversity is also borne out by the life histories in this study: the Boko Haram members were diverse in every dimension except that they are all Muslims and joined when they were relatively young, ranging from 16 to 33 years of age at the time of joining, with an average age of 24. In all other dimensions, the life histories show considerable variation. While this is not surprising given the scholarly literature on profiling, it does debunk several salient preconceptions about Boko Haram, particularly related to ethnicity, gender, education and the moment of joining the organization.

In ethnic terms, Boko Haram is often presented as a Kanuri problem. Kanuri is the major ethnic group in Borno and surrounding states, and many prominent Boko Haram members have Kanuri backgrounds. But Boko Haram has attracted many non-Kanuri, in important roles as well as in the rank-and-file. The life histories comprised people with Igala, Babur, Hausa, Mandara, Manga and Wula backgrounds alongside the large majority of Kanuri people. There were several Kanuri with clear leadership positions, but also non-Kanuri who held vital roles – for example as the key supplier of food stuffs and as a personal aide to the first Boko Haram leader, Mohammed Yusuf.

In terms of gender, Boko Haram has often been portrayed as a misogynistic organization, solely aiming to repress and abuse women. Yet as Matfess (2017) and ICG (2016), among others, have argued, the position of women in Boko Haram has been far more complex. For some women, Boko Haram offered opportunities that were not accessible outside of the group, including education, protection from bodily harm, access to material resources and the opportunity to take direct action in pursuit of (religious) ideals. Life for women in north-eastern Nigeria was sometimes better inside Boko Haram than outside it, as illustrated by several of the life histories in this study. For example, one woman had lived under strict wife seclusion (*kulle*) for over a decade. After the death of her husband, she moved back into her parents' house, but found it difficult to adapt. Her elder brother then introduced her to Boko Haram, which not only offered opportunities to find a new husband but also allowed her to become a teacher and preacher within the movement (LH56).

With regard to education, Boko Haram is widely seen to be against Western secular education and supported largely by young boys and men without any formal schooling. In particular, *almajirai* (or students at local Qur'anic schools) are blamed for instigating Boko Haram violence. However, as Table 6.1 shows, the life histories cover a wide range of educational backgrounds, from no education at all to both Islamic and tertiary secular education. About 90 per cent of the sample has some form of education, most commonly Islamic schooling; but about half also have some form of secular education.

Within Islamic education, Qur'anic schools are the predominant form, but very often combined with secular schooling. The table clearly under-

Table 6.1 Highest levels of Islamic and formal (secular) education of Boko Haram members

[redacted]					
				1	**1**
	3	3	7	3	**16**
	18	4	10		32
	1		1		2
	6	1	1		8
	28	**8**	**19**	**4**	**59**

(Source: Fieldwork, 2014)

lines that Boko Haram members are not made up largely of *almajirai* from Qur'anic schools – a point well documented by Hannah Hoechner (2018). In fact, there is evidence that people with modern secular education may be more attracted to radical and sometimes even violent Salafism than people with a grounding in traditional Islamic learning, as argued by Gambetta and Hertog (2016). This pattern has been documented in the literature on Salafism in Nigeria (Umar 1993, 2001; Loimeier 1997; Kane,2003; Thurston 2016) and West Africa (Niezen 1990; Launay 1992 Kaba 1993;; Brenner 2001; Kobo 2009, 2012) as well as in other regions of the Islamic world (Azra 2004; Meijer 2009).

Moreover, the educational profile of Boko Haram members shifts over time, as shown in Tables 6.2a and 6.2b, reflecting transformations in the religious character of Boko Haram. If we compare the life histories of the members who joined before and after 2009, the turning point of Boko Haram towards violent jihadism, we see that the early joiners were, on average, more highly educated than those who joined later. While this pattern should be approached with the caution of possible selection bias, it is statistically significant. Moreover, it contrasts sharply with the Islamic educational backgrounds of the members, which shows no difference before and after 2009, as shown in Table 6.2b. The decline in secular education alongside a lack of variation in Islamic education supports the notion that high levels of secular education may be correlated with support for Salafism but not with support for jihadism – a point observed and insightfully analysed by Kobo (2009) in his comparative study of Ghana and Burkina Faso.

Table 6.2a Secular education levels of Boko Haram members and their time of joining the movement

[redacted]

Tertiary	4	0
Secondary	12	7
Primary	4	4
No secular education	9	19
Total	**29**	**30**

(Source: Fieldwork, 2014)

Table 6.2b Levels of Islamic education of Boko Haram members and their time of joining the movement

[redacted]

Adult Arabic-Islamic studies	1	0
Islamiyya	9	7
Tsangaya	16	16
Islamiyya and tsangaya	1	1
None	2	6
Total	**29**	**30**

(Source: Fieldwork, 2014)

Pathways to Boko Haram

The diversity of the Boko Haram 'profiles' sketched out above also gives rise to a diversity of pathways through which the individuals joined the organization. This section will examine these pathways by describing the barriers to membership, the main push factors away from the mainstream, and the pull factors into Boko Haram membership.

BARRIERS TO BOKO HARAM MEMBERSHIP

Although all the respondents were closely acquainted with Boko Haram members, none claimed to have had any serious interest in joining the organization. This lack of interest in joining, though likely coloured by a desire to avoid negative judgements, provides an insightful starting point to thinking about the barriers that hinder people from joining the movement. Even though Boko Haram, at its peak, could boast thousands of members and likely many more supporters, the vast majority of northern

Nigerians neither joined nor actively supported the movement; in fact many opposed the ideology and the violence of Boko Haram. In other words, many people whose profile may have matched that of Boko Haram members, chose not to join. What do the interviews tell us about the reasons that held them back?

Interview respondents gave a wide variety of answers to this question. Some did not join because they did not believe in Yusuf's teachings, or stopped attending Boko Haram's preaching after it became clear its leaders were advocating violence. For most Nigerian Muslims, the Qur'an sanctifies human life and expressly forbids murder, providing believers with a moral injunction prohibiting indiscriminate violence against innocent people.

Others did not like Boko Haram because they felt the organization was not sincere: they saw Boko Haram as more interested in power and money than religion, and felt it was 'taking advantage of the sentiments of poor youths and the lapses of government' (LH19). Still others were interested in Western education and, as such, found their ambitions incompatible with the injunctions of Boko Haram against Western education. Finally, some respondents reasoned that they had businesses and family to take care of, which prevented them from joining Boko Haram.

These findings are important because they underline the values and social bonds that served as counter-radicalizing forces. Neither their mundane nature nor their violation by violent radicals diminishes their powerful potential as starting points of counter-radicalization interventions. Furthermore, it is important to situate the barriers to joining Boko Haram within the wider lack of support for the group among the majority of northern Nigerian Muslims. Several studies have shown this lack of broad-based support for the group. For example, a Gallup survey conducted in February 2012 indicates that 'Nigerians do not embrace the anti-Western rhetoric of Boko Haram' (Rheault and Tortora 2012). In fact, about two-thirds of the respondents in the north-eastern states – the home base of Boko Haram – held that greater interaction with the West is more of a benefit than a threat – a statement that runs directly against Boko Haram doctrine.

PUSH FACTORS

Given the lack of widespread public support and the many barriers that respondents identified to joining the movement, what were the factors that drove those who did join? This question turns attention to the push and pull factors identified in the 59 life histories. On the 'push' side, these include not only the ubiquitous problem of poverty, but also the more specific threat of violence at the hands of the Nigeria security forces, the vagaries of precarious livelihoods, and tensions within the family.

With regard to poverty, the life histories (see Table 6.3) suggest that the Boko Haram members were seen as relatively poor in the areas where interviews were held. The information presented here is based on the subjective assessment of the interviewees, and the ratings are relative to the general population in the region where many people are considered poor.

Table 6.3 Relative wealth of Boko Haram members' families

Members' family economic status	
Wealthier than average	3
Average	11
Poorer than average	45
Total	**59**

(Source: Fieldwork, 2014)

Surprisingly, however, poverty was only explicitly mentioned as a cause of joining Boko Haram in a handful of life histories. This was despite the fact that virtually all respondents mentioned poverty as a *general* reason why people joined Boko Haram. This contrast suggests that we should think carefully – and empirically – about the precise role of poverty as a push factor into violent radicalization, and be cautious not to overstate its importance. Studies in radicalization across the globe have shown the limits of the poverty hypothesis (Krueger and Maleckova, 2003; Bhui et al., 2014). Moreover, if poverty is an important push factor, what is holding back the majority of poor Nigerians who do not join violent radical movements?

A related push factor involves the insecurity of livelihoods of young people in the northeast. Although it is difficult to demonstrate clear causal links here, several of the life histories showed individuals with precarious livelihoods choosing to join Boko Haram. For example, some people were reported to have joined 'as a result of doing nothing' (LH20), or because they were surviving through 'any available odd job' (LH1; LH11), often including *achaba* (motorcycle taxi) driving (e.g. LH12; LH14). In some cases, precarious livelihoods overlapped with criminal activities or political thuggery: although this was not found in any of the interviews cases, several respondents mentioned that one of the factions of post-2009 Boko Haram was made up mainly of criminals and political thugs. The seasonal use of political thugs in Nigerian politics around election time may create a push factor in the 'off-season', when specialists in violence look for alternative gainful employment – in this case, in the ranks of Boko Haram (Adeoye, 2009; Adenrele, 2012). Of course, it is difficult to disentangle the 'pushing' nature of precarious livelihoods from the 'pulling' attraction of livelihood opportunities within Boko Haram – a factor that will be discussed in the subsequent section.

In addition to poverty and precarious livelihoods, physical insecurity was also highlighted as a key push factor for people to move towards Boko Haram. Given that north-eastern Nigeria is a volatile and unsafe region, joining Boko Haram was seen as a form of security and protection both against the violence perpetrated by Boko Haram itself, and against the violence of the security forces. For example, one of the Boko Haram members joined because of the scrutiny, and possibly harassment, from the security forces due to his brother's existing membership in Boko Haram (LH 18). Kalyvas and Kocher's (2007) also note that (random) violence by security forces increases the likelihood of people joining rebel organizations.

Family relations could also constitute a push factor. While almost all life histories mentioned the importance of social ties in pulling people into Boko Haram, there were also cases where family tensions may have produced disaffection and pushed people to join the movement's ranks. For example, one person was said to have joined Boko Haram partly because he was always fighting with his parents, 'giving them a lot of trouble' (LH 21). However, for most Boko Haram members their membership of this radical movement was itself a cause for family tensions. The most we can say, therefore, is that family tensions appears to have been a push factor in some of the life histories; although the interviews provide far stronger support for family and other social ties as pull factors into the movement.

PULL FACTORS

Although public discourse often focuses on the push factors as explanations for Boko Haram, the life histories clearly underline the various ways in which the movement's own appeal accounts for recruitment and radicalization. In particular, factors of religious conviction, social ties, socio-economic opportunities, and the practicalities of place were flagged as pull factors into the organization. Violence has a special place in this list, given that it 'pulls' people into radicalism by force rather than persuasion. Importantly, the relative importance of these pull factors shifted over time, as Boko Haram changed as an organization. In particular, religious motives for joining appear to have been much stronger before 2009, while economic and other non-religious inducements (including violent coercion) increased in importance after the death of Mohammed Yusuf.

Religion

Prior to joining Boko Haram, several of the Boko Haram members had affiliations with other Islamic organizations, mostly with Izala, but many were not members of any Islamic organization. In quite a few cases, religion was explicitly mentioned as a step on the path towards Boko Haram. It is important to note, however, that all Boko Haram members who were motivated by religious preaching joined the organization before the violent crisis in 2009, after which Boko Haram became outlawed and lost its ability to preach and recruit openly. This shift of motivations away from religious considerations after 2009 is an important finding in itself. Moreover, even before 2009, religious motivations could take different shapes. Some Boko Haram members joined because they were part of the Salafist group where Mohammed Yusuf began preaching in Maiduguri (in particular the Indimi mosque in Maiduguri). Others joined because they believed in the Boko Haram teachings and were convinced by the charismatic Boko Haram leadership, particularly when Mohammed Yusuf was still alive.

This raises the important issue of whether Salafism draws Muslims into violent radicalization. There is a widespread view of Salafism as puritanical, exclusivist, intolerant and prone to violence (Habib 1978; Gold, 2003; Hussain 2011; al-Rasheed 2007; Schwartz, 2008). This view of Salafism has gained more currency owing to the prominent roles of Saudi nationals (all presumed to be Wahhabi/Salafis) in the attack on the World Trade Center in New York in September 2001, as well as the violent challenges to the Saudi regime by radicalized Wahhabi intellectuals and activists. Yet the common association of Salafism with violent radicalism has been challenged by evidence of non-violent forms of Salafism, and or non-Salafi Muslims engaging in violent radicalization (Woodward et al. 2013). In fact, the extensive literature on Salafism reveals an ongoing struggle between the radical/political tendencies of extremist Salafists, and the quietist/apolitical tendencies frequently associated with mainstream forms of Salafism (Wagemakers 2012; Lacroix 2004; Thurston 2016).

As indicated in Chapter 2, it is jihadism rather than Salafism per se that is linked to violent radicalization. The origins of what has been termed 'Salafi Jihadism' remain controversial (Meijer 2009, 244–320). One plausible source of the merger of Salafism and Jihadism can be traced to the influence of Muhammad Qutb, the brother of Sayyid Qutb, who was perhaps the most influential among members of the Egyptian Muslim Brothers who taught in Saudi Arabian Islamic universities following their exile from Egypt in the late 1960s. Sayyid Qutb has been dubbed 'the Philosopher of Islamic Terror' (Berman 2003). Yet the ideological roots of Jihadism are not purely Islamic. They reflect tensions between Islamic and Western ideological influences (Euben 1997; Larsen 2011). Euben notes:

> Qutb's critique of modernity ensures that his project is profoundly engaged with and influenced by such distinctively modern phenomena

> as Enlightenment philosophy, Marxism, socialism and liberalism. Thus ... his version of a purified Islamic worldview [is] not the expression of some kind of unadulterated Islamic thought, but rather reflect the interaction ... with a world where colonialism and the influence of modern Western political thought have set the terms of debate ... Qutb's Islamic fundamentalist political thought cannot be understood as premodern ... it is both a child of modernity and one of its fiercest critics. (Ibid., 449)

In their early confrontations with Nigerian security forces, Boko Haram were described as the 'Nigerian Talibans', thus underscoring the ideological similarity with the Saudi-linked Salafi Jihadism of the Taliban in Afghanistan. Boko Haram's later pledge of allegiance to ISIS reaffirmed Boko Haram's ideological affinity with Salafi Jihadism. The important point to note here is that violent jihadis are a minority within the broader universe of radical Salafi thought in Nigeria. Given the limited acceptance of jihadism among Salafis and the diverse tendencies among Nigerian Salafis (Thurston 2016, 2017), it is not surprising that Nigerian Salafis have been vocal in their opposition to Boko Haram's violent ultra-Salafism (Anonymous 2012; Umar 2015). The identification of Salafism with violent radicalism does not withstand careful scrutiny.

Social ties

Beyond religious motives, social ties to people already in Boko Haram constituted a powerful pull factor. With the exception of a handful, all of the respondents had friends or family members in Boko Haram before they joined the organization; a large majority of the histories mentioned relatives or friends explicitly as a crucial step in the pathway into the organization. As a typical example, LH17 describes a person who joined 'due to the influence of friends in the market place and neighbourhood where he lives. Any time they wanted to go the [Boko Haram] preaching, they [would] carry him along because the preaching venue is close to his house'. Over time, then, the person was convinced to join and began to evangelize for the sect independently.

Family connections, and social bonds in general, have been widely reported as a common pathway of radicalization into violent movements, including in Boko Haram (Mercy Corps 2016). Although apparently intuitive, family ties and social connections can lead to violent radicalization in various ways: recruitment facilitated by family bonds, the desire to avenge loss of relatives killed in confrontation between security forces and radical movements, the honour or even financial reward that may accrue to families whose members have been 'martyred' in the 'noble struggle'.

The specific roles of friends and family members in the life histories of the male Boko Haram members varied in all these ways. Some people were convinced by either siblings or friends to join. Interestingly, none of the members were led to join by their fathers, but there are several stories where fathers were not happy with the actions of their sons/daughters. One life history notes that after Boko Haram's return from exile in 2009 they conducted a concerted recruitment drive aimed primarily at recruiting family members of existing Boko Haram members. Some were drawn in by family members, such as a brother who had already joined the group. Some were married, often with children, but others were not.

But while the men's social ties leading to Boko Haram were diverse, women showed a more consistent pattern centred on their husbands. Typically, the histories depict women who married Boko Haram members, either knowingly or not. After their marriage, they were then coerced or convinced into joining the organization; in many cases, with time, the women then became strong advocates of the movement in their own right. Husbands were thus focal points in the radicalization process of most female members, although in a few cases other family members were also important (e.g. an older sister). This points to an important form of social connection that underlies – perhaps counterintuitively – many of the radicalization trajectories in these life histories: love. For example, LH48 tells us how

> It was during her days as a student at the polytechnic that she met a young man and fell in love. They were always seen together in school. This young man finally convinced her to marry him; she agreed but unbeknownst to her and her parents, he was by then a Boko Haram member who was moving up in the ranks. So after he graduated they got married and he tried to get her out of the polytechnic, but she resisted until she graduated. After her graduation, he introduced her to the Boko Haram teachings until she finally gave in and abandoned her university ambition and followed her husband.

Opportunities

Boko Haram drew in people not only through religion and social connections, but also by offering members different kinds of opportunities. Most obviously, perhaps, after 2009 the organization allowed members to engage in violence and thus acquire wealth (e.g. through looting or criminal activities such as smuggling), status (e.g. by gaining a fearsome reputation), or even a wife (through the much-reported practice of kidnapping and forced marriages). These opportunities provided particular groups with strong incentives to join the movement – for example, political thugs, criminals and other specialists in violence. Most respondents confirm that Boko Haram became factionalized after 2009, with some 'Yusufiyya' groups remaining 'loyal' to Mohammed Yusuf and his successor Mamman Nur, while others followed Abubakar Shekau. For many respondents, this distinction overlapped with a conflict between the political/religious goals of the Yusufiyya, and the more explicitly criminal and violent activities in the Shekau faction. Both factions thus offered opportunities for violence; but the specific payoffs were likely different between the two.

Particularly after 2009, therefore, pull factors into Boko Haram were increasingly influenced by an interest in the movement's violent and criminal activities. However, our life histories suggest that these violent opportunities, for which Boko Haram has become so notorious, obscure a range of other benefits that accrued to membership of the group. We want to highlight some of them here: access to finance, employment, security and personal freedom.

As others have found, Boko Haram often operated as an investor in the business ventures of its prospective members (Mercy Corps 2016). These investments then tied the prospective members to Boko Haram, not least by convincing them of the value of the organization. For example, one life history describes how Boko Haram leaders provided someone with the start-up capital to set up a telecommunications business and helped him to open up the shop (LH10). As they continued to help him sell his goods, they convinced him to join the movement. Similarly, another person received capital to start a provision store, allegedly from Mohammed Yusuf himself (LF15).

Beyond providing capital, Boko Haram has also provided opportunities for employment of its members in their fields of expertise. At its peak in 2014, respondents estimated Boko Haram's membership to be up to 15,000, creating needs for a range of specialized skills. Craftsmen were recruited to continue their activities within Boko Haram. One respondent talked about a tailor who was made one of the official Boko Haram tailors, sewing the insurgent uniforms and other clothes for the members (LH19). Similarly, some of those with experience in transport, for example as *keke napep* (motorized tricycle) or lorry drivers, were utilized in the same functions within the organization (LH12). And a blacksmith who joined Boko Haram became a weapons manufacturer (LH13).

Opportunities were also created to work in a range of social services and organizational activities. One respondent explained that there was a formal organizational structure, with a Shura council, a Hisbah (police), educational bodies and women's wing. Many members could find opportunities for personal development in these functions, including many women. To some, Boko Haram was a space of opportunities that were inaccessible in normal life, given the constraints of poverty and 'traditional' Islamic lifestyles. For example, one woman found opportunities to teach and even preach within Boko Haram, while she had been a divorcee living with her parents in the outside world (LH56). Others were engaged in recruitment (LH48), organizing weddings or secret transportation (LH40). These findings resonate with earlier work on women in Boko Haram, which also highlights the complexity of the organization's mix of misogyny and practical opportunities, and the agency it offered to many of its female members (Matfess 2017; ICG, 2016).

Proximity

In the early years of Boko Haram, before the 2009 crisis, respondents also mentioned the proximity of the movement's base as a pull factor of importance. For several Boko Haram members, respondents highlighted that they resided, or worked, close to the area where Boko Haram operated: Markaz, in the central area of Maiduguri. This led these men to come into close contact with the Boko Haram organization and be exposed to their preaching, as a result of which they befriended existing members and joined their organization. For example, one life history depicts a young man who was popular in his neighbourhood, and whose house was close to the Markaz. Oftentimes, friends who were members of Boko Haram would walk by and stay in his house, which eventually led to an introduction to Mohammed Yusuf and subsequent membership (LH11). Similarly, another member joined because his shop was close to the Markaz and membership was both a good business decision and a way to solidify his social networks (LH17).

Security

Finally, a brief mention of security as a pull factor into to the movement, which has been well-documented elsewhere (e.g. Thurston 2018). While it was a terrifying source of insecurity for many, Boko Haram's coercive powers offered relative security and predictability to some of those who were faced with violence in the normal world. Several respondents noted that Boko Haram was tightly organized, for example because 'after every lecture they will accompany each member to their house' and because they have an effective system of communication (LH13). Boko Haram's tight organization thus provided security to some, but was used to threaten and coerce others.

PATHWAYS TO VIOLENCE

Now that we have outlined the barriers and the push and pull factors that emerged from the life histories, we can begin to put them together into an analysis of pathways of radicalization. One of the key insights from the radicalization literature is that individual factors rarely explain violent radicalization by themselves. They need to be seen in conjunction with each other, as part of a complex and contingent social process that ends up – in some cases – in the decision to engage in violence. Such sequences – or pathways – are composed of the barriers and the push and pull factors described above, along with the decisions made by the individuals along the way. They can be simple and more or less linear, as proposed in Moghaddam's (2005) ladder. However, pathways can also be varied and complex, incorporating critical junctures, feedback loops, poor information, and irreversible decisions (Ehrhardt 2019). The life histories collected for this study can give us a first glance into the variety of pathways that have led people to Boko Haram; more research is needed to flesh out the dynamics at play. Here, we make three arguments about Boko Haram pathways, related to their normalcy, the multiple configurations of push/pull factors they involve, and positive feedback.

One striking aspect of most of the life histories is the sense of normalcy that pervades them. While Boko Haram is often perceived as an aberrant organization, a violent outlier on the social spectrum of religious and political movements, there is little in these interviews to suggest that its members were abnormal before they joined. Respondents generally viewed future Boko Haram members as socially connected and well-adjusted individuals, often even engaging in activities that would later – under Boko Haram – be punished harshly. For example, LH16 tells the story of a young man who was a 'fun-loving guy' and a 'normal university student and graduate'. In fact, he

> loved music and dancing so much that he was known to be a very good dancer among his peers. [At university] he was always seen among students that had money or those who had parents who were rich and were spending a lot of money on campus. He was also known to be among those that were always organizing parties on campus. When he graduated he was full of life, outgoing, womanizing a little, and he loved going night clubbing. He is also very peaceful person, jovial and with a good sense of humour. Due to some of his antics, and because he was a friend to children of the rich, he was popular among his peers.

This story leads to Boko Haram when the protagonist, after graduation, was gradually converted to Salafism, which appears to convince him to abandon his 'fun-loving' behaviour. Over time, this affiliation brings him in contact with Mohammed Yusuf and into the fold of what was to become Boko Haram (LH16). But it would have been difficult to predict this outcome as a product of the university experience. Similarly, several of the female members were described as 'normal' and 'decent' girls, with good relations to their parents and social environment (e.g. LH45; LH46). What led them to Boko Haram was often love and marriage, and persuasion or pressure from husbands and other family members.

Although Boko Haram's activities have been recognized as extraordinarily violent, the life histories suggest that many paths that led people into the organization were surprisingly ordinary – perhaps not so fundamentally different from the paths to other life choices. This is not to deny that many Boko Haram members were coerced into the movement, through threats or direct mental or bodily harm. These paths have been well documented, particularly after 2009 (e.g. Thurston 2017). Rather, the point here is to underline the multiplicity of paths into the movement, many of which were perhaps not recognizably 'radicalizing' at the time, particularly in the period before the organization became violent.

The second argument about pathways relates to their multiplicity, in particular the different configurations and sequences of barriers and push and pull factors that featured in them. As for the profiles, the life histories show no single sequence of factors and decisions that uniformly led to radicalization and Boko Haram membership. At the same time, however, there were several emergent patterns that indicate the need for further systematic research in this area. We present three of them here as stylized ideal-types that are not mutually exclusive but have distinct internal logics.

The ideological path

This pathway occurred more regularly prior to 2009 and generally included, in varying order but prior to Boko Haram membership, social persuasion or pressure to attend prayers and preaching by Mohammed Yusuf (or his successors) and a genuine conversion to Yusuf's beliefs. In this pathway, the decision to engage in violence appears to have occurred after joining the movement; in a way, the Boko Haram members seem to have been radicalized in tandem with the organization as a whole. The 2009 crisis was a turning point in this move towards violence as members were mobilized against the state security forces. There is some evidence in the life histories that the ideological path continued into the Yusufiyya faction led by Mamman Nur after Yusuf's death, but this requires further research.

The relationship path

While obviously not exclusive to women, this path appears most often in the female life histories in this project. It centres on marriage and the persuasion and pressure between the husband and wife. The paths leading to the marriage are diverse. In some cases, the pull of Boko Haram began only after the wedding, as one of the partners revealed their (secret) membership and persuaded/pressured the other one to come along. In others, Boko Haram membership was explicitly seen as a way to find a suitable life partner. In yet others, forced marriages were used explicitly as the means for recruitment. In the case of forced marriage of abducted women, subsequent birth leaves the women with little option but acquiesce to their situation. But in all these different situations, marriage was the vehicle by which radicalization occurred and persisted (often, in time, with the ostensible acquiescence of both partners).

The opportunity path

This path includes those members who joined for rational, self-interested reasons, to take advantage of the benefits of Boko Haram membership. This could include the promise of financial or other livelihood support, including loans to finance entrepreneurship. Similarly, the opportunity path led people into Boko Haram through other opportunities for self-development, including opening up markets for their products or by enabling them to utilize specific skills sets (including specialisms for violence). It could also include those who joined for protection, as their security was threatened by the heavy-handed tactics of the state security forces, the Civilian Joint Task Force (CJTF), and Boko Haram itself. Others were simply hired guns who needed cash payment for carrying specific tasks, including logistical support as well combat operations. Yet another set seized the opportunity to settle scores with their adversaries. The opportunistic path is thus diverse, but held together by the logic of joining the movement for the benefits of membership.

These vignettes reveal the value of developing empirically driven, context-specific models for radicalization and action pathways. They can help shed light on the specific configurations of 'causes' that produce violent radicalism and specify the processes through which this occurs with higher validity than most generalized theoretical approaches (e.g. Moghaddam 2005). We will return to this point.

Finally, the life histories highlight the presence of strong reinforcement mechanisms – or positive feedback (Pierson 2004) – following the decision to join Boko Haram. Some of this feedback is social, for example when family relations become acrimonious after someone decides to join. The state security forces also added to this feedback, as being part of Boko Haram became increasingly seen as a crime. But the reinforcement is also partly economic, in a broad sense, as people invested heavily in their membership, for example by building social, emotional and financial relations within the movement. These investments tied members ever more strongly to the organization. Finally, the feedback was also related to Boko Haram's tight organizational structure, which seems well designed to keep members in when they had decided to join.

These positive feedback mechanisms reinforced membership of the organization and strengthened the barriers to exit after joining. In other words, they strengthened the path-dependent and perhaps even irreversible nature of the decision to join. Their impact is painfully illustrated by recent stories of women returning home from Boko Haram, only to be met with deprivation, stigma, suspicion and even violence – to the point where many express the wish to return to the movement (Nwaubani 2018; Moaveni, 2019). The positive feedback mechanisms of membership are thus not only important for understanding pathways of radicalization; they also help understand the specific barriers to demobilizing and de-radicalizing Boko Haram members and can provide important entry points for intervention.

Conclusion

This chapter has presented the findings from life histories of past and current Boko Haram members, highlighting important features of the movement's dynamics as well as avenues for intervention. The life histories confirm the consensus in the relevant literature that there is no single Boko Haram profile (e.g. Onuoha 2014; Mercy Corps 2016; Botha and Abdile 2017). They also suggest important shifts in profiles before and after 2009: it seemed that religious and ideological motivations for joining were replaced by more coercive and opportunistic motives after Boko Haram became an underground terrorist organization.

The focus on barriers to radicalization is also an important observation, as radicalization studies often focus on the reasons for radicalization rather than the barriers that terrorists have overcome. Moreover, where many analyses emphasize push factors as the main drivers of radicalization, these life histories put more weight on the pull factors of Boko Haram membership. Many of the pull factors identified resonate with other studies, such as the importance of religion, social ties, opportunities and security (Onuoha 2014; Mercy Corps 2016; Botha and Abdile 2017). In focusing on pull factors, respondents prioritize the *positive* reasons that drew people to join Boko Haram, over the *negative* reasons that pushed them away from mainstream activities and affiliations. This has potential policy implications that suggest a need to take greater account of the appeal of radical movements as well as focusing on underlying grievances or injustices. It is important to note that the appeal of radical groups may be less about religious ideology than a thirst for economic opportunity or visions of a different future, raising important questions about the relevance of deradicalization programmes.

We have presented three findings about the nature of radicalization pathways into Boko Haram. First, the life histories suggest that many of the pathways into Boko Haram are not necessarily 'abberant', even if their endpoint may have resulted in atrocious violence. They may even resemble the processes of joining other, less violent organizations. Second, and relatedly, we have begun to draw out patterns in the variation of pathways, specifically by highlighting three possible ideal types: the ideological pathway, the relationship pathway, and the opportunity pathway. These offer an empirically grounded starting point for a deeper understanding of the way Boko Haram grew and persisted. Finally, we highlighted some of the mechanisms of positive feedback, reinforcing radicalization after the decision to join Boko Haram had been made.

Together, the findings presented in this chapter further develop our understanding of the multiple factors and complex processes that drove people to Boko Haram and often kept them there, even as the movement transformed and became more violent. More work, however, is necessary to put the life histories presented here in the wider context of north-eastern Nigeria in this period. For example, how do the motivations of Boko Haram members differ from those who joined the Civilian JTF? Of course, this vigilante-turned-state-force has been hailed widely as an effective counterforce to Boko Haram, but it has also engaged in gruesome and extra-legal violence, as did the Nigerian official security forces (Thurston 2017). Comparing the life histories and pathways of joining the CJTF with those joining Boko Haram could give valuable insights in the meaning of radicalization in this region and the driving forces and processes behind it.

Finally, much has been made of the international connections of Boko Haram, particularly since it became allied officially with the Islamic State. The development of the Islamic State of West-Africa Province (ISWAP) faction of the movement has been the latest trend in this regard, but Boko Haram's international linkages have been hotly debated at least since Mohammed Yusuf fled to the Middle East. What, then, has been the role of international connections in the patterns of mobilization and recruitment of Boko Haram, and what impact have they had on patterns of local radicalization? None of the life histories alluded to international factors, and it is widely accepted that Boko Haram is a home-grown insurgency. What kinds of international linkages have been most influential in the rise of Boko Haram – linkages with Middle Eastern countries seeking greater influence among Nigerian Muslims, or connections with Islamic terrorist networks? Have international connections played more of an ideological or an operational role? These issues would repay further research, which may cast important light on trajectories of violent radicalization in Nigeria and other parts of the Sahel and West Africa.

Bibliography

Adenrele, A.R., 2012, 'Boko Haram Insurgency in Nigeria as a Symptom of Poverty and Political Alienation', *IOSR Journal of Humanities and Social Science* 3 (5), 21–6.

Adeoye, O.A., 2009, 'Godfatherism and the Future of Nigerian Democracy'. *African Journal of Political Science and International Relations* 3 (6), 268–72.

Al-Fahad, A.H., 2004, Commentary 'From Exclusivism to Accommodation: The Doctrinal and Legal Evolution of Wahhabism', *New York University Law Review* 79 (2), 485–519.

al-Rasheed, M., 2007. *Contesting the Saudi State: Islamic Voices from a New Generation*, Cambridge, UK: Cambridge University Press.

Anonymous, 2012. 'The Popular Discourses of Salafi Radicalism and Salafi Counter-radicalism in Nigeria: A Case Study of Boko Haram', *Journal of Religion in Africa* 42 (2), 118–44.

Azra, A., 2004, *The Origins of Islamic Reformism in Southeast Asia: Networks of Malay-Indonesian and Middle Eastern 'Ulama' in the Seventeenth and Eighteenth Centuries*. Honolulu: University of Hawaii Press.

Bandura, A., 2004, 'The Origins and Consequences of Moral Disengagement: A Social Learning Perspective', in F.M. Moghaddam and A.J. Marsella (eds), *Understanding Terrorism: Psychosocial Roots, Consequences, and Interventions*. Washington, DC: American Psychological Association, 224–39.

Bartlett, J. and Miller, C., 2012, 'The Edge of Violence: Towards Telling the Difference Between Violent and Non-Violent Radicalization', *Terrorism and Political Violence* 24 (1), 1–21.

Berman, P., 2003, 'The Philosopher of Islamic Terror', *New York Times*, 23 March, www.nytimes.com/2003/03/23/magazine/23GURU.html, accessed 17 March 2010.

Bhui, K., Warfa, N. and Jones, E., 2014, 'Is Violent Radicalisation Associated with Poverty, Migration, Poor Self-Reported Health and Common Mental Disorders?' *PloS One* 9 (3), e90718.

Bjørgo, T., 2005, *Root Causes of Terrorism: Myths, Reality and Ways Forward*, London: Routledge.

Borum, R., 2011a, 'Radicalization into Violent Extremism I: A Review of Social Science Theories', *Journal of Strategic Security* 4 (4), 7–35.

Borum, R., 2011b, 'Radicalization into Violent Extremism II: A Review of Conceptual Models and Empirical Research', *Journal of Strategic Security* 4 (4), 37–61.

Botha, A. and Abdile, M., 2017, 'Reality Versus Perception: Toward Understanding Boko Haram in Nigeria', *Studies in Conflict & Terrorism* 42 (5), 493–519.

Brenner, L., 2001, *Controlling Knowledge: Religion, Power, and Schooling in a West African Muslim Society*, Bloomington: Indiana University Press.

Comolli, V., 2015, *Boko Haram: Nigeria's Islamist Insurgency*, Oxford: Oxford University Press.

Crenshaw, M., 1981, 'The Causes of Terrorism', *Comparative Politics* 13 (4), 379–99.

Crone, M. and Harrow, M., 2011, 'Homegrown Terrorism in the West', *Terrorism and Political Violence* 23 (4), 521–36.

Dapel, Z., 2018, 'Three Decades of Poverty Mobility in Nigeria: The Trapped, the Freed, and the Never Trapped', Center for Global Development Working Paper 485, https://papers.ssrn.com/sol3/papers.cfm?abstract_id=3208845, accessed 29 March 2019.

Davis, P.K. and O'Mahony, A., 2013, *A Computational Model of Public Support for Insurgency and Terrorism: A Prototype for More-General Social-Science Modelling*, Santa Monica, CA: Rand Corporation.

De Long-Bas, N., 2004, *Wahhabi Islam: From Revival and Reform to Global Jihad*, New York: Oxford University Press.

Ehrhardt, D., 2019, 'Radicalization in Northern Nigeria: Stories from Boko Haram', in Mirjam de Bruijn (ed.), *Biographies of Radicalization: Hidden Messages of Social Change*, Berlin: De Gruyter, 114–33.

Euben, R., 1997, 'Premodern, Antimodern or Postmodern? Islamic and Western Critiques of Modernity', *The Review of Politics* 59 (3): 429–59.

Euben, R., 1999, *Enemy in the Mirror: Islamic Fundamentalism and the Limits of Modern Rationalism*, Princeton: Princeton University Press.

Gambetta, D. and Hertog, S., 2016, *Engineers of Jihad: the Curious Connection between Violent Extremism and Education*, Princeton, NJ: Princeton University Press.

Gold, D., 2003, *Hatred's Kingdom: How Saudi Arabia Supports the New Global Terror*, Washington DC: Regnery Publishing.

Habib, J., 1978, *Ibn Sa'ud's Warriors of Islam: The Ikhwan of Najd and Their Role in the Creation of the Sa'udi Kingdom,1910–1930*, Leiden: Brill.

Hoechner, H., 2014, 'Traditional Quranic Students (Almajirai) in Nigeria: Fair Game for Unfair Accusations?' in M. Pérouse de Montclos (ed.), *Boko Haram: Islamism, Politics, Security and the State in Nigeria*, Leiden: African Studies Centre, 63–84.

Hoechner, H., 2018, *Quranic Schools in Northern Nigeria: Everyday Experiences of Youth, Faith, and Poverty*, Cambridge, UK: Cambridge University Press.

Horgan, J., 2008, 'From Profiles to Pathways and Roots to Routes: Perspectives from Psychology on Radicalization into Terrorism', *Annals of the American Academy of Political and Social Science* 618 (1), 80–94.

Hussain, E., 2011, 'Should Egypt Fear the Rise of Salafis?' *The Atlantic*, 4 December.

ICG, 2016, *Women and the Boko Haram Insurgency*, Africa Report No 242, Brussels: International Crisis Group, www.crisisgroup.org/africa/west-africa/nigeria/nigeria-women-and-boko-haram-insurgency, accessed 29 March 2019.

Kaba, L., 1993, 'Islam in West Africa: Radicalism and the New Ethic of Disagreement, 1960–1990', in N. Levtzion and R. Pouwels (eds), *The History of Islam in Africa*, Athens: Ohio University Press.

Kalyvas, S.N. and Kocher, M.A., 2007, 'How "Free" is Free Riding in Civil Wars? Violence, Insurgency, and the Collective Action Problem', *World Politics* 59 (2), 177–216.

Kane, O., 2003, *Muslim Modernity in Postcolonial Nigeria: A Study of the Society for the Removal of Innovation and Reinstatement of Tradition*, Leiden: Brill.

Kendhammer, B. and McCain, C., 2018, *Boko Haram*. Athens: Ohio University Press.

Kobo, U., 2009, 'The Development of Wahhabi Reforms in Ghana and Burkina Faso, 1960–1990: Elective Affinities between Western-Educated Muslims and Islamic Scholars', *Comparative Studies in Society and History* 51 (3), 502–32.

Kobo, U., 2012, *Unveiling Modernity in West African Islamic Reforms, 1950–2000*, Leiden: Brill.

Krueger, A.B., and Male ková, J., 2003, 'Education, Poverty and Terrorism: Is There a Causal Connection?' *Journal of Economic Perspectives* 17 (4), 119–44.

Lacroix, S., 2004, 'Between Islamists and Liberals: Saudi Arabia's New "Islamo-Liberal" Reformists', *Middle East Journal* 58 (3), 345–65.

Larsen, J.M., 2011, 'A Western Source of Islamism – Soundings in the Influence of Alexis Carrel on Sayyid Qutb', Aarhus: Centre for Studies in Islamism and Radicalisation.

Launay, R., 1992, *Beyond the Stream: Islam and Society in a West African Town*, Los Angeles: University of California Press.

Loimeier, R., 1997, *Islamic Reform and Political Change in Northern Nigeria*, Evanston, IL: Northwestern University Press.

Matfess, H., 2017, *Women and the War on Boko Haram: Wives, Weapons, Witnesses*, London: Zed Books.

McCauley, C. and Moskalenko, S., 2008, 'Mechanisms of Political Radicalization: Pathways Toward Terrorism', *Terrorism and Political Violence* 20 (3), 415–33.

Meijer, R. (ed.), 2009, *Global Salafism: Islam's New Religious Movement*, London: Hurst

Mercy Corps, 2016, *Motivations and Empty Promises: Voices of Former Boko Haram Combatants and Nigerian Youth*, www.mercycorps.org/sites/default/files/Motivations%20and%20Empty%20Promises_Mercy% 20Corps_Full% 20Report.pdf, accessed 29 March 2019.

Moaveni, A., 2019, 'What Would Make a Woman Go Back to Boko Haram? Despair', *The Guardian,* 14 January, www.theguardian.com/commentisfree/2019/jan/14/woman-boko-haram-nigeria-militant-group, accessed 29 March 2019.

Moghaddam, F.M., 2005, 'The Staircase to Terrorism: A Psychological Exploration', *American Psychologist* 60 (2), 161–9.

Mustapha, A.R. (ed.), 2014, *Sects & Social Disorder: Muslim Identities & Conflict in Northern Nigeria*, Woodbridge: James Currey.

Mustapha, A.R. and Ehrhardt, D. (eds), 2018, *Creed & Grievance: Muslim-Christian Relations & Conflict Resolution in Northern Nigeria*, Woodbridge: James Currey.

Nesser, P., 2012, 'Research Note: Single Actor Terrorism: Scope, Characteristics and Explanations', *Perspectives on Terrorism* 6 (6), 61–73.

Niezen, R.W., 1990, 'The "Community of Helpers of the Sunna": Islamic Reform among the Songhay of Gao (Mali)', *Africa: Journal of the International African Institute* 60 (3), 399–424.

Nwaubani, A., 2018, 'The Women Rescued from Boko Haram Who Are Returning to Their Captors', 20 December, www.newyorker.com/news/dispatch/the-women-rescued-from-boko-haram-who-are-returning-to-their-captors, accessed 29 March 2019.

Onuoha, F.C., 2014, 'Why do Youth Join Boko Haram?' Special Report, Washington DC: US Institute of Peace,www.files.ethz.ch/isn/180882/SR348-Why_do_Youth_Join_Boko_Haram.pdf, accessed 29 March 2019,

Pérouse de Montclos, M.A. (ed.), 2014, *Boko Haram: Islamism, Politics, Security and the State in Nigeria*, Leiden: African Studies Centre.

Pierson, P., 2004, *Politics in Time: History, Institutions, and Social Analysis*, Princeton: Princeton University Press.

Rheault, M. and Tortora, B., 2012, 'Northern Nigerians' Views Not in Line with Boko Haram's', *Gallup World,* 20 February, www.gallup.com/poll/152780/northern-nigerians-views-not-line-boko-haram.aspx, accessed 23 March 2019.

Schwartz, S., 2008, *The Other Islam: Sufism and the Road to Global Harmony*, New York: Random House.

Smith, M., 2015, *Boko Haram: Inside Nigeria's Unholy War*, London: IB Tauris.

Sykes, G.M. and Matza, D., 1957, 'Techniques of Neutralization: A Theory of Delinquency', *American Sociological Review* 22 6, 664–70.

Thurston, A., 2016, *Salafism in Nigeria: Islam, Preaching, and Politics*, Cambridge, UK: Cambridge University Press.

Thurston, A., 2017, *Boko Haram: The History of an African Jihadist Movement*, Princeton, NJ: Princeton University Press.

Umar, M.S., 1993, 'Changing Islamic Identity in Nigeria from 1960s to the 1980s: From Sufism to Anti-Sufism', in Louis Brenner (ed.), *Muslim Identity and Social Change in Sub-Saharan Africa*, Bloomington: Indiana University Press, 154–78.

Umar, M.S., 2001, 'Education and Islamic Trends in Northern Nigeria: 1970–1990s', *Africa Today* 48 (2), 127–50.

Umar, M.S., 2015, 'Salafi Narratives against Violent Extremism in Nigeria', Center for Democracy and Development Monograph (CDD M01), August 2015.

Victoroff, J., 2005, 'The Mind of the Terrorist: A Review and Critique of Psychological Approaches', Author(s): *The Journal of Conflict Resolution* 49 (1), 3–42.

Wagemakers, J., 2012, 'The Enduring Legacy of the Second Saudi State: Quietist and Radical Wahhabi Contestations of *al-Wala'a wa al-Bara'a*', *International Journal of Middle Eastern Studies* 44 (1), 93–110.

Woodward, M., Umar, M.S., Rohmaniyah, I. and Yahya, M., 2013, 'Salafi Violence and Sufi Tolerance? Rethinking Conventional Wisdom', *Perspectives on Terrorism* 7 (6), 58–89.

7

Gender norms & female participation in radicalization

ZAINAB USMAN,
SHERINE EL TARABOULSI-McCARTHY
& KHADIJA GAMBO HAWAJA

Introduction

The kidnapping of 276 school girls in April 2014 in Chibok in Borno State in northern Nigeria, brought the *Jama'atul Ahlul Sunna li Da'wati Jihad*, commonly referred to as 'Boko Haram', into global headlines. This singular event highlighted multiple dimensions of a chronic crisis: expanding Islamist terrorism in northern Nigeria, the government's ongoing failure to address the insurgency, critical data gaps on Islamist radical groups, as well as the position of women in northern Nigeria and in this group. Gender has become one of the many terrains on which battles – ideological and otherwise – are fought, often in the guise of Islamic purity. Yet, northern Nigerian women have not just been passive victims; they have contributed to resisting, and sometimes to shaping radicalism.

Much of the available literature has lamented women's victimization and celebrated their struggle for empowerment but has shied away from the other side of the coin: women's active participation in radical movements and their active engagement in forms of counter-radicalization. Sit-ins and protests led by women pressing government to 'Bring Back Our Girls' are an example of the agency of women and their resistance to forms of victimization such as the kidnapping of the girls in Chibok. At the same time, news about willing female suicide bombers in Boko Haram brought up a different side to women's presence in a charged public space, as perpetrators. Current studies of the role of women in Boko Haram tend to restrict their focus to the role of women as victims and perpetrators (Matfess 2017), yet the reality of women in northern Nigeria today transcends and challenges those binary perspectives. Victims can also be active agents of change and vice versa. Northern Nigerian women do not only exercise agency as participants in violent groups, but can also be agents of positive forms of change. The purpose of this study therefore is to examine how social norms shape the role of women in Boko Haram – both as victims and as willing participants – but also as active players in countering violent radicalization.

The relationship between gender and Islamic radicalism is complicated by issues of economic injustice and identity politics. Radicalized individuals often perceive themselves as activists or resistance fighters and may well be perceived by their followers as such. While Boko Haram is recognized globally as a violent organization, it is perceived by its followers as resisting inequities and injustices of the status quo. Relative deprivation theory can provide an interesting lens to understanding some of the drivers of radicalism: 'people become dissatisfied if they feel they have less than they should and could have' (Agbiboa 2012). Perspectives on oppressive gender roles in Nigeria have also been used to account for vulnerability to violent radicalization (Matfess 2017).

In northern Nigeria, the relationship between gender and radical Islamic movements is further complicated by intensifying fragmentation within Islam that creates variations in gender norms and relations. Nigerian Muslims are divided into several groupings that include Sufi brotherhoods, Salafi reformists, generic Sunnis, Shi'ite, Ahmadiyya and the Qur'aniyyun. Gender roles, motivations and modes of engagement in social change vary across these various groups, requiring more differentiated analysis of the relationship between Islam and gender roles, as well as a serious interrogation of stereotypical images of faith-based organizing. A study conducted on perceptions of radicalization and deradicalization among British South Asian Muslims in Birmingham, UK, highlighted the importance of Islamic political engagement in countering radicalization. It argued that effective political participation and representation of Muslims, far from promoting radicalization, can be tools for the prevention of extremism (Tahir and Siddique 2011, 120).

Of course, women's participation in radicalism and violent extremism, which has gripped the public imagination recently, is not a new phenomenon. Mia Bloom (2007, 94) argues that women have participated in 'insurgency, revolution, and war for a long time', playing prominent roles in the Russian Narodnaya Volya in the nineteenth century, the Irish Republican Army, the Baader-Meinhof organization in Germany, the Italian Red Brigades, and the Popular Front for the Liberation of Palestine. In recent decades, the participation of women in combat roles, especially suicide bombings has been salient. Gonzalez-Perez (2011, 50–51) sees the phenomenon of women suicide bombers as a clear indication of how what is often called Islamic radicalism or political Islam has far less connection with religion than it does with utilitarian and pragmatic concerns of strategic and military tactics, systematically drawing on radical and aberrant reinterpretations of religious doctrine to justify political violence that is widely prohibited by Islam.

In addition to economic, social and political motivations at the national level, international and regional dimensions of Islamic radicalization cannot be overstated. Recent events on the African continent, particularly in neighbouring countries such as Mali and Libya, have demonstrated that the role of women in supporting and fighting against Islamist radical movements is not only about Nigeria. It is essentially the continent's fight and women are active players in the locale within which much of the fighting is taking place. Reflection on shifts in gender roles in light of similar instances beyond Nigeria is thus in order.

METHODOLOGY

This chapter examines how societal norms shape women's participation in violent Islamist groups, with a focus on Boko Haram. It is structured around the following questions:

1. How do society's gender norms shape the radicalization of women in northern Nigeria?
2. What are the modes of women's participation in Boko Haram?

The chapter explores the various dimensions of women's participation in Islamist radicalization in Nigeria in general and in Boko Haram in particular, as victims, as perpetrators and as agents of counter-radicalization. It examines their motivations, modes of participation and how their roles are translated across the different realms in which they move – the family, the radical group and public space more broadly. We aim to capture the socio-economic, cultural, ideological, as well as structural facets of women's participation in radical movements in line with Juergensmeyer's (2000) identification of the political, social and ideological dimensions of violent radicalism.

The study is based on in-depth interviews with 30 women and men from North West Nigeria (Kano and Kaduna), from Borno State in the North East, from Plateau State in the North Central zone, as well as from the capital, Abuja. Interviews explored the roles of northern women in radicalization, and initiatives by women against radicalism. Respondents included senior political figures, community leaders, civil society activists, journalist and religious figures. A focus group discussion was held with the management of a Muslim women's non-governmental organization (NGO) in Kaduna, along with informal discussions with residents of the cities of Kaduna, Kano and Maiduguri. There was also a participant observation of the Bring Back Our Girls sit-outs and protests in

Abuja over a period of two weeks. The fieldwork was carried out between April and May 2014. The rapid escalation of violence meant it was not possible to interview either male or female insurgents in the Boko Haram movement, and thus a range of secondary sources were used, including information from the life histories of female Boko Haram members, transcription of videos released by Boko Haram, especially those featuring the leader, Abubakar Shekau, research reports, academic sources, and media reports on women's involvement in Boko Haram.

Respondents in the qualitative study represented a wide range of experiences. These include women who belonged to different Islamic sects (Sufi, Salafi, mainstream Sunni, and Shia), women who were actively involved in civil society and women who were working with the federal government on countering terrorism, opinion leaders, high-ranking women in some of the prominent religious movements, journalists, female Civilian Joint Task Force (CJTF) members, victims of Boko Haram (widows, teachers), and other Maiduguri, Kano and Kaduna residents. Men were also included in the interviews to present their own views on radicalism in Nigeria and how they saw women as forces for or against those Islamist movements. The men interviewed also covered some of the dominant Islamic sects in northern Nigeria.

However, the importance of ethnic variation among northern Nigerian Muslims should also be noted. Gender norms vary considerably by ethnicity. Muslim women living in northern Nigeria include women from southern parts of Nigeria (largely Yoruba and Auchi women from the South West, and women from minorities in the North Central zone) whose gender norms are quite different from those for indigenous northern Nigerian ethnic groups, including the Hausa, Fulani and Kanuri. While Boko Haram emerged from the Kanuri ethnic heartlands of north-eastern Nigeria, safety and language constraints confined our fieldwork to the North West, where respondents largely belonged to Hausa and Fulani ethnicities. In this chapter, we focus on women from northern Nigerian ethnic groups, mostly of Hausa and Fulani origins, two groups that have also been prominent in the spread of and resistance to Boko Haram.

Gender norms and drivers of radicalization among women

Women's engagement in radical Islamic movements is the result of their social circumstances, economic vulnerability and limited pathways to self-realization. The socio-cultural context of many women's lives in northern Nigeria of early marriage, marital seclusion, and dependence on men shape their limited access to economic opportunities. The region has the lowest levels of educational attainment in the country and some of the worst human development indicators in the world. This is within a general environment of declining economic opportunities in northern Nigeria, affecting men as well as women. These human development indicators include access to education, finance, formal sector employment, proportion of tax paid and ownership of land title. Similarly, access to health care is dismal. With restricted income-generation opportunities, women's pathways to empowerment, social respectability and self-realization are heavily dependent on the men in their lives – their fathers and brothers, and later their husbands.

Within a social context characterized by high levels of female dependence on the male figures in their lives, women are particularly vulnerable to economic pressures to engage in radical movements. Boko Haram is known to give money and other welfare benefits to its members, including women, and has a dedicated fund for widows of insurgents.[1] This contrasts sharply with minimal efforts by the state to compensate victims of violence. Two respondents[2] who had lost their male breadwinners stated that they had received no assistance from the government. It has been confirmed that some women who participate in extremist violence are left poor, economically disempowered and without means of sustenance when their husbands are in custody or have been killed in attacks. Other women were drawn to join the sect by their husbands who were active Boko Haram members. In cases where the husband who is a member of Boko Haram dies, the widow is often married to another member of the movement. Voluntary participation of women in the insurgency may be legitimized by their desire to play the roles of 'good' Muslim women, as companions and supporters of their husbands, as nurturers and home makers within the Boko Haram camps.

This highlights the reality that not all women who participate in violent Islamic movements in northern Nigeria are radicalized. On the one hand, involvement may be motivated by economic need or by familial obligation. On the other hand, Islamic movements run a wide gamut between faith-based community organizing, used to fill the vacuum of state presence in the north, to more radical groups like Boko Haram – differences that are not always evident to participants at the outset. This chapter will emphasize the following key points about women's participation in Islamist movements. First, women are not a single unit of analysis, and drivers for participation are as varied as the circumstances within which women

[1] Under interrogation by security officials, Abu Qaqa, the then spokesperson of Boko Haram said that money obtained from bank robberies was shared to five groups: the less privileged, widows of those that died in the Jihad, Zakat (obligatory alms giving), those that brought in the money and the last to the leadership, to be used in prosecuting the Jihad (Uzendu and Mari 2012).

[2] Interviews with widow whose husband was killed by insurgents, and an elderly woman whose son was similarly murdered by insurgents, Maiduguri, Borno, 23 and 28 April 2014.

live. Those circumstances are, however, determined by three main factors: institutional malfunction and poor governance; the socio-religious discourse on women's rights and duties; and women's struggles to reconcile their individual, cultural and Islamic identities. Second, understanding the role of women is inextricably bound to understanding the role of men within those organized groups. In the lives of those women where family is the primary institution in the country, men are husbands, sons, brothers and an inextricable part of their existence. Women are highly dependent on men for status and access to resources, and their participation in Islamic movements is conditioned by that of male members of their family. While faith-based agenda are important and can, on rare occasions, include tendencies towards violence, some of the reasons why women participate in violent groups are extremely mundane and much more about their own family narratives than a collective ideology.

INSTITUTIONAL MALFUNCTION AND POOR GOVERNANCE

Structural economic challenges bedevil northern Nigeria in general, and the North East in particular. Deindustrialization and closure of state-protected manufacturing industries, agricultural decline, climate change, creeping desertification and thinning out of foreign investments have disrupted livelihoods and narrowed employment opportunities. According to 2014 estimates, young people under the age of 30 constitute over 62.5 per cent of the approximately 177 million Nigerians (CIA 2014). The unemployment rate in Nigeria is growing at the rate of 16 per cent per year with young people of the 15 to 24 age range accounting for 37.7 per cent of the general unemployed.[3] Transitions to adulthood are stalled and young people are stuck within a 'waithood' period.[4] This makes them into easy targets for radical groups; a situation that is exacerbated by the disconnect between the education they receive and the needs of the job market.

For women, the situation is far worse. The North East and the North West have the lowest levels of educational attainment and the highest levels of illiteracy in Nigeria. As Figure 7.1 shows, women aged 15–24 years in Nigeria's North East (41.9 per cent), North West (38%) and North Central (62%) have a far lower level of educational attainment than their counterparts in the South East (95.4%), South South (94.8%) and South West (92.6%). The figures on educational attainment for rural women in the North are much lower than these regional averages. Similarly, northern women have very limited access to healthcare services. As Figure 7.2 shows, the top 15 states in Nigeria where women do not have

3 See National Bureau of Statistics 2011; Salami 2013.
4 See Salehi-Isfahani and Dhillon 2008.

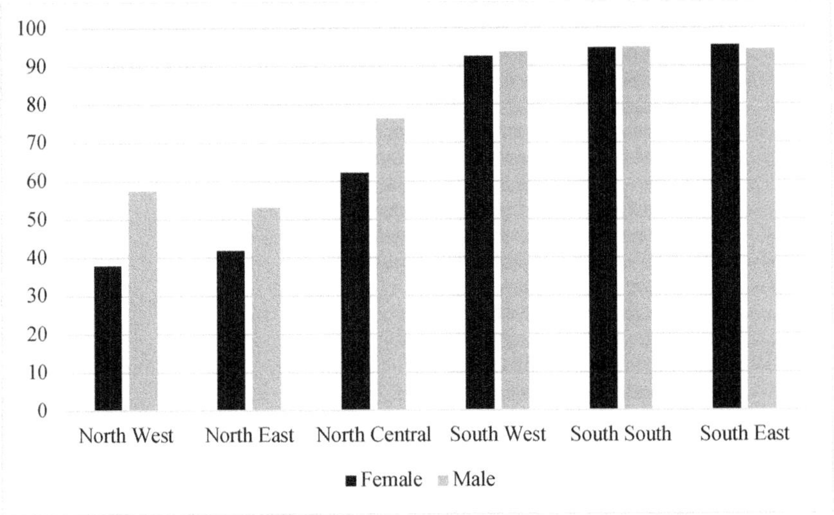

Figure 7.1 Percentage of women and men age 15-24 years who are literate (2016–17)

Source: Authors' calculations based on data from the Nigerian Bureau of Statistics (2017) *Statistical Report on Women and Men in Nigeria*

antenatal care hospital visits are all in the north. The highest percentages are found in Sokoto (63.9%), Zamfara (57.8%) and Yobe (57.4%), whereas the lowest percentages are in Anambra (1.3%), Osun (2.4%) and Lagos (3.1%)

With little education or access to the job market, women are left with very few options. They find themselves dependent on the men in their family; either the husband, the brother or the father and often have little autonomy. The failure of education to empower youth in general, and women in particular, and help them carve out a path in the job market once they graduate was reiterated in the interviews. According to one respondent: 'Education is important because it is empowerment; it gives you power'. Education, according to him, gives you a 'voice'. Yet, a vast disconnect between education and the job market has rendered university degrees mere 'paper qualifications, not real qualifications'. One respondent added: 'Boko Haram have a point; what is the use of an education that does not help you find a job? But the way they are fighting is not right'. 'How do you right a wrong by perpetuating a wrong?' Reports note that Boko Haram thrived initially by providing micro-finance and other social welfare benefits to its followers, a service not provided by the state.[5]

[5] Mohammed Yusuf was reported to have received funds from a range of sources which include external Salafi contacts, notably Osama bin Laden, and the former governor of Borno State, Sheriff. These funds were channelled towards a micro-credit scheme for followers, food, welfare and shelter to refugees and unemployed youth (International Crisis Group 2014, 11).

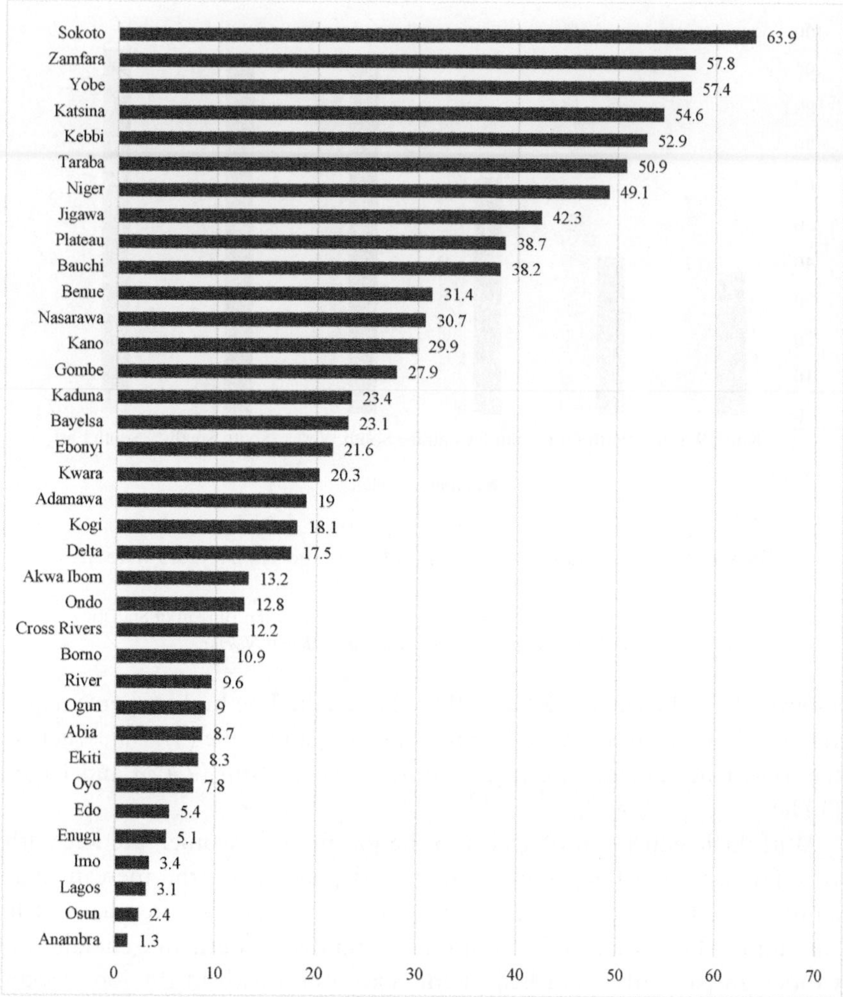

Figure 7.2 Percentage distribution of women without antenatal care visits 2016–17

Source: Authors' calculations based on data from the Nigerian Bureau of Statistics (2017) *Statistical Report on Women and Men in Nigeria*

The failure of the state to address livelihood challenges and the deficit in basic services in northern Nigeria has exacerbated a sense of abandonment and injustice, strengthening the recourse of many in northern Nigerian society to Islamic norms and institutions.

THE SOCIO-RELIGIOUS DISCOURSE ON WOMEN'S RIGHTS AND DUTIES

Muslims in northern Nigeria have crafted a primary identity around Islam. Islam is regarded as the overarching framework guiding their existence, outlining their rights and duties and shaping the social, political and economic interactions among Muslims and with other groups in the country. Given the diversity of ethnic groups and Islamic sects in northern Nigeria, gender roles vary considerably according to cultural practices as well as Islamic sects, and how they interpret Islamic injunctions in the Qur'an and the Prophet Muhammad's traditions. As Adamu (1999) posits, ideas about gender relations are derived from interpretations of Islam, and these ideas are enacted either through legislation or public opinion. However, these interpretations are neither homogenous nor monolithic. Ahmed (1992) argues that 'fundamentally different "Islams"' arise in different readings and interpretations of religious texts. Barlas (2002) points to the role of the state and interpretive communities in the interpretation of Islamic texts and, by implication, the definition of women's status and roles in Muslim societies. It is these varied interpretations among Islamic groups which delineate gender roles, rights and duties, and individual and group interrelationships.

In this context, rights and duties are interconnected, and for women, their rights are meant to enable them to perform their duties better. With considerable divergence among respondents, women's duties in Islam revolve around their being a good supportive wife, a devoted mother, a daughter and a sister. As one of our respondents, a senior member of Muslim NGO, *Women in Da'awah*[6] said:

> A Muslim woman is the overall. You are the mother, you are the teacher, you are the role model, because you are the first teacher for your child. So as a woman, you have to know … the responsibility that is being placed on you … As a mother, you need to contribute to the well-being of the family in particular, and the nation at large. Because if you are not adding value to where you are then there is no reason for your existence anymore.

Thus, a woman's role is to maintain order, and stability in the home and, by implication, in the society in raising children with the right (religious and moral) values or *tarbiyya*.[7] Most respondents recognized women's rights or *hakki* as guaranteed by the Qur'an to enable them to

[6] Interview, Abuja, 4 April 2014.
[7] Most of the female respondents emphasized the critical role played by women in instilling values or *tarbiyya* in their children.

Figure 7.3 Relationship between women's rights and duties
Source: Authors' illustration

worship Allah effectively and be better Muslims. More progressive views contend that women's rights give them the freedom to pursue education, access to healthcare, pursue a livelihood etc. to enhance their ability to carry out their duties better – as a wife, mother, daughter, sister and for the betterment of the community, as moral pillars of society. These societal duties are expected to make women good Muslims. From this perspective, women's rights do not exist independently of duties but are contingent on them as illustrated in Figure 7.3.

The relationship between a woman's duty to Allah, which comes first, her duty to the family and community, and her rights can be envisioned as three steps in a staircase. To be an exemplary Muslim woman is contingent on how she is able to discharge her obligations to the husband, to the family and, by implication, to the community. For Muslim civil society activists, educational and economic empowerment enhances a woman's ability to discharge these duties. According to Werthmann (2000), educated women in northern Nigeria define education in particular and a livelihood outside the home more broadly, as a religious obligation for women, stressing its importance as a means of serving the community. Adamu (2008a; 2008b) notes that, even after the introduction of Sharia law for the criminal and economic legal systems in parts of northern Nigeria in 1999, some Muslim women's movements sought to work within this system to further the rights of women. Thus, according to respondents, the right to education, pursuit of livelihoods – done in accordance with limits set by Islam, and sanctioned by the husband or other male guardians – and the 'rights to be respected and consulted in decisions' exist in Islam.[8]

Across much of northern Nigeria, traditional Islamic views of the rights and duties of women diverge from this idealized notion. Adamu (2008b) for instance points out that the negative bias in the implemen-

[8] Interview with Sheikh Tukur Abdullahi 'al-Manar, Kaduna, 9 April 2014; Werthmann (2000, 264) argues that the women strike patriarchal bargains by securing the support of male relatives to pursue education or livelihoods outside the home.

tation of Sharia against women's concerns curtails their mobility and visibility, and affects their access to education and their involvement in politics and governance. Among our respondents, although there was no explicit articulation of the idea that women are inferior to men, there was a strong emphasis by male clerics of the physiological and psychological differences among the sexes. Women are regarded as weak, emotional, less physically powerful than men and possessing a pacifist nature that makes them best suited for managing domestic affairs. These physical and physiological differences 'naturally' constrain women's ability to exercise certain rights. Significantly, these distinctions are perceived to be reflective of a hierarchy conferred by nature which delimits gender roles and duties. Sheikh Ahmad Gumi, son of the Izala leader Sheikh Abubakar Gumi, while an active proponent of encouraging women's education,[9] explained:

> Islam has not put a ceiling to the education of any gender. Islam has not put a limit to knowledge of any gender … The way of acquiring the knowledge, that's where the problem comes … A woman should study anything as a man to the best of her ability with no limitations and no restrictions. But what brings about limitations … is nature … Even in America, I have seen statistics which show that most women are in nursing, teaching, clerical [work] than other fields like engineering … There are jobs that have a certain predilection for women and others with a predilection for men. It is our nature that determines our jobs. This division is not caused about by any limitation by law but by nature. The restrictions by Islam [are] not only on women, but on men. This brings stability and balance in life.

Yet, this emphasis on physiological differences and divinely ordained duties limits women's divinely ordained rights guaranteed by the Qur'an. Greater weight is given to women's obligations and responsibilities as opposed their Islamic rights.[10] As a cleric and proprietor of Darrul Hadith Foundation, a school that combines Islamic education with a Western curriculum in Kano explained:[11]

[9] Interview with Sheikh Ahmad Gumi, Kaduna, 10 April 2014. This was a view similarly articulated by another cleric, Sheikh Tukur Abdullahi 'al-Manar' who acknowledged the rights of women to be educated but emphasized restrictions placed on the women both by their 'primary responsibilities to take care of the home', and also on the physiological and psychological differences which 'elevate men above women', Kaduna, 9 April 2013.

[10] As Hajjar (2004, 7) notes, gender inequality is acknowledged and justified in religious terms on the grounds that God made men and women essentially different; that these differences contribute to different familial roles, rights and duties which are complementary; and that this complementarity is crucial to the cohesion and stability of the family and society.

[11] Interview, Kano, 12 April 2014.

> It is widely acknowledged that women are calmer and more methodical than men. There are [occupational] fields that would benefit from women's pacifist and calm nature. Yet society saddles so much responsibilities on women – marital duties, child rearing, etc.

An important dimension of these obligations conditioned by the physiological and psychological gender differences is that it confers on men the power over women. As Barkindo et al. (2013, 10) note, as a protector and provider for the woman, the man of the house reserves the right and has the sole responsibility in Islamic law to determine what is necessary for her (their) safety, security and protection. Although it is a religious obligation for a man to be compassionate and not to unreasonably restrict women's freedom of movement, the law remains open to misinterpretation, abuse and misapplication (ibid.). The individuality of women in this context is at great risk. Sheikh Tukur Abdullahi of 'al-Manar' academy in Kaduna, a Salafi-leaning institution that combines Islamic education with a Western curriculum emphasized: 'A woman from birth to death is the responsibility of a man. She does not take responsibility for herself'.[12]

Margaret Gonzalez-Perez (2008) contends that women's engagement in violent political activity is linked to prospects of changing hierarchical restrictions imposed on women through gender roles. She argues that an examination of women's participation in terrorism in the period following the Second World War shows that 'women choose to become active and involved in domestic terrorist organizations because they anticipate a greater potential for change in their hierarchical status' as opposed to terrorist organizations with a wider international agenda (ibid., 1). She argues that women 'seek to overthrow the agents of the society that they believe restrict their influence and limit their potential' (vii). In northern Nigeria, however, women who join Boko Haram seem to be less motivated by the desire to overthrow gender hierarchies than by a desire to perform them through observation of their duties towards radicalized family members (supporting a husband, for example, who is a member of Boko Haram), their duty to marry, and their perceived duty to God.

WOMEN'S STRUGGLES TO RECONCILE THEIR INDIVIDUAL, CULTURAL AND ISLAMIC IDENTITIES

One of the drivers of radicalization is the struggle to reconcile women's personal aspirations, and Islamic identity with societal gender norms. A tendency to use Islamic injunctions to constrain women rather than to enable them to become better Muslims and role models has created tensions between Islamic injunctions and women's rights. According to

12 Interview, Kaduna, 9 April 2014.

a female journalist and activist, many Muslim societies have monopolized the Islamic injunctions and used them to box in and circumscribe women, denying them freedoms to which they had a right. She made a clear distinction between Islamic religious injunctions, how society practised them, in general, and how men, in particular, used them as a weapon to disempower women. She argued that there are many layers to women's struggles:

> A lot of things that women have to fight. You have to fight because you are a woman. You have to fight because you are a Muslim. You are always set up against some kind of obstacle ... Some major decisions, you are not listened to ... You are not allowed to be an individual. You are constantly stereotyped.[13]

This tension between what Islam ordains, how it is practised in northern Nigerian society and how this socio-cultural context constrains women's individuality is also evident in the practice of polygamy. One respondent distinguished between the Islamic injunction and the practice. The journalist explained: 'I don't have a problem with polygamy, but the way it is practised'.[14] Having been in a polygamist family herself, she described it as follows:

> You are all placed into one house and you live like chicken in a cage. You ... all have the same quarters, the same kitchen, the same bathroom. And I am an individual. I am supposed to have rights and to be myself. It's like living in a school dormitory. You cannot bring up your own children the way you'd like to ... you practically have to fight for everything ... that's not the way the Prophet practiced Islam.

The tension between women's Islamic self-expression and traditional Islamic practice is so prevalent that, despite the rich heritage of Muslim women scholars in northern Nigeria, many men are reluctant to allow women to access education opportunities for fear of losing 'control'. Nana Asma'u Usman 'dan Fodio was an influential female scholar in the nineteenth-century Sokoto Caliphate. She taught men and women in Fulfude, Arabic and Hausa and promoted the reformation of Islam at the time.[15] There is also a rich history of female Sufi scholars in places like Kano (see Hutson 2001). A respondent who was the founder of an organization in Kaduna that provides humanitarian support to young girls, women, widows and divorcees, and combines an Islamic curriculum with Western

13 Interview, Respondent 1, Abuja, 4 April 2014.
14 Ibid.
15 Mack 2019.

education, explained that some men deliberately refused to allow their wives participate in such activities for fear of 'losing control'.

Cultural differences in Islamic practice were also highlighted. With the rise of Salafism originating in Saudi Arabia, a number of Saudi cultural practices are seeping into northern Nigerian Islam. One respondent claimed: 'Your culture determines how you practise the faith', emphasizing the different ways that Muslims around the world wear the veil. In Saudi Arabia, for instance, they wear black, while in Nigeria the mode of dress is different. Women cover up, but in colourful clothes that express their personal and cultural identities. One respondent articulated the struggle: 'You are up in a battle against your own religion but it is not supposed to be that way … I am fighting against the societal connotation of hijab, not the religious one.'[16] The respondent declared emphatically that there is a need disentangle Islamic identity from Arab identity, expressing the need to 'liberate Islam from the Arabs'. While this may not be the pervasive view among Nigerians in the north, it does shed light on the multiple tensions of gender, culture and Islamic identity faced by northern Nigerians.

Some women manage to address these religious struggles via organizing groups and organizations, e.g. *da'wa* (prosletysing activities to call people into the faith of Islam) and women-led initiatives, to assert their presence as active players within the public sphere, often couched within an Islamic message. The Muslim Sisters Organization (MSO) is an example. At the MSO conference in 1984, the need for sensitivity towards the rights of women was vehemently articulated through this platform, and out of it, a federation of Muslim women (FOMWAN) was launched in Nigeria. According to the journalist and activist who was one of the founding members, there was a pressing need for a body that would speak and represent Muslim women's concerns.[17] The first branch was established in 1985. Today, those women run 250 schools and hospitals and they have several affiliates. Sectarian differences are less relevant in those organizations because their primary concerns are related to the problems of women.

Another way through which women's presence in the public sphere is asserted is through *da'wa* work. One respondent, the leader of an Izala-leaning *da'wa* organization[18] emphasized a woman's role as 'a teacher, a teacher of generations. A teacher in a multi-faceted manner'. They added that the need for *da'wa* work emerged from their conviction that women had potential and were capable of putting together an agenda. In Izala and other Salafi-related groups, the importance of converting other Muslims from local Nigerian sects to Salafist views was accompanied by an emphasis on the role of women in the public sphere. Priorities along-

16 Interview, Respondent 1, Abuja, 4 April 2014.
17 Ibid.
18 Interview, Respondent 2, Abuja, 4 April 2014.

side spreading the word of Islam and extending their circles of influence include education and health and, more recently, rights-based groups and approaches, election monitoring and income-generation activities.

It is important to note that some radical Islamic actors articulate 'progressive' ideas about day-to-day life, social interactions and gender relations, and rights and duties relative to the more mainstream Sunni-Maliki tradition in northern Nigeria. For instance, Hutson (2001) describes how, in the *Tijaniyya* Sufi order, Muslim women who held positions of spiritual authority as *muqaddamat* or initiators had some agency and autonomy. The Shi'ites under the banner of the Islamic Movement in Nigeria (IMN) have a strong female and youth component, as the leader of a state chapter and the leader of the female wing both explained.[19] Institutions of higher learning constitute the most important pool from which their membership is recruited and they include women in their annual processions, lectures and seminars. They also have a tradition of female scholars and teachers and therefore emphasize the importance of female religious education, and they even celebrate Women's Day to commemorate the birth of Fatima, the Prophet's daughter.[20]

In Boko Haram as well, at the onset, processions to mosques for prayers also included women according to a Maiduguri resident.[21] Women participated in gatherings that were led by the Boko Haram leader, Mohammed Yusuf. On women's presence, the respondent described that, in Maiduguri, there were debates between the *ulama* that women should not be in public spaces. Mohammed Yusuf came with the idea that it is the responsibility of the husbands to teach their wives, allowing them to attend the mosque as long as they are covered and stand behind or separately from the men. This decision on allowing women to pray in mosques was a radical departure from the norm in most parts of northern Nigeria where only elderly women or children were permitted. On education and women, Mohammed Yusuf called for a provision in schools for women not to mix with men. He later changed his mind and advocated that women should not attend school at all.[22] This was taken one step further when he called for men not to attend state schools because they are based on a Western model, not Islam.

This suggests that radical groups may receive some measure of popular support, and are able to thrive because they are more inclusive of women

[19] Interviews, 6 April 2014.

[20] Interviews with leader of a state chapter of the IMN, and the leader of the female wing of same state chapter of the IMN, 6 April 2014. See also Alkali et al. 2012, 14.

[21] Interview with Maiduguri resident who witnessed the rise of Boko Haram in the early 2000s as a student of the University of Maiduguri, Abuja, 3 April 2014. Interviews with leader of a state chapter of IMN, and the leader of the female wing of same state chapter of IMN, 6 April 2014.

[22] Ibid.

and young people, demographics which are largely marginalized by the mainstream. In such circumstances, radical movements and their practices that deviate from the monotony of the mainstream may initially become attractive options.

Modes of female participation in radical movements

While Boko Haram initially introduced some progressive and attractive innovations that improved women's access to education and the public sphere, women have also played active roles in the more violent dimensions of the movement. They have participated in Boko Haram as wives, helpers, fighters and suicide bombers. The exact nature of this engagement will be analysed in this section. Women have participated in Boko Haram as 'activists' as well as 'victims'. Many respondents held that the role of women in direct violence was minimal, despite media coverage of incidents in which women took an active role in the insurgency. However, women are also visible in a third capacity, as active forces for counter-radicalization across a spectrum of activities: as relief and aid workers, and as vigilantes on the frontlines of the war on Boko Haram.

WOMEN AS VICTIMS

In examining women's participation as victims, three dynamics can be discerned. First is the coercive element which distinguishes this dimension from the voluntary nature of active participation,[23] Coercion could involve forceful indoctrination into radical ideology, threats to the lives of the women, their families and other loved ones, and the use of drugs and hypnosis.

Second, this involuntary mode of participation is sometimes driven by the need to have women who can serve the traditional role of companions and for tactical military expediency in supportive combatant roles. As escapees who were abducted in Gwoza, Borno, have revealed, abducted women were forced to marry insurgents and perform other domestic chores.[24] The insurgents believe Islam gives them the right to abduct non-Muslim girls and women as 'slaves', as a legitimate part of combat,

[23] Some pressure and coercion are often employed by Boko Haram husbands to convince and compel their wives to join the group. Thus, the distinction between the use of coercion for women activists and victims may not be very clear-cut.

[24] Ibid.; testimony by abducted girls from Gwoza in Borno, *Sahara Reporters* (2014a). According to Human Rights Watch (2013, 6), Boko Haram fighters would take girls away by storming into the homes and throwing sums of money at their parents, with a declaration that it was the dowry for their teenage daughter. Some of the girls returned months later, showing signs of pregnancy or babies born during their captivity.

based on practices in ancient warfare.[25] Boko Haram rationalize these acts by referring to Qur'anic verse (4:24) which says: 'And all married women (are forbidden) unto you save those (captives) whom your right hands possess'. The insurgents believe this verse permits them to capture women and property of the 'enemy', and confers vast rights over them – to subject captives to forced marriage, domestic, sexual and other servitude and treat them as prisoners of war. Indeed, Abubakar Shekau, the Boko Haram leader, threatened and promised in several video messages to abduct 'infidel' women of the police and other government officials and sell them in the market.

Third, this dimension of women's engagement with Boko Haram reflects their growing instrumentalization in the insurgency in Boko Haram's operations, culture and ideology (Barkindo et al. 2013). As Zenn and Pearson (2014) argue, the instrumentalization of women marked a new phase in the insurgency from 2012 when Abubakar Shekau threatened severally to kidnap the wives of government officials in response to the government imprisoning the insurgents' wives and children. In January 2012, he said in a video: 'we attacked the securities base because they were arresting our members and torturing our wives and children. They should know they have families too, we can abduct them. We have what it takes to do anything we want.'[26] Shekau was more emphatic in another video later in the year in September 2012:

> [N]ow they have continued capturing our women, this week about seven women were captured and we don't even know where they are, but they are being held by infidel enemies of Allah ... Since you are now holding our women, just wait and see what will happen to your own women. Just wait and see what will happen to your own wives according to Shari'ah law, just wait and see if it is ... convenient for you.[27]

A spike in mass female abductions in 2014 may have been informed by this retaliation, to be used as bargaining strategies, to undertake duties carried out by the insurgents' imprisoned companions, and to be used in supportive combat roles. Similarly, threats of slaughtering female security and intelligence officials were carried out.[28] Furthermore, the state of

[25] Conversation with journalist who has interviewed Boko Haram insurgents, 3 May 2014.

[26] Transcript of Shekau's video message, Oboh 2012.

[27] Transcript of Shekau's video message, September 2012.

[28] In a statement sent to journalists in August 2012, the sect's spokesperson said: 'We are also aware of the activities of some women who have been recruited to spy on us. This is a final warning to all of them. Whenever we catch any woman spying on us, we would slaughter her like a ram' (*Sahara Reporters* 2012). Within the year, Boko Haram recorded on video, the 'execution' by beheading of a female Department of State Security (DSS) official they had caught who had compiled substantial intelligence on the group.

emergency in Borno, Yobe and Adamawa States from May 2013, which made it increasingly difficult for them to move about freely, encouraged the utilization of women to undertake the roles of logisticians, recruiters and suicide bombers.[29] Therefore, the co-option of women in various roles in the insurgency appears to be driven by pragmatic imperatives for women companions and other traditional roles in the camps, and as leverage and in operational roles due to the evolving combat strategies of the insurgents.

These coerced participants have also been caught in cross-fire between Boko Haram and security forces. A recent Amnesty International report[30] shows that many women and children detained from 2015 in the Giwa barracks detention centre in Maiduguri, were victims of abductions or forced marriages by Boko Haram and were detained by the military for being so-called 'Boko Haram wives' instead of being rescued.

WOMEN AS PERPETRATORS

To examine the various dimensions of women's *active* role in radical movements, Cragin and Daly's (2009) delineation of the categories of activities that women terrorists engage in provides a useful starting point. Based on a study of 22 terrorist groups, they identify the following five roles women insurgents play:

- Logisticians: they courier money and weapons to various terrorist cells. They typically conceal these items and smuggle them past security officials.
- Recruiters: they seek out new members and filter through grassroots volunteers typically by exploiting family ties or other personal relationships. The new recruits are often women but could also include men.
- Suicide bombers.
- Operational leaders and fighters who carry weapons during combat.
- Political vanguards: strategic thinkers in the central committees or senior leaders in terrorist cells.

Within the context of Boko Haram in Nigeria, the evidence suggests that women engage in the first four roles, with little evidence to support their participation in the fifth role of political vanguards. In the capacity of logisticians, as information from the life histories of female Boko Haram

[29] Observers say the Boko Haram leaders are now using women as cover, because of the traditional and religious immunity given to them. While it is very common to see men being asked to get out of their vehicles and form long queues to be searched by security operatives, women get lighter treatment when entering important places like government offices, police and military barracks, among others (Idris and Sawab 2013).

[30] Amnesty International 2018.

members shows, women store, conceal and transport weapons and improvised explosive devices (IEDs) to be used in operations elsewhere or for delivery to Boko Haram militants in other camps. They also undertake rebel intelligence gathering and baiting of security forces to be ambushed, according to female members of CJTF, the anti-Boko Haram vigilante group.[31] One of them said they found a pistol strapped to the thigh of a woman at the market.

As recruiters, female members were involved in preaching to and recruiting other women to the group. In many ways, this activity bore a similarity with *da'wa* activities in non-violent Salafist groups. As revealed in the life history of a female Boko Haram member in Borno in her early 30s, recruitment of women is a role undertaken especially by the wives of commanders and other high-ranking members: they recruit women and young girls to be married off to male insurgents, they organize secret weddings between widows of deceased insurgents and members who want to marry and they cater to, and 'train', the newly arrived women, For instance, in July 2015, three female Boko Haram members, who had been allegedly recruiting widows and young girls into Boko Haram by luring them with the prospects for marriage to male insurgents, were arrested.[32]

At the onset of the insurgency, there was relatively little verifiable evidence of women operating as suicide bombers and operational leaders and fighters. There is now a well-documented trend of female suicide bombers.[33] This may be attributed to the rapidly evolving nature of Boko Haram combat tactics and the expediency of using women, who are less likely to arouse suspicion. There is also little evidence of women in strategic and leadership roles, as political vanguards, within the sect although the *ameeras* or wives of senior commanders are given some responsibility to coordinate the general activities of women, mobilize them for attending sermons and other gatherings and to cater to them. Some *ameeras* have been reported to participate in executions of captors in the camps.[34] Specific

[31] Interview with three CJTF members in Maiduguri, Borno, 23 April 2014; interview with Hajja, an escapee, confirmed this dimension of women's participation (Brock 2013).

[32] *Premium Times* 2014.

[33] Some later incidents of suicide bombing have featured female suicide bombers. These include the attack in Lagos on 25 June 2014 aimed at igniting several gasoline depots in Apapa where Nigeria's main seaports are located, which is a hub for shipping, manufacturing, storage of petrochemical products and other economic activity (*Sahara Reporters* 2014b). On 27 July 2014, a female suicide bomber unsuccessfully attempted to attack Northwest University in Kano on Eid day, while another female bomber attacked a Roman Catholic church in the same city. The next day, two female suicide bombers were responsible for the twin attacks in Kano at a fuel station and a trade fair complex. Newspapers reported that the Kano suicide bombers are in their teens (*Thisday* 2014).

[34] Hajja (see footnote 31) also revealed that among those who killed captors and 'enemies' was the Muslim wife of the leader *Nglayike*, the only other woman in the band of fighters (Brock 2013).

accounts of women's participation in combat roles in Boko Haram are more limited.

Understanding the role of women in the insurgency is as much about motivation as it is about activities. Economic dependence and a pervasive sense of injustice perpetrated by the state is a factor in radicalizing women and in legitimizing their 'activist' participation in extremism and violence in various capacities. *Al-Qisas* is the Islamic term for 'retaliation'. It means equality in punishment – justice in an 'eye for an eye' fashion. For example, if a person is murdered, a member of the family has the right to demand the execution of the murderer or carry out the execution on his own. In the Qur'an, *al-Qisas* is linked to 'life': 'And there is [a saving of] life for you in al-Qisas, O men of understanding, that you may become righteous' (2: 179). In the literature on Islamic criminal jurisprudence, *al-Qisas* is one of four pillars: *Hadd* (violation of the right of God), *Ta'zir* (violation of the right of an individual), *al-Qisas* (a violation of the right of God through the violation of the right of the individual) and finally, *Siyasah* (violation of the right of the state).

In interviews, retaliation was described as central to the outbreak of violence. A respondent related that it was not violent in the beginning but then the activities of Boko Haram became restricted by the state, which expected them to comply with state regulations such as traffic rules. Boko Haram members claimed that they did not need to comply with policies that were not mandated by Islam. They also believed that Islam as practised in Borno State was not according to the teachings of the Prophet. Their point of departure was initially 'reform' rather than a toppling of the state altogether. They were, as one respondent related, 'very calm, quiet'. Respondents related that Mohammed Yusuf's preaching was successful because he

> brought stories from the times of the prophet. And he convinced them that the Prophet lived in a particular manner and so the Muslim world should follow suit. He wanted them to emulate the life of the prophet. The women were always at home and some of them stopped going to schools. They were not seen. They move in groups and their presence is barely perceptible.[35]

A clash between the police and followers of Boko Haram ensued and this was followed by the killing of Yusuf. According to the respondent, 'when they killed Yusuf, they said they killed him because he was preaching Islam because he was not violent. His murder was considered a "declaration of war"'.[36] As a result, a radical worldview

[35] Interview with Maiduguri resident who witnessed the rise of Boko Haram in the early 2000s as a student of the University of Maiduguri, Abuja, 3 April 2014.
[36] Ibid.

based on *al-Qisas* or retaliation was propounded and adopted by Boko Haram:

> You tell them that those people are killing Muslims and that if you kill them you get rewarded with Heaven. They do believe that they are doing 'jihad'. [That] they are killing the infidels ...Who are the 'infidels'? The non-Muslims and the security forces because they are 'enemies' and so it would be halal to kill them.

Among women, legitimacy for radicalism was explained by respondents needing to avenge the death of husbands, sons, fathers and other male figures who are victims of state brutality – the police, the army and other security forces. This desire for vengeance as a motive was confirmed by respondents in Borno, particularly Civilian JTF.[37] As one respondent mentioned:

> You know men cannot search women. That is why we the female CJTF go out (to the checkpoints) to search women. Some of the women have been abandoned by their husbands, and they still yearn for them ... [Some] are women whose husbands were Boko Haram militants killed in combat, and who are desperate to seek vengeance on their behalf.[38]

Another respondent who spoke with female detainees stated:

> The insurgents told us: 'we are not allowed to preach in our mosques. They [security agencies] invade our mosques and they kill us ... so the person who does that to you, you have a right to kill that person. They kill us and drive us out of our mosques, simply because we are Muslims, then '*kan su ya halatta*' [taking their lives becomes legitimized]. There are security forces whom we didn't know whether they were Christians or Muslims when they were doing the killings. So once they are security forces, we kill them.' That's their justification and the women actually do believe this.[39]

Cragin and Daly's (2009) analysis however does not cover the domestic roles women play in terrorist groups. In this capacity, they undertake the traditional roles of companionship and management of domestic chores to the insurgents. They also play other supporting and non-domestic roles. We propose that women's activist participation in the Boko Haram insurgency is both in voluntary and supportive capacities either domestically

[37] Interview with three CJTF members in Maiduguri, Borno, 23 April 2014.
[38] Ibid.
[39] Interview with female civil society activist, Abuja, 3 April 2014.

or in combat spheres, to the men – who are the main actors. Within the context of Islamically defined gender norms in northern Nigeria, any leadership that is exercised by women within the Boko Haram movements would be within the boundaries of women's roles in the domestic realm. For instance, supervising cooking, fetching water, washing clothes and other domestic chores, training and integrating new arrivals and 'spousal' (either voluntary or forced) companionship.[40] In addition to the *ameera*s who wield some authority, escapees have also recounted the existence of active 'senior' female Boko Haram members in the camps who cater for, 'train' and assign duties, and integrate newly abducted ones.[41] We are unable to determine the extent to which these women exercise significant decision-making power.

So far, the evidence points to marriage to male Boko Haram members as the main route through which women, as active participants, are introduced to the group. Female members who voluntarily undertake specific roles vital to the group's existence tend to be wives of members, particularly those with significant authority. Yet, even as wives, their radicalization and conversion to Boko Haram ideology is not an automatic and inevitable outcome. As information from the life histories reveal, there is often a time lag between a man's radicalization and participation in violent extremism, and his wife's similar conversion and active participation. In between this period is when the radicalized husband convinces and pressurizes his wife to join the group. Some coercion may be involved with threats of divorce to the woman or to her family's well-being, financial vulnerability of the woman, etc. However, once the wives become members, many seem to accept and internalize their new roles in Boko Haram, and even become strong advocates regarding this new position as their duties to their husbands, and their duties to God. It appears difficult for them to renounce their membership, even when their husbands die, although they may scale back on their active participation. Widows tend to be courted by and married to other Boko Haram members, reflecting conventional local injunctions against women remaining unmarried. In addition, even women who are recruited by female members are attracted not just by individual membership of the group, but by the prospect of marriage to male insurgents given the social significance of marriage to the transition to adulthood, and the necessity of having a man to cater for a woman.

The ability of Boko Haram to respond to socio-economic needs of women is evident in the tendency of some to return to the group even

[40] Cf. note 34.

[41] Conversation with journalist, Abuja 3 May 2014; Baba Goni, a teenage boy who also escaped from one of the camps recounted that 'many of them [insurgents] lived with women who had come voluntarily into the camp' (Jones 2014).

after rescue. Since 2015, some women who escaped or were rescued from Boko Haram camps, have gone back to the insurgents. This tendency was particularly noted among women in internally displaced persons (IDP) camps in Maiduguri, who were subjected to the deplorable living conditions in these camps.[42] While many IDPs are absorbed in communities, thousands are in camps in Adamawa, Bauchi, Borno, Gombe, Taraba and Yobe. Reports of severe food shortages, overcrowding, and other instances of economic deprivation, and limited healthcare services indicate that life after Boko Haram simply plunges women back into conditions of deprivation and injustice such as those from which they sought relief.[43] Dire living conditions for the large number of IDPs have been compounded by exploitation and abuse by relief workers and security officials. Reports abound of women trading sexual favours for food and, in some cases, being coerced and subjected to sexual violence, while their husbands are forcefully separated from them, detained and physically abused. The lack of accountability of some relief workers and security personnel who perpetrate these abuses contrasts with experiences in Boko Haram camps, where justice of a crude form is swiftly served. Motivations behind the return of these women to Boko Haram tend to be expressed less in terms of radical religious beliefs than a desire for socio-economic security. For some of these women: 'Life in the forest felt freer and more dignified than living in the dust of an internally displaced persons' camp, dependent on international aid groups for a meal a day'.[44]

WOMEN AS AGENTS OF COUNTER-RADICALIZATION

Women also play an important role of countering radicalization that defies the binary of a coerced and subjugated victim or active perpetrator of violence. This dimension of women's involvement in counter-radicalization spans a spectrum of activities, from relief work with IDPs and other victims of violence, to activism and active engagement on the frontlines of the war on Boko Haram. Through these efforts, women in northern Nigeria are exercising autonomy, finding a greater sense of purpose in contributing to their communities, finding new ways of undertaking their religious duties and gaining empowerment and visibility beyond traditional domestic roles.

The insurgency has created an imperative for the active involvement of women from northern Nigeria to rebuild their communities in the

42 UNHCR (2019) Operations Portal – Refugee Situations: Nigeria Situation. https://data2.unhcr.org/en/situations/nigeriasituation#_ga=2.196338860.1463812103.1556897273-1427840102.1556897273, accessed 2 August 2019.

43 International Crisis Group 2016.

44 Moaveni 2019.

aftermath of violence in a variety of ways. In Borno and beyond, women from the region are serving as nurses, relief workers, activists and journalists, founding various not-for-profit initiatives. The platforms include government agencies and relief efforts, international NGO initiatives, local civil society and media outlets. Perhaps the most prominent civil society initiative is the Bring Back Our Girls movement, co-founded by Hadiza Bala Usman and Oby Ezekwesili, which promoted cooperation between northern and southern Nigerian women and men.[45] Through sit-ins, marches and other forms of peaceful protest, they collectively demanded government action to rescue the abducted Chibok girls and other kidnapped victims in Boko Haram custody. Others such as Fatima Abubakar, a photojournalist from Maiduguri, have received international acclaim for creative use of social media to provide a nuanced and humane perspective on the everyday reality of people living, affected by and surviving Boko Haram in Borno State.[46] In many respects, these women see their role in activism and relief initiatives as an extension of their duties to their families, their communities and to their religion. This expression of agency can come with immense rewards as well as great personal cost. For instance, northern women relief workers have been victims of attacks on IDP camps by Boko Haram. Some, such as Hauwa Mohammed Liman, have also been abducted and executed by the militants.[47]

At the other end of the spectrum of women's counter-radicalization role is their presence on the frontlines in the war on the insurgency. Operating within the umbrella of vigilante groups in north-eastern Nigeria, informally known as the 'Civilian Joint Task Force' (CJTF), women actively provide support to security forces. It is not clear how many of the estimated 26,000 CJTF members are women, but they do exist. Drawing on our interviews with female vigilantes, as well as secondary sources, we identify at least three specific roles they play. First, they gather intelligence on suspected militants within their communities and report to security agencies. Second, they operate checkpoints and, in particular, they search and frisk women. Third, female vigilantes participate in arresting and apprehending female Boko Haram suspects and in a few reported cases have been involved in actual combat with the insurgents. A 27-year-old divorcee and mother of one, educated up to secondary school level, explained the role of female vigilantes as follows:

> We have apprehended both male and female suspects. We [female CJTF] are allowed to do what our male counterparts do. You know we women talk amongst ourselves, this puts us in a better position than the

45 See profile in Wallis 2014.
46 Searcey 2016.
47 Busari and Adebayo 2018.

> men to know exactly what is going on in the neighbourhood, because the men are usually out at work or earning money. That is why we [female CJTF] are able to apprehend the criminals [young men] here.[48]

The respondent provides more details on how they have arrested suspected female Boko Haram members:

> [A]t Shuri House, we once caught a woman carrying a bomb. Her name was Shatu. She is the only female we have caught so far ... You know men cannot search women. That is why we the female CJTF go out [to the checkpoints] to search women ... Some of the women have been abandoned by their husbands, and they still yearn for them ... that is why we are able to catch them. These are women whose husbands are Boko Haram fighters killed in combat, and who are desperate for vengeance on their behalf.[49]

There are similarities in the profiles of these female vigilantes but they are not uniform. These women tend to be in their 20s and 30s, often unmarried, divorcees or widows, although there are some who are married. Like their male counterparts, they are volunteers, some are students and or unemployed; others are petty traders and small-scale entrepreneurs. Increasingly, they have been receiving paramilitary training from security agencies, and in some cases, a stipend from the government.

The varied motivations of female participation in the CJTF are often personally underlined by a sense of duty to their families and communities. In many cases, the death of a family member, neighbour or others from Boko Haram attacks inspires them to join vigilante groups. A 25-year old single student in one of the higher education institutes in Borno explained her motivations for joining the vigilante as follows:

> As a woman, I joined the CJTF, to be honest, because we [the community] have been too frustrated. Young men simply shoot and kill people in this neighbourhood outside their homes, in the market. When I was pursuing my diploma at [name of institution withheld], a quarter up to half of the class were affiliated with Boko Haram. They were there to spy and infiltrate and everyone was scared of them back then. They would go to Ramat and kill people.[50]

She explained further that her parents initially disapproved of her participation in vigilante activities but she persevered. She and other women

[48] Interview with female CJTF member, Maiduguri, Borno, 23 April 2014.
[49] Ibid.
[50] Interview, Maiduguri, Borno, 23 April 2014.

were able to report a neighbour's son, suspected to be a militant, to security officials. Another respondent, the divorcee mentioned earlier, explained her motivations as follows:

> It was the love for my country … you see a lot of young people taking up arms and killing indiscriminately. They create a lot of widows and orphans … You know it is us women who bear the burden of raising a child in the father's absence. What happens is that young men take guns, kill people, and then come back to the neighbourhood … that's why I made the decision to stand out, and provide information to the soldiers to arrest these young men [the perpetrators].

They explain that they were motivated to join when they realized that the information they provide to soldiers is treated confidentially and acted upon. There are also cases where women, like their male counterparts, joined the CJTF out of fear of intimidation and harassment from security forces to expose insurgents, but later found the efforts rewarding. In all cases, there seems to be an implicit zeal to actively contribute to their communities through new ways beyond the realm of domestic duties. Those we interviewed seemed enthusiastic at doing physical drills and other paramilitary training, being on the government's payroll, being issued ID cards and uniforms and working with others in a group.

Conclusion

This chapter has explored the various dimensions of women's participation in Boko Haram and Islamist radicalism in Nigeria. It examined how gender norms in northern Nigerian society have shaped women's engagement with Boko Haram. A key finding is that not all women who participate in radical Islamist movements are themselves radicalized. Indeed, northern Nigerian women have engaged with Boko Haram in a variety of ways, for a variety of reasons, participating variously as victims, as perpetrators, and as agents of counter-radicalization. In general, the empirical analysis reveals the following key points about women's participation in Boko Haram:

1. Northern Nigerian women are highly differentiated by sect, ethnicity, education and socio-economic status. These factors interact with highly patriarchal gender norms of traditional Islamic practice in northern Nigeria to create various forms of Islamic activism, from progressive civil society groups to violent Islamic sects. However, pervasive illiteracy, severe economic deprivation, and high levels of dependence on

male breadwinners increase the vulnerability of poor northern women to being drawn into violent movements such as Boko Haram.

2. Understanding how northern Nigerian women are drawn into radical Islamic groups requires an understanding of their economic dependence on men and the traditional Islamic embedding of their roles and rights within their family duties. The evidence presented here shows that joining Boko Haram was more about carrying out traditional gender roles than about resisting female subordination. Female members of Boko Haram did not operate independently of the men and oftentimes their participation was conditioned by that of male members of their family.
3. While faith-based ideologies sometimes play a role, many of the reasons behind women's voluntary participation are linked to personal family narratives and experiences rather than involving a commitment to violent ideologies.

For the women directly involved in Boko Haram, we have identified three main forms of engagement. They can be coerced victims, active participants, or can contribute towards counter-radicalization efforts. We find that both coerced and active female participants in Boko Haram are largely in a subordinate position to the men to whom they are married or attached to individually, and to the male leadership of the group as a whole. This is a reflection and a reproduction of the larger society's gender norms where the most exemplary women are not expected to act as individuals, but whose actions and existence are largely conditioned by their support to the male figures in their lives – fathers, brothers and especially husbands. In both cases, the necessity of having women in a supportive capacity – to undertake domestic chores, for companionship, and for tactical deployment in violent activities – has driven the voluntary recruitment and coercion of women into the sect. This echoes the findings of studies on the gender dynamics in suicide attacks in the global literature, which finds that female participation is associated with personally focused recruitment through peer-pressure, retaliation and exploitation, whereas recruitment driven by ideological factors occurs more frequently for males (Jacques and Taylor 2008, 316; Bloom, 2011, 9–10).

Both coerced and active participants often end up performing relatively similar support roles in Boko Haram. Active participants could initially be coerced, then accept and internalize radical doctrine, and actively propagate it even in the event of their husband's death, by remarrying into the group. Those who remain coerced participants on the other hand undertake these roles under duress, without necessarily becoming radicalized, and are willing to escape when an opportunity presents itself. Women's authority within the group tends to be based on authority over other women, as in the case of wives of senior commanders, the *ameeras*, who were responsible for organizing the activities of subordinate women. Active participation in perpetrating violence also showed a combination of coercion and active participation, as in the case of female suicide bombers, many of whom were coerced.

Contrary to the prevailing literature on Boko Haram, however, women also play an important role in countering radicalization that defies the binary of a subjugated participant or active perpetrator of violence. This dimension of women's involvement in counter-radicalization spans a spectrum of activities, from relief work with IDPs and other victims of violence, to local and international activism against radicalism, and even active engagement on the frontlines of the war on Boko Haram. Women's active engagement in counter-radicalization draws from a long history of Islamic women's civil society organizations that pursue socially progressive objectives of advancing women's welfare and rights within religious framing of their rights and duties. Through these efforts, women in northern Nigeria are exercising autonomy, finding a greater sense of purpose in contributing to their communities, finding new ways of undertaking their religious duties and gaining empowerment and visibility beyond traditional domestic roles. In many cases, such women have drawn inspiration from some of northern Nigeria's progressive historical traditions of female scholarship and women's rights.

Bibliography

Abbas, T. and Siddique, A., 2011, 'Perceptions of the Processes of Radicalisation and De-Radicalisation among British South Asian Muslims in a Post-Industrial City', *Social Identities* 18 (1), 119–34, accessed, 28 March 2016.

Abdellatif, O. and Ottaway, M., 2007, 'Women in Islamist Movements: Toward an Islamist Model of Women's Activism', Carnegie Papers 2, http://carnegieendowment.org/files/cmec2_women_in_islam_final1.pdf, accessed 20 July 2014.

Adamu, F.L., 1999, 'A Double-Edged Sword: Challenging Women's Oppression within Muslim Society in Northern Nigeria', *Gender and Development* 7 (1), 56–61, accessed 8 February 2014.

—— 2008a, 'Women's Struggle and the Politics of Difference', *Inhalt*, www.fu-berlin.de/sites/gpo/tagungen/tagungfeministperspectives/fatima_l_adamu.pdf, accessed 8 February 2014.

—— 2008b, 'Gender, Hisba and the Enforcement of Morality in Northern Nigeria', *Africa* 78 (1), 136–52, accessed 8 February 2014.

Alkali, M.N., Monguno, A.K. and Mustafa, B.S., 2012, 'Overview of Islamic Actors in Northeastern Nigeria', Working Paper 2, Nigeria Research Network, Oxford, www3.qeh.ox.ac.uk/pdf/nrn/WP2Alkali.pdf, accessed 20 June 2014.

Alubo, O., 2009, 'Citizenship and Identity Politics in Nigeria', in *Citizenship and Identity Politics in Nigeria: Conference Proceedings*, Cleen Foundation, Nigeria, www.cleen.org/Citizenship%20and%20Identity%20Crisis%20in%20Nigeria.pdf, accessed 20 April 2014.

Amnesty International U.K., 2018, 'Nigeria: Boko Haram Survivors Raped and Starved by Military "Rescuers" – New Report', Amnesty International, UK, www.amnesty.org.uk/press-releases/nigeria-boko-haram-survivors-raped-and-starved-military-rescuers-new-report, accessed 20 January 2019.

Audu, O., 2014, 'Boko Haram: Shekau Claims Responsibility for Attack on Giwa Barracks, Threatens to Attack Universities, Civilian-JTF', *Premium Times*, 24 March 2014, www.premiumtimesng.com/news/157374-boko-haram-shekau-claims-responsibility-attack-giwa-barracks-threatens-attack-universities-civilian-jtf.html, accessed 20 April 2014.

Baker, A., 2014, 'How ISIS is Recruiting Women from Around the World', *Time*, 6 September, http://time.com/3276567/how-isis-is-recruiting-women-from-around-the-world, accessed 28 March 2016.

Barkindo, A., Gudaku, B.T., Wesley, C.K., 2013, 'Our Bodies, their Battleground: Boko Haram and Gender-Based Violence against Christian Women and Children in North-Eastern Nigeria since 1999', Nigeria's Political Violence Research Network (NPVRN) Working Paper 1, Open Doors International, Amsterdam.

Barlas, A., 2002, *Believing Women in Islam: Unreading Patriarchal Interpretations of the Qur'an*, Austin: University of Texas Press.

Ben Chuks, O., 2004, 'Literacy/Numeracy and Vocational Training among Rural Women in Nigeria for a Good Livelihood and Empowerment', *International Journal of Lifelong Education* 23 (3), 287–99.

Bloom, M., 2007, 'Female Suicide Bombers: A Global Trend', *Daedalus* 136 (1), 94–102.

—— 2011, 'Bombshells: Women and Terror', *Gender Issues* 28 (1–2), 1–21.

British Council, 2012, 'Gender in Nigeria Report 2012: Improving the Lives of Girls and Women in Nigeria, Issues, Policies, Action', 2nd edition.

Brock, J., 2013, 'Insight: Boko Haram, Taking to Hills, Seize Slave "Brides"', *Reuters*, 17 November, www.reuters.com/article/us-nigeria-security-islamists-insight/insight-boko-haram-taking-to-hills-seize-slave-brides-idUSBRE9AG04120131117, accessed 2 January 2014.

Brown, K., 2014, 'Analysis: Why are Western Women Joining the Islamic State?' *BBC*, 6 October 2014, www.bbc.co.uk/news/uk-29507410, accessed 28 March 2016.

Busari, S. and Adebayo, B., 2018, 'Second Aid Worker Held by Boko Haram Executed as Negotiation Deadline Expires', *CNN International*, 16 October, www.cnn.com/2018/10/16/africa/second-nigerian-aid-worker-killed-intl/index.html, accessed 20 January 2019.

CIA, 2014, *The World Factbook: Nigeria*, Central Intelligence Agency, www.cia.gov/library/publications/the-world-factbook/geos/ni.html, accessed 31 July 2014.

Cook, D., 2005, 'Women Fighting in Jihad?' *Studies in Conflict & Terrorism* 28 (5), 375–4, accessed 28 March 2016.

Cragin, R.K. and Daly, S.A., 2009, *Women as Terrorists: Mothers, Recruiters, and Martyrs.* Santa Barbara, CA: Praeger Security International.

Cunningham, K.J., 2003, 'Cross-Regional Trends in Female Terrorism', *Studies in Conflict & Terrorism* 26 (3), 171–95.

Erulkar, A.S. and Bello, M., 2007, 'The Experience of Married Adolescent Girls in Northern Nigeria', Population Council, www.ohchr.org/Documents/Issues/Women/WRGS/ForcedMarriage/NGO/PopulationCouncil24.pdf, accessed 21 August 2019.

Gonzalez-Perez, M., 2008, *Women and Terrorism: Female Activity in Domestic and International Terror Groups*, New York: Routledge.

—— 2011, 'The False Islamization of Female Suicide Bombers', *Gender Issues* 28 (1), 50–65.

Hajjar, L., 2004, 'Religion, State Power, and Domestic Violence in Muslim Societies: A Framework for Comparative Analysis', *Law & Social Inquiry* 29 (1), 1–38.

Hill, J.N.C., 2010, 'Sufism in Northern Nigeria: Force for Counter-Radicalization?' Strategic Studies Institute, https://ssi.armywarcollege.edu/pdffiles/PUB989.pdf, accessed 23 August 2019.

Human Rights Watch, 2013a, 'Nigeria: Massive Destruction, Deaths from Military Raid', Human Rights Watch, May, www.hrw.org/news/2013/05/01/nigeria-massive-destruction-deaths-military-raid, accessed 8 February 2014.

——2013b, 'Nigeria: Boko Haram Abducts Women, Recruits Children', Human Rights Watch, November, www.hrw.org/news/2013/11/29/nigeria-boko-haram-abducts-women-recruits-children, accessed 8 February 2014.

Hutson, A.S., 2001, 'Women, Men and Patriarchal Bargaining in an Islamic Sufi Order: The Tijaniyya in Kano, Nigeria, 1937–Present', *Gender & Society*, 15 (5), 734–53.

Idris, H. and Sawab, I., 2014, 'Women as Boko Haram's New Face', *Weekly Trust*, 6 July, https://allafrica.com/stories/201307081607.html, accessed 23 August 2019.

International Crisis Group, 2014, 'Curbing Violence in Nigeria (II): The Boko Haram Insurgency', International Crisis Group, Africa Report 216, 4 April 2014, www.crisisgroup.org/en/regions/africa/west-africa/nigeria/216-curbing-violence-in-nigeria-ii-the-boko-haram-insurgency.aspx, accessed 7 April 2014.

—— 2016, 'Nigeria: Women and the Boko Haram Insurgency', Africa Report 242, 5 December 2016, www.crisisgroup.org/africa/west-africa/nigeria/nigeria-women-and-boko-haram-insurgency, accessed 20 January 2019.

Jacques, K. and Taylor, P.J., 2008, 'Male and Female Suicide Bombers: Different Sexes, Different Reasons?' *Studies in Conflict & Terrorism* 31 (4), 304–26.

Jones, B, 2014, 'Defiled and Bloody, Tethered to a Tree, School Uniforms Ripped: The Moment I Rescued Two Girls from Boko Haram', *MailOnline*, 17 May 2014, www.dailymail.co.uk/news/article-2631546/Defiled-bloody-tethered-tree-school-uniforms-ripped-The-moment-I-rescued-two-girls-Boko-Haram.html, accessed 8 June 2014.

Juergensmeyer, M., 2000, *Terror in the Mind of God: The Global Rise of Religious Violence*, Berkeley: University of California Press.

Kendall, B., 2015, 'What Drives Women to Extreme Acts?' *BBC*, 28 July, www.bbc.co.uk/news/world-33600267, accessed 28 March 2016.

Last, M., 2011, 'Governance and the Public at the Local Level: From Revenue-Raising to Benign Neglect, 1960–2010', unpublished paper.

Leadership, 2014, 'Our Ordeal in Hands of Rapists in Boko Haram Camps', 9 March 2014, http://leadership.ng/features/353367/ordeal-hands-rapists-boko-haram-camps, accessed 15 March 2014.

Mack, B., 2019, 'Nana Asma'u bint Usman 'dan Fodio', *Oxford Bibliographies Online*, www.oxfordbibliographies.com/view/document/obo-9780195390155/obo-9780195390155-0262.xml, accessed 20 January 2019.

Matfess, H., 2017, *Women and the War on Boko Haram: Wives, Weapons, Witnesses*, London: Zed Books.

Moaveni, A., 2019, 'What Would Make A Woman Go Back To Boko Haram? Despair', *International Crisis Group*, 14 January, www.crisisgroup.org/africa/west-africa/nigeria/what-would-make-woman-go-back-boko-haram-despair, accessed 20 January 2019.

Mshelizza, I., 2012, 'Boko Haram Rules Out Talks with Nigeria Government', *Reuters*, 21 March, http://reut.rs/11bV2DT, accessed 20 June 2014.

National Bureau of Statistics, 2011, '2011 Annual Socio-Economic Report', National Bureau of Statistics, Abuja.

——2018, '2017: Statistical Report on Women and Men in Nigeria', February, National Bureau of Statistics, Abuja.

Ness, C., 2005, 'In the Name of the Cause: Women's Work in Secular and Religious Terrorism', *Studies in Conflict & Terrorism* 28 (5), 353–73.

News Rescue, 2012, 'Nigeria Muslims: Christians Behind Many Alleged Boko Bombings', 21 June 2012, http://newsrescue.com/nigeria-muslims-say-christians-behind-many-alleged-boko-bombings, accessed 31 July 2014.

Nigeria Research Network, 2013, 'Islamic Actors and Interfaith Relations in Northern Nigeria', Policy Paper 1, Oxford, www.qeh.ox.ac.uk/research/research-networks/nrn/nrn-pb, accessed 30 July 2014.

Nigerian Tribune, 2014, 'Jonathan Should Call Asari-Dokubo To Order – Lagos Lawmaker', 31 July 2014, www.tribune.com.ng/news/news-headlines/item/12129-jonathan-should-call-asari-dokubo-to-order-lagos-lawmaker, accessed 31 July 2014.

Oboh, M., 2012, 'Boko Haram Leader Tape Threatens Nigeria Forces', *Reuters*, 27 January, www.reuters.com/article/2012/01/27/us-nigeria-bokoharam-tape-idUSTRE80Q1YL20120127, accessed 20 June 2014.

Premium Times, 2014, 'Nigerian Military Arrests Three Female Boko Haram Recruiters', 5 July, www.premiumtimesng.com/news/164389-nigerian-military-arrests-three-female-boko-haram-recruiters-dhq.html, accessed 5 July 2014.

Punch, 2014, 'B'Haram Leader: I Ordered Apapa, Lagos Bombing', 14 July 2014, www.punchng.com/news/bharam-leader-i-ordered-apapa-lagos-bombing, accessed 28 July 2014,

Qazi, F., 2011, 'The Mujahidaat: Tracing the Early Female Warriors of Islam', in *Women, Gender and Terrorism*, L. Sjoberg and C.E. Gentry (eds), Athens: University of Georgia Press.

Sahara Reporters, 2012, 'Boko Haram Claims Responsibility for Attack on VP Sambo's Home', 1 August, http://saharareporters.com/2012/08/01/boko-haram-claims-responsibility-attack-vp-sambo%E2%80%99s-home, accessed 20 June 2014.

—— 2014a, 'Gwoza Christians Release Disturbing Details about Six Girls Kidnapped by Boko Haram Militants in 2013', 5 June, http://saharareporters.com/news-page/gwoza-christians-release-disturbing-details-about-six-girls-kidnapped-boko-haram-militants, accessed 6 June 2014.

——2014b, 'Lagos Explosion Was a Car Bombing', 26 June, http://saharareporters.com/news-page/lagos-explosion-was-car-bombing, accessed 25 July 2014.

'Sako Zuwa Ga Duniya' (A Message to the World), *YouTube*, http://youtu.be/txUJCOK-TIuk, accessed 20 July 2014,

Salami, C.G.E., 2013, 'Youth Unemployment in Nigeria: A Time for Creative Interventions', *International Journal of Business and Marketing Management* 1 (2), 18–26.

Salehi-Isfahani, D. and Dhillon, N., 2008, 'Stalled Youth Transitions in the Middle East: A Framework for Policy Reform', Middle East Initiative Working Paper, Wolfensohn Center for Development and Dubai School of Government, The Brookings Institution, Washington, DC.

Sayne, A., 2012, 'Rethinking Nigeria's Indigene-Settler Conflicts', United States Institute of Peace (USIP), Special Report 311, July, www.usip.org/sites/default/files/SR311.pdf, accessed 20 June 2014.

Searcey, D., 2016, 'From Boko Haram's Birthplace, Instagram Posts Beyond "Death and Despair"', *The New York Times*, 30 June 2016, www.nytimes.com/2016/06/30/world/africa/boko-haram-nigeria-maiduguri-bitsofborno.html, accessed 19 January 2019.

The Economist, 2014, 'Africa's new Number One', www.economist.com/news/leaders/21600685-nigerias-suddenly-supersized-economy-indeed-wonder-so-are-its-still-huge, accessed 11 July 2014.

Thisday, 2014, 'Again, Three Female Suicide Bombers Strike in Kano, Kill 3, Injure 16', 29 July, www.thisdaylive.com/articles/again-three-female-suicide-bombers-strike-in-kano-kill-3-injure-16/184848, accessed 29 July 2014.

Toft, D.F., Philpott, D. and Shah, T.S., 2011, *God's Century: Resurgent Religion and Global Politics*, New York and London: W.W. Norton.

Udo, B., 2014, 'There Will Be Bloodshed if Jonathan Loses in 2015, says Asari-Dokubo', *Premium Times*, 9 September, www.premiumtimesng.com/news/144368-there-will-be-bloodshed-if-jonathan-loses-in-2015-says-asari-dokubo.html, accessed 31 July 2014.

Uzendu, M. and Mari, A., 2012, 'How We Share Boko Haram Loot – Abul Qaqa', *allAfrica*, 12 February, http://allafrica.com/stories/201202140935.html, accessed 20 June 2014.

Victor, B., 2006, *Army of Roses*, London: Constable and Robinson.

Wallis, W., 2014, 'Women of 2014: Hadiza Bala Usman', *Financial Times*, 12 December, www.ft.com/content/08738682-7fa7-11e4-adff-00144feabdc0, accessed 20 June 2014.

Werthmann, K., 2000, '"Seek for Knowledge, Even If it is in China!" Muslim Women and Secular Education in Northern Nigeria', in T. Salter and K. King (eds), *Africa, Islam and Development: Islam and Development in Africa*, Centre of African Studies, University of Edinburgh.

Williams, B.G., 2014, 'The Brides of Allah: The Terror Threat of Black-Widow Suicide Bombers to the Winter Olympics', *HuffPost*, www.huffingtonpost.com/brian-glyn-williams/the-brides-of-allah-the-t_b_4761027.html, accessed 10 July 2014.

Zenn, J. and Pearson, E., 2014, 'Women, Gender and the Evolving Tactics of Boko Haram', *Journal of Terrorism Research* 5 (1), 46–57.

8

An inquiry into possible factors contributing to radicalization in childhood & youth in northern Nigeria

MURRAY LAST

Introduction

The experience of childhood in northern Nigeria varies widely, of course, across the groups and environments that make up the north. Nonetheless I will try here to spell out some of the factors that might be involved in turning a youth into the path of radical religious politics. Much of what I will write is based on living two years within a large farmstead in southern Katsina; I go back there every year and have seen the very young grow up into adults over the last 47 years.[1] But I have also shared a house with adult *almajirai* for a year in Birnin Zaria, and studied (*karatu*) Arabic Islamic texts alongside them.[2] In the 1990s, Hausa colleagues and I for several years did field research on youth in Kano.[3] Above all, I have been a guest of many friends and colleagues in various towns in northern Nigeria, and chatted for many hours, gradually (I hope) understanding better how Hausa social life works.

I admit I have not been in Maiduguri or Potiskum in the Kanuri-speaking heartlands of Nigeria for many years, so this analysis is predominantly Hausa-focused. Indeed, one of the key questions among the people of Kano today is why so few supporters, apparently, of the *Jama'atul Ahlul Sunna li Da'wat wal Jihad*, also known as Boko Haram, are found there.

1 My work in Gidan Jatau focused primarily on traditional modes of managing health and illness. Essays were published as Last 1979, 1991b, 1992, 2000a, 2011, 2019.

2 A brief account of *almajiranci* (traditional Islamic studies).was published in Last 1993b. But Dr Hannah Hoechner's 2018 book on young *almajirai* in Kano is more up to date and extensive. Rudolph Ware (2014) gives an account of *almajirai* in Dakar from an American Muslim perspective.

3 Some results were published in the 1991 report, 'Youth & health in Kano today', *Kano Studies*, special issue. Other essays on youth (and exclusion) are Last 1993a, 2000b, 2005, 2008. A more recent essay is by Conerly Casey (2008).

It is true that no one knows precisely the make-up of the forces that Boko Haram draws in: we know their fighters and spokesmen come from different groups – Igbirra (for example, their spokesman 'Abu Qaqa'), Igbo (e.g. Aminu Sadiq Ogwuche in Abuja), as well as Kanuri and related north-eastern groups including some from the Niger Republic, Cameroon and Chad. We know, too, that bombs have gone off in Lagos, Kaduna and Jos, kidnappings have taken place in Kebbi and Katsina, in Gombe and Bauchi, and Ansaru (*Jama'atul Anṣarul Muslimina fi Biladis Sudan* –Vanguards for the Aid of Muslims in Black Africa) operated for a while out of Kano; murders have occurred there as they have too in Zaria. Traditionally, after independence in 1960, many *almajirai* were still being sent in groups as young boys from the villages of Katsina and Kano to study the Holy Qur'an in western Borno where the best teachers (*malamai*) and their schools (*tsangaya*) were to be found, and where Qur'anic calligraphy was finest. But many children I saw in southern Katsina *c.* 1970 were being taught locally, rising about 5 a.m. to light a big fire and recite the Qur'an from their boards (*allo*), while in Sokoto I knew of elderly women who specialized in providing hostels for very young local *almajirai*. Dr Hamidu Bobboyi, in one study, showed that Mohammed Yusuf, when under pressure from the state Government in Maiduguri, had issued a call to his former students (who were now teaching the Qur'an all over the north) to come with their *almajirai* and join in the defence of his *ahl al-sunna* in Maiduguri. And indeed many very young *almajirai* did go, to the fury or anxiety of their parents (as reported in the media). In which case, we can assume that the early core of what became Boko Haram was drawn from all over the north, though the leaders apparently are still Kanuri-speakers from Yobe and Borno. It is also possible that former *'yan Tatsine* who had survived the killings in Kano and later in Adamawa (as well as in Borno) also responded to Mohammed Yusuf's appeal for help, making Boko Haram still more a multi-ethnic, polyglot group. Thus we need to analyse Boko Haram not from an ethnic but from an Islamist perspective.

However, the lingua franca of Boko Haram seems, unsurprisingly, to be Hausa (and Arabic?). But in recent years it seems probable that young men passing through Niger en route to Libya and Europe may have turned to earning money by joining Boko Haram 'on contract' (e.g. for a month): the pay, I have been told by a reliable source, was apparently good (GBP £325, US $400 per month), and the risk was seen to be low (first month only logistics and training). Such recruits have been hardened by their suffering on the journey so far; some originate from distant Mandinka- and Wolof-speaking areas like The Gambia, Senegal, Mali (the route via Mauretania/Morocco is closed as it has too many mines – hence the re-routing via Niger). Many of these asylum-seekers have joined armed gangs in Niger, for protection as well as for profit: there is, it seems, a level of lawlessness on the margins of Nigerien society that escapes police control.[4] If all this is true, then the origins of *this* segment of Boko Haram's recruits lie in their determination to leave home and seek a new life in Europe: it will not lie in religious radicalization from youth, but in an exceptional courage and restlessness, a sense of adventure and ambition. If they are joining Boko Haram, it is temporary (and out of desperation?) – but it may well confuse any simple analysis of how young men come to join. They are indeed 'foreign fighters', but not in the sense that the media usually presume. They may not even be, at root, 'Islamists'.

Indeed it is important to realize how normal it is in reformist movements for them to start out as primarily ideological, only to be taken over by more military-minded recruits in the second or third year. These then transform what started as a jihad into a guerrilla war, retaining the *baraka* (charisma) of the jihad's original Shaikh or Amir but otherwise largely ignoring the Sharia, and in some instances, causing the Shaikh to modify his Sharia rulings to permit some of the excesses that his new troops insist upon. This pattern is not, of course, confined to Nigerian history; it has recently occurred in both Libya and Syria; indeed ISIS, with its extraordinary levels of cruel violence and its focus on dramatic, public killings of fellow Muslims, may well have then been in the midst of such a transition. Such extreme, dramatic violence has its own attraction to certain youth; it is not only exciting, adrenalin-fuelled, but is so transgressive that it creates a unique bond between the perpetrators, a bond that cannot be broken – or so they say. Such new recruits to dramatic violence, then, have not necessarily been radicalized in childhood; it is more their current isolation from their old home milieu that lets them act in ways wholly new to them (and previously recognized by them as wholly evil). It seems probable that Boko Haram has been through such a transition: Shekau as the charismatic leader may still be in charge, performing as the key figure in all the videos that Boko Haram releases to the press, but his military commanders who determine day-to-day tactics may be more strategists than scholars. We know that was true of Ansaru in Kano. Indeed, since 2016, Boko Haram has been split into two with, it seems, the more moderate commanders under al-Barnawi having moved to an island in Lake Chad from which they send out their expeditions. For them, proper Islamic government is their explicit policy for the towns they capture, with fewer executions.[5]

Nonetheless, the question remains, what might turn a young person into a potential angry radical, and make him willing, one day, to join in extreme violence? For surely, at root in these extreme dissident groups,

4 A personal account of this is given in Kalilu Jammeh (2009).

5 An unusually useful analysis of the groups within Boko Haram, from a Chadian perspective, is by Corentin Cohen (2015).

is an anger, a disillusion with society or simply a strong dislike for their immediate milieu, that justifies for them behaviour that encodes large elements of revenge (*ramuwa*), even hatred (*gaba, fushi*), anger (*hasala*). Yet one should not ignore the idealism over how a properly pious Muslim *jama'a* should live: before that ideal can come about, it may require, say idealists, extreme, shocking violence to force ordinary Muslims to change their old ways and comply – that was the theory of, say, the French revolutionaries, the Khmer radicals, the Red Guards. As has been pointed out elsewhere, that theory comes more obviously out of modern or modernizing Europe than out of Islamic thought in Hausaland. Even in the Sokoto jihad the death toll from fighting was relatively low; as Muhammad Bello said (in *al-Dhikra* – recitation), more people died from disease and hunger than from actual fighting (and that is true of many a war, including the extraordinarily lethal American civil war). In the Sokoto jihad, victors tended instead not to kill their enemies but take them as prisoners, who could then be re-settled as slaves on farms or sold off to the merchants that followed behind an army in order to monetize whatever either side took as loot (including people) after a battle or a raid. In short, I suggest that here the institution of slavery (along with ransoming) actually *saved* lives, albeit in a very disruptive, harsh way. Death was never the obsession in the jihad that it seems to be today for some extremist groups, such as Boko Haram or ISIS (Last 2018). The *takfir*-based punishment in the jihad was not death but enslavement or enforced switching of sides.[6] Again, I would suggest that Hausa culture has never been so obsessed with death, graveyards or even bodily mutilation as some cultures are, though some *jihadi* poetry gloried in killing. Boko Haram, in short, I suggest is not now behaving in a way that follows traditional Hausa or Kanuri values, however much it may have sprung originally from a long-established tradition of Islamic dissent (Last 2014). So, back to the subject of Hausa childhood!

Childhood

Key elements in a northern Nigerian childhood are a deep sense of (a) justice (*adalci*) and (b) respect (*girma*; *mutunci* – Hausa). Although these are adult values, in a large compound with many children (the farmstead I lived in had some 60 children in 1971, and now has over 350), these values were crucial to keeping order if not harmony around a house where elder siblings looked after their younger ones. Mothers explicitly made sure their children recognized not just the values' importance, but

6 A very few executions were done by crucifixion or by impaling; spies were beheaded by the sword. The last impaling was on Friday/Saturday, 13/14 March 1903.

also rebuked their children if they were being 'negative' (*kushe*; *tsulmi*) towards others. Children grew up conscious of their own worth vis-à-vis other children, and took care to respect those older than them: seniority was crucial, and exact ages were known by children too. An older child learned to earn and try to keep the respect of his or her juniors – or suffer humiliating ridicule from a crowd of other kids in the house. A marked feature of a Hausa household, in my experience, is the lack of tantrums, 'melt-downs' by 2- or 3-year olds of a kind so often seen in 'Western' households where such tantrums should be just a stage in growing up. I assume it is the way other, slightly older children care for, and play with, their younger siblings that eliminates such highly irritating behaviour. But the notion of patience (*hakuri*) and self-restraint is also deeply inculcated into the young. Even pain might elicit the minimum of noise – one rarely heard adults howl or scream in agony, say, at a child's death (though it did sometimes happen). Great pain and grief might be seen on the dour face of a woman, but otherwise silence reigned: indeed the extreme silence that enveloped the house at night when a death occurred would actually wake me up. Even wounds were borne in silence, as were such operations as circumcision, opening an abscess (*sakiya*), re-setting a broken leg or managing a guinea-worm (*kurkunu*). Children learned early to be restrained in expressing their hurt. I also never saw any child being deliberately cruel to an animal or pulling apart, say, a living insect (as one sometimes sees in Europe): pain was not something you inflict on other beings, let alone sadistically. Hunting, yes; but gratuitous torture, no.

The farmstead was also a world in which children were not usually beaten even if they behaved badly: other children's long-term disapproval and ridicule could be enough punishment. Ridicule (*ba'a*; *zambo*) plays a major role in Hausa criticism of misbehaviour – one can see it among adults when, say, a servant has done something wrong: his deliberately bizarre, absurd explanation to his boss in public is designed to bring on mocking laughter from the other servants watching his confession of misconduct. It is public self-humiliation as the penalty for doing something wrong. To be able really to feel shame (*kunya*) is an essential element of good behaviour: the shameless, like those who do not fear God (*tsoron Allah*), are truly beyond the pale. The two attributes are linked – Allah expects you to repent, to seek forgiveness, yet the shameless do not. 'Fearing Allah' is a characteristic that earns genuine praise and admiration – and it can apply to non-Muslims as well as Muslims. Children learn then to feel shame (*kunya*) and to expect it in other children. But underlying all this is a pervasive sense of justice, of fairness for all.

Clearly, children blush when embarrassed and learn to spot blushing in others; there are other conventional ways of showing embarrassment, lowering eyes or the head – just as one can show anger by turning the head away, by overtly not paying attention when in conversation. But there are also rules about not hitting another person, in some cases not even touching them. Hausa modes of 'beating' (*buga*), say, within the house may be nothing more than a fingertip pressed briefly on another's forehead or flicking their nose: as 'domestic violence', this can be classed as gross even though it leaves no mark. Again, foreigners may be thinking a rod or a whip is required in 'beating', but that would be very rare, not least as the more senior you are, the less physical action you take: one might get a servant to use a stick on someone, but as a *mai gida* (head of house) that is below what your status allows. Violence is the domain of the young, the juniors in the community – it is a mark of their subordination that they behave roughly. Elders use their brains, not their bodies, to reprimand their subordinates. In the countryside, where police are absent, it is the young boys that take action to defend their environment, whether against armed robbers or dangerously armed madmen: as a group they are ready to kill the intruder. But once they are adult, joining the police or the army is *not* an appropriate career: such professional violence is not for a self-respecting, grown-up *baHaushe* (Hausa male) – at least not in the minds of the elders. In the past, violence was the province of slaves. Similarly today, married men do not take part in riots or demonstrations (although they may organize them).

Boys in the countryside have had to learn to be brave, whether they are out on their own herding livestock all day armed just with a stick, or they have been sent on errands to another distant farmhouse. Girls too may be sent on lonely paths to carry goods for sale at the local market, often returning late. The countryside might well seem safe, but there are dangers – strangers, dogs, even hyenas or snakes. Children may till distant fields alone, and need to ensure other people's livestock, including herds of cattle, do not stray into the crops; and they climb trees (where snakes are) to get fodder. In the rainy season, a sudden storm can soak them far from home. In short, children learn to endure daily hardship and fears, to be 'country-wise' if not street-wise; and some are smarter than others in coping, some better leaders, or have distinct skills, say, in foraging for things to eat. Hunger and thirst are commonplace, as is tiredness.

So in such a tough milieu, if the *mai gida* or a father did harshly punish a son of his, and did so unjustly in the eyes of the boy, then the father might find he was never forgiven: the son, even a senior son, could leave his father's house and never return. Just as in a marriage, a disgruntled wife may leave the house temporarily (*yaji*) until her husband repairs the offence he has caused, so too a son may put himself beyond reach of his father (though his whereabouts are known to his brothers), and nothing makes him return. This sense of *yaji*, of deep injustice *and* humiliation that the injustice invokes, is I think central to our understanding of radical dissent and vengeance, even on a political plane.

It is important to recognize how central justice (and the processes of justice) has been to political movements over the centuries in northern Nigeria. As one important research project showed, Islamic justice was explicitly preferred to traditional justice by ethnic elders in parts of Gongola state as it put the responsibility for a 'crime' on the individual who had committed the crime and not on the group as a whole: Sharia was cheaper, faster and not subject to prolonged negotiation – the penalties were already down in writing and could be paid by the culprit immediately.[7] Similarly, the Sokoto jihad centred around justice, focusing as it did on implementing Sharia government against the arbitrary exploitation of peasants, pastoralists and citizens by those in power in the great cities. Indeed as I have witnessed in recent years, what gave a village or district head his standing (and popular support) in the wider community was his reputation for providing mediation and proper justice for his community: much less important was any demonstration of power or connections, any display of his wealth or his following.

So too with an elderly *mai gida*: he seldom went out or was seen far from his room – there he sat, ready to offer advice and settle disputes, an often silent figure underwriting the (spiritual) security of the household. In many ways this role was hard, yet essential, for the *mai gida* as changes in the world outside made conflicts inside more difficult to manage: households could fall apart (as I witnessed) if the *mai gida* failed, whether through greed or recourse to a *dodo* (a personal demon with extra-legal power). Therefore any violation of this all-pervading sense of justice, if experienced by a son (who must respect, above all, his father) cuts deep into the son's acceptance of the cultural structures surrounding *girma* (seniority). The diminution of his respect for his father diminishes his own humanity (*mutunci*); and, by abandoning his natal home, he loses too the possibility of developing in time into a *mutumin kirki* – a distinctively honourable elder recognized as such within his local world.

In short, such a son, young though he is, has gone into 'exile', to make a new, much reduced life in some distant anonymous town, earning a living as best he can in a rented room or two. Once there, so much depends on whom he joins up with, what friends and support he can find. Essentially, much of urban life for the migrant young initially depends on groups or gangs that flourish on the margins of the great cities – the *daba* or 'lairs' of gangs of teenagers under the leadership of an older 'thug' (Dan Asabe 1991). These are tightly structured with a hierarchy into which a

[7] The unpublished D.Phil thesis by Dr Abdul-Mumin Sa'ad in 1989 compares traditional, Islamic and magistrate courts and analyses the cases they heard. Although focused on cases in Gongola (where all three court systems operated, and Fulfulde and Hausa are the lingua franca), his analysis suggests legal cultures there were not very different from elsewhere in northern Nigeria. I am very grateful to Dr Sa'ad for lending me a copy while in Kano.

newcomer can find a place: as a young boy he finds support by way of food and shelter, but also responsibilities and duties from which he may earn some money of his own.

The life they live is semi-criminal, they go armed or ready to fight: big men or politicians can recruit their services to intimidate opponents at political rallies (as *'yan banga*). But they can be sites of fun, too, for the migrant boy: smoking cannabis or taking some other concoction, kidnapping young girls for a week-end somewhere out of town (as *'yan hiace*), or going hunting with dogs over the mud walls of city houses. The migrant boy learns the skills of street-life, how to survive fights, how to pick up cash in one way or another, how simply to get by, avoiding police or *hisba* (religious 'police').

Eventually, as the boy grows into being a young man, he may become dissatisfied with being a *dan daba*, or simply tire of such a negative lifestyle (perhaps thinking of marriage and a family). In this context the persuasiveness of a radical Islamic preacher may be enough to make him change course, and become religious once again. On the evening streets of Kano metropolitan as in the marketplaces of small towns there are preachers of all kinds, often in groups, haranguing hearers against such common sins as smoking or drugs or brothels – and very effective they are too. Due to these touring preachers, in many a rural village tobacco sales have fallen to zero; brothels and beer parlours have been taken over by Christians, spirit possession (especially in its cult form, *bori*) has become rare – so too have still more non-Muslim traditions such as *bagiro*, which uses a bull-roarer in darkness. In some places I know, even the group recitation (*dhikri*) in Sufi mosques has fallen quiet. So for the urban migrant seeking a new lifestyle there are several different close-knit, ultra-pious groups ready to receive him and take him on a radically Islamic journey – and all are supremely confident that theirs is the *right* path, whereas the common establishment's path is a compromise that leads ultimately to hell.

Nonetheless there are in big cities other routes to support, food and companionship. For example, small football clubs offer a camaraderie in their rituals of regular 'training'; and together they have to find ways of raising money, usually in semi-legal ways (e.g. getting cash for not damaging a car), in order to pay for balls, boots, clothes or whatever they need for matches or for getting access to pitches (Haruna and Abdullahi 1991). Traditionally, city quarters had their own gangs that defended their quarters' territory against outsiders and rival gangs from neighbouring quarters. Even in the countryside a big house or a village would have its own football teams with fierce rivalries; but again it was not necessarily the matches that mattered as much as the regular training and its comradeship where the extra-special skills of some players were recognized. Although there were forms of pre-colonial football (with balls made from the intestines of sheep or cattle), more commonly young boys from the neighbourhood went off hunting together, shooting birds with catapults and then roasting them on a campfire. But there were also larger-scale occasions for the young to foregather: after the market had closed, boys would have wrestling matches (watched by the girls) and show off their prowess. But perhaps the major site of local collective identity in the early 20th century were the mock assemblies, where boys and girls took spoof titles (such as *Sarki*, *Magajiya* or *Alkali*, *Joji*) and mimicked the posh roles of formal adult life – and these titles lasted a lifetime. Thus there was, in the countryside, a real unity among the young: to leave it all for the dangerous loneliness of a big city could be a major turning point for any restlessly ambitious or angry youth.

So far, I have been mainly discussing rural childhood, but both boys and girls growing up in a big city learn to be street-wise: girls are often sent hawking the cooked foods their mother has made, but so too may boys be out on the streets selling items at traffic junctions. There is enough legitimate trade in a big city – compared to, say, smaller rural towns – that boys can learn a trade without getting lured into petty criminality simply to stave off the pangs of hunger. Many boys (and girls too) in villages as well in the big city still attend a local Qur'anic school for at least part of the day, but many daughters of a big house can be taught within the house by some of the learned women: indeed in many old quarters of a city, women are the main teachers of the Qur'an to the young. I have known a boy be taken from the farmhouse I was living in to a *malam* in a town some 50 miles away: I don't think the boy (or his mother) had much say in the matter – it was the father's project. Reportedly he was not happy at the plan, and is now angry with the way his father treated him.

Another young man I knew went on Qur'anic studies to a remote area (beyond Birnin Gwari) to try to become in time a *malam*, but after many years he has given up: the humiliations of seeking money for his Islamic services, the humiliation of being so poor and initially wifeless were more than he could bear. He now farms. In short, from what people tell me, it is hard these days living as a *malam*: there are fewer alms, less respect – society's values, they say, are changing. Even the disabled – the blind, the crippled – get less support, whether in the big cities (which is where they congregate in separate communities, as big-city people are thought to be more generous) or in rural towns. My broader point here is that even among Muslims the Islamic values that insist that the well-off give alms to the poor are today at risk, prompting among pious young boys a real anger with contemporary society and disillusion with the elite whom Allah has blessed, apparently, with so much wealth. That anger can be organized and brought to bear on the institutions and agents of the state – especially in a state that flouts Sharia law (as ordinary people understand the Sharia) in the way it runs the business of the nation.

There are, nonetheless, plenty of well-off Muslims (and others) in northern Nigeria who *do* give alms and feed those who are starving, but such acts of piety are no longer so generalized as they used to be: only certain houses put out bowls of food each evening for anyone to eat.[8] Instead, money is used not to relieve the poor but to make more mundane gains – a very big city is too anonymous, too vast, too busy, too fragmented to create even local cohesive communities, let alone a single city-wide one. Even the ancient systems of quarters and wards have begun to lose their distinct identities. The countryside still can have such communities – but that is not where the young today want to be.

To sum up on childhood: I have not found any obvious avenue for radicalization except in the breakdown of relations between a son and his father, leading to the son's acute sense of anger and alienation from a home he considers to have been unjust in humiliating him. On growing up, boys do, anyway, automatically leave home: sons, once they are mature, do not have rooms that open inside the family's house: they are formally marginal to the home – their rooms, instead, look out on to the street. In that sense, there is not only social 'avoidance' (*kunya*) of the father but also a physical relocation vis-à-vis the mother. In practice, though, affection and respect both between parents and children and between brothers and sisters persist long into adulthood: seniority never fades. Only in exceptional circumstances might the family unit break. But could it be that in recent years those 'exceptional circumstances' include migration, itself a kind of exile,[9] to the cities? Have cities, then, become a kind of new 'bush', a 'forest' that is dangerously wild and poorly mapped – but with exciting possibilities for the independent and brave?

8 In cities like Sokoto, a big house may be sending out cooked food to a hundred or more needy households each evening. As a student living locally, I was a grateful recipient of these meals – and still am, but now as a guest.

9 It is perhaps worth noting that 'exile' has had great significance in northern Nigerian history. As long-term imprisonment was never a pre-colonial mode of punishment, the guilty were banished, sent into 'exile' – sometimes in lieu of a more extreme sharia punishment such as stoning (as in Muhammad Bello's time in *c.* 1820s Sokoto). To leave your ('home') town 'for ever' could be a highly symbolic act – as it was for Ahmad Baba in 1607, who specifically shook the sand from off his sandals once he was beyond the city walls. A striking instance of self-imposed exile is the decision, 1806-08, by the Hausa Emirs of Kano, Daura, Zaria and Katsina, and even the Mai Barno, all to evacuate their cities before the *jihadi* forces besieged them: each Emir sought to start again, with his Muslim followers, elsewhere. 'Exile' meant a new beginning.

Youth

My argument in this section is that young boys who have left (for whatever reason) their rural homes for a big city require not only shelter and food but also ways of getting the companionship that both protects them and offers them a new way forward in life, a way forward that has both meaning and moral value within the Hausa context. The huge numbers that have migrated in recent decades to the great cities of Hausaland and Borno (and indeed to Lagos too) have fuelled all kinds of groupings, ranging not only from the legitimate to the criminal, but also from the pious to the extremist. My suggestion here is that it is this urban migration that has supplied recruits for such radical religious groups as an *ahl al-sunna* (of which Boko Haram originally was but one example), enabling them to expand their *jama'a* within even a big city.

This urban migration is a new phenomenon; it can empty farmsteads of their young men, not just for the dry season (as did *cin rani* – dry-season migrant labour – in the past) but for the whole year. We need to remember this phenomenon is wider than Nigeria: urbanization is a marked problem throughout the West African region, but so too is the urge to migrate even further, beyond the cities in Africa and on, by a very dangerous passage harassed by both police and highwaymen, to European cities as 'asylum-seekers' or simply seekers after a new life, a better career.

Unsurprisingly, this novel re-orientation towards the great city has affected dissident Islamic leaders too. The first Shaikh to re-settle his large following in a major city was Muhammad Marwa, known as *Mai Tatsine*: *c.* 1978 his followers took over a run-down quarter of Kano city while he occupied a strongly defensible house nearby. His followers, numbering over 4,000, preached and harangued young Kanawa over their love of modern gadgets, but they clashed with the police too. Joining such a group even in the late 1970s was an attractive option for youth in Kano, and it had considerable *implicit* support from much of Kano's population which had become tolerant of such pious radicalism. Hence, Mohammed Yusuf's *ahl al-sunna*, before he moved it to Maiduguri, also enjoyed support in the wider Kano urban world. Interestingly, even al-Zakzaky's movement, now re-oriented towards Shi'ism, has recently expanded hugely within the Zaria conurbation, drawing pilgrims on foot from rural towns 70–80 miles away. In short, new religious sects flourish in *cities* in a way they never did before the 1970s and 1980s. Thus radicalism became predominantly urban (though rural radicals still exist), at just the time when young men were migrating to these same cities. For them, such radicalism was new and exciting – even a group like *Kala Kato* can attract the young migrants in a city like Zaria, and they now take it back home to the countryside.[10] In short, cities are

[10] *Kala Kato* are distinctive in that they do not prostrate at prayer but remain standing up.

both where the exciting, radical preachers are and where there are plenty of young men discovering a new life far from home. For these young men such new ways of thought and faith separate them from the mind-sets of their fathers: just as the *'yan Izala* preachers showed their young audiences in the rural marketplaces what a stricter, more-modern Islam stood for, so too the new wave of radicalism, for many, pushes aside not only once-radical *Izala* but also the long-established Tijani and the neo-Qadiri ways of expressing one's faith.[11]

Previously, such *ahl al-sunna* groups had all withdrawn deep into the countryside, well away from the great cities and from government. There they could live out the Islamic model of life and prayer they advocated, quietly and undisturbed by the urban-focused administration. But these deep-rural sects do not expand, do not attract new followers, as the newer groups do: they represent the past extreme piety of their parents and grand-parents who confronted colonialism by withdrawing into isolation.[12] The new groups, then, represent a modernity that distances itself from fathers and the political elite. By their very youthfulness they are expected to be fervent, even violent in ways no proper adult would be. Radicalization, I suggest, is a horizontal process, not top-down: it spreads peer-to-peer, not father to son. If so, we need to examine what peer-to-peer groupings exist to both accommodate and inspire the migrant young amid the disorder and hardship of a new life in a great city.

It is often said that fathers today neglect their sons, and it is this that leads boys into joining gangs and criminal activities. There is certainly a tradition of 'avoidance' (*kunya*), especially for eldest sons, that may mean they seek support from other relatives, from uncles in particular, or other close mentors. But that is true of many children, daughters as well as sons, who find a special someone to whom they can relate closely, thereby learning some particular, idiosyncratic skill in farming or trade: parents are not the only resource a child has in developing a career or a talent (such as healing or hunting). Children are agents, actors in their own right, and not just pawns moved by parents. So I would argue that parental 'neglect' is not the issue. More important influences come from the particular set of friends or 'mates' that boys make outside the house. In a rural area, such

(contd) They say they are following *only* what is in the Holy Qur'an and not anything in Hadith or Sunna. Some of my rural neighbours in Katsina are young *Kala Kato*.

11 By neo-Qadiris I mean followers of Shaikh Nasiru Kabara who, in 1960s Kano, developed a Qadiri *tariqa* that used musical instruments in group *dhikri* and had spectacular processions once a year – a noisy mass movement very different from the traditional, quietist Qadiri sufism of individual scholars and *almajirai* in old Sokoto.

12 My introduction to these communities was via the late Alhaji Garba Sa'id, who as a senior member of Nigeria's Mahdiyya was very welcome whenever he visited them. The Digawa (eastern Kano) and the Salihawa (southern Katsina) are some of the oldest such pre-colonial communities that still exist; the millenarian Isawa, in response to Kano's persecution, moved to northern Zaria and became Christian in the 20th century.

groups are under everyday observation as they head off together; among them often a leader emerges, who determines what 'risky' ploys they may get up to – not just hunting but travelling to a nearby town: some boys are bolder, and one may indeed earn himself the nickname 'Risky' after some extra-daring acts.

In the city, by contrast, boys that have moved to town *on their own* need to join some existing group, which will be tougher, more criminal, than any such group they knew at home. What sort of group picks them up may well be a matter of chance, though traditionally motor parks or lorry parks were sites for all kinds of touts, especially those in pursuit of women abandoning their husbands and now in urgent need of shelter somewhere. Boys too could find work there, carrying baggage etc., or loading and unloading lorries.[13] They could sleep there too, and find food from the stalls supplying travellers. If not at the motor park, then the marketplace was the site for odd jobs, left-over food, and a place to sleep (the deserted booths offer shelter overnight). There is often a night-time community of the ultra-poor in marketplaces and lorry parks; although traditionally there was an official supervisor for such places (under the old Native Authority), much of the bureaucratic structures that once controlled them (and, crucially, provided the intelligence the security services required) have lost their edge – if indeed they remain. The constant surveillance that nervous colonial officials, fearing sedition, once instituted is no longer in place: the sheer size of cities and the mobility within them makes migrants harder than ever to track.

Until recently, a young boy could take the job of a free-lance motorcycle taxi driver (a *dan achaba*). Suitable motorbikes were available for rent from bourgeois housewives, with slightly differing contracts, some of which handed the 'machine' over to its driver after a fixed number of years. It was hard yet independent work that a money-short newcomer could break into, once he learned the geography of his new town. The maintenance of the motorbikes brought him into contact with like-minded specialists, often at permanent workshop sites. There were risks of injury, of course, but it was perhaps the *only* good work a young newcomer could find. However, state governments were against the *'yan achaba* and banned them (on health grounds, the governments said); one state government banned a particular make of motorbike (the Indian-made Boxer) because, it said, Boko Haram operatives rode them. Ordinary people liked the great convenience of *'yan achaba*, enabling one to travel anywhere cheaply, but that seemed not to convince state governments, who are more concerned with keeping their capital

[13] A particularly vivid novel set in Kano about such a boy is *The Reckless Climber* by my former colleague Ahmed Beita Yusuf (1978).

unsullied.[14] The arbitrary ban left many young men in the cities without work, angry and feeling persecuted by government – perhaps a recipe for joining a cell of Boko Haram, if not in Borno, at least in their new city.

However, there are other routes – for example, each quarter of a big city, as I have said, will have one or two gangs defending its territory from rival gangs, and these gangs may be very old, with traditions and hierarchies that bond their members closely. A newcomer to the city might well need protection and the comradeship that such a quarter-wide gang offers; as a newcomer he will have to show he is brave, resourceful and can fight. Quickly he will have to become 'street-wise' in a way that borders on the criminal. He will acquire a new name – a nickname – and need to develop a distinct personality: being a *dan kauye*, a 'country bumpkin', simply will not do.

Other such groups, but not located to specific city quarters, are the *'yan daba*, also already mentioned. These have their own camps in wasteland in the metropolitan area or in one of the many buildings under construction but temporarily abandoned by the builders. They may use drugs, intimidate local shopkeepers, or help run roadside petrol suppliers – any activity that brings in some little money that can supply their often rather minimal needs. A newcomer to the city might find shelter with them, and serve his seniors in the *daba*. It is a risky way of life that leads nowhere except, perhaps, to more organized criminality like robbery or burglary. For, in big cities too, there are organized criminal gangs not linked to city quarters but run over many years by older men (like the late *Makahon Ingla* in Kano) who presumably had come to some understanding with the local police.[15] Normally, there is a local *Sarkin Baraye* or Master of Thieves who exerts some control over regular, local criminals: it is from him that you go to recover, for a fee, your lost property after a burglary – sometimes you do get it back but not always. Children are often used for break-ins (through narrow windows), but items like motorbikes are simply stolen off the street. Not all criminals, then, come under a *Sarkin Baraye*, but a young newcomer might well find him a helpful contact to work with. The best pitches for begging or any semi-criminal activity are controlled by local bosses

[14] Boko Haram chose to use motorcycles in the big cities as they could then outrun any police in pursuit of them: Boxers were faster than anything the police had, and could go up alleyways to escape pursuers. A pillion passenger would carry the gun. Their small tricycles (*Keke NAPEP*) were not as mobile but could carry the petrol needed to set a target alight (and carry away any wounded). Similarly, in Borno's Sambisa 'forest', motorcycles can move easily and fast on paths that the army's four-wheeled vehicles cannot use; motorcycles also cost less, use less fuel, can be repaired – and are easy to steal.

[15] *Makahon Ingla* was the nickname of Kano's long-time 'top' manager of criminals; he was famous as always being based in Beirut Road, Kano, a modern shopping area. However, I did not know him personally.

who will beat up any intruder: a young newcomer cannot just move in wherever he wishes. Even gangs of disabled are run as a unit by a boss, with some of the apparently 'disabled' only pretending to lack a leg or an arm. A newcomer could join one of these 'disabled' gangs, but there are more attractive careers, it seems, in Islamic activism.

I have focused here more on criminal or semi-criminal groups that could offer shelter and work to a young boy coming for the first time to a city where he has no relatives or friends to look after him. Most such boys do indeed have contacts from their home village, but not all can look after the newcomer. If he is religiously minded he could find shelter in a *malam*'s entry-hall (the *zaure*), and sleep there: he will find other boys, usually from within the house, already sleeping there – doors to the outside are not always closed, let alone locked. Alternatively he could sleep in one of the many small mosques, whether attached to big houses or not. He might also be able to learn the long prayers for the recitation (*dhikri*) of a particular Sufi brotherhood (*tariqa*), and join in the Friday afternoon recitations, becoming a new member of a young coterie of Sufi students and the pious. Again, he would get some status in the immediate community and be given alms occasionally, but above all he would be within a new community with its own rules and patterns of acceptable behaviour. In this way it is conceivable that he might eventually drift into Islamism, as the competition between preachers, between sects, offers him more exciting possibilities – possibilities that include a newly pious lifestyle, a promise of paradise, even martyrdom. For someone currently at the bottom of the social heap, surely the promise of so much better a future is irresistible, no matter how much it may require acts that conflict with what he was taught as a child, and with the cultural milieu he knows as 'Hausa' or 'Kanuri'.

Conclusion

In this essay, I have focused on childhood and youth in a northern Nigerian, Muslim context as I have seen it over the last 50 years. I offer the essay tentatively, as no doubt many readers will have had markedly different insights through their own lifetimes. But I think it is worthwhile to open a conversation – dialogue rather than debate – and see what develops from a pooling of our insights into the crises that can occur within families and within individual lives in northern Nigeria. One dimension is clear to me: modes of growing up have changed enormously in Hausaland, yet there are many parents and children seeking to maintain, against the odds, the values that they inherited from the past and want to retain into the future.

So what have I suggested as a route to radicalization in Hausaland? First, that cities, rather than the countryside, is where radical sects now recruit their most active followers. Their followers are more often immigrants into cities rather than locally born: the local-born have their family structures in place, and have ways of earning money and getting jobs that young new immigrants do not have. In short, radical sects offer a *replacement* moral context and comrades ('brothers', *ikhwan*) for newcomers who have left behind their original, rural context. Furthermore, city governments have banned the young man's classic occupation of *achaba*, almost to spite them as a despised, unkempt, drug-addicted (and politically suspect) group that opposed the agents of government's new, often wilful *hisba*. Next, I emphasize that there is indeed a long tradition, in Nigeria as elsewhere, for youth to be the main vehicles, the key agents, of radical reform and are usually empowered by society to perform, if necessary, the acts of violence that implement reforms against any opposition either from the old or from outside. In short, isn't youth doing what all youth does, once it is beyond the older generation's control? I do not think there is any special, extraordinary element in Hausa or Kanuri culture that in itself promotes Islamic radicalism in the very young. The crucial element has been the inner drive to migrate to the big cities, and to find a new life there. Once the countryside starts to empty, why stay there, why *not* go with the tide?

Thus Boko Haram, with its charismatic, articulate preachers, offered what seemed a very rare opportunity to any migrant young man who was looking to make a good future somehow for himself. Excitingly radical religious movements, especially ones that claim also to be both 'ultra-modern' and 'global', do not come by often in northern Nigeria – and this one was making promises that sounded convincing; and many were already joining it. Furthermore, the remarkable 'victories' that Boko Haram was having in its jihad against the government would suggest that Allah had given His blessing to Boko Haram's cause. I doubt if the bloodthirsty element – the killings and the loot – was then as obvious or as off-putting as it is now to us outside observers looking back. Instead, Boko Haram may have seemed, to the naïve at least, as their last chance to behave righteously before the Day of Judgement, arguably imminent, came upon them. If they passed up this opportunity, would there ever be another one in their lifetime?

Finally, that 'new life' involves a radically new *identity* and the shedding of the familiar old one. No longer has the migrant an acceptable career ahead of him, as farmer or craftsman, and his family's home and name to inherit. No longer can he be sure of soon being given a wife with whom to start a household of his own. Indeed his old identity (*asali*, *iri*) could be a liability in the city: he might even be bearing the old-fashioned, ineradicable *asali*/identity marks cut onto his cheeks:[16] laughed at (or cheated) as a country bumpkin (*dan kauye),* he is an easy victim of the city-slickers (*'yan birni*). However, another part of that old identity was also his very pious upbringing, of saying (even leading) the family prayers without fail: more than once have I come across young girls running at home a miniature *madrasa,* regularly teaching the Qur'an (and some Arabic) to their siblings. Inside households there is often a genuine 'fear of Allah' (*tsoron Allah*) that permeates daily life – to the extent that if a small child's death should take place on a *Friday*, it can be piously accepted as specifically a blessing from Allah. My suggestion, then, is that, for a young migrant from such a culturally pious milieu, joining the *jama'a* of a charismatic preacher offers a new, highly prized identity, as well as a new career, and maybe even a new bride. All successful Shaikhs in northern Nigeria have had given them the financial means for providing for the social welfare of their *jama'a* – whether 'Uthman 'dan Fodio in the past or more recently Muhammad Marwa (with his *'yan Tatsine*) and al-Zakzaky (with his *'yan Shia*). In the quest for a respected new identity, is not one like theirs impossible to resist?

But, one might ask, if it is so irresistible, why do not all of northern Nigeria's migrant youth join? An answer, I think, lies partly in a deep-set distaste, even contempt, for violence in Hausa culture, most obviously among the mature but also among all the young whom I have known. Boko Haram's recruits, if they are Hausa, have had to put that distaste to one side – is that the price they accept for their new, prized identity? But this core-cultural ambivalence over violence may underlie the widespread yet necessarily tacit, secret sympathy that is shown to such groups, as was heard in 1980, to the surprise of researchers in Kano, after the army's destruction there of all the *'yan Tatsine.* The Hausa population, at heart, may be 'radical' but not rashly revolutionary.[17] So it is their young who,

[16] These marks are rarely inscribed on very young boys nowadays, but in the pre-colonial past they were invaluable for broadly identifying the origins of children or adults who had been abducted. They mainly indicated Hausa-speaking sub-ethnic groups (such as *Kanawa, Kutumbawa, Katsinawa, Katukawa, Gobirawa,* etc.) but also, humorously, a recent Mercedes model with a striking rear-end (*baGobiri*).

[17] It is important to keep in mind when discussing violence that sharia distinguishes between the rules for jihad (*siyar*) and what is allowed for a raid (*ghazw*). Jihad can only be *defensive*, when the Muslim *jama'a* has already been attacked by government forces: hence Shaikh 'Uthman Dan Fodio *c.* 1804 explicitly launched his jihad only after his people were attacked by Gobiri forces. So too with *Mai Tatsine* and Boko Haram's Mohammed Yusuf; the police, they both said, harassed their people first. Much of the subsequent fighting was then done under rules for raiding; only the rare major 'battles' were fought under jihad rules. Raiding was done to get supplies for the *jama'a* and raise from loot or ransoms the finance to fund and arm the jihad. The actual, detailed economy of the Sokoto jihad, and now of Boko Haram, has to be researched seriously (Last 2018). Local people may in principle support jihad, but dislike the raiding: they may change sides over time. This at root is the dilemma – and tragedy – of violence for the leaders, the led and their victims: ideals perish too. But do histories try to cover up the resulting, disturbing dismay?

at the start of a Boko Haram attack on an urban police station, were once heard saying repeatedly to onlookers that they were doing 'Allah's work' (*aikin Allah*), yet often also politely adding, to anyone put in danger by it, a courteous *gafara dai* ('excuse me').[18]

[18] As told to me by a local resident there at the time, my colleague the late Garba Ilyasu of Rijiya Hudu. The attackers, with grenades in a bag and AK-47s, were dressed neatly in clean trousers and shirts and arrived, and left two hours later, in a smart if stolen Honda Civic (supposedly Boko Haram's favourite car). The goods of traders nearby were unspoilt.

Bibliography

Beita Yusuf, A., 1978, *The Reckless Climber*, Ibadan: Onibonoje Publishers.

Casey, C., 2008, '"Marginal Muslims": Politics and the Perceptual Bounds of Islamic Authenticity in Northern Nigeria', Special issue: Muslim West Africa in the Age of Neoliberalism, B. Soares and M.N. LeBlanc, guest editors, *Africa Today* 54 (3), 67–94.

Cohen, C., 2015, 'Boko Haram and the Impossible Political Sociology of an Armed Group: Catalysing Armed Violence Region-wide', *Afrique contemporaine* 3 (255), 71–87.

Dan Asabe, A.U. 1991, 'Yandaba: The 'Terrorists' of Kano Metropolitan?' in Youth & Health in Kano Today, *Kano Studies*, special issue, edited by M. Last, Kano: Bayero University, 85–111.

Haruna, M.A. and Abdullahi, S.A., 1991, 'The "Soccer Craze" and Club Formation among Hausa Youth in Kano, Nigeria' in Youth & Health in Kano Today, *Kano Studies*, special issue, edited by M. Last, Kano: Bayero University, 113–24.

Hoechner, H., 2018, *Quranic Schools in Northern Nigeria: Everyday Experiences of Youth, Faith, and Poverty*, London: International African Institute; Cambridge, UK: Cambridge University Press.

Jammeh, K., 2009, *Journey of Misery*, Fulladu: Banjul.

Last, M., 1979, 'Some Economic Aspects of Conversion in Hausaland', in N. Levtzion (ed.), *Conversion to Islam*, New York: Holmes & Meier, 236–46.

—— 1991a, 'Adolescents in a Muslim city: The Cultural Context of Danger and Risk', in 'Youth & Health in Kano Today', *Kano Studies*, special issue, edited by M. Last, Kano: Bayero University, 3–17.

—— 1991b, 'Spirit Possession as Therapy: Bori among Non-Muslims in Nigeria', in I.M. Lewis, A. Al-Safi and S. Hurreiz (eds), *Women's Medicine: The Zar-Bori Cult in Africa and Beyond*, Edinburgh: Edinburgh University Press, 49–63.

—— 1992, 'The Importance of Extremes: The Social Implications of Intra-Household Variation in Child Mortality', *Social Science and Medicine* 35 (6), 799–810.

—— 1993a, 'The Power of Youth, Youth of Power: Notes on the Religions of the Young in Northern Nigeria', in H. d'Almeida-Topor, C. Coquery-Vidrovitch, O. Goerg and F. Guitart (eds), *Les jeunes en Afrique*, Paris: L'Harmattan, 375–99.

—— 1993b, 'The Traditional Muslim Intellectual in Hausaland: The Background', in T. Falola (ed.), *African Historiography*, Harlow: Longman, 116–31.

—— 2000a, 'Children and the Experience of Violence: Contrasting Cultures of Punishment in Northern Nigeria', *Africa* 70 (3), 359–93.

—— 2000b, 'Social Exclusion in Northern Nigeria', in Jane Hubert (ed.), *Madness, Disability and Social Exclusion: The Archaeology and Anthropology of 'Difference'*, London: Routledge, 217–39.

—— 2005, 'Towards a Political History of Youth in Muslim Northern Nigeria 1750–2000', in J. Abbink and I. van Kessel (eds), *Vanguard or Vandals: Youth, Politics and Conflict in Africa*, Leiden: Brill, 37–54.

—— 2008, 'The Search for Security in Muslim Northern Nigeria', *Africa* 78 (1), 41–63.

—— 2011, 'Another Geography: Risks to Health as Perceived in a Deep-Rural Environment in Hausaland', *Anthropology & Medicine* 18 (2), 217–29.

—— 2014, 'From Dissent to Dissidence: The Genesis & Development of Reformist Islamic Groups in Northern Nigeria', in A.R. Mustapha (ed.), *Sects & Social Disorder: Muslim Identities & Conflict in Northern Nigeria*, Woodbridge: James Currey, 18–53.

—— 2018, 'Slavery or Death in Sokoto: Tactics, Legality and Sources', in T. Green and B. Rossi (eds), *Landscapes, Sources and Intellectual Projects of the West African Past*, Leiden: Brill, 422–42.

—— 2019, 'Medical Ethnography Over Time: Penetrating "the Fog of Health" in a Nigerian Community, 1970–2017', *Anthropology in Action* 26 (1), 52–60.

Sa'ad, A.-M., 1989, 'In Search of Justice for Nigeria: A Critical Analysis of Formal and Informal Justice in Gongola State', D.Phil. thesis, University of Sussex.

Ware, R., 2014, *The Walking Qur'an: Islamic History, Embodied Knowledge and History in West Africa*, Chapel Hill: University of North Carolina Press.

9

Informalization & its discontents
The informal economy & Islamic radicalization in northern Nigeria

KATE MEAGHER & IBRAHIM HARUNA HASSAN

Introduction

The economic factors underlying violent radicalization are often less clear cut than political and religious factors. High levels of poverty, unemployment and illiteracy in northern Nigeria have been contrasted with lower levels of deprivation in southern Nigeria, particularly in the South West of the country. However, very few poor northern Nigerian Muslims have succumbed to radicalization, and not all Islamic radicals are poor, raising questions about why some poor northern Muslims become radicalized while others do not, and what other factors intervene in the process of radicalization. This study moves away from a general poverty perspective on drivers of radicalization to focus more explicitly on how dynamics of economic informality have shaped and sometimes mitigated radicalization processes, often in unexpected ways.

In northern Nigeria, a particularly negative convergence of high rates of population growth, low levels of educational attainment and a collapse of formal economic opportunities in the wake of market reforms have devastated the local economy. In the Nigerian context where few can afford open unemployment, the stresses of poverty and joblessness are largely played out in the informal economy. In Nigeria's large informal economy, which accounts for 80 per cent of the non-agricultural employment, poverty and disaffection interact with ethnically and religiously based forms of economic organization, creating tensions and opportunities that cast important light on the trajectories of Islamic radicalization (ILO 2018; Meagher 2009, 2013). An informal-economy-centred analysis offers a more complex understanding of how poverty and unemployment interact with issues of competition, disaffection, religious networks and experiences of the state. Instead of focusing on the failure of the formal economy to provide jobs, this study will concentrate on the radicalizing and counter-radicalizing implications of structures and networks within the informal economy, which shapes how the overwhelming majority of northern Nigeria's formally unemployed actually live, work and experience the state.

This chapter will explore whether, in absorbing the unemployed and disaffected, the informal economy serves as an incubator of radicalization or as a buffer against it. Attention will focus on how high unemployment has interacted with shifting patterns of educational attainment, political claims, and new religious movements to restructure channels of economic opportunity and political expression among the informally employed. In the process, this study will draw attention to the emergence of pressures within the informal economy that may exacerbate dynamics of radicalization, while highlighting the potential as well as the limits of the informal economy as a field of counter-radicalization.

The chapter will begin with a background section covering policy perspectives and economic and religious realities in northern Nigeria. It will then outline the methodology used in the study, and turn to an exploration of five dimensions of radicalizing pressures building up in the northern Nigerian informal economy. These five dimensions include pressures on ownership of informal businesses, the penetration of indigeneity politics into the informal economy, competition from more-educated entrepreneurs, new Salafist pressures, and the strain of security measures on informal livelihoods. This will be followed by concluding thoughts about how to move ideas about radicalization and counter-radicalization beyond abstract notions of poverty, unemployment and informality to engage with the specific risks and institutional processes that shape the drivers of Islamic radicalization in northern Nigeria.

Informality, radicalization and counter-radicalization

Understanding the economic context of radicalization requires an assessment of the religious context within which dynamics of aspiration, marginalization, and disaffection have given rise to violent religious extremism. This section will review prevailing policy perspectives on economic informality and religious violence and consider how they intersect with the economic and religious climate of radicalization in northern Nigeria.

REFLECTIONS ON POLICY PERSPECTIVES

Research and policy reflections on the role of the informal economy in driving or mitigating violence and social conflict tend to fall into two broad categories: those who view the informal economy as a driver of conflict and social radicalization, and those who view it as a counter-radicalizing force that mitigates unemployment and social tensions. Mainstream economic thinking tends to see the informal economy as a drag on growth and job creation, as well as associating informality with criminality and a 'culture of non-compliance', owing to its association with lack of registration, non-payment of taxes, and a tendency to live and operate businesses on the wrong side of the law (ILO and WTO 2009; Perry et al. 2007; Bayart et al. 1999). Others see the informal economy as a breeding ground for anger and disaffection as informally employed youth are subject to marginalization and poverty. A report from the Brookings Institution (Bhatia and Ghanem 2017,10) sees educated youth as particularly vulnerable to radicalization when lack of jobs forces them to 'join the informal sector where wages are low and where there is no job security or social protection. Whether unemployed or underemployed in the informal sector, educated youth feel that they have a serious grievance against society.'

The predominantly ethnic and religious structure of informal enterprise networks in many African informal economies, including Nigeria, has also raised concerns about the vulnerability of the informal economy to religious radicalization. For example, Muslim Hausa-Fulani networks dominate butchering, as well as livestock, grain and currency trading, while Christian Igbo networks are the dominant players in auto-parts, electrical goods and used clothing (Hashim and Meagher 1999; Meagher 2010; Onokheroye 1977). These long-standing specializations have bred a significant degree of efficiency and institutional development within these activities. However, they have also embedded ethnic and religious differences within the structure of the informal economy. Studies of religious conflict have emphasized the importance of ethnically and religiously integrated organizations as key to preventing conflict (Varshney 2001; Armakolas 2011). From this perspective, the structure of the Nigerian informal economy suggests a vulnerability to conflict rather than stabilization, given the ethno-religious structure of many informal economic networks and associations.

A contrary trend in the literature argues that, far from increasing social vulnerability to conflict and radicalization, the informal economy tends to limit conflict and stave off pressures associated with radicalization. Studies of youth unemployment in Africa emphasize the importance of the informal economy for creating employment and absorbing unemployed youth (Ibrahim Forum 2012; African Development Bank et al. 2010; Meagher 2016). De Soto (2014) and others argue that violent radicalization is not a product of poverty and informality, but of negative encounters of informal actors with the state, where they are routinely subject to harassment, extortion and negative policy attitudes on the part of officials. These studies highlight the role of the informal economy as a source of youth entrepreneurship and ingenuity, and emphasize its potential for reducing unemployment and feelings of desperation, which have been identified as drivers of radicalization.

A number of studies of religiously based informal enterprise networks in developing countries have highlighted their ability to bridge ethnic and religious divides through symbiotic economic relations and the development of integrative business institutions (Jha 2007; Lovejoy 1980; Meagher 2007, 2013). Far from fostering divisions, evidence from India and West Africa indicates that symbiotic patterns of occupational specialization along religious lines are associated with inter-religious cooperation and economic growth and efficiency. Research on northern as well as southern Nigeria has detailed the role of informal enterprise networks in resolving conflict and stemming radicalization through economic interdependence, cross-religious credit networks, and social ties between Muslim and Christian informal business groups (Meagher 2009; 2013).

The main weakness of perspectives that view the informal economy as either a driver of radicalization or counter-radicalization is that they tend to encourage a view of the informal economy as a force that stands outside society, fostering or absorbing vulnerabilities to radicalization within the wider society. The reality is that the informal economy exists within these societies, and the pressures and opportunities that affect social order also strengthen or weaken the organizational capacities of the informal economy. A clearer understanding of how contemporary economic pressures and opportunities have reshaped the informal economy in northern Nigeria is essential to evaluating who wins and who loses from these changes, and the implications for radicalization or counter-radicalization.

The northern Nigerian informal economic context

Situating processes of Islamic radicalization requires a closer consideration of the effects of contemporary economic restructuring in Nigeria. A decade of economic resurgence, averaging 7 per cent annual growth rates, has been accompanied by rising poverty and unemployment. Despite robust growth performance, poverty has actually increased from 52 per cent of the population living on less than US $1 per day in 2004 to 61 per cent in 2010 (National Bureau of Statistics hereafter NBS 2010, 5). By May 2018, Nigeria overtook India for the highest number of people in extreme poverty (Kharas et al. 2018). By late 2018, youth unemployment and under-employment stood at 55.4 per cent (NBS 2018). With a young population growing at 3.2 per cent per year, unemployment and informality are set to expand further (NBS 2017, 12).

These worrying statistical trends are rendered even more alarming by the pronounced regional inequalities in their distribution. Poverty, illiteracy and unemployment are markedly higher in the north than in the southern zones of the country. Poverty levels in the core northern states are some 40 per cent higher than in the South West zone, unemployment is three times as high, and illiteracy is four times and high – 64 per cent of the population has no Western education at all (NBS 2010, 5; National Population Commission 2011, 13, 16). These patterns reflect the ways in which pressures of economic restructuring and globalization have exacerbated rather than eased long-standing patterns of regional inequality. A history of educational disadvantage in the Muslim north has left the population poorly equipped to seize the new opportunities created by Nigeria's economic resurgence. Employment in the educationally disadvantaged northern states was dominated by agriculture and formal sector employment, both of which have declined dramatically. Rapid population growth, declining investment in smallholder agriculture and problems of recurrent drought have decimated the northern rural economy, while legacies of indirect rule, resistance to Western education, and the downsizing of public employment have gutted the urban economy. The textile industry, once the nation's largest industrial employer, was concentrated in the northern states of Kano and Kaduna, and has all but collapsed under the pressures of economic liberalization. Low levels of formal education have left northerners poorly positioned to take up new formal sector opportunities in the financial and service sectors, which demand high levels of education and technical skills (Treichel 2010).

Since the 1980s, policies aimed at restructuring the formal economy have also restructured the informal economy. In particular, unemployment and falling real incomes in the formal sector have dramatically altered the social composition of the Nigerian informal economy. Since the 1990s, the class, gender, ethnic and religious profile of informal activities in Nigeria has changed markedly (Meagher 2007, 2010). These changes have involved increased entry into the informal economy by more-educated and middle-class actors, a greater incursion of men into lucrative women's activities, and the penetration of new ethnic and religious groups into formerly ethnically specialized activities. New religious movements have also played a key role in processes of informal economic restructuring, particularly evangelical Christianity and reformist Islam (Kane 2003; Meagher 2009). There is also evidence that repeated rounds of violent religious conflict in the wider society have begun to erode institutions of inter-religious cooperation within the informal economy (Meagher 2013). These tumultuous changes have intensified competition within the informal economy, leading to greater polarization along class as well as ethnic and religious lines, and increasing vulnerability to aggressive forms of religious mobilization.

Economic informality and the religious climate

The social restructuring of the Nigerian informal economy has not undermined its remarkable economic dynamism, but responding to new economic challenges has triggered intensifying internal differentiation and inequality. The heart of the matter lies in way poverty and inequality have been mediated through religious and political processes. Two issues are central to the ways in which religious and political processes have shaped the vulnerability to extremism within the northern Nigerian informal economy. These involve the role of Islamic reformist movements in economic transformations within the informal economy, and the intensification of religious and political intolerance toward poor and marginal Muslims. Key among the new religious movements are the Wahhabist movement *Jama'tu Izalatil Bid'a wa Iqamat al-Sunna* (Society for the Eradication of Innovation and Reinstatement of Tradition), popularly known as 'Izala', established in 1978, followed by fully Salafist movements in the 1990s, some of whom referred to themselves as *Ahl al-Sunna* (Thurston 2016).

Ousmane Kane (2003) and others have highlighted the role of Izala and other Wahhabi/Salafi movements in promoting an ethic of frugality and economic advancement through an emphasis on piety, education, modesty, minimal ceremonial expenditure, and the greater economic and educational advancement of women (Thurston 2016). In particular, Salafist movements have appealed to northern Nigerian artisans, small traders and aspiring middle classes hard hit by the depredations of structural adjustment (Kane 2003; Labazee 1995). From above, however, Wahhabi/Salafi movements have led campaigns for the Islamic capture of state institutions, accompanied by intensifying religious intolerance, which have spread across the core northern states since the turn of the millennium. Salafi encouragement of increased political engagement has been accompanied by increasingly sharp denunciation of non-Salafi Muslims (Wakili 2009; Mustapha 2014). Commentators have drawn attention to the tendency of pro-Sharia politics in Kano and other northern states to elide Muslim identities with discourses of ethnicity, indigeneity and Islamic propriety in ways that have intensified discrimination not only against Christians but against ethnic minority Muslims and the poor (Casey 2008; Sanusi 2003; Hashim and Walker 2014). In the process, new economic opportunities within the informal economy have been accompanied by new tensions between successful and less successful informal actors, and between poor migrants and the state.

Far from acting as a driver of or bulwark against radicalization, the northern Nigerian informal economy has been transformed in the process of absorbing new pressures and opportunities. It has served as a site of new opportunity for some, while being subject to rapid entry and greater social and economic polarization. How have these changing realities interacted with processes of Islamic radicalization? Can the northern Nigerian informal economy continue to absorb mounting numbers of unemployed without dysfunctional levels of competition or erosion of livelihoods? Have new technologies and new religious movements transformed the potential of the informal economy for accumulation and employment generation? Focusing on the way in which these various pressures and opportunities are playing themselves out offers a lens into the dynamics of radicalization within the northern Nigerian informal economy.

Methodology

In order to explore the structure of the northern Nigerian informal economy and its implications for Islamic radicalization, this study examines the characteristics of a range of Muslim-dominated informal activities in economically dynamic northern Nigerian cities. For reasons of security and time constraints, it was not possible to carry out the research in the North East zone. Instead, the research was carried out in the North West cities of Kano and Kaduna in 2014, when Boko Haram was still active in both cities. Three categories of activities were selected for the study:

- *Modern activities* (tailors, motorized rickshaw operators, and CD and phone-card distributors – also referred to as media distributors): these activities involve modern technology, social status befitting educated entrants, and offer significant opportunities for economic advancement;
- *Traditional activities* (butchers and traditional restaurants/food sellers): these activities lack modern technology, have low social status but offer opportunities for economic advancement; food sellers represent the only female dominated activity;
- *Survival activities* (hawkers, load carriers and motorcycle taxi operators): these activities may or may not use modern technology, but are arduous, low status, and offer little or no prospects for economic advancement.

While different categories of informal activities involve variations in socio-economic background, economic prospects and gender composition, they also involve different experiences with the state. More respectable modern activities are relatively shielded from negative experiences with the state owing to their location and social standing. Conversely, lowly survival activities or those dominated by women are more vulnerable to official harassment and more exposed to the dangers of violence and insecurity. To the extent possible, matching activities were investigated in the two cities. However, some variation was necessary owing to the banning of motorcycle taxis in Kano but not in Kaduna, necessitating minor adjustments in activity coverage in order to maintain balance in the three activity categories.

Fieldwork involved identifying the main concentrations of stationary activities, and the main gathering points of mobile activities, and contacting informal actors in their shops, gathering points and associational headquarters across the two cities. Information was gathered through 18 interviews with leadership and branch executives of 12 key enterprise associations in the various activities; 35 interviews with rank-and-file members across the various activities, and 8 focus group discussions across a variety of activities. Interviews were used to develop a brief survey of key characteristics and attitudes, which was administered by trained research assistants and one researcher to 187 informal operators across the 8 study activities (tailors, motorized rickshaw operators, compact disk (CD) and phone-card distributors, butchers, traditional restauranteurs, load carriers, motorcycle taxis drivers and hawkers), involving 90 in Kano and 97 in Kaduna. The survey focused on education, past activities, economic concerns, changes in religious affiliation, experiences of religious violence, attitudes to the state, and experiences with the police and security services. By analysing variations in the experience of informal actors, this study explores how economic prospects, social status, interaction with the state, and vulnerability to religious violence interact with a range of social characteristics to shape vulnerability to radicalization. Rather than focusing on the experience of Boko Haram members, the study focused on identifying stresses that heightened the risk of Islamic radicalization among some informal actors, while noting what made others less vulnerable to radical mobilization.

Informal activities in Kano and Kaduna: characteristics and perspectives

A look at the social profile of the informal operators (firm heads) in Kano and Kaduna reveals some important developments (Table 9.1). Given the focus on northern Muslims, the low participation of women is not surprising owing to the widespread practice of female seclusion, particularly among the less privileged sectors of society. While women perform a range of informal activities inside their compounds, the short

Table 9.1 Selected informal firm characteristics in Kaduna and Kano (percentage of firm heads)

City	Female	State indigene	Aged 15–30 years	Secondary education or more	Previous formal job	Previous activity
Kaduna	16.5	36.1	36.1	32.0	11.3	55.7
Kano	17.8	75.6	40.0	53.3	14.4	53.3
Average	17.1	55.1	38.0	42.2	12.8	54.5

(Source: Fieldwork, 2014)

research period made it impossible to cover such activities (Hill 1969). However, female representation in the sample was ensured through the inclusion of traditional restaurants, an activity performed in the open air by northern Muslim women. This activity constitutes the bulk of women in the sample, with the exception of a few women tailors and phone-card distributors of southern and Middle-belt Muslim origins.

A further issue to note is the comparatively high participation of state indigenes. Many of these informal activities, particularly lowly activities such as hawking and load carrying, have historically been the preserve of poor migrants. However, high unemployment and religious violence has shifted participation toward indigenes, who make up 55 per cent of the sample, and over three-quarters of those interviewed in Kano. Equally notable is the high participation of youth.[1] Young people aged 30 and under make up 38 per cent of the sample, rising as high as 40 per cent in Kano. Perhaps the most striking characteristic, particularly given the northern Nigerian context and the prominence of a range of fairly lowly activities such as butchers, load carriers and hawkers, is the comparatively high level of education of informal sector participants. More than 40 per cent of operators in the sample have secondary school education or more. Indeed, more than 10 per cent of the sample are diploma or degree holders – an issue that will be explored in more detail below. It is also noteworthy that fewer than 13 per cent of the sample has ever held a formal job, although more than half of the sample in both cities has engaged in previous economic activities, including farming, house guard, black market petrol seller, bus conductor, butcher, bricklayer and trader in various commodities.

Table 9.2 indicates the distribution of the three strata of informal activities: modern, traditional and survival activities. The activities are relatively evenly distributed across the two cities, with roughly one-third of actors in each city in each activity category. Only 15 per cent of the activities are

[1] The age range 15–30 was chosen as a compromise between the international (15–24) and the Nigerian (15–35) definitions of youth.

Table 9.2 Formal registration and distribution of modern, traditional and survival activities in Kaduna and Kano (percentage of firm heads)

City	Modern activity	Traditional activity	Survival activity	Registered
Kaduna	37.1	30.9	32.0	13.4
Kano	33.3	33.3	33.3	17.8
Average	35.3	32.1	32.6	15.5

(Source: Fieldwork, 2014)

formally registered, including a few CD distributors, tailors and butchers, and a significant share of load carriers who are required to register formally in certain sectors of porterage. However, registration alone does not constitute the only boundary of informality. Even registered concerns remain embedded in informal economic relations of taxation, labour relations and business systems (Meagher 2010).

Interviews confirmed that many actors in the modern and traditional activities feel that they can make a good living from their activity, including funding personal advancement, education and, where desired, education of children. However, some actors in both categories, particularly butchers and motorized rickshaw operators, expressed concerns that increased entry of competition was pushing down incomes in their activity. Those in survival activities tended to associate their activities with getting by, though 21 per cent of them used survival activities to fund further education in the hope of moving on to something better.

A final general observation relates to the importance of these activities in informal employment. Estimates by tailors' associations put the number of tailors in Kano and Kaduna at about 20,000 in each city, while the butchers' association in Kano estimated their number to be about 10,000 in Kano alone. The motorized rickshaw operators' association in Kano showed a registered membership of 27,449, while the motorcycle taxi association in Kaduna put their numbers at 23,400 in late 2011. Even these patchy numbers indicate employment levels approaching 100,000 across barely half of the study activities in two cities. This signals the importance of these activities in informal employment if these numbers were scaled up across northern Nigeria.

Differentiation, economic change and radicalization within the informal economy

Examining informal activities from the perspective of stratified activity categories gives a clearer sense of cooperative structures and fault lines

Table 9.3 Gender, indigeneity and age by activity type (percentage of firm heads)

Activity type	Female	Indigene	Age 15–30	Age 31–45	Age 46–60	Age over 60
Modern	7.6	63.6	45.5	43.9	9.1	1.5
Traditional	45.0	58.3	18.3	56.7	16.7	8.3
Survival	0.0	42.6	49.2	41.0	6.6	3.3
Average	17.1	55.1	38.0	47.1	10.7	4.3

(Source: Fieldwork, 2014)

within the northern Nigerian informal economy. Despite a fairly even distribution of activity categories across the two study cities, Table 9.3 shows a concentration of indigenes in the most lucrative category: modern activities. By contrast, women are concentrated in traditional activities, though this is largely an artefact of the main female activity chosen. Also striking is the heavy concentration of youth in modern and survival activities; nearly 50 per cent of actors in both activity categories are aged 30 or under. By contrast, traditional activities are biased toward older age categories, with only 18 per cent being aged 30 or under, owing to a combination of traditional training hierarchies and social norms that restrict traditional restaurants to divorced and widowed women.

Using the lens of stratified activity categories, a closer look at contemporary developments in Kano and Kaduna reveals a number of emerging tensions. These centre around ownership, indigeneity, education, religion and security. Drawing on evidence from interviews and the survey, these issues will be taken up one by one.

OWNERSHIP

The different activity categories show important variations in activity history. As shown in Table 9.4, both modern and survival activities have a much higher share of involvement in previous activities, and a greater incidence of prior involvement in formal sector activities. Half of those in modern activities have worked in a previous activity, and nearly 20 per cent have worked in the formal sector, in jobs like civil servants or white collar activities such as teachers or bank employees. In survival activities, a surprising 80 per cent were involved in prior activities, but just over 10 per cent previously held a formal sector job, dominated by workers in private companies. Given fairly similar age profiles and length of time in their current activity – both around 10 years – modern activities are more indicative of a process of working one's way up through

Table 9.4 Activity history and ownership status by activity type (percentage of firm heads)

Activity type	Previous activity	Formal sector activity	Years in this activity	Owner	Hire-purchase	Work on commission
Modern	50.0	18.2	10.4	73.8	7.7	18.5
Traditional	33.3	8.3	15.3	79.3	1.7	19.0
Survival	80.3	11.5	9.6	53.3	16.7	30.0
Average	54.5	12.8	11.7	68.9	8.7	22.4

(Source: Fieldwork, 2014)

the informal system or of access to capital to enter at a fairly lucrative level, while survival activities suggest a context of economic instability and lack of opportunity to move beyond the survival level. By contrast, those in traditional activities show more stable occupational histories and less exposure to formal sector work. With an average of 15 years in their current occupation, only one-third had a previous activity, and fewer than 10 per cent have held a formal sector job.

What is particularly striking about the ownership profile is the significant level of hire-purchase and work on commission in what are perceived to be owner-operated enterprises. In such cases, those identified as heads of informal firms are not necessarily the owners of the firms. Predictably, modern and traditional activities show comparatively high levels of owner-operated businesses, with more than 70 per cent in both categories owning their businesses. However, even in these more stable categories of activity, there is a notable level of hire-purchase in modern activities, and nearly 20 per cent work on commission in both categories. Hire-purchase in modern activities is attributable largely to motorized rickshaw operators, over one-third of whom bought their vehicles on hire-purchase arrangements or received them through political hire-purchase job-creation initiatives, though in interviews some commented that such arrangements were un-Islamic. Commission work is concentrated among motorized rickshaw operators and some tailors, who operate businesses owned by civil servants or other middle-class actors that own the machines but do not run the business. In a focus group discussion, some tailors referred to this as a modern way to enter the tailoring business, by running tailoring enterprises as an investment in which trained tailors are hired as workers for an absentee entrepreneur who supplies the capital.

By contrast, the table (9.4) shows that barely half of those in survival activities run their own business, with 17 per cent, particularly motorcycle taxis in Kaduna, working on hire-purchase arrangements. This includes some load carriers who do not own their wheelbarrows outright.

A worrying one-third of survivalists work on commission, spread across motorcycle taxi operators, load carriers and hawkers, who worked for the owners of the equipment or the trade goods and paid a commission on the daily turnover. Given an average time in the activity of 10 years, the high share of survivalists who do not own their business cannot simply be put down to the process of getting started. Indeed, the average number of years in business of survivalists who owned their business, relative to those engaged in hire-purchase arrangements and those working on commission was nine years in each category. Rather than serving purely as entrepreneurial opportunities for the unemployed, informal activities are being turned into an investment opportunity for some elements of the middle class.

INDIGENEITY

In the face of jobless growth in the formal sector, and rapid entry of a growing youth population into various types of informal employment, indigeneity has become a point of contestation over access to informal activities. In Nigeria, many forms of access to public sector benefits, such as scholarships or public sector employment, are obtained on the basis of being an indigene of a given state, rather than on the basis of national-level citizenship (Mustapha 1998). Conventionally invoked in struggles over public sector jobs, in this study indigeneity was widely invoked in struggles over access to informal work, even in some of the lowliest sectors, such as load carriers. Across a range of lowly as well as lucrative informal activities, concerns were raised about non-indigenes crowding out indigenes and driving down incomes. As shown by Table 9.5, indigenes make up over 40 per cent of operators in survival activities. What is particularly striking is the large number of indigenes in modern and survival activities that have secondary school education or more. Even in the educationally disadvantaged north of Nigeria, 43 per cent of indigenes in modern activities, and nearly one-third of those in survival activities, have comparatively high levels of education, rather than being forced into the informal economy by inadequate education.

The majority of informal actors in all three categories of activities felt that the share of indigenes in their activity had been rising – a perception shared by non-indigenes as well as indigenes. An elderly load carrier in Kano, himself an indigene, commented that the activity used to be the preserve of poor migrants from the drier areas of the far north and Niger. But, with the collapse of formal sector industry, and the lack of alternatives sources of income, indigenes were rushing into load carrying and other menial informal activities. Among motorized rickshaw operators – a particularly politicized activity owing to its centrality

Table 9.5 The roles of state indigenes in informal economy participation by activity type (percentage of firm heads)

Activity type	Share of indigenes	Indigenes with secondary education or more	Perception of rising share of indigenes in activity	Negative attitude to entry of non-indigenes
Modern	63.6	42.8	84.6	34.4
Traditional	58.3	13.3	60.3	30.0
Survival	42.6	31.1	63.3	42.6
Average	55.1	29.4	69.9	35.7

(Source: Fieldwork, 2014)

in security concerns as well as political job-creation schemes – there was a strong resistance to the entry of non-indigenes in the business. It was repeatedly claimed that non-indigenes did not know the town properly, overcharged customers, had rough driving habits, and were a security risk. Many also expressed concerns about saturated markets, and the importance of keeping non-indigenes out of the business in order to prevent incomes from falling. Particular concerns were expressed about the influx of former motorcycle taxi operators from Kano after the activity was banned there.

Tailors, butchers and traditional restaurants operators were generally more positive about the skills and variety gained from the entry of non-indigenes, and about the ability of the market to absorb them. A stronger sense of occupational solidarity appeared to pervade these activities, particularly among traditional activities where there was little pressure from secondary-educated indigenes. Negative attitudes to the entry of non-indigenes were particularly pronounced in survival activities, given their low incomes and a comparatively high share of secondary-educated indigenes, with 43 per cent indicating that the entry of non-indigenes was not good for business. In modern activities, by contrast, higher incomes and barriers to entry produced less resistance to the entry of non-indigenes, despite higher levels of secondary-educated indigenes in these activities. It is significant, however that, even in activities where concerns were more moderate, roughly one-third of informal actors were resistant to the entry of non-indigenes.

Some non-indigenes in these activities experienced the growing hostility to their presence in terms of discrimination at the hands of local officials. Those operating in migrant neighbourhoods, or in activities known to be dominated by non-indigenes, felt that they were subject to unfair taxation. Skilled hand-embroiderers in Kaduna – an activity dominated by non-indigenes – complained of a recent doubling of rents in their section of the market amid continued state neglect and lack of basic services such as electricity or sanitation. By contrast, activities dominated by indigenes generally indicated that local taxes and fees were not a problem, since officials largely left them alone during the security crisis.

EDUCATION

While Islamic extremism in Nigeria is associated with a rejection of Western education, what is immediately evident in the northern informal economy is the rising level of Western education across all levels of activities. As Table 9.6 indicates, only 25 per cent have no Western education, rising to 38 per cent among traditional activities. More than 40 per cent of those in modern activities have completed secondary school, along with 20 and 28 per cent of those in traditional and survival activities respectively. Even more striking is that 18 per cent of those in modern activities, and 12 per cent of those in survival activities have post-secondary qualifications, including one tailor with a university degree. During interviews, we also came across a load carrier in Kano with a university degree, and one in Kaduna with a post-secondary diploma. There has been a growing awareness of university students and graduates working as waste pickers scavenging in garbage dumps for recyclable waste, either to pay their fees, or as a solution to unemployment after graduation (Balogun 2014; Sessou et al. 2014). Interestingly, more than two-thirds of those with post-secondary qualifications were state indigenes.

The majority in all levels of activities noted an increase in the levels of education of people entering their activity. Tailors spoke of graduates unable to find jobs who would turn to tailoring to make a living. Motorized rickshaw transport was attracting a range of people from other professions, including teachers, taxi drivers and business people, as well as unemployed graduates, making it a much more middle-class activity than the motorcycle taxi business had been. Many also finance higher education by working in informal activities at all levels. Indeed, one quarter of those in modern activities, and one-fifth of those in survival activities indicated that they are using their informal activity to finance further education. This was also true of one in seven of those in traditional activities, largely butchers.

A majority, particularly in modern and survival activities, felt that the entry of more educated people is a positive development. More-educated entrants bring innovations, such as modern disposable take-away containers in traditional restaurants, improved meat hygiene and more-modern technology among butchers, and more-innovative marketing networks in tailoring. However, more-educated entrants have also brought new tensions. At the level of survival activities, the prospects

Table 9.6 Highest education levels in informal activities by activity type (percentage of firm heads)

Activity type	No Western education	Primary certificate	Secondary certificate	Post-secondary diploma or degree	More educated people entering the business	Educated entrants good for business	Activity offers good prospects for own level of education
Modern	10.6	28.8	42.4	18.2	84.8	75.8	69.2
Traditional	38.3	36.7	20.0	5.0	65.0	58.3	58.6
Survival	26.2	34.4	27.9	11.5	67.2	81.0	54.4
Average	24.6	33.2	30.5	11.7	72.7	71.7	61.1

(Source: Fieldwork, 2014)

for resentment and frustration of post-secondary degree holders working as hawkers and load carriers is obvious. The potential for disaffection is accentuated when the majority of those with post-secondary qualifications are state indigenes. Survival activities have the lowest share of operators indicating that their activity offered good prospects for their level of education. Only 54 per cent felt that this was the case, compared to nearly 60 per cent of those in traditional activities, and just short of 70 per cent of those in modern activities. The lowly character of most survival activities is particularly degrading for those with high levels of education, unless they can see their way to working toward something better. In addition to low incomes and harsh working conditions, both the resources and prospects for marriage are poor, as is the capacity to support a family. Given that most of those interviewed had been in their activity for nearly a decade, the scope for optimism is low. While the quality of education received by those working in the informal economy is clearly an issue, it does not detract from the sense of disaffection experienced by graduates facing a future in lowly survival activities.

A further point of tension arose within traditional and modern activities, among those who developed skills via traditional channels, and are feeling crowded out by educated entrants who capture contracts and monopolize markets. Butchers in Kano expressed some concern about competition from more-educated entrants, particularly in view of government initiatives toward upgrading hygiene and slaughtering facilities. The chairman of a local branch of the butchers' association felt that government modernization plans excluded the association, while others are concerned about being crowded out of their own profession by more-educated entrants and more technically and financially demanding development programmes. Similarly, in a focus group discussion with Kano tailors, less educated tailors expressed resentment against graduates who use their education to get contracts and take business away from those with proper artisanal training. One complained that *'yan boko* (Western-educated people) were dominating the business despite their lack of proper artisanal skills.

These two points of stress – highly educated indigenes reduced to working in demeaning low-income activities, and artisanally trained actors feeling crowded out by more-educated entrants – suggest two ways in which rising levels of education in the informal economy is inflaming resentment against *boko* – Western education. The tendency to associate Islamic radicalism in northern Nigeria with a backward Muslim dislike of Western education ignores more complex social realities. Alternative paths to radicalization may also emerge from rising education and a lack of economic opportunity. Increasing levels of education (although often of poor quality), disappointed entitlement, and the incursion of graduates into the livelihood spheres of those with fewer social and economic advantages are creating mounting tensions in northern Nigerian society. While the majority are managing these stresses constructively, and even generating economically successful innovations, cracks are beginning to show. Contemporary processes of religious change and the politicization of these processes have exacerbated tensions around access to livelihoods, indigeneity and education, as well as giving them a religious expression.

RELIGION

Interviews across all categories of activities suggest a picture of comparative religious harmony within the informal economies of Kano and Kaduna, both between Muslims and Christians and among Muslims. Informal actors in the sample were keen to emphasize their good relations with Christians in their midst. Indeed, they expressed more unease about the economic impact of the Chinese than about local Christians. Butchers highlighted good relations with Christian butchers in Kano as well as Kaduna. Christians do not slaughter, but sell meat and are members of the local butchers' associations. Load carriers expressed dismay about the departure of Christian shop owners amid extreme insecurity since 2011, leading to a serious decline in work. In Kano and Kaduna, they described how Igbo, Edo and Yoruba Christians would bring in trailers full of goods, and develop personal relations with trusted Muslim load carriers to handle their loads. Since the rise of extremist violence, many Igbo traders have left town, and others from southern Nigeria have stopped coming to northern cities, reducing available work for load carriers. Igbo traders also gave out goods on credit for locals to send up to contacts in Yobe and Borno, and return the proceeds at the end of two weeks. Food sellers in these markets also provided food for Igbo businessmen on credit, to be paid off at the end of their stay. Indeed, there was a strong sense across a number of activities that business cooperation across religious lines was more supportive than relations with ones' own ethnic and religious leaders. As one load carrier explained, an Igbo will take a Hausa boy and train him, while their own leaders leave them in poverty.

Accounts of close relations with Christian customers, suppliers and colleagues mirrored accounts from earlier research in 2011 (Meagher 2013), though this time it was accompanied by laments about the loss of business and institutional support because Christians were moving out of Kano or into segregated neighbourhoods in Kaduna. Tailors in Kaduna drew attention to their lack of work in the week before Easter, expressing dismay at the collapse of business from Christian customers too afraid to come into Muslim areas. Some maintain links with Christian customers by phone, but this represents only a fraction of former inter-religious business relations. Among media distributors, who tend to specialize by Islamic sect, a number of distributors will carry a small section of Christian religious media if there are specific items that are selling well. One distributor even noted that, in Kano, there were some Igbos who produce Islamic films. In hard times, the market is as important as the message.

Yet, years of extreme religious violence are taking their toll on previously integrative inter-religious relations. Fear, segregation and restrictions on movement are leading to the unravelling of cooperative strategies that once linked Muslim and Christian informal businesses. In the past, tailors in Kano indicated that they used to employ Christian tailors to make suits for them, while Christians used to send their embroidery to Muslim specialists (Meagher 2013). But tailors indicated that these practices are disappearing. Christian tailors in Kaduna have begun to hire Muslim embroiderers to train them to do the embroidery themselves, because they are too afraid to come into Muslim areas. Media distributors also indicated that Christians used to dominate their business, but there are now only a few Christian media distributors in Kano, and Muslims now dominate the business. As Christians withdraw into their own neighbourhoods, or leave the north altogether, symbiotic economic structures and social relations are being eroded, creating space for greater polarization, religiously based agendas of competition within certain activities, and greater vulnerability to opportunistic mobilization along religious lines.

Within Islam as well, the rise of Islamic reformist movements has altered the distribution of opportunity and created new tensions within the informal economy. The rise of Izala and other Salafist movements from the late 1970s has been central to processes of modernization and economic consolidation within the informal economy in the punishing economic conditions of economic reform. A strident modernizing force within northern Nigerian society, Salafis encourage a strong emphasis on education, frugality and individual achievement – reminiscent of an

Islamic version of the Protestant ethic (Kane 2003; Masquellier 1999; Meagher 2009). As Sani Umar (1993, 178) points out, the 'reorientation from a communal to an individualistic mode of religiosity seems to be more in tune with the rugged individualism of capitalist social relations.'

The rise of Salafist movements has produced a significant fragmentation in religious affiliation within society, and within the informal economy in particular. Nearly one-third of informal actors in the sample had changed their religious affiliation, and belonged to a different affiliation from their parents. This was highest among modern activities, rising to nearly 40 per cent, and lowest among traditional activities, where general Islam and Sufi brotherhoods continued to dominate, as shown in Table 9.7. Salafis still constitute a minority among northern Muslims, amounting to only one-third of Muslims in the sample. Non-aligned or 'general' Muslims constitute the majority in the sample and in northern Nigerian society as a whole, while Sufis constitute an important traditional affiliation, along with minor allegiance to 'other sects', including Shi'ites and other small groups.

What is particularly striking is the concentration of Salafist groups, overwhelmingly dominated by Izala, in modern activities. Traditional activities are dominated by general Muslims, while participation in Sufi brotherhoods is the dominant trend among those in survival activities. Salafis are not only concentrated in lucrative modern activities, but they are the most highly educated group across all activity categories. Analysis of educational level by religious affiliation showed that 54 per cent of Salafis have secondary education or better, compared to only 38 and 33 per cent of general Muslims and Sufis respectively. The general feeling among informal actors was that shifts in religious affiliation had not been disruptive of good relations in the informal economy. In interviews, respondents consistently replied that religious affiliation was a private thing, that they were barely aware of the religious affiliation of those in their activities, and that differences in religious affiliation were not a source of divisions. Even among media distributors, who tend to specialize by religious affiliation, there was an emphasis on congenial relations between the various sects.

However, there was some evidence of tensions arising from changing religious affiliations within Islam. The Salafi ethos of frugality and efficiency has facilitated new processes of accumulation among middle-level informal actors, but have tended to weaken redistributive relations between more-successful informal actors and those less fortunate, leading to Salafi converts being branded as 'selfish' by their Sufi critics (Kane 2003; Meagher 2009; Masquellier 1999; Loimeier 2005). Conventionally, successful tailors or CD distributors would keep on a few 'boys' who run errands in return for a little food or money. Salafi enterprise heads spoke of letting their boys go when business is slow, and were known for refusing to give alms to Qur'anic students (Mustapha and Bunza 2014;

Table 9.7 Religious affiliation by activity type (percentage of firm heads)

Activity type	General Muslim	Sufi	Salafist	Other	Changed religious affiliation	Different religious affiliations bring division
Modern	25.8	21.2	51.5	1.5	37.9	20.3
Traditional	55.0	23.3	21.7	0.0	23.3	17.2
Survival	31.1	37.7	26.2	4.9	29.5	6.7
Average	36.9	27.3	33.7	2.1	30.5	14.8

(Source: Fieldwork, 2014)

Umar 1993; Hochner 2014). Gains in efficient resource use and accumulation are experienced as a loss of social support among the less advantaged, intensifying economic pressure and disaffection among the poor.

Alongside a more individualist orientation, more-politicized Salafis have shown a propensity to aggressive tactics of institutional capture, particularly with the rise of pro-Sharia politics since the turn of the millennium (Wakili 2009; Thurston 2016; Umar, Chapter 2 this volume). While Salafist movements are strongly oriented toward reform of the state, they are explicitly against violence. However, tendencies toward intolerance, provocation and institutional capture have bred increasing conflict and resentment among those marginalized by these tactics (Casey 2008; Mustapha and Bunza 2014). Within the sample, the incursion of more individualistic and educated Salafi operators has tended to exacerbate tensions between more and less educated informal actors. While people were generally reluctant to speak of religious divisions within Islam, 20 per cent of those in modern activities, and 17 per cent of those in traditional activities indicated that diversification in religious affiliation brought divisions within their activities.

There was some evidence to suggest a growing incursion of Salafi entrants into large, well-connected enterprise associations with significant profit potential, such as the nationally federated National Butchers Union and the motorized rickshaw operators' association, which enjoy access to state-level and even federal-level politicians as well as to state development assistance (*This Day* 2013; Meagher 2013). While Salafists made up only 20 per cent of the participants in small informal enterprise associations, such as neighbourhood tailors' unions, or market-based hawkers' associations, they constituted 40 per cent of those in politically connected associations. These developments have created tensions within associations, uncomfortable with the potential for associational takeovers by educated newcomers.

Both the incursion of more-politicized and more-educated Salafi entrants, and the decline of symbiotic inter-religious business relations between Muslims and Christians are worrying developments. They threaten to undermine the conflict-mitigating effect of informal business activities by undermining symbiotic relations and introducing new tensions from within. Salafi activism has produced countervailing tendencies of modernist values and religious intolerance, new avenues of accumulation and declining mechanisms of redistribution, and Islamic engagement with the state alongside intensified state violence against marginal Muslims. While mainstream Salafism has not instigated violent radicalization, it has exacerbated a climate of exclusion, resentment and desperation, particularly among non-indigenes from other parts of northern Nigeria.

SECURITY

While insecurity resulting from religious extremism poses a threat to informal livelihoods, the disruptive activities of security forces were also a major focus of concern. Physical insecurity and heavy-handed security measures have severely undermined informal markets and threatened previously viable livelihoods. Modal estimates across all activity categories put the decline in business since 2011 at 40 to 50 per cent. Respondents spoke of the inability to operate during periods following attacks, loss of out-of-town customers owing to fears for their safety, and the disruption or destruction of business networks resulting from the fleeing or relocating of Christians. Tailors spoke of the loss of customers who used to come in from all over northern Nigeria, while media distributors lamented the drying up of business from Niger, Burkina Faso, Mali and Sudan. For butchers, food sellers and load carriers, the withdrawal and fleeing of Christians, and restriction of movement within the town posed serious problems for demand. There was also a more general sense that it was riskier to offer credit because insecurity could prevent people from coming back to repay it, eroding the financial networks that facilitate business in the cash-strapped environment of the informal economy.

A number of respondents indicated that the collapse of markets was driving smaller operators out of business, with CD distributors indicating that loss of customers was running down capital, leading to many bankruptcies among weaker players. They pointed to dwindling numbers of operators even among Muslims in the business. Women operating traditional restaurants made a similar point, explaining that only the more established operators were still able to survive in the current climate. Many women were leaving the business to go into something less risky, such as petty trade. The implication of these developments is increasing differentiation within informal activities, as better-off operators get by, while once-established smaller operators are driven under.

Economic pressures rather than religious extremism were widely seen as the greatest threat to informal livelihoods. Although extremist violence and insecurity were disruptive, they were not defined as the greatest livelihood threat in any activity. Across all activity categories, lack of capital was most widely listed as the greatest concern, followed by too much entry into the activity, and, in the case of survival activities, official harassment. For the most part, religious violence came a distant fourth or fifth behind power cuts and rising input costs.

Focusing in on occupationally specific problems, religious extremism was still not seen as a primary threat. Media distributors saw piracy as their most serious problem. They raised issues about the understaffing and underfunding of the copyright board across the country, which was unable to take any effective measures against piracy, despite high levels of taxes paid by film producers, and the significant contribution of the Nigerian film industry to national growth revealed in the rebased GDP statistics (Ogunlesi 2014). This situation has serious implications for the rise and perpetuation of extremism. Despite significant regulation of the Nigerian film industry, with federal as well as state-level censorship boards, and copyright authorities, and also heavy self-censorship within the film industry associations themselves in order to avoid falling afoul of censorship authorities, there is no regulatory control of religious media, particularly preaching. Preaching CDs are produced live at mosques and other preaching venues rather than in studios, are not subject to the oversight of censorship authorities, and feed into a media distribution system which is dominated by piracy. Distributors indicated that as much as 80 per cent of media distribution in Nigeria is made up of pirated copies, while the film makers and distributors capture only about 20 per cent of sales. Beyond the market, some distributors lamented that young people with few resources circumvent the market altogether by downloading films and religious content onto memory sticks.

Among women, specific concerns also focused on livelihoods rather than security. Women running traditional restaurants in Kano did not indicate significant worries about personal insecurity resulting from religious violence, although they were concerned about loss of business owing to insecurity as well as disruptive security responses. A number of food sellers only remembered the electoral violence of 2011 as a time of significant personal insecurity, and did not associate recent extremist attacks with a sense of personal vulnerability. What they did comment on was the weakening of the market, and the difficulties faced by new entrants in making a living in the activity. Comments from tailors suggest that female tailors also face greater difficulty making a living owing to the constraints of insecurity on the mobility of female customers (see also Meagher 2013). Lower levels of capital, constraints of seclusion and a narrow customer base make women tailors more vulnerable to hard economic times. One food seller noted that women face an increasingly desperate situation in which they are less able to rely on male incomes, owing to unemployment and insecurity, but are struggling to make a living in the activities accessible to them.

Overall, threats to livelihoods were seen as more immediate problems than religious violence, and in interviews, extremism and insecurity were widely seen as consequences rather than causes of a lack of access to decent livelihoods. Indeed, many saw the problem of insecurity as a problem of unemployment rather than a religious problem. As a Kaduna tailor put it: 'If I have something to do, I can't think of doing bad things, because I have hope. But if you bring money, an amount I can't get in five years, you can get me to do things'.[2] In Kaduna, there was a greater propensity to regard security as a more direct concern. A longer exposure to extremist violence has devastated the local economy and produced a more acute sense of threat. A tailor in Kaduna's Kakuri Market commented, 'if there is no peace, light and capital won't help'.

Despite concerns about insecurity, and an awareness that extremist violence has damaged livelihoods, security measures were felt to be as much part of the problem as part of the solution. There was a general recognition that security measures were necessary in the context of extremist attacks, but there was also a strong feeling that security measures often do more harm than good. While 31 per cent of actors felt that security measures were not a problem, rising as high as 46 per cent among those in traditional activities, the majority in all activities experienced heightened security measures as harming their livelihoods in various ways (Table 9.8). Across a range of activities, concerns were raised about the negative effects on local livelihoods of the motorcycle taxi curfew, roadblocks, and extraction of bribes. Roughly one-third of operators across all three activity categories felt the motorcycle curfew significantly undermined incomes. Tailors, butchers, hawkers and load carriers often depend on motorcycles for travelling to and from work. Evening curfews for motorcycle riding forced them to leave work early so as to be home before the curfew, preventing night work or staying late to deal with the needs of customers. Motorcycle taxi operators were also prevented from working at night, and were put out of business entirely in Kano where the activity was banned outright from January 2012. Traditional restaurants in some locations also depend on custom from men returning from work, who now had no time to stop at restaurants because of the need to beat the motorcycle curfew. Tailors also complained of a loss of customers who

[2] Interview, tailor, Central Market, Kaduna, 15 April 2014.

Table 9.8 Effects of security measures on business by activity type (percentage of firm heads)

Activity type	Security measures not a problem	Motorbike curfew a problem	Roadblocks a problem	Bribes a problem	Security helps
Modern	25.8	33.3	47.0	24.2	0.0
Traditional	45.8	25.4	38.9	6.8	5.1
Survival	23.0	37.7	42.7	14.8	8.2
Average	31.2	32.3	43.0	15.0	4.2

(Source: Fieldwork, 2014)

were unable to come by after work, a key time for customers to attend to business with tailors. By contrast, motorized rickshaw operators gained economically from motorcycle curfews, which diverted business to them, particularly in Kano. However, a number of other aspects of security measures were more problematic for this group as well.

Security roadblocks, and the behaviour of security officials manning roadblocks were perceived as problematic by roughly 40 per cent of informal actors. Those in survival activities as well as the more successful motorized rickshaw operators noted that roadblocks complicated routes, and wasted petrol, as well as exposing them to higher than average levels of official harassment. Motorized rickshaw and motorcycle taxi operators also spoke of routine humiliation at the hands of security forces, including being subject to frog jumps, beatings and heavy fines for the slightest mistake. Tailors, media distributors and food sellers complained that roadblocks discouraged customers, seriously affecting business. Customers found it more difficult and sometimes expensive to get to their shops, leading to a significant decline in business. Bribery by security personnel was highlighted as a specific problem by 15 per cent of actors, rising to almost a quarter of those in modern activities. A small share of informal actors managed to benefit from security measures. In interviews, some media distributors indicated that police helped them to limit piracy by seizing pirated CDs at roadblocks.

In addition to negative effects on livelihoods, informal actors have faced direct losses and physical harm as a result of extremist attacks and the excessive action of security forces. This includes theft and destruction of property, torture and molestation, as well as the killing of parents, siblings, children and other relatives. It is worth noting that the majority of respondents had not suffered personally from extremist violence. With regard to extremist violence, Table 9.9 shows that 68 per cent of the sample suffered no property losses or physical harm to themselves or to

Table 9.9 Losses resulting from extremism and security force actions by activity type (percentage of firm heads)

Activity type	No personal harm from extremist attacks	No personal harm from security forces	Property loss from extremist attacks	Property loss from security forces	Physical harm from extremist attacks	Physical harm from security forces	Unjust arrest by security forces
Modern	65.2	59.1	6.1	3.0	13.6	12.1	25.8
Traditional	70.0	88.3	15.0	0.0	8.3	0.0	11.7
Survival	68.3	54.1	8.3	4.9	11.7	6.6	31.1
Average	67.7	66.8	9.7	2.7	11.3	6.4	23.0

(Source: Fieldwork, 2014)

loved ones. A similar proportion, 67 per cent, had experienced no property losses or physical harm at the hands of security forces, indicating that among the common people, security forces represented a comparable source of personal insecurity. Both property loss and physical harm were greater at the hands of extremists, around 10 per cent of respondents, while amounting to only 3 per cent and 6 per cent at the hands of security forces. However, unjust arrest by security forces was a significant source of concern, affecting 23 per cent of actors overall.

The pattern of property loss and physical harm is of significance. Losses are more generalized across all activity groups in the case of extremist attacks, while harm at the hands of security forces is concentrated in modern and survival activities, particularly among youth aged 30 and under. Traditional activities, by contrast, are dominated by older actors, and seem to be less subject to negative effects of security forces. A much more significant share of those in modern or survival activities experienced unjust arrest of themselves or those close to them in the context of security interventions, amounting to one-quarter of those in modern activities, and nearly one-third of those in survival activities, again with a bias toward youth.

There were notable differences in the distribution of personal losses between cities. In Kaduna, only 57 per cent had suffered no personal harm from extremist attacks, compared to nearly 80 per cent in Kano. The share of people affected by property loss was eight times higher in Kaduna than in Kano, and physical harm to self or loved ones was twice as high. By contrast, those affected by personal losses resulting from the action of security forces was more evenly distributed between the two cities, with a significantly lower share in Kaduna suffering from losses at the hands of security forces relative to extremist violence, and the reverse in Kano. The higher level of harm suffered from extremist violence relative to security forces in Kaduna appears to have led to greater prioritization of security over economic concerns.

Overall, insecurity has tended to exacerbate problems of economic stress that feed into local processes of radicalization. Extremist disruption of business activities has severely undermined livelihoods across all activity categories, and has subjected some 20 per cent of informal actors to direct property and physical losses. However, excessive interventions by security forces have also been a source of significant insecurity and personal losses among the popular classes. Security measures have exacerbated the negative effects on livelihoods, owing in part to a lack of coordination with local livelihood needs, and in part to the predatory and undisciplined behaviour of security forces (see Sanda, Chapter 5 this volume). To make matters worse, security forces are associated with direct harm to local populations, particularly youth, exacerbating a sense of grievance against a state that ignores their livelihood needs, and harms and humiliates them into the bargain.

Conclusion

Despite its remarkable dynamism, the northern Nigerian informal economy has been subject to mounting economic and social tensions. These tensions have not only weakened counter-radicalizing tendencies operating within the informal economy, but have exacerbated pressures that drive violent radicalization, including crushed aspirations, economic grievances, and corruption and brutality at the hands of state agencies. Given that the informal economy constitutes the bulk of the non-agricultural labour force in urban northern Nigeria, understanding how processes within the informal economy affect the dynamics of violent radicalization are essential to the formulation of effective policy solutions, as well as for avoiding new rounds of extremist violence in future.

Attention has been focused on the increasing saturation of the informal economy and new struggles over the access to informal livelihoods centred on indigeneity, education and formal sector actors attempting to harness informal activities for their own profit. In the face of decades of persistent unemployment and poverty in the north, the absorptive capacity of the northern Nigerian informal economy is under severe stress. It is no longer absorbing youth as entrepreneurs, but increasingly as indentured operators or workers making returns from their low incomes to better-off traders and middle-class actors. Despite participation in a given activity for an average of 10 years, nearly one-third of operators were working on commission or hire-purchase terms, rising to 50 per cent in survival activities.

Narrowing livelihood opportunities in the informal as well as the formal sector have triggered rising contestation by indigenes and the educated over access to informal activities – even activities that used to be the preserve of uneducated migrants. This is manifested in increasing participation of indigenes in even the lowliest informal activities, and a growing resistance to entry of non-indigenes, particularly in survival activities. The increasing incursion of graduates into the informal economy has intensified competition over access to informal livelihoods, especially in modern and survival activities. Worst affected are those with post-secondary qualifications working in lowly survival activities, and skilled artisanally trained operators being crowded out by graduates. In both cases, Western education adds a new level of indignity to intense competitive pressures within the informal economy.

The monopolistic tendencies of aggressive Salafi activists and the excesses of security forces have tended to intensify these tensions, as well as associating them with an increasing sense of injustice among those demeaned, crowded out and brutalized by economic and political forces. The expansion of Salafist movements and their increasing politicization within northern states has introduced a tone of religious intolerance into existing tensions of indigeneity, educational competition and intense livelihood competition. More individualistic values are disrupting solidaristic forms of occupational organization, generating a tendency to crowd out less educated or non-indigenous actors while narrowing opportunities for redistribution through religious and communal networks. The heavy-handedness and indiscipline of security interventions have added insult to injury as informal actors struggle to maintain livelihoods in the face of pervasive insecurity. In addition to predatory behaviour, humiliation, and unjust arrest, levels of personal harm suffered at the hands of security forces were similar to levels suffered as a result of extremist violence. Religious and state aggression contributes to an atmosphere of resentment, economic threat and desperation, while closing down legitimate channels for voicing concerns.

The majority of informal operators manage to cope with the frustrations and livelihood pressures of the current economic climate, but mounting poverty and desperation, combined with the heavy-handed response of state security services, have pushed some over the edge into violence, particularly among poor northern migrants. It is not by accident that Boko Haram recruits in Kano and Kaduna were concentrated in the poor migrant neighbourhoods. Yet extremist violence in north-western Nigeria was considerably more limited than in the North East. Not only did Boko Haram not emerge in centres of Salafi radicalism such as Kano and Kaduna, but its reign of terror was more quickly contained in the North West, largely disappearing by 2015.

Yet the North West performs only slightly better than the North East in terms of inequality and access to services. There is still much that holds society together, but mounting tensions continue to eat away at its foundations. While counter-radicalizing tendencies persist in informal economic relations, they are under increasing stress, and risk being further weakened by policy solutions that treat the informal economy as a sponge for rising unemployment in the wider Nigerian economy. Shifting away from viewing informality as a soak pit for surplus labour, toward a more informed understanding of its strengths and weaknesses, opens the possibility of using policy to stem divisive tensions and shore up the ability of informal occupational groups, enterprise associations and local communities to continue acting as bulwarks against radicalization, rather than turning them into incubators of extremism.

Bibliography

Africa Center for Strategic Studies, 2012, 'Preventing Youth Radicalization in East Africa', Program Report, 22–27 January, Kigali, Rwanda.

African Development Bank, Organisation for Economic Co-operation and Development, United Nations Development Programme and United Nations Economic Commission for Africa, 2012, *African Economic Outlook: Promoting Youth Employment*, Paris: OECD.

Armakolas, I., 2011, 'The "Paradox" of Tuzla City: Explaining Non-Nationalist Local Politics during the Bosnian War', *Europe-Asia Studies* 63, 229–61.

Aryeetey, E., 2005, 'Informal Finance for Private Sector Development in Sub-Saharan Africa', *Journal of Micro-finance/ESR Review* 7 (1).

Babou, C.A., 2013, 'The Senegalese "Social Contract" Revisited: The Muridiyya Muslim Order and State Politics', in M. Diouf (ed.), *Tolerance, Democracy, and Sufis in Senegal*, New York: Columbia University Press.

Balogun, B., 2014, 'How Nigerian Undergraduates Live on Scavenging', *Vanguard*, 17 May.

Bayart, J.-F., Ellis, S. and Hibou, B., 1999, *The Criminalisation of the State in Africa*, Oxford: James Currey.

Bhatia, K. and Ghanem, H., 2017, 'How Do Education and Unemployment Affect Support for Violent Extremism?' Brookings Global Working Paper Series, Washington, DC, The Brookings Institution.

Casey, C., 2008, '"Marginal Muslims": Politics and the Perceptual Bounds of Islamic Authenticity in Northern Nigeria', *Africa Today* 54 (3), 67–92.

CBN/FOS/NISER (Central Bank of Nigeria / Federal Office of Statistics / Nigerian Institute for Social & Economic Research), 2001, *A Study of Nigeria's Informal Sector*, Vol 1, *Statistics on Nigeria's Informal Sector*, Abuja: Central Bank of Nigeria.

Dawson, J. and Oyeyinka, B., 1993, 'Structural Adjustment and Urban Informal Sector in Nigeria', ILO Working Paper 65, May, World Employment Programme Research, International Labour Office (ILO), Geneva.

De Soto, H., 2014, 'The Capitalist Cure for Terrorism', *The Wall Street Journal*, 10 October, www.wsj.com/articles/the-capitalist-cure-for-terrorism-1412973796, accessed 3 October 2015.

Diouf, M. (ed.), 2013, *Tolerance, Democracy, and Sufis in Senegal*, New York: Columbia University Press.

Garcia, M. and Fares, J. (eds), 2008, *Youth in Africa's Labour Market*, Washington, DC: World Bank Publications.

Hashim, Y., and Meagher, K., 1999, 'Cross-Border Trade and the Parallel Currency Market – Trade and Finance in the Context of Structural Adjustment: A Case Study from Kano, Nigeria', Research Report 13, Nordiska Afrikainstitutet, Uppsala.

Hashim, Y. and Walker, J.-A., 2014, '"Marginal Muslims": Ethnic Identity and the Umma in Kano', in A.R. Mustapha (ed.), *Sects & Social Disorder: Muslim Identities & Conflict in Northern Nigeria*, Woodbridge: James Currey, 126–46.

Hill, P., 1969, 'Hidden Trade in Hausaland', *Man* 4 (3), 392–409.

Hoechner, H., 2014, 'Experiencing Inequality at Close Range: Almajiri Students and Qur'anic Schools in Kano', in A.R. Mustapha (ed.), *Sects & Social Disorder: Muslim Identities & Conflict in Northern Nigeria*, Woodbridge: James Currey, 98–125.

Ibrahim Forum, 2012, 'African Youth: Fulfilling the Potential', Dakar, Mo Ibrahim Foundation.

ILO (International Labour Organization) and WTO (World Trade Organization), 2009, *Globalization and Informal Jobs in Developing Countries*, Geneva: WTO and ILO.

—— 2018, *Women and Men in the Informal Economy: A Statistical Picture*, third edition, Geneva: ILO.

Jagun, A., Heeks, R. and Whalley, J.L., 2008, 'The Impact of Mobile Telephony on Developing Country Micro-Enterprise: A Nigerian Case Study', *Information Technologies and International Development* 4 (4), 47–65.

Jha, S., 2007, 'Maintaining Peace across Ethnic Lines: New Lessons from the Past', *Economics of Peace and Security Journal* 2 (2), 81–93.

Kane, O., 2003, *Muslim Modernity in Postcolonial Nigeria: A Study of the Society for the Removal of Innovation and Reinstatement of Tradition*, Leiden and Boston, MA: Brill.

Kharas, H., Hamel, K. and Hofer, M., 2018, 'The Start of a New Poverty Narrative', The Brookings Institution, Washington, DC, 19 June, www.brookings.edu/blog/future-development/2018/06/19/the-start-of-a-new-poverty-narrative, accessed 29 March 2019.

Labazee, P., 1995, 'Enterprises, promoteurs et rapports communautaires. Les logiques economiques de la gestion de liens sociaux', in *Entreprises et entrepreneurs africains*, S. Ellis and Y.A. Fauré (eds), Paris: Karthala-ORSTOM.

Loimeier, R., 2005, 'Playing with Affiliations: Muslims in Northern Nigeria in the 20th Century', in *Entreprises religieuses transnationales en Afrique de l'Ouest*, L. Fouchard, A. Mary and R. Otayek (eds), Ibadan and Paris: IFRA-Karthala, 349–71.

Lovejoy, P.E., 1980, *Caravans of Kola: The Hausa Kola Trade, 1700–1900*, Zaria: Ahmadu Bello University Press.

Masquellier, A., 1999, 'Debating Muslims, Disputed Practices: Struggles for the Realization of an Alternative Moral Order in Niger', in J.L. and J. Comaroff (eds), *Civil Society and the Political Imagination in Africa: Critical Perspectives*, Chicago, IL: University of Chicago Press, 219–50.

Meagher, K., 2007, 'Manufacturing Disorder: Liberalization, Informal Enterprise and Economic "Ungovernance" in African Small Firm Clusters', *Development and Change* 38 (3), 473–503.

—— 2009, 'Trading on Faith: Religious Movements and Informal Economic Governance in Nigeria', *The Journal of Modern African Studies* 47 (3), 397–423.

—— 2010, *Identity Economics: Social Networks and the Informal Economy in Africa*, Oxford: James Currey.

—— 2013, 'The Jobs Crisis Behind Nigeria's Unrest', *Current History* 112 (754), 169–74.

—— 2016, 'The Scramble for Africans: Demography, Globalisation and Africa's Informal Labour Markets', *The Journal of Development Studies* 52 (4), 483–97.

Meagher, K. and Yunusa, M.-B., 1996, 'Passing the Buck: Structural Adjustment and the Nigerian Urban Informal Sector', Geneva: UNRISD.

Mustapha, A.R., 1998, 'Identity Boundaries, Ethnicity and National Integration in Nigeria', in O. Nnoli (ed.), *Ethnic Conflicts in Africa*, Dakar: CODESRIA, 27–52.

—— (ed.), 2014, *Sects & Social Disorder: Muslim Identities & Conflict in Northern Nigeria*, Woodbridge: James Currey.

Mustapha, A.R. and Bunza, M.U., 2014, 'Contemporary Islamic Sects & Groups in Northern Nigeria', in A.R. Mustapha (ed.), *Sects & Social Disorder: Muslim Identities & Conflicts in Northern Nigeria*, Woodbridge: James Currey.

NBS (National Bureau of Statistics), 2010, 'Nigeria Poverty Profile 2010 Report', Nigeria.

—— 2011, 'Annual Socio-Economic Report', Nigeria.

—— 2017, 'Demographic Statistics Bulletin', May, Nigeria.

—— 2018, 'Labor Force Statistics', vol. I, 'Unemployment and Underemployment Report, (Q4 2017 – Q3 2018)', December, Nigeria.

National Population Commission (Nigeria) and RTI International, 2011, 'Nigeria Demographic and Health Survey (DHS) EdData Profile 1990, 2003 and 2008: Education Data for Decision-Making' 2011. Washington, DC: National Population Commission and RTI International.

Nigeria Stability and Reconciliation Programme (NSRP), 2014, 'Winners or Losers? Assessing the Contribution of Youth Employment and Empowerment Programmes to Reducing Conflict Risk in Nigeria', NSRP, Abuja.

Oduh, M., Eboh, E., Ichoku, H. and Ujah, O., 2008, 'Measurement and Explanation of Informal Sector of the Nigerian Economy' AIAE Research Paper 3, African Institute for Applied Economics, August, Enugu.

Ogunlesi, T., 2014, 'Rebasing Highlights Nigeria's Inequalities', *Financial Times*, 18 April, www.ft.com/intl/cms/s/0/09e27808-c598-11e3-97e4-00144feabdc0.html#axzz-39Rn2hxI6, accessed 4 August 2014.

Onokheroye, A.G., 1977, 'Occupational Specialization by Ethnic Groups in the Informal Sector of the Urban Economies of Traditional Nigerian Cities: The Case of Benin', *African Studies Review* 20 (1), 53–69.

Onyebueke, V., and Geyer, M., 2011, 'The Informal Sector in Urban Nigeria: Reflections from almost Four Decades of Research', *Town and Regional Planning* 12, 65–76.

Osterbo, T., 2012, 'Islamic Militancy in Africa', Africa Security Brief 23, November, Africa Center for Strategic Studies, Washington, DC.

Perry, G.E., Maloney, W.F., Arias, O.S., Fajnzylber, P., Mason, A.D. and Saavedra-Chanduvi, J., 2007, 'Informality: Exit and Exclusion', World Bank, Washington DC.

Sanusi, S.L. 2003. 'The Shari'a Debate and the Construction of a "Muslim" Identity in Northern Nigeria: A Critical Perspective', paper presented at seminar 'The Shari'a Debate and the Construction of Muslim and Christian Identities in Northern Nigeria', University of Bayreuth, Germany, 11 and 12 July, www.gamji.com/sanusi/sanusi34.htm, accessed 27 August 2014.

Schneider, F., 2002, 'Size and Measurement of the Informal Economy in 110 Countries around the World', paper presented at a workshop of the Australian National Tax Centre, Canberra, Australia.

Sessou, E., Ajayi, O., Adeyeri, A. and Anyaegbu, A., 2014, 'How I Turn Waste to Wealth – Graduate Scavenger', *Vanguard*, 17 May.

This Day, 2013, 'Kano's Ultra Modern Butchers', www.thisdaylive.com/articles/kano-s-ultra-modern-butchers/145725, accessed 12 December 2014.

Thurston, A., 2009, 'Why is Militant Islam a Weak Phenomenon in Senegal?' Working Paper 09-005, Institute for the Study of Islamic Thought in Africa (ISITA), Buffett Center, International and Comparative Studies, Northwestern University, Evanston, IL.

—— 2016, *Salafism in Nigeria: Islam, Preaching, and Politics*, Cambridge, UK: Cambridge University Press.

Treichel, V., 2010, 'Putting Nigeria to Work: A Strategy for Employment and Growth', Directions in Development, World Bank, Washington, DC.

Umar, M.S., 1993, 'Changing Islamic Identity in Nigeria from 1960s to the 1980s:

From Sufism to Anti-Sufism', in L. Brenner (ed.), *Muslim Identity and Social Change in Sub-Saharan Africa*, Bloomington: Indiana University Press, 154–78.

UN Data, 'Population Below the National Poverty Line – Total', Millennium Development Goals Data Base, Statistics Division, http://data.un.org/Data.aspx?d=MDG&f=seriesRowID%3A581, accessed 25 July 2014.

Varshney, A., 2001, 'Ethnic Conflict and Civil Society: India and Beyond', *World Politics* 53, 362–98

Wakili, H., 2009, 'Islam and the Political Arena in Nigeria: The Ulama and the 2007 Elections', Institute for the Study of Islamic Thought in Africa (ISITA) Working Paper 09-004, Northwestern University, Evanston, IL.

World Bank, Data, GINI Index, http://data.worldbank.org/indicator/SI.POV.GINI, accessed 25 July 2014.

—— Data, Poverty Headcount Ratio at $2 a Day, http://data.worldbank.org/indicator/SI.POV.2DAY, accessed 25 July 2014.

Part Three

Seeking a Way Forward

10

Endgames: The evolution of Boko Haram in comparative perspective

M. SANI UMAR & DAVID EHRHARDT

Introduction

As the Boko Haram insurgency heads into its second decade, it seems no quick end is in sight. What are the possible scenarios for the future trajectory of Boko Haram, and in particular what is its endgame? While predicting the future is a very hazardous business, plausible endgame scenarios can be envisioned based on reflection on the metamorphoses of Boko Haram, careful analysis of the dynamics of its current situation, and prognosis of its emergent trends. The formal declaration of the Boko Haram Caliphate and its territorial control over much of Borno State are no more. Yet the 'technical military defeat' proclaimed by President Muhammad Buhari in 2015 has not prevented Boko Haram from carrying out attacks not only in rural areas, but in big towns and even military bases, often killing Nigerian soldiers – as many as 100 soldiers in one attack. Negotiations leading to the release of Boko Haram captives in exchange for freeing incarcerated leaders of the insurgency came about more than a year after the proclamation of the technical defeat. It seems that decisive defeat leading to complete surrender and total cessation of hostilities is not on the immediate horizon. Yet what scenario is likely to unfold?

This chapter explores this question by drawing insights from the literature on the growth, decline, and end of past insurgent insurgencies and civil wars. Theoretically, one may argue that there are only a few possible outcomes to an insurgency: the government may defeat the insurgents; the insurgents may defeat the government; both parties may reach a negotiated settlement; there may be a stalemate; or the insurgency may transform into something else, such as organized crime. We suggest that rather than one distinct ending, Boko Haram is likely to continue its previous patterns of transformations and factionalization, precluding decisive outcomes. Unless distinctively different approaches are taken by the state, likely endgames include a negotiated settlement with some factions, the further entrenchment of the war economy with its continuous menacing of rural areas by others, and some elements potentially becoming absorbed into the global terrorist networks of the Islamic State.

Comparative perspectives on possible trajectories

To begin with, it is important to keep in mind that while the literature on civil wars and (counter)insurgency has a long history, it also faces serious methodological challenges. These challenges include vague and unsystematic conceptualization, measurement problems, and highly complex causal chains with few opportunities for systematic controlled comparison. Consequently, few theories have been systematically tested and much of the empirical evidence is contradictory and difficult to compare. Rather than aspiring to predictions from clear-cut theories, this chapter seeks to decipher the mechanisms and factors at play and to sketch their possible impact on the future trajectory of Boko Haram.

WHAT EXPLAINS INSURGENCY OUTCOMES?

To begin with, insurgency outcomes are affected by structural factors, such as the capacities of the state and the insurgents, deeply rooted grievances, and entrenched narratives of victimhood, that influence outcomes but can only be changed in the long run. Second, outcomes are also influenced by dynamic factors, such as conflict duration, strategy, role of civil society, and foreign intervention, and may be changed in the short or medium term.

With regard to structural factors, Shelton et al. (2013) argue that state capacity in both military strength and effectiveness of the administrative system, affects outcomes of insurgencies. They argue that a strong bureaucratic state may be more likely to defeat the insurgency. While strong states offer many advantages, the direction of their effect on insurgency outcomes is contested. Stronger rebel forces increase the likelihood to a rebel victory or negotiated settlement (ibid., 529). Moreover, the strength of a government military force becomes less and less likely to help the government win the war as the insurgency drags on (ibid.). The positive effect of rebel military strength on rebel victory in turn is contingent upon the level of unity of the rebel movement: factionalization of insurgent groups makes their victory against the state less likely. In some cases militarily strong insurgent forces can be a handicap, because they make for more easily distinguishable targets than more lightly armed and mobile (asymmetric) insurgent forces (Connable and Libicki 2010). In the simplest terms, strong states are likely to be the winners in insurgency conflicts, as are relatively strong rebel movements. But these structural variables can be affected by the dynamic variables that can constrain the choices of strategies on both sides.

Dynamic factors that can influences conflict outcomes in the short run include the duration of the conflict, (counter)insurgency strategies, roles of civil societies and foreign intervention. While insurgencies are on average lengthy affairs, significant variation exists in conflict duration, with some conflict actors benefiting more from long, drawn-out violence, and others from quick and decisive victory. Rational actors will try to achieve their preferred outcome, and push to end or draw out conflicts accordingly. In some contexts, duration of the conflict can affect outcomes, independently of the interests and strategies of the actors – although there is disagreement about whether a longer duration benefits rebels or governments (Shelton et al. 2013; Connable and Libicki 2010).

Conflict strategies are also dynamic factors that normally enable the stronger party to prevail (Blattman and Miguel 2010). They have two basic forms: enemy-centric (or attrition) and population-centric (or hearts and minds – HAM). This becomes more complex, however, where insurgencies are asymmetric conflicts. Findley and Young (2007) argue for the relative efficacy of HAM strategies, based on a mathematical model. Shelton et al. (2013), however, note that there is no clear-cut evidence to support either strategy over the other. Instead, they suggest that enemy-centric strategies focused on defeating opponents militarily may be more effective if they are undertaken by militarily strong actors, while population-centric strategies require a stronger bureaucracy, or strong internal cohesion and organizational capacity in the case of rebel groups. Arreguín-Toft (2001, 2005), by contrast, views strategies as either direct (enemy-centric) or indirect (population-centric, or aimed at the enemy's will to fight) and argues that rebels win if the warring parties use opposite strategies (direct vs. indirect), while governments win if they use matching strategies (direct vs. direct or indirect vs. indirect) (Enterline et al. 2013).

Strategically, indiscriminate violence has been uniformly negative: both governments and rebels are more likely to lose the war if they employ indiscriminate violence on large parts of the population (Kalyvas and Kocher 2007; Shelton et al. 2013; Connable and Libicki 2010). This may be because indiscriminate violence by rebels erodes support among the population (Connable and Libicki 2010, 103), or because such violence by the government changes the relative costs and benefits of participation in a rebel movement (Kalyvas and Kocher 2007). Whatever the mechanism, it seems clear that indiscriminate violence is a tactic that backfires on those employing it because of its effects on loyalty of a population (Findley and Young 2007).

Civil society organizations constitute a dynamic factor that deserves more attention in the literature (e.g. Marchetti and Tocci 2009). The growth in number and roles of civil society organizations, including human rights activism, peace movements, international humanitarian organizations, and women's associations, have enabled them to play an important role in pushing violent conflicts toward a conclusion, whether victory for one side, or negotiated settlement. Examples include the roles played by the business community in apartheid South Africa, the women's groups in Sierra Leone and civil initiatives in Northern Ireland. As a third set of players standing apart from the warring parties, civil society organizations can influence the outcomes of violent conflict in various ways, including mediation, redressing some of the underlying grievances, and offering opportunities and funding for post-conflict reconstruction, resettlement and reconciliation.

Connable and Libicki (2010) argue that foreign support – the fourth dynamic factor – greatly improves the chances of insurgent victory, while the withdrawal of such support has often presaged rebel defeat. The provision of sanctuary by external actors to rebel groups can greatly improve the likelihood of rebel victory, and insurgent groups rarely survive without some sanctuary outside the state they are fighting, even where unwittingly provided (ibid., xvii). External support for government forces has a less clear effect (Shelton et al. 2013; Connable and Libicki 2010).

Drawing out the major trends of this section, there are four main observations. First, insurgencies are messy and protracted, but long duration is not necessarily an indication of future rebel victory. Second, it is likely that state capacity and regime type have effects on the outcome of an insurgency, but they are also structural variables that are hard to change. As we will discuss in more detail below, Nigeria's status as an 'anocracy' (or a semi-democracy, in between autocratic and democratic regimes) with a relatively strong military but weak bureaucratic capabilities (Vreeland 2008), and the fragmented nature of Boko Haram represent a combination of variables that do not favour a quick victory for the government forces.

Third, while there are clear indications that conflict duration, strategic choices, and civil society engagement are important for insurgency outcomes, the direction of their effect is difficult to predict and is often conditional on other variables. Finally, there are three factors with less equivocal impact on insurgency outcomes, and hence clearer implications for strategies for resolving insurgencies: (i) the importance of tailoring government strategy to the strategy of the rebels, taking into account both enemy-centric and population-centric tactics; (ii) the negative impact of indiscriminate government violence on the likelihood of government victory (not to mention the impact of government strategy on the incentives for joining rebel groups); and (iii) the negative effect of obvious foreign support on government victory, and the positive effect of external support for insurgents, and particularly sanctuary, on rebel victory.

Case studies

Building on the overview of factors that affect insurgency outcomes, we will now analyse three case studies of insurgencies that resemble the Boko Haram insurgency in significant ways. Table 10.1 gives the main reasons for case selection. First, the case al-Gama'ah al-Islamiyya (GI) of Egypt was selected because of the similarity between the GI and Boko Haram in their Salafi/Islamist ideological orientations, Muslim nativist rejection of Western culture, emergence in the context of general Islamic radicalism, and the patterns of confrontation with the state (Ashour 2007; Mitchell 1969; Ibrahim 1996; Leiken and Brooke 2007; El-Ghobashy 2005). Second, the Ugandan history with the Lord's Resistance Army (LRA) is comparable to the Boko Haram insurgency because of the regional concentration of the movements, their complex religious origins,

Table 10.1 Reasons for case study selections

Country	**Egypt**	**Uganda**	**Northern Ireland**	**Nigeria**
Outcome	***Government victory***	***Transformed***	***Negotiated settlement***	***Ongoing***
Regional concentration insurgents	•	•	•	•
Religious framing of insurgency	•	•	•	•
Porous borders and safe havens		•		•
Decentralized insurgent organization		•	•	•
Factionalized insurgent organization			•	•
Centralized insurgent organization	•			
Weak state capacity		•		•

the porous borders around their areas of operations, and the LRA's decentralized organizational structure (Jackson 2002; Behrend 2000; ICG 2010; Jackson 2002). Finally, the British and Irish experiences with the Irish Republican Army (IRA) can help to inform our scenarios for Boko Haram because of the regional concentration of the violence, the religious undertones of the conflict, the complex factionalization of the militant groups, and the decentralized guerrilla tactics of the insurgent groups (Dixon 2001; Bamford 2005; Mac Ginty et al. 2007; Barnes 2005; Whyte 1986; Brewer et al. 2014). Although only the Egyptian case is an Islamic insurgency, all three are centred around strong religious identities. Looking beyond Islam to wider dynamics of religious insurgencies can prove useful in seeing beyond some of the stereotypes that constrain analyses of Islamic extremism.

In addition to the comparability of the insurgent movements, the cases were also selected because they present different types of scenarios that might happen in Nigeria: one government victory (Egypt); one conflict that has relocated and transformed (LRA); and one case of a negotiated settlement (IRA). Given that rebel victory is highly unlikely, this type was not included in the analysis. Moreover, given the extensive literature on all these movements, there is no need for a lengthy discussion of each. Instead, we summarize the key points for each insurgency and present our analysis of the possible future trajectories of Boko Haram in light of its similarities with each. We will also examine the peculiarities of Boko Haram that may lead to multiple outcomes, and preclude certain outcomes, such as achieving the unrealistic aim of creating an Islamic polity. The prospect of forming an independent Caliphate has significant ideological power, but suffers from a lack of empirical capacity, given Boko Haram's fragile financial and organizational character, the lack of broad-based popular support, and the lack of political vision for a viable system of governance through public goods provision rather than compelling obedience through a reign of terror (Thurston 2017, 226). This has led to different outcomes between hardliners and others.

Case 1 Egypt: Al-Gama'ah al-Islamiyya

Al-Gama'ah al-Islamiyya (GI, The Islamic Group) used to be 'the largest armed Islamist movement in Egypt' (Ashour 2007) during the 1980s–1990s. It started in the 1970s in the context of the new policy adopted by the regime of President Anwar Sadat of encouraging Islamic movements, especially within Egyptian universities. President Sadat hoped that the Islamic movements would serve as a counterforce against the Nasserists and leftists, the secular opposition groups. More broadly, the emergence of both movements has to be located also in the long history of organized Islamic activism of the Muslim Brothers (al-Ikhwan al-Mus-

Case 1 Egypt: Al-Gama'ah al-Islamiyya (GI, The Islamic Group)

- Duration: 1974–1997/8
- Outcome: Government victory resulting in cease-fire
- Variables that help to explain this outcome:
  - *Strong state capacity*
  - *Ruthless suppression by the authoritarian regime of Hosni Mubarak*
  - *Cohesive nature of the GI, with strong leadership capable of imposing its decisions on the rank and file*
  - *Lack of popular support*

limun), founded in 1928 by Hassan al-Banna (d. 1949), and the recurrent violence in its confrontations with the Egyptian state. Equally relevant are the Muslim Brothers' strong Islamist ideological orientation, its cohesive organization, centralized leadership, hierarchical structure, and populist appeal to the professional elites and the masses as well (Mitchell 1969; Ibrahim 1980). In fact, the Muslim Brothers can be seen as the inspiration and the template for the emergence and organization of the GI.

According to Ashour (2007, 605–15), GI evolved in five phases. The first phase, lasting from 1974 to 1981, saw the building of the movement out of several groups in Egyptian universities that sprang up in the wake of the President Sadat's encouragement. Some of the new groups were absorbed into the Muslim Brothers, which, as a group, renounced its previous violence and embraced the overtures of President Sadat to collaborate with the regime against secular leftists (Leiken and Brooke 2007; El-Ghobashy 2005). But the groups not attracted to the new pragmatism of the Muslim Brothers coalesced around a strong Salafi ideological orientation, with its puritanism and intolerance of other Islamic tendencies. Such groups also adopted the radical political activism developed by the Muslim Brothers in the 1950s–1960s; they also embraced wholeheartedly Sayyid Qutb's articulation of Islam as revolutionary ideology. Strong leadership, grassroots mobilization, hierarchical structure, cohesive organization, as well as mass mobilization strategies were all borrowed from the earlier phases of the Muslim Brothers, and used as additional building blocks for the subsequent emergence of the violent radicalism of the GI in the second phase.

The massive arrests and detentions following the assassination of President Sadat opened the second phase in the radicalization of the GI. The brutality, torture, and humiliating conditions of imprisonment provided fertile ground for the growth of what has been termed jihadism: the ideological transformation of the traditional conceptions of jihad as just war into a mixture of cosmic and holy wars, with Salafi puritanism adding some Islamic veneer. Building on Qutb's articulation of jihadism, the imprisoned members of GI debated the finer points of where and against which political manifestation of *jahiliyya* (era of ignorance) they should start their jihadist campaigns. These debates led to the production of substantial writings in a new genre called *fiqh al-unf* (jurisprudence of violence).

The third phase can be traced to the strategy developed by the imprisoned leaders of the GI. The first batch of the leaders released from prison in 1984 began the gradual building of mass following through *da'wa* in the major urban centres, especially Cairo. As with the ideological transformation of jihad into jihadism, radical Islamists have also adapted and transformed *da'wa*. In contrast to societal conversion to Islam following political conquest through jihad, *da'wa* is the missionary strategy traditionally pursued by Muslim clerics and mystics of inviting people to join Islam by persuasion from below through preaching, performance of miracles and provision of social support services. But in the hands of radical Islamists, *da'wa* means not converting non-Muslims but the recruitment of supporters among the Muslim masses to radical Islamic movements to serve as foot soldiers for the eventual jihadist campaign. Thus, not surprisingly, the second batch of GI detainees released in 1985 were charged with the responsibility of using the people recruited through the *da'wa* of the first batch to establish GI presence in Cairo and other cities, while the third batch of detainees released in 1988 had 'the task of building the two branches of the armed wing' (Ashour 2007, 610).

According to Ashour (ibid.), the first branch of the armed wing of GI 'would be trained locally with light arms for quick and small-scale operations', meant to protect GI recruitment against the state security and paramilitary forces. The second branch 'was called the military wing and its members were supposed to be the nucleus of [a GI] army' (ibid.). With some members sent to Afghanistan in 1988 to obtain 'more sophisticated military training', the third phase in the radicalization of the GI came to an end, having prepared the ground for the eruption of violence in the next phase, characterized by GI insurgency.

The transition to the violent fourth phase had a more dramatic beginning with the spectacular assassination attempt targeting the incumbent interior minister in 1989. Interestingly, this phase had an equally dramatic ending with the GI declaring a totally unexpected unilateral ceasefire in 1997. In addition to the high importance of ideology in the formation of the GI, careful organizing and military training were other crucial features that made for a very a cohesive insurgency capable of inflicting heavy losses on the Egyptian state despite its strong army and formidable administrative machinery. There is no need to go into the details of the violent confrontations between GI fighters and Egyptian security forces from 1989 to 1997. Ashour quotes the official fatality figures thus: 471 GI members, 401 security forces, 306 Egyptian civilians and 97 tourists. The main strategies used in waging and resisting the GI insurgency included

> a rise in the use of terror tactics, many assassinations/assassination-attempts, bombings, extra-judicial killings, mass-murders, systematic torture in prisons, 98 military show-trials, regular curfews in many Upper Egyptian towns and villages, and the destruction of hundreds of acres of arable land [to] force possible guerrillas from their hideouts inside these cultivated lands. (Ibid., 612)

After the notorious attacks on Luxor in November 1997, GI declared a ceasefire and, in the years following, most of its leaders explicitly renounced violence. This outcome should be understood partly in terms of the strong capacity of the Egyptian state to militarily repress the movement and make its activities too costly to continue (Gunaratna and Ali 2009). But it should also be viewed in terms of the cohesive organization with strong leadership, hierarchical structure and clear ideological orientation that enabled the leadership of the Islamist insurgent movement to convince its mass membership to accept the decision to end their insurgency, and also prevent defection and factionalization. The authoritarian regime of Hosni Mubarak was willing to use brute force while Islamist insurgency was active, and to grant concessions and inducements once the ceasefire began (Ashour 2007, 620–24). Finally, indiscriminate violence against civilians and the brutal response of the authoritarian regime combined to repel the vast majority of Egyptians, and make them very receptive to the termination of the insurgency.

Case 2 Uganda: The Lord's Resistance Army

The long conflict between the Ugandan state and the Lord's Resistance Army (LRA), an insurgent movement that began in 1987, has been a classic insurgency. The LRA grew out of the short-lived prophetic movement led by Alice 'Lakwena' Auma and adopted some its religious discourses (Behrend 2000). Lacking the broad support Lakwena had enjoyed, LRA leader Joseph Kony was forced to organize the LRA more along the lines of a guerrilla organization. In the first years of the war until 1991, the fighting mainly took place between the LRA and Ugandan government forces. When it became clear that the movement could not defeat the government, which had used an intensely violent campaign targeted not only at the LRA but also the wider Acholi population of the area, the

Case 2 Uganda: The Lord's Resistance Army (1987 to *c.* 2006 in Uganda, regionally ongoing)

- Outcome: transformed
- Duration: >30 years
- Variables that help to explain this outcome:
  - *Low state capacity, Uganda as a democratizing anocracy*
  - *Geographically and politically peripheral to Ugandan state*
  - *Unclear political aims of insurgency; use of religious framing*
  - *Mismatched state-rebel strategies: state exclusively enemy-centric, and rebels deploying low-level, small-scale guerrilla tactics (including abductions) from safe haven outside of Uganda*
  - *Indiscriminate violence by both state and insurgents*
  - *External support (from Sudan) and safe haven for insurgents*

LRA increasingly turned against Northern Uganda civilians, particularly the Acholi.

The outcome of the LRA insurgency is difficult to categorize. Since 2006 the Ugandan government has successfully curtailed LRA operations within Uganda and forced the movement across the borders into South Sudan, the Democratic Republic of the Congo (DRC), and the Central African Republic (CAR). But the movement has now existed and fought for over 30 years and continues to wreak havoc on civilians in the poorly regulated border regions of the three failing states in Uganda's vicinity (ICG 2010). As such, we classify the outcome of this insurgency as a transformation: the shift from domestic to regional insurgency, as the Ugandan government pushed the movement out of its territory.

Several factors help to understand this outcome and long duration of the LRA insurgency. One lies in the relative capabilities of the government and rebel forces. For many years, the Ugandan government lacked strong incentives to end the insurgency in the politically marginal north, which explains part of the outcome. Second, there was a persistent mismatch between the government's enemy-centric strategy and the LRA's guerrilla tactics, including widespread abductions (Jackson 2002; Pham et al. 2008). However, given the protracted nature of the LRA conflict, the strategic choices of both government and insurgents are complex. On the LRA side, the lack of a strategic objective beyond survival allowed it to develop low-level, decentralized tactics that successfully exploited the LRA fighters' knowledge of the terrain and the weaknesses of law enforcement in Northern Uganda. But the LRA's successful post-1994 strategy was contingent on one last necessary condition: the support, both tacit and active, of the Sudanese government.

As the International Crisis Group (2004) notes, Sudan had long been the external supporter of the LRA, purportedly in retaliation for the support Uganda gave the Sudan People's Liberation Movement/Army (SPLM/A) in their independence struggle for southern Sudan. While some of this support was expressed in funding or supplies (including weapons), arguably the most important aspect of the Sudan-LRA relationship has been that the LRA was able to establish its bases in southern Sudan, outside the reach of the Ugandan government. The fact that the LRA could stage all its operations from an external safe haven has been one of the main reasons for its tenacity – a mechanism that has also been highlighted above. Together with the other factors, this external support is important in understanding the trajectory of the LRA and its current outcome as a transformed (and relocated) regional insurgency.

Case 3 Northern Ireland: 'The Troubles'

In its most simplified form, Northern Ireland's 'Troubles' were a period in which the nationalists/republicans fought the unionists/loyalists for the constitutional future of Ireland's six most contested counties (Dixon 2001). It was a complicated conflict, building on centuries of previous contestation and violence, and had at least three main dimensions: the political contest over Northern Ireland's constitutional status as part of the United Kingdom; the religious tension between the largely Catholic nationalists/republicans and the largely Protestant unionists/loyalists and the perceived inequalities between them; and violent struggle between the various militant groups and armed forces on all sides. It was also a long conflict: while the violence began and peaked in the late 1960s and early 1970s, the peace process only began in earnest with the 1998 Good

Case 3 Northern Ireland: 'The Troubles' (1969–2007)

- Outcome: negotiated settlement
- Duration: 38 years (including peace process)
- Variables that help to explain this outcome:
  - *Complex, multi-level, dynamic, and factionalized actors*
  - *Zero-sum political problem, use of religious framing*
  - *Involved states are liberal democracies; both strong and constrained*
  - *Strategic choices that led to mutually harmful stalemate*
  - *Extensive and influential external support on both sides*

Friday Agreement, concluded in 2007. The violence that characterized this struggle was varied, and fluctuated over time, but between 1969 and 1998, Dixon (2001) estimates that about 3,720 people were killed in violence related to the conflict.

Although some of the violent splinter groups (e.g. the Real IRA) are still operating, the level of the threat they currently pose is insufficient to be labelled an insurgency. As such, the outcome of the 'Troubles' may be categorized as a negotiated settlement. Despite the strength of both the Irish and British states, the conflict became protracted because of: (i) the complexity of the warring parties; (ii) the deep and intractable constitutional/political problem underlying the conflict; (iii) the relative strengths of the insurgent, paramilitary and state forces; (iv) the legitimacy of both sides among local populations; and (v) the extensive external support given to the militant groups within Northern Ireland on both sides of the conflict (Mac Ginty et al. 2007; Barnes 2005; Whyte 1986; Brewer et al. 2014). At the same time, the negotiated settlement was made possible because of the mutually hurting stalemate that arose in the 1980s, and the shifting incentives and roles of important internal and external actors that reinforced the strength and bargaining power of both warring parties.

In sum, the complex and protracted conflict in Northern Ireland suggests that under certain circumstances, the long duration of an insurgency may create incentives for a negotiated settlement. In this particular case, the contributing circumstances to the negotiated settlement included strong, but constrained state actors without winning strategies, a resulting mutually hurting stalemate, and a shifting role of external actors and support, moving from direct support to warring parties on both sides to support for the negotiations and broader peace process. The conflict may also have been affected by global shifts such as the end of the Cold War and the War on Terror – both of which provided liberal-democratic and 'Western' governments with incentives to stop supporting militant groups and shore up their support for peace processes, especially in allied states. Even so, despite the incentive shifts away from violence and for peace, the fact remains that the peace process itself took 9 years to settle after the 1998 Good Friday Accords were signed and continues to be fragile, as illustrated by the current impact of the Brexit process on Northern Ireland intercommunal relations.

Case 4 Boko Haram

Although there is much confusion and misinformation about the current activities of Boko Haram, scholarship on its origins and earlier incarnations has improved steadily over the last few years. As this volume has also shown, more and more studies are empirically informed, based on interviews or in-depth analyses of relevant speeches and texts, helping us

Case 4 Boko Haram

- Outcome: not yet in sight
- Duration: 2009 onwards
- Variables that may shape outcome:
  - *Complex, multi-level, fragmented conflict*
  - *Use of religious framing but without clear political ambitions*
  - *Weak state capacity and apparent regime unwillingness to end the insurgency*
  - *Mismatch of state and insurgent strategies, indiscriminate violence against the civilian population by the insurgent and state forces*
  - *Extensive and influential external support for state, external refuge and ideological support for militants*

to get an increasingly clear picture of the trajectory of the movement. Yet there remains much to uncover, and the nature of the movement remains subject to intense public and political debate in and outside of Nigeria.

If we divide Boko Haram's trajectory into two phases, the first one can be traced to the early 2000s when Mohammed Yusuf articulated his 'ultra-Salafi' radicalism that departed significantly from most of the Nigerian Salafis' doctrinal positions on a host of religious, social and political issues. In particular, Yusuf's argument that modern secular education is religiously forbidden sets him at odds with many of his fellow Salafis, who vigorously disagreed with him. His contention that employment under the secular state of Nigeria is also religiously forbidden sets him not only apart from his fellow Salafis, but also on a dangerous path that led to violent confrontations with the security forces (Anonymous 2012; Kassim and Nwamkpa 2018; Thurston 2017). Despite localized skirmishes with communities and police, this earlier phase of Boko Haram's evolution was characterized not by violence but by ideological radicalization and grassroots mobilization of mass support, especially when compared with the ferocious conflagration in July 2009 that marked the beginning of the second phase.

There are several accounts of the 2009 confrontations between Mohammed Yusuf and Nigerian security forces that erupted simultaneously in Borno, Yobe, Bauchi, Kano and Jigawa states. The fierce fighting that lasted for about a week claimed over a thousand lives, left many more traumatized, and created property damage estimated at over N1.5 billion (Mohammed 2010; Pérouse de Montclos 2014; Botha et al. 2017; Mustapha 2014).

The success of government security forces in flushing the insurgents from their embedded cells within urban centres, especially in Maiduguri, has forced the insurgents to retreat into the forest, from where they have been devastating rural areas that are not adequately protected or policed (see Monguno and Umara, Chapter 3 this volume). Boko Haram has significantly shifted its targets of attack from specifically targeting arms-bearing agents of the Nigerian state, police informants, and Christians to the indiscriminate violence that has engulfed anything and anyone that present a target of opportunity, including the 50+ students slaughtered while sleeping in their hostels at the Yobe State Institute of Agricultural Training. To be sure, however, Boko Haram insurgents have continued to attack security forces, including the bold assaults on military barracks (see Chapter 5).

At risk of repeating many of the arguments made in other parts of this book, we want to briefly highlight some of the main factors that produced the current situation. First, factionalization and fragmentation are important dynamic factors often observed in insurgencies. As the insurgency has dragged on since 2009, Boko Haram has split into factions, which have used violence in different ways. The faction that was willing to swap captives with incarcerated leaders of the insurgency has demonstrated the possibility of negotiated end of the insurgency, while the belligerent faction continues to fight on even if the victory against Nigeria is no longer realistic, especially after losing much of the territory it controlled prior to 2015.

Second, like GI in Egypt, Boko Haram very effectively used *da'wa* to generate support, especially in the earlier, non-violent years of the movement. *Da'wa* has been particularly effective among the northern Nigerian poor, given high levels of poverty, lack of access to basic services, and lack of livelihood opportunities (see the Introduction and chapters by Monguno and Umara, and Meagher and Hassan, this volume). Throughout the movement's existence, Islam has been an important organizing principle and has served as a strong frame in the movement's rhetoric to its members as well as the outside world. Yet after the collapse of its Caliphate in 2015, there appears to be no clear political objective to the insurgency. Different factions may have different objectives, and parts of the movement as well as elements within the state appear more interested in sustaining the conflict (and its profitable war economy) than ending it (see the Introduction and Sanda, Chapter 5 this volume).

Third, the Nigerian government has displayed remarkable weakness and unwillingness to put in the effort required to fully defeat the movement. Although the government's approach has fluctuated over time and become gradually more effective in military terms, the continuing insecurity in large parts of the North East underline its inability or reluctance to implement the combination of enemy-centric and hearts-and-minds strategies that are required to end the insurgency (see Chapter 5). This government failure was originally connected to Nigeria's federal politics, in which ending the insurgency was not treated as a priority. This changed somewhat under President Buhari, who won the 2015 elections promising to defeat Boko Haram; but even he has struggled to coordinate an effective strategy beyond traditional military operations. This approach has resulted in a mismatch of strategies, where the government's heavy-handed enemy-centric approach has struggled to defeat the insurgents' guerrilla tactics. At the same time, both warring parties have engaged in extensive indiscriminate violence, which has alienated the population and intensified a pattern of violent escalation increasingly woven into national dynamics of electoral cycles and political corruption (see the Introduction).

The Boko Haram insurgency has been shaped by international dimensions. For one, the porous borders around Lake Chad have allowed the movement to seek refuge and support outside Nigeria (see Monguno and Umara, Chapter 3 this volume). It is also very likely that the movement has attracted fighters from outside Nigeria, including from other Sahelian countries and Libya. Moreover, factions of Boko Haram have explicitly sought an alliance with the so-called Islamic State (IS) and there have been indications of earlier ties with Al Shabaab and Al-Qaeda in the Islamic Maghreb (AQIM) (Comolli 2015; Thurston 2017). Although the depth of these connections is limited, the fact that one of Boko Haram's factions was renamed as the Islamic State's West Africa Province (ISWAP) indicates the strategic advantage this link is perceived to have for the faction officially recognized by IS, as well as the desire of this faction to distance itself from Shekau faction, particularly over the prohibition against killing innocent Muslims (Thurston 2017).

Finally, the Nigerian government has also received substantial support in its campaign, notably from neighbouring countries (Cameroon and Chad in particular) as well as the US and EU. While helping to rein in the insurgency, some feel that international coalitions have contributed to the over-militarization of the crisis, and allowed international actors greater latitude in pursuing their own agendas within Nigeria (Thurston 2017, 283; Ibrahim 2018). There is also a sense that the intervention of such a large number of actors on both sides 'heightens unpredictability' (Thurston 2017, 299).

Possible endgames of the Boko Haram insurgency

Taken together, these brief case studies allow us to construct scenarios for Boko Haram's endgame and discuss their relative likelihood. We will discuss the following possible scenarios:

- Nigerian government defeats the Boko Haram insurgency, for example by massive deployment of troops and eliminating its capacity to carry out violent attacks (similar to the GI case).
- Boko Haram achieves victory, for example, by creating and defending a polity in the rural areas of the North East, or by persisting as an entrenched Islamic insurgency.
- Negotiated settlement, which may for example involve the Nigerian government granting amnesty and compensation in return for Boko Haram disarmament and complete renunciation of violence (similar to the IRA case).
- Boko Haram transforms into a less ideological, more opportunistic militia operating like roving bandits with no territorial ambitions (similar to the LRA case).

To assess the relative likelihood of these outcomes, let us first consider the similarities and differences between the Boko Haram insurgency and the three other case studies analysed above. Table 10.2 summarizes some of the main features of the cases.

On the basis of this schematic overview, it is clear that no deterministic conclusions are possible. But we might conclude that, while all cases have some important elements in common, the LRA case is most similar to the current Boko Haram crisis. But the dynamics of factionalization suggests the likelihood of a twist that Boko Haram may end up with at least two different outcomes for different parts of the organization. Let us now examine the structural and dynamic factors that could shape the various scenarios for the end of the Boko Haram insurgency and then reflect on the possibility of fragmentation and a 'mixed' outcome.

NIGERIA DEFEATS BOKO HARAM

A clear victory by Nigerian government over Boko Haram is possible, even if it does not seem likely at the moment. Structurally, the Nigerian state could marshal the military and security capabilities to degrade the capacity of Boko Haram to continue as a viable insurgency, if not eliminating it altogether. The liberation of most of the territories hitherto controlled by Boko Haram reveals the capability of the Nigerian military to dislodge the insurgents, forcing them into hideouts in remote areas. The continued aerial campaigns by the Nigerian air force can be intensified to destroy any Boko Haram hideout. If sufficient military and security forces can be deployed in a coordinated and sustained offensive, they can defeat the insurgents. But this will involve overcoming current entrenched coordination and corruption problems.

This outcome becomes all the more possible if the Nigerian govern-

Table 10.2 Summary of case study findings

Insurgent group	**GI**	**LRA**	**IRA**	**Boko Haram**
Outcome	***Government victory***	***Transformation***	***Negotiated settlement***	***Ongoing***
Duration	*23 years*	*>30 years*	*38 years*	*Ongoing*
State bureaucratic capacity low		•		•
State military capacity low		•		•
Insurgent fragmentation			•	•
Democratizing (anocracy)	•	•		•
Mismatched conflict strategies		•	•	•
Enemy-centric strategy of state	•	•		•
Indiscriminate state violence		•		•
Indiscriminate rebel violence	•	•		•
International support for insurgents		•	•	•

ment is also able to consider the dynamic factors laid out above. First, this requires matching the military strategy with a strategy to win the 'hearts and minds' of north-eastern Nigerians. This will require systematic provision of security and other public goods and services, possibly in collaboration with the extensive international humanitarian efforts, as well as through a credible media campaign to rally public support. Second, the Nigerian security and military forces should refrain from threatening and harming members who are no longer fighting for Boko Haram, and provide safe haven for those who wish to defect. Finally, Nigeria should further strengthen its intelligence and military collaboration with the neighbouring Cameroon, Chad and Niger, although there is need for attention to US and EU activities in neighbouring countries. This collaboration proved vital in the successful 2015 campaign that destroyed the Boko Haram Caliphate, and can be used more effectively in current counter-insurgency efforts.

A defeat of Boko Haram has potential benefits. It can serve as a deterrent against other possible insurgencies, and also send clear signals to all the perpetrators of the pervasive insecurity in other parts of the country, including rural banditry, cattle rustling, and kidnapping for ransom. Yet at the same time, military interventions without complementary hearts-and-minds activities are very likely to fail; more perniciously, overly repressive military tactics can backfire by further destroying livelihoods and creating fresh grievances among its victims. Therefore, the temptation for the government to pursue this outcome should be wisely considered. That requires addressing the vested interests that appear no longer to be keen on ending the insurgency since it 'became an ATM machine [for politicians, the military and security forces] for taking money out of the treasury', creating a material interest in perpetuating the insurgency (Odunsi 2017).

Even if the Nigerian military secured a decisive victory by taking a comprehensive offensive against all the enclaves, hideouts and training camps of Boko Haram, it is important to keep in mind that insurgencies tend to outlast their military defeats by mutating into different kinds of unrest, or resurfacing under new leadership or organization. Boko Haram did re-emerge barely one year after the crushing defeat by security forces in 2009. In states with weak bureaucratic capacity to address the underlying structural causes of unrest, such as Nigeria and Uganda in this study, the patterns of military defeat followed by resurgent rebellion has occurred regularly. In other words, unless underlying causes are addressed, recurring insurgencies have the tendency to elude definitive government victory.

BOKO HARAM DEFEATS NIGERIA

Insurgent victories can take different guises. Arguably, right now Boko Haram can claim victory given its remarkable resilience after the brutal suppression of its first major confrontation with the Nigerian state in 2009, as well as the President Buhari's declaration in 2015 of its 'technical defeat'. In fact, many insurgencies have reckoned their victory not necessarily in clear defeat of government forces or toppling the adversary regime, but also in terms of their ability to persist and resist total elimination. Given the low standards of insurgents' victory, they can claim victory in so far as they can continue to cause havoc and chaos, long after government forces have crushed the backbone of the insurgency, thereby stealing victory out of defeat.

But some of the possible 'victories' of Boko Haram are clearly less likely than others. A full defeat of the Nigerian state, or gaining sovereignty over a significant part of Nigerian territory, is improbable, owing to the size and strength of Nigerian military might, the overwhelming lack of popular support for the insurgency, and the military and political limitations on the part of Boko Haram. Nigeria is also of too much strategic importance for the international community to allow such a victory, not only because of Nigeria's wealth in petroleum and other resources, but also because of its large population and strategic importance to economic and regional stability in West Africa. The French campaign that ousted the Islamists from northern Mali is indicative of the likely response to any significant resurgence of Boko Haram.

Moreover, Boko Haram has not, on the whole, demonstrated the political and bureaucratic capacity to successfully govern, even if it were able to retain long-term military control over part of the north-eastern region. Despite a remarkable ability to amass and operate sophisticated weapons, the insurgency under Shekau has not tended to focus on developing the indispensable political skills needed to hold and administer territories. Boko Haram discourses reveal an obsession with religious puritanism and violence, but little else. An increasing focus on recruitment through abductions and cash payment, indiscriminate slaughter of innocent civilians, sexual violence against women, and destruction of property and infrastructure all undermine the sustainability of life under Boko Haram. The already observed pattern of mass exodus of populations from areas that Boko Haram has controlled tends to drain people out of any possible territorial jurisdiction that the insurgency may establish.

At this point, Boko Haram also lacks the advantage of significant external support of its own. The recognition of ISWAP by IS has not significantly changed the dynamics of confrontation between Boko Haram and the Nigerian military, nor has it contributed materially to the Boko Haram cause. However, the rise of ISWAP is about more than factionalization of the insurgency. There is growing evidence of ISWAP shifting to a strategy of winning the hearts and minds of the local population (Hassan 2018; Bukarti 2018; Kelly 2019). In line with Islamic State ideology, ISWAP has publicly denounced the killing of innocent Muslims, allows civilians to leave conquered settlements if they wish, and punishes the harming of innocents by Boko Haram (Maclean 2019). Recent reports have also documented the development of basic administrative capacity in ISWAP territories around Lake Chad, involving systems of taxation, enforcement of Sharia law, provision of basic infrastructure and services such as wells, seeds, safe pasture for herders and protection from attacks by Shekau's faction of Boko Haram (Bukarti 2018; Reuters 2018). Far from being degraded by factionalism and the Nigerian military campaigns, ISWAP seems to have given Boko Haram a new lease of life, with a fighting force that was estimated in 2018 to have risen to between 3,000 and 5,000, and now stands at twice that of Shekau's faction, which is being drained by desertion (Reuters 2018).

While clear military victory that could lead to the establishment of a functional Islamic polity still seems far-fetched, the rise of ISWAP suggests that there is still no room for complacency. Prospects for persistently evading defeat, or building up loyalty in areas around Lake Chad long neglected by the state remain plausible outcomes. The failure on the part of Nigerian government to decisively end the Boko Haram insurgency, the potential for further international connections (in particular of the ISWAP faction), and the shift of ISWAP to a hearts-and-minds strategy in Nigeria's abandoned peripheries, indicate an ongoing risk of Boko Haram establishing some sort of de facto Islamic polity in hard-to-reach territory of the north-eastern borderlands. Whether this initiative will take root, and whether it would involve a move towards closer connections to international jihadist networks like IS or Al-Qaeda remains to be seen.

BOKO HARAM TRANSFORMATION

If we take the LRA as a 'model', a third scenario is for the status quo to continue, with Boko Haram insurgents conquering, holding and losing some territories within Nigeria and neighbouring border areas, if the incoherent response of Nigerian government remains unchanged. This may well involve a transformation in the nature of the insurgency towards more economic and criminal motivations: a move towards what we might call the 'double economies of extortion'. In this situation, the government continues to turn the Boko Haram insurgency into a source of rent extraction, and the insurgents create more widespread raids into local markets and engage increasingly in the extraction of 'taxes' from the population, as has occurred in many parts of the Democratic Republic of the Congo (Raeymaekers 2010; Oxfam 2012). These economies of extortion carry the insidious possibility of removing any desire on both sides to end the conflict in so far as it creates a steady stream of revenue to both sides, thereby undermining incentives bring it to a close. This scenario could include a further regionalization of the insurgency, as happened with the LRA, turning into a system of cross-border raiding or roving banditry.

The two main structural factors determining state efficacy against insurgencies – weak state and regime performance on the part of Nigeria, and a strong capacity to acquire and deploy sophisticated weapons and wage asymmetric warfare on the part of the insurgency – combine to suggest this trajectory as a plausible outcome, particularly with regard to Shekau's faction of Boko Haram. The incoherent strategy of the Nigerian government seems set to allow the insurgency to continue festering. But ongoing indiscriminate violence by both sides is likely to elicit growing pressure and possibly intervention by the international community. This scenario of militarized criminalization of the region, with ongoing military and humanitarian intervention, resembles an East African Great Lakes scenario in the Chad Basin, playing out Janet Roitman's (2005) violent vision of the region.

While such criminalized instability has persisted for 25 years over vast swaths of the DRC and neighbouring countries, the very different nature of West African states is more likely to contain it within the peripheries (Meagher 2014). However, unlike the LRA, Boko Haram is no longer likely to secure safe-havens in the neighbouring countries. Despite various challenges, regional collaboration with of the neighbouring countries will restrict the ability of Boko Haram to regroup in those countries, since each of those countries has its own incentives for not granting sanctuary to Boko Haram combatants, and only a few of them (Chad and Central African Republic) suffer from the levels of political disorder prevalent across South Sudan and the DRC. However, the very prospect of such a scenario in the more heavily populated and strategic context of West Africa should concentrate minds on alternatives.

Given the many changes required for a clear victory or defeat by either the Nigerian government or Boko Haram, such an unstable and messy scenario remains a plausible outcome, at least in the near future, particularly if the ISWAP experiment fails. It is clearly a destructive outcome, not only because of the high political, economic and social costs it would entail, but also because previous experience shows that such an outcome can persist for a long time. The only possible silver lining to such a scenario can be discerned in the Northern Irish Troubles: in the long run (more than one generation), this scenario can lead to pressure from all sides to end the conflict. Under the right circumstances, such a stalemate may be a step towards a negotiated settlement.

NEGOTIATED SETTLEMENT

Given that both structural and dynamic factors appear to rule out the feasibility of clear and decisive victory or defeat by either side, could this mean that the two parties may eventually come to the negotiating table?

Based on the Northern Irish case, such a negotiated settlement can occur after the development of a stable and long mutually hurting stalemate, in which neither party can win and the costs of continuing hostilities is too high but, as in the Northern Irish case, this can take decades. Buoyed by its ability to attack, and sustained by its powerful religious zeal, Boko Haram may not, right now, see the need or the wisdom in changing course. In the coming months and years, the double-edged potential of long duration may allow Boko Haram to continue wreaking havoc, or even reconquer towns and territories it once held but was unable to keep. At the same time, more belligerent factions would pose a threat as 'spoilers' of any seriously attempted peace process. The lack of a unified organizational structure characterizing Boko Haram makes it a highly problematic negotiating partner. While the Nigerian government has engaged some factions in negotiations that led to the swapping of captives and detainees, it still seems bent on carrying on with costly and indecisive military campaigns. In the Nigerian context, the lack of developed democratic states on both sides of the struggle as existed in the Northern Irish scenario suggests that growing disorder would overwhelm the possibility of negotiation over time. Prospects for effective negotiation look more likely sooner rather than later.

Perhaps a more relevant comparison is the Nigerian approach to the Niger Delta insurgency. There, amnesty and monetary incentives appear to have succeeded in reducing the violence considerably. However, important differences obtain. Despite its eventual degeneration into criminality, the Niger Delta insurgency was based on a more socially and politically acceptable narrative of marginalization in the context of resource extraction and environmental damage, and pursued more targeted insurgency strategies. While poverty, marginalization and environmental degradation are also part of the story of Boko Haram, their history of brutality and indiscriminate violence makes any form of amnesty, much less monetary incentives, highly problematic, and potentially politically explosive (Tucker and Mohammed 2018). This would require something more akin to the transitional justice arrangements of the Sierra Leonian and South African peace settlements, which, while not religious insurgencies, involved brutality against the population that undermined prospects for legitimate negotiation.

That said, thinking more creatively about such 'Nigerian' negotiated settlements may prove a fertile approach to the short run reduction of violence – even if it may not solve the deeper structural problems that helped Boko Haram to develop into the violent organization that has wreaked so much havoc. A more concerted effort from the Nigerian government for a negotiated settlement with members willing to defect can continue to isolate the hardliners and reduce their options. But that could also engender more determination or desperation in the ranks of the hardliners, giving them stronger incentives to function as 'spoilers' to any attempts at settlement.

MIXED OUTCOME

Given the fragmented nature of Boko Haram and the various pressures that the factors identified in Table 10.2 exert on these factions, a final possible outcome is a mixed scenario in which different factions end up in different scenarios. For example, such a mix could include negotiated settlements with willing factions or defectors and incarcerated Boko Haram insurgents; the creation of a rudimentary Islamic polity in the peripheral reaches of Lake Chad under the auspices of ISWAP with possible connections to transnational jihadi networks, and the continuation of more indiscriminate jihadi violence perpetrated by the most committed members of Shekau's faction; and the transformation of breakaway groups into disparate criminal elements wreaking havoc on peripheral rural areas. A version of this mixed outcome is likely in the current situation of fragmentation, lack of options, and lack of decisive military strategy or governance reforms on the part of the Nigerian state. A sober consideration of these prospects offers an opportunity for the Nigerian government to develop a more decisive and effective strategy by engaging constructively with some factions, waging serious military campaigns against the more intransigent elements, and above all, addressing the causes of Boko Haram violence by addressing the pervasive poverty, inequality, joblessness, lack of service provision and widespread despair across the north-east of the country.

Conclusion

Clearly, the end of the Boko Haram insurgency cannot be predicated with any certitude. The average duration of insurgences is at least eight years (Fearon and Laitin 2003; Pilster and Böhmelt 2014), and current developments suggest that the Boko Haram insurgency may last for a few more years. The trajectory of the LRA insurgency in Uganda demonstrates the unacceptable hazard of failure to end such an insurgency, instead allowing it to mutate into festering unrest ravaging innocent populations, while the ISWAP turn reveals the risks of allowing an insurgency to embed itself in the population through continued state neglect and insecurity. The Nigerian government should resist the temptation to consider the status quo a regrettable but tolerable outcome that does not threaten the regime or the nation.

Of the possible endgames examined here, government victory currently looks the least likely under current conditions. The state has failed to mobilize the economic, military and governance resources to defeat Boko Haram, and a unilateral ceasefire similar to the one made by the Islamist insurgency in Egypt is a pious dream – which the fractious structure of Boko Haram lacks the capacity to impose on its members even if it wanted to. The Nigerian government should note seriously the tendency of insurgencies to become long, messy and difficult to terminate. The terrible costs of that fact should provide a strong incentive to find the political will to work towards the expeditious ending of Boko Haram insurgency through a combination of focused military strategy, socio-economic rehabilitation, and improved governance. It is vital that a sustained and coordinated military offensive into all the remaining strongholds of Boko Haram be accompanied by committed and well-resourced population-centric strategies in order to drain Boko Haram of support and reduce the likelihood of recurrence.

Pursuing any kind of negotiated resolution will require diplomacy and constructive engagement with all Boko Haram factions, members and detainees who are willing to cease hostilities, or who have been victims of circumstance. But who can be the interlocutors in these communications? And what political incentives are required at what levels to make constructive engagement possible? One potential path of engagement is religious. An important lesson to be learned from the Egyptian insurgency is the central role of religious doctrine and ideological commitment in radicalizing movements, as well as providing justifications for ending the violence. Prominent Nigerian Islamic scholars have already spoken against Boko Haram violence and more might be needed; some could also function as brokers and interlocutors in more constructive engagement with the movement. Other candidates could be local traditional authorities or politicians with connections and trust on both sides. But the risks to such individuals are tremendous, and creating a 'safe space' for such engagement would require creative political entrepreneurship and genuine political commitment to honour any negotiated terms of settlement. Without that, negotiations are bound to be a wasteful exercise instead of a way to end the bloodshed and terminate the misery of millions of innocent people.

Bibliography

Adesoji, A.O., 2011, 'Between Maitatsine and Boko Haram: Islamic Fundamentalism and the Response of the Nigerian State', *Africa Today* 57 (4), 98–119.

Agbiboa, D.E., 2013, 'Living in Fear: Religious Identity, Relative Deprivation and the Boko Haram Terrorism', *African Security* 6 (2), 153–70

Anonymous, 2012, 'The Popular Discourses of Salafi Radicalism and Salafi Counter-radicalism in Nigeria: A Case Study of Boko Haram', *Journal of Religion in Africa* 42 (2), 118–44.

Arreguín-Toft, I., 2001, 'How the Weak Win Wars: A Theory of Asymmetric Conflict', *International Security* 26 (1), 93–128.

——2005, *How the Weak Win Wars: A Theory of Asymmetric Conflict*, Cambridge University Press.

Ashour, O., 2007, 'Lions Tamed? An Inquiry into the Causes of De-Radicalization of Armed Islamist Movements: The Case of the Egyptian Islamic Group', *Middle East Journal* 61 (4), 596–625.

Bamford, B.W.C., 2005, 'The Role and Effectiveness of Intelligence in Northern Ireland', *Intelligence and National Security* 20 (4), 581–607.

Barnes, L.P., 2005, 'Was the Northern Ireland Conflict Religious?' *Journal of Contemporary Religion* 20 (1), 55–69.

BBC, 2003, 'Security Forces Aided Loyalist Murders', 17 April, http://news.bbc.co.uk/2/hi/uk_news/northern_ireland/2954773.stm, accessed 27 April 2019.
BBC, 2014, 'Pat Finucane Murder: "Shocking State Collusion", says PM', 12 December, www.bbc.com/news/uk-northern-ireland-20662412, accessed 27 April, 2019.
Behrend, H., 2000, *Alice Lakwena & the Holy Spirits: War In Northern Uganda 1986–97*, 1st edn, Oxford, Kampala, Nairobi and Athens, OH: Ohio University Press.
Bell, J.B., 1997, *The Secret Army: The IRA*, New Brunswick, NJ.: Transaction Publishers.
Bergesen, A.J., 2008, *The Sayyid Qutb Reader: Selected Writings on Politics, Religion, and Society*, New York: Routledge.
Berman, P., 2003, 'The Philosopher of Islamic Terror', *New York Times*, 23 March, www.nytimes.com/2003/03/23/magazine/23GURU.html, accessed 17 March 2010.
Blattman, C. and Miguel, E., 2010, 'Civil War', *Journal of Economic Literature* 48 (1), 3–57.
Botha, A., Ewi, M., Salifu, U. and Abdile, M., 2017, 'Understanding Nigerian citizens' perspectives on Boko Haram', ISS Monographs 196, Institute for Security Studies, Pretoria.
Brewer, J.D., Higgins, G.I. and Teeney, F., 2014, *Religion, Civil Society, & Peace in Northern Ireland*, Oxford: Oxford University Press.
Brigaglia, A., 2012, 'Ja'far Mahmoud Adam, Mohammed Yusuf and Al-Muntada Islamic Trust: Reflections on the Genesis of the Boko Haram Phenomenon in Nigeria', *Annual Review of Islam in Africa* 11, 35–44.
Bukarti, A.B., 2018, 'The Battle for Hearts and Minds in the Lake Chad Basin', Tony Blair Institute for Global Change, https://institute.global/insight/co-existence/battle-hearts-and-minds-lake-chad-basin, accessed 9 September 2019.
Burke, J., 2018, 'Nigerian Islamists Kill Scores of Soldiers in Military Base Attack', *The Guardian*, Friday 23 November.
Carey, S.C., 2007, 'Rebellion in Africa: Disaggregating the Effect of Political Regimes', *Journal of Peace Research* 44 (1): 47–64.
Carsten, P. and Kingimi, A., 2018, 'Islamic State Ally Stakes Out Territory around Lake Chad' *Reuters*, 30 April, https://uk.reuters.com/article/uk-nigeria-security/islamic-state-ally-stakes-out-territory-around-lake-chad-idUKKBN1I11BP, accessed 9 September 2019.
Cochrane, F., 2007, 'Irish-America, the End of the IRA's Armed Struggle and the Utility of "Soft Power"', *Journal of Peace Research* 44 (2), 215–31.
—— 2013, *Northern Ireland: The Reluctant Peace*, New Haven, CT: Yale University Press.
Comolli, V., 2015, *Boko Haram: Nigeria's Islamist Insurgency*, Oxford: Oxford University Press.
Connable, B. and Libicki, M.C., 2010, 'How Insurgencies End', RAND Corporation, Santa Monica, CA, www.rand.org/pubs/monographs/MG965.html, accessed 27 April 2019.
Dixon, P., 2001, *Northern Ireland: The Politics of War and Peace*, New York: Palgrave Macmillan.
El-Ghobashy, M., 2005, 'Metamorphosis of the Egyptian Muslim Brothers', *International Journal of Middle East Studies* 37, 373–93.
Enterline, A.J., Stull, E. and Magagnoli, J., 2013, 'Reversal of Fortune? Strategy Change and Counterinsurgency Success by Foreign Powers in the Twentieth Century', *International Studies Perspectives* 14 (2), 176–98.
Fearon, J.D. and Laitin, D.D., 2003, 'Ethnicity, Insurgency, and Civil War', *American Political Science Review* 97 (1), 75–90.
Findley, M.G. and Young, J.K., 2007, 'Fighting Fire with Fire? How (Not) to Neutralize an Insurgency', *Civil Wars* 9 (4), 378–401.
Firestone, R., 2012, *Holy War in Judaism: The Fall and Rise of a Controversial Idea*, Oxford: Oxford University Press.
Fletcher, H., 2008, 'Egyptian Islamic Jihad (aka: Al-Jihad, Egyptian al-Jihad; New Jihad; Jihad Group, Al-Qaeda)', Council on Foreign Relations, www.cfr.org/egypt/egyptian-islamic-jihad/p16376, accessed 27 April 2019.

Gent, S.E., 2008, 'Going in When It Counts: Military Intervention and the Outcome of Civil Conflicts', *International Studies Quarterly* 52 (4), 713–35.

Gunaratna, R. and Ali, M.B., 2009, 'De-Radicalization Initiatives in Egypt: A Preliminary Insight', *Studies in Conflict & Terrorism* 32 (4), 277–91.

Hashmi, S.H., 2012, *Just Wars, Holy Wars, and Jihads: Christian, Jewish, and Muslim Encounters and Exchanges*, Oxford: Oxford University Press.

Hassan, I., 2018, 'The Dangers of a Better-Behaved Boko Haram', *The New Humanitarian* (formerly *IRIN News*), 21 August, www.thenewhumanitarian.org/opinion/2018/08/21/opinion-nigeria-militancy-peace-boko-haram, accessed 9 September 2019.

Ibrahim, J, 2018, 'Telling Ourselves the Truth About the Boko Haram Insurgency', *Premium Times*, 18 December.

Ibrahim, S.E, 1996, *Egypt, Islam, and Democracy: Twelve Critical Essays*, Cairo: American University in Cairo Press.

ICG (International Crisis Group), 2004, 'Northern Uganda: Understanding and Solving the Conflict', www.crisisgroup.org/en/regions/africa/horn-of-africa/uganda/077-northern-uganda-understanding-and-solving-the-conflict.aspx, accessed 27 April 2019.

—— 2005, 'Shock Therapy for Northern Uganda's Peace Process', www.crisisgroup.org/en/regions/africa/horn-of-africa/uganda/B023-shock-therapy-for-northern-ugandas-peace-process.aspx, accessed 27 April 2019.

—— 2006, 'Peace in Northern Uganda?' www.crisisgroup.org/en/regions/africa/horn-of-africa/uganda/B041-peace-in-northern-uganda.aspx, accessed 27 April 2019.

—— 2010, 'LRA: A Regional Strategy beyond Killing Kony', www.crisisgroup.org/en/regions/africa/horn-of-africa/uganda/157-lra-a-regional-strategy-beyond-killing-kony.aspx, accessed 27 April, 2019.

Jackson, P., 2002, 'The March of the Lord's Resistance Army: Greed or Grievance in Northern Uganda?' *Small Wars and Insurgencies* 13 (3), 29–52.

Johnson, J.T., 1997, *The Holy War Idea in Western and Islamic Traditions*, University Park: Pennsylvania State University Press.

Juergensmeyer, M., 2003, *Terror in the Mind of God: The Global Rise of Religious Violence*, Berkeley: University of California Press.

Kalyvas, S.N. and Kocher, M.A., 2007, 'How "Free" is Free Riding in Civil Wars? Violence, Insurgency, and the Collective Action Problem', *World Politics* 59 (2), 177–216.

Kassim, A. and Nwankpa, 2018, *The Boko Haram Reader: From Nigerian Preachers to the Islamic State*, London: Hurst.

Kelly, F., 2019, 'ISWAP Killed "Dozens" of Nigeria and Chad Troops near Baga in July 29 Clashes', *The Defense Post*, 1 August, https://thedefensepost.com/2019/08/01/nigeria-baga-iswap-borno, accessed 7 August 2019.

Last, M., 2009, 'The Pattern of Dissent: Boko Haram in Nigeria 2009', *Annual Review of Islam in Africa* 10, 7–11.

—— 2011, 'Northern Nigerian Militancy: Who and What are Boko Haram?' *African Arguments*, 15 July.

Leiken, R.S. and Brooke, S., 2007. The Moderate Muslim Brotherhood, *Foreign Affairs* 86 (2), 107–21.

Loimeier, R., 2012, 'Boko Haram: The Development of a Militant Religious Movement in Nigeria', *Afrika Spectrum* 47 (2–3), 137–55.

Maclean, R., 2019, 'They say Boko Haram is gone: One Mother's Terror Tells Another Story…', *The Guardian*, 2 February, www.theguardian.com/world/2019/feb/02/election-nigeria-boko-haram-refugees, accessed 9 September 2019.

Mac Ginty, R., Muldoon, O.T. and Ferguson, N., 2007, 'No War, No Peace: Northern Ireland after the Agreement', *Political Psychology* 28 (1), 1–11.

Marchetti, R. and Tocci, N., 2009, 'Conflict Society: Understanding the Role of Civil

Society in Conflict', *Global Change, Peace & Security* 21 (2), 201–17.

Meagher, K., 2014, 'Smuggling Ideologies: From Criminalization to Hybrid Governance in African Clandestine Economies', *African Affairs* 113 (453), 497–517.

Mitchell, R.P., 1969, *The Society of the Muslim Brothers*, London: Oxford University Press.

Mohammed, A., 2010, *The Paradox of Boko Haram*, Kano: Moving Image.

Mustapha, A.R., 2014, 'Understanding Boko Haram', in A.R. Mustapha (ed.), *Sects & Social Disorder: Muslim Identities & Conflict in Northern Nigeria*, Woodbridge: James Currey, 147–98.

O'Brien, B., 1995, *The Long War: The IRA and Sinn Fein*, Dublin: The O'Brien Press.

Odunsi, W., 2017, 'Jonathan, Loyalists Turned Boko Haram Insurgency into ATM', *Daily Post*, 27 April, http://dailypost.ng/2017/04/27/jonathan-loyalists-turned-boko-haram-insurgency-atm-obasanjo, accessed 27 April 2019.

Oxfam, 2012, 'Commodities of War', Oxfam Briefing Paper, www.oxfam.org/sites/www.oxfam.org/files/bp164-commodities-of-war-drc-protection-201112-en.pdf, accessed 9 September 2019.

Pérouse de Montclos, M.A., 2014, *Boko Haram: Islamism, Politics, Security and the State in Nigeria*, West African Politics and Society series, Leiden: African Studies Centre.

Pham, P.N., Vinck, P. and Stover, E., 2008. 'The Lord's Resistance Army and Forced Conscription in Northern Uganda', *Human Rights Quarterly*, 30, 404–11.

Pilster, U. and Böhmelt, T., 2014, 'Predicting the Duration of the Syrian Insurgency', *Research & Politics* (July–September), 1–10, https://journals.sagepub.com/doi/pdf/10.1177/2053168014544586, accessed 27 April 2019.

Raeymaekers, T., 2010, 'Protection for sale? War and the Transformation of Regulation on the Congo-Ugandan Border', *Development and Change* 41 (4), 563–87.

Roitman, J., 2005, *Fiscal Disobedience: An Anthropology of Economic Regulation in Central Africa*, Princeton, NJ: Princeton University Press.

Shelton, A.M., Stojek, A.M. and Sullivan, P.L., 2013, 'What Do We Know about Civil War Outcomes?' *International Studies Review* 15 (4), 515–38.

Stedman, S., 1997, 'Spoiler Problems in Peace Processes', *International Security* 22 (2), 5–53.

Thurston, A., 2017, *Boko Haram: The History of an African Jihadist Movement*, Princeton, NJ: Princeton University Press.

Tucker, D. and Mohammed, J.A., 2018, 'Through Our Eyes: People's Perspectives on Building Peace in Northeast Nigeria', Kukah Centre and Conciliation Resources Policy Paper, April, Abuja and London.

Vindevogel, S., Coppens, K., Derluyn, I., De Schryver, M., Loots, G. and Broekaert, E., 2011, 'Forced Conscription of Children during Armed Conflict: Experiences of Former Child Soldiers in Northern Uganda', *Child Abuse & Neglect* 35 (7), 551–62.

Vreeland, J.R., 2008, 'The Effect of Political Regime on Civil War: Unpacking Anocracy', *Journal of Conflict Resolution* 52 (3), 401–25.

Whyte, J.H., 1986, 'How Is the Boundary Maintained between the Two Communities in Northern Ireland?' *Ethnic and Racial Studies* 9 (2), 219–34.

Wright, L., 2008, 'The Rebellion Within: Al-Qaeda Mastermind Questions Terrorism', *The New Yorker*, 2 June.

11

Conclusion
Toward a whole-of-society approach to counter-radicalization

ABDUL RAUFU MUSTAPHA, KATE MEAGHER, DAVID EHRHARDT, IBRAHIM HARUNA HASSAN, KHADIJA GAMBO HAWAJA, RAHMANE IDRISSA, MURRAY LAST, ABUBAKAR K. MONGUNO, JULIE G. SANDA, SHERINE EL TARABOULSI-McCARTHY, M. SANI UMAR, IBRAHIM UMARA, ZAINAB USMAN

Rethinking counter-radicalization policy

After a decade of failed counter-insurgency, there is a need to rethink prevailing approaches to defeating Boko Haram. The sobering endgame scenarios outlined in the previous chapter highlight what is at stake if the Nigerian state and international community continue to press ahead with current strategies. Over the past few years, there has been a growing recognition of the need to shift away from a focus on security and humanitarian responses toward a holistic approach that engages more fully with the causes of conflict and the societal resources for resolving it (Tucker and Mohammed 2018, 4; Thurston 2018; *Daily Post* 2014). Indeed, since 2014, strategies of the Nigerian state for dealing with Boko Haram have advocated the need to supplement military strategies with a 'whole-of-society approach' as articulated in the previous administration's National Counter Terrorism Strategy (NACTEST):

> [W]e have moved from a whole of government to a whole of society approach in our counter terrorism thinking. We believe that we can win the war against terror by mobilizing our family, cultural, religious and national values.... Government is partnering with faith based organizations, community based organizations, NGOs and other stakeholders to deliver counter radicalization programs at community levels. (*Daily Post* 2014)

The notion of a 'whole-of-society approach' has percolated through subsequent incarnations of counter-radicalization policy, and has been reaffirmed in President Buhari's National Action Plan for Preventing and Countering Violent Extremism, signed in 2017, which 'adopts a 'whole-of-government' and a 'whole-of-society approach' centred on engagement with civil society in the delivery of counter-radicalization measures (Musa 2017, 2).

As this book has argued, a whole-of-society approach requires a 'whole-of-society' understanding of causes of the conflict, and a commitment to engaging the vast institutional resources within society in the design as well as the delivery of counter-radicalization policy. This concluding chapter will consider more precisely what a whole-of-society approach must mean if it is to provide an effective resolution to the conflict. It will draw together the insights of the preceding chapters on the forces driving the rise and persistence of Boko Haram, to develop a clearer policy vision for ending the conflict. An effective response requires both the Nigerian state and the international community to confront their demons: corruption, mismanagement, counter-terrorism protocols that are fundamentally inappropriate to engagement with a Muslim majority context, and a persistent unwillingness to address the failure of liberalizing economic policies to include the less advantaged. Reforming security and social programming will not resolve the scourge of Islamic insurgency if the underlying economic and political causes are left unaddressed.

Throughout, this chapter will emphasize the importance of aligning counter-radicalization policy with the needs and capacities of northern Nigerian society, and with a national policy vision, rather than with detached international notions of best practice, inappropriate counter-terrorism protocols and disruptive economic policies. Starting with a brief critique of the limitations of prevailing policy strategies, this chapter will go on to distil alternative policy perspectives that engage more effectively with wider social and political realities, focusing on four dimensions: religion and the state, the military, poverty alleviation and employment, and the role of women and civil society.

Beyond Prevailing Approaches

As the years go by, criticisms of Nigeria's counter-insurgency efforts have mounted. Successive initiatives have been accused of being too security-focused, too inconsistent, too gender-blind, too depoliticized and too costly (Thurston 2018; Tucker and Mohammed 2018; Matfess 2017; Mercy Corps 2016). There is much truth in these critiques, but there is a tendency to then use them as wedges to push sectoral and external priorities into the policy process, rather than helping to refocus policy on the underlying drivers of conflict and the needs of northern Nigerian society. Expanding international cooperation through increasingly multinational joint task forces and engagement with international aid agencies have brought greater military expertise, resources, territorial coverage and humanitarian support into the campaign. But they have also shifted the dominant interests and interpretations of the conflict further away from national counter-radicalization plans, economic causes, and social realities on the ground, with the result that much is being lost in translation.

A number of commentators have raised concerns about how the formulation and implementation of policies designed to end the conflict are distorted by international protocols and practices. As Luisa Enria (2012) has pointed out in the context of Sierra Leone, international policy priorities and abstract notions of 'best practice' tend to promote standardized policy packages detached from local realities, turning local populations into objects rather than subjects of peace building. Technocratic priorities and pressures to involve the private sector take precedence over genuine engagement with local needs. The 'new humanitarianism' has accentuated the involvement of the global private sector in humanitarian activities as well as peace-building initiatives, from logistics and shelter building to project financing. While this may bring in much needed resources and capacities, it also biases practices and goals away from local concerns in the interests of international policy pressures, profit, financialization and datafication (ODI 2016, 39; Duffield 2018).

Further concerns have been raised about the tendency of multinational forces to use the Boko Haram conflict to pursue foreign policy objectives at the expense of local sovereignty, expanding international military presence within the region (Ibrahim and Bala 2018; Thurston 2018). International pressures also influence outward-facing national policy concerns. The push for return and reintegration of displaced people prioritizes humanitarian policy fashions and domestic political appearances over the experience and security of north-eastern Nigerian populations. Pressures to return, and repeated rounds of Boko Haram attacks have forced some local communities to flee towns like Bama as many as three times (Maclean 2018, 2019). Similarly, peace-building models privileging negotiation and rapid reintegration of former Boko Haram members is felt by many local communities to prioritize the needs of insurgents over those of victims (Tucker and Mohammed 2018). A joint report of the Kukah Foundation and Conciliation Resources notes that 'The deeply entrenched belief that existing reintegration, reconciliation and negotiation processes in north-east Nigeria offer impunity for perpetrators and limited justice for the victims is at the heart of communities' resistance…' (ibid., 8). Balancing the need for reintegration with local fears and concerns, and ensuring that material support and training are not targeted at perpetrators to the exclusion of equally poor and more long-suffering members of the surrounding communities is key to fostering peace rather than rewarding or inciting conflict (Knight 2008, 47).

Tensions between international protocols and local realities have embedded deep contradictions at the heart of the demand for 'soft' approaches to counter-extremism. Despite a growing international emphasis on a 'multidimensional, whole-of-society approach' in rehabilitation and reintegration (R&R) programming to combat violent extremism, prevailing counter-terrorism protocols and programming priorities militate against genuine community engagement. Calls for a 'soft approach' are accompanied by counter-terrorism protocols that marginalize and bureaucratize civil engagement, particularly in Muslim societies. Demands to make R&R programming 'age appropriate' and 'gender-sensitive', and to ensure that civil society partners are 'neutral' and able to engage with the private sector and media, severely constrain who is allowed to contribute to processes of counter-radicalization (Nemr and Bhulai 2018). As a result, society-focused approaches mandate a range of best practices on how society can be brought in, often screening out those with the greatest local knowledge. Community participation becomes a mechanical process of contracting qualifying locals to roll out internationally formulated counter-extremism programmes, reducing the role of community actors to one of service provision rather than shaping programme content (Njoku 2018).

The Global Community and Resilience Fund (GCERF) has taken this form of engagement to a new extreme in its pilot partnership with Nigeria to support local resilience in contexts of violent extremism by providing small grants to local civil society organizations. The eligibility criteria for local organizations include experience and capability in programme design and management, experience in financial management and accounting for international donor grant funding, as well as experience in working with or forming a consortium – effectively targeting funding well above the heads of most local civil society groups in north-eastern Nigeria (GCERF 2018). More to the point, the fund has elected to focus on the North Central zone rather than the North East, given less attractive risk profiles in areas where violent extremism is pervasive (GCERF 2017).

As a wider number of international and corporate actors move in, there are growing pressures to financialize counter-radicalization through 'blended and innovative financing', 'social impact bonds' (GCERF 2016), and what the World Economic Forum (2017) has referred to as 'a market for impact investment in humanitarian challenges'. The idea of turning humanitarian crises into investment opportunities, however benevolently intended, is not only disturbing but may well steer funding away from areas most in need owing to unprofitable risk calculations. Alongside dubious promises to bring in more resources, such processes of projectization and financialization of societal engagement in counter-terrorism generate an increasingly anarchic and fragmented arena of counter-radicalization policy, ever more detached from local realities and the requirements of informed and coherent policy planning.

Policy insights from a whole-of-society perspective

Using a 'whole-of-society approach' to engage with local strengths requires a reconnection with the perspectives and capacities detailed throughout this book. While international perspectives, inputs and resources offer valuable support, it is vital that they be used to inform rather than to determine or distort policy choices. National priorities, local realities and a clear understanding of northern Nigerian political and social dynamics remain the real crucible in which effective approaches to counter-radicalization must be forged. Refocusing the discussion of counter-radicalization policy on local realities takes us back to the three arguments made at the beginning of the book: that Boko Haram is more about politics than religion; that counter-radicalization is not only about jihadis, but about the embedded societal capacities for reigning in extremism; and that Boko Haram is a product of the structural dynamics of poverty and inequality. These arguments, and the evidence presented in the course of this book, propose a significant reframing of counter-radicalization policy in Nigeria. Decoding the policy message of Boko Haram has less to do with understanding jihadi ideology or global terrorist networks, than with grasping less exotic notions of subaltern political protest in the face of extreme economic inequality, cast in the idiom of an Islamic society. The remainder of the chapter draws out key implications for more effective counter-radicalization policy across the four key domains of religion and the state, the military, poverty alleviation and employment, and the role of women and civil society.

RELIGION AND THE STATE

While some segments of the *ulama* have played a central role in provoking radicalization, Umar (Chapter 2) documents the central importance of the vast majority of moderate *ulama* in counter-radicalization processes. He emphasizes the need for Islamic messaging through preaching, and conventional as well as social media, drawing on Qur'anic verses, traditions of the Prophet Muhammad, and also doctrines and tenets in the traditions of Islamic learning deployed to reject violence and to demonstrate the Islamic acceptance of difference and diversity in religious convictions. The existence of several different schools of Islamic law and theological interpretation as well as numerous verses that celebrate difference show that diversity is part of the Islamic DNA, opening opportunities to celebrate it, while reiterating existing scriptural warnings against reckless accusations of apostasy (*takfir*). The case of al-Gama'ah al-Islamiyya in Egypt highlights the power of religious doctrine in ending violence even among committed extremist groups. Repeated exposure to popular suffering and Islamic prohibitions of violence against innocents are a source of constructive ideological power from within Islam. A similar process of religious revulsion against the massacring of innocents appears to be at work within the Islamic State's West Africa Province (ISWAP), opening potential for new avenues for potent messaging and moral challenges.

To be effective, however, counter-radical religious messaging must be about more than propagating religious tolerance and quietist doctrines. The challenge of making these messages credible to the millions of disaffected youth across the north must go beyond emphasizing the Qur'anic credentials of quietism and decrying the suffering of victims of Boko Haram. The relevance of counter-radical messaging requires that scriptural support for peace and pluralism must be connected to non-violent discourses about justice, economic rights, anti-corruption and democracy. If the price of counter-radicalization is that Muslims can no longer be critical citizens, efforts at religious messaging are likely to backfire (Brown and Saeed 2015). That genie is already out of the bottle. It is the lack of conventional political space for voicing popular social and economic protest that drove much of the appeal of Yusuf's sermons, and will drive support for new Yusufs if political and religious space is not created for Muslims to engage in non-violent social and political critique. Anything less will damage the credibility of moderate Islamic scholars, particularly among disaffected youth. Peaceful expressions of Islam need to demonstrate that they too can offer a vision of an alternative future.

The task of creating a framework for social cohesion cannot be left to religion alone. Lessons from Niger Republic highlight the failure of Nigerian federalism to safeguard social cohesion, as well as the loss of regulatory capacity to limit extremist mobilization, particularly in the domains of education and preaching. The key issue is to control anti-democratic and violent forms of mobilization, not all political mobilization by Muslims. While Nigeria's federal governance structures – and perhaps also its much larger and more heterogeneous population – are less suited to centralized policy making, there is a need to restore basic political mechanisms for controlling religious and opportunist excesses and promoting a national vision. Effective state coordination of religious practice is not about draconian new laws or top-down control, but about reinstating mechanisms to curb the propensity of religious competition to foster extremist tendencies.

The contributions by Umar and Idrissa emphasize the need for central state oversight over preaching and education in order to contain radical tendencies and competitive religious pressures. Far from calling for greater centralization of powers or constraints on religious freedom, state regulation is primarily about the revival of pre-existing institutions and enforcement of laws that already exist. The restoration and appropriate funding of preaching boards that operated in the early 1980s, and of state-level bureaux of Islamic affairs to monitor Islamic school curricula and quality of instruction in the burgeoning Islamic school sector, would go a long way to containing the pressures that have propagated violent extremism (Umar 1993; Mustapha 2015). Given aggressive tendencies toward institutional capture among particular sects, special attention is needed to ensure and enshrine representative balance among Islamic sects in the constitution and staffing of these bodies. These Islamic regulatory bodies should not be confused with the more recent involvement of Islamic scholars in a range of new bodies such as the Sharia Implementation Committee or the Hisbah. While the former focus on the mutual harmonization of religious practice and educational priorities with national law, the latter involve the politicized mobilization of religious authority in confrontation with national law.

Preaching could also be better regulated through enforcement of existing laws against hate speech, incitement to violence and threat to public order, which would also go a long way to containing extremist pressures. Greater enforcement of existing laws, rules, regulations and guidelines governing the licensing of private media organizations, and production and sale of religious media is also vital. The use of copyright bodies to collect fees for the state needs to be complemented with a greater role in monitoring for extremist content. There is also a need for greater monitoring of the discourses recorded and spread in portable media, through surveying new releases in the market as well as by monitoring what is spreading on social media. Rather than creating a basis for censorship, this should be subject to existing laws against incitement, and could be used as an indicator of rising tensions and a basis for religious debate. Where problematic discourses are identified, learned and influential members of the *ulama* should be approached to offer timely and measured rebuttals, robustly challenging misreadings and reckless interpretations of the scriptures, contributing to a spirit of religious debate and robust regulation rather than repression.

As Idrissa has shown in this volume, effective agendas of social cohesion do not arise spontaneously, and do not prevail unaided. In addition to being promoted through coordination between the *ulama* and the state, they must be nurtured in the nation's school system and protected through its regulatory agencies. The Niger case shows that an education policy that puts a premium on the need for curricula to promote national cohesion, religious tolerance, and respect for democracy strongly contributes to providing balance and ideological resilience even in a cash-strapped state and impoverished society such as Niger. More attention is needed to curricular oversight and coordination between Ministries of Education and revitalized bureaux of Islamic affairs. It is also vital to ensure adequate funding and organizational arrangements to allow these institutions to carry out their duties. It would be worth investigating the share of funding, professional training, and institutional organization provided for preaching boards, Islamic bureaux and educational oversight in Niger relative to Nigeria. These lessons from Niger mitigate fears of a contagion effect within the region, given the stronger institutions of secularism and centralized control of education and preaching within many Francophone West African states (Idrissa 2017).

Finally, more explicit attention must be paid to the limited role of actual religious radicalization in Boko Haram membership so that deradicalization strategies can be more effectively targeted. As several of the studies presented here have shown, a range of other motives including social loyalties, poverty, economic opportunity, revenge, coercion and criminality account for the bulk of Boko Haram membership (see Umar and Ehrhardt, Chapter 10; Monguno and Umara, Chapter 3 this volume). A greater focus on separating genuinely radicalized adherents from the destitute, socially loyal, opportunistic and coerced, not to mention the unjustly arrested, would facilitate more timely and effective reintegration, with a focus on addressing the problems of poverty, injustice and criminality among non-radicalized members, while concentrating the more demanding process of deradicalization on the much smaller numbers who actually show signs of extremist radicalization.

THE MILITARY

An effective military is central to ending the Boko Haram insurgency, making it essential that counter-radicalization strategies focus on improving the performance and integrity of the military as an institution. The need for an overarching national security policy cannot be overemphasized. A national security policy would provide a framework for effective cooperation among the various arms of the security services, as well as providing for a long-term and institutionalized approach to security as opposed to the ad hoc and reactive manner that has become the norm. While Obasanjo put the military back in the barracks in 1999, the military has managed to extend the barracks across the whole of society.

Active in at least 32 out of 36 states, the military has extended its reach into a wide range of internal security operations. Such over-militarization is damaging both to society and to the military. The need to protect the integrity of the military requires confining it to clearly defined roles and minimizing its use outside of those roles, to ensure that the military operates within rather than above the law.

Effective use of the military calls for handing over primary responsibility for internal security to the Nigeria Police Force as soon as order is restored in towns and cities. The police force is underutilized under the guise of being overwhelmed by the security situation, and is often required to stand aside for the military to normalize the situation. There is need for an integrated plan that would involve the police progressively resuming civil policing duties when the fighting is done, while the military rolls back its activities. Timely return to civil policing is complicated by the erosion of the police force over many years by resource constraints, and the deployment of up to one-third of the existing force to private protection duties in the face of growing insecurity. Out of a force of nearly 400,000 police officers, more than 150,000 are assigned to guard state officials and wealthy individuals (Ibrahim and Bala 2018). There is clearly a case for increased recruitment and training of police officers. This dovetails with the need to demobilize the Civilian Joint Task Force (CJTF), which, with appropriate screening and training, could be integrated into the police force or into forms of community-led policing. The CJTF is an unusual model that needs to be re-organized under an appropriate regulatory framework to avoid its degeneration into a disruptive force. The efforts of the Borno State government toward re-organizing the group and training its members must be continued until all members suited to remaining in law enforcement are trained. It is imperative for government to develop an effective and comprehensive policy for managing the CJTF post-insurgency. This would entail a more nuanced understanding of the composition of the group and resolution of the allegations of abuse levelled against some of its members.

While over-militarization has contributed to over-stretching the military, the insurgency has also exposed and in some cases exacerbated serious weaknesses in military capacity. The military has an estimated force strength of 181,000 deployed across 32 states (Ibrahim and Bala 2018, 5). Such understaffing has confined soldiers to long tours of duty – some on the front lines in fighting Boko Haram have been on duty for 3–5 years without a break, seriously undermining morale (Durmaz 2019). President Buhari has recently commented that the military are suffering from 'battle fatigue' (*The Defense Post* 2019). While the army is losing morale, Boko Haram has been re-energized by the rise of the newer ISWAP faction. Events linked to ISWAP more than tripled in 2018 compared to 2017, and fatalities increased by nearly 60 per cent (Olojo 2019). Lethal attacks continue to punctuate the course of 2019, and ISWAP is reputed to have created state-like structures in five local governments in the north-eastern corner of Borno State (Samuel 2019; *The Defense Post* 2019). This kinder, gentler brand of violent extremism continues to win local hearts and minds by filling gaps in basic infrastructural, security and social welfare services, while seige tactics and abuses by the military continue to alienate local populations.

The under-performance of the military is linked to the need for continuous upgrading of specialized training curricula in light of dynamic security realities. Even after 10 years of counter-insurgency operations, the military remains ill-trained in asymmetric warfare which is central to dealing with Boko Haram. It is imperative that some of the huge budgetary resources devoted to security be invested in appropriate training and equipment for effective engagement with Boko Haram. At the other end of the scale, in a context of increasing international collaboration, the military as an institution needs to be protected from the disruptive effects of international assistance. In line with comments above, it is vital to align international assistance programmes with Nigerian military doctrines and strategies in order to prevent organizational disruption and planning incoherence.

Amid these disruptive pressures, 10 years of internally and internationally complex counter-insurgency has taken a toll on the institutional coherence and performance of the Nigerian military. In the process, it has tended to exacerbate two central weaknesses which are undermining the goals of counter-radicalization: corruption and military heavy-handedness. While embarrassing to the government, the issue of military corruption must be squarely addressed if there is to be any hope of ending the insurgency in the near future. As various sources have pointed out, corruption within some elements of the military has become the real war economy (Ndujihe 2018; Olufemi 2015). While insurgents draw on kidnapping, bank robbery, gun running and the fish and pepper trades, this pales into insignificance against the billions of dollars siphoned out of the national treasury through inflated security budgets and rampant diversion of resources. Corruption within the military has both undermined access to adequate military logistics and supplies at the front line, and created high level economic interests in the continuation of the conflict. These problems are further exacerbated by frequent changes of Operation Commanders, which only intensify perverse incentives.

Corruption has also exacerbated problems of military demoralization and heavy-handedness. Lack of appropriate training and equipment constrain efforts at improving human rights performance. In addition to improving the working conditions of soldiers, effective counter-radicalization requires that human rights abuses are brought to justice. It is vital that relevant authorities address allegations made against security personnel in incidents of severe abuses, as well as addressing grievances among military personnel to enable them to perform their duties with dignity.

The economic incentives behind corruption and over-militarization of the conflict cannot be laid solely at the door of the Nigerian military. At the international level, the arms trade and humanitarian aid machinery are generating more globalized forms of war economy. In April 2018, US President Trump celebrated a $593 million deal with Nigeria for military aircraft, previously blocked owing to human rights concerns which Trump dismissed as 'not good reasons' (Gould 2018). As hundreds of millions of dollars are spent on new weapons, while donor resources, consultants, and employment opportunities slosh through the Nigerian economy, global economic interests are biasing incentives against more socially embedded approaches to conflict resolution.

POVERTY ALLEVIATION AND EMPLOYMENT

Despite repeated insistence by politicians, public figures and scholars that the Boko Haram insurgency is not about poverty, this book joins the growing crescendo of voices insisting that poverty is a central issue, along with the economic policies and governance failures that have allowed such extreme and regionally unequal patterns of poverty to emerge and persist. Discussions of poverty and inequality presented in the Introduction and the chapter on Borno make it abundantly clear why Boko Haram emerged in the North East, as well as highlighting the extreme risk of similar forms of violent unrest emerging in the Islamic North West, which is on aggregate poorer than the North East, if slightly less plagued by internal inequality. Contributions by Last, and Meagher and Hassan draw attention to worrying pressures of poverty and inequality in the North West, with particular attention to declining opportunity in the rural economy and within the urban informal economy – the main economic options of poor northern youth.

The contribution by Monguno and Umara (Chapter 3) on Borno State reveals the extreme combination of economic calamities afflicting the state, which suffers from catastrophic levels of poverty, environmental crisis, infrastructural marginalization, and inequality of opportunity, both between Borno State and other parts of the country, and within particular parts of Borno State. A detailed and lucid account of the varied nature of the conflict within Borno State shows how grievances about poverty and inequality took ethnic as well as religious form. Membership in Boko Haram offered angry local youth a means of venting frustration and settling scores against the structural monopolization of opportunities by Christian indigenes in southern Borno and by Muslim migrants around Lake Chad. Difficult terrain and porous borders have facilitated the entrenchment of bellicose elements, but poverty and inequality are central features of the social and physical environment conducive to conflict. Religious messaging alone will not end the insurgency if it is not accompanied by broad-based improvements in dignified livelihood opportunities and the rebuilding and upgrading of basic social and physical infrastructure. As Ibrahim (2018) starkly declared, 'to win the war, we have to lift the standard of life and build livelihoods for the people, so that it becomes clear that governments – federal, state and local – have a better offer for the people than the insurgents'.

The contribution by Last (Chapter 8) draws attention to the need for greater economic attention to the rural economy across the north. While existing counter-insurgency policy continues to focus on the promotion of commercial agriculture, it is smallholder family farming and nomadic pastoralism that employ the vast majority of the population in the North East as well as the North West, particularly among the poor (World Bank 2015). Low productivity in this sector has a great deal to do with the abysmally low federal budgetary allocation to agriculture, which has been below 2 per cent for nearly a decade, representing a tiny fraction of recommended levels (Iorember and Jelilov 2018). The neglect of small-scale rural livelihoods is spilling unemployed unskilled Muslim youth into urban areas in droves, and tipping a growing number into rural banditry (Mustapha 2014; Thurston 2018; Higazi 2019). Few if any of the footloose millions of northern Nigerian youth would have the resources or the education to take advantage of commercial farming opportunities or new ranching proposals. This is one of the many examples of how 'best practice' visions from above lead to the mistargeting of economic policy. Effective rural engagement requires a renewed focus on supporting, upgrading and diversifying existing rural livelihoods where the majority of people work, rather than allowing policy to be led by concerns of investors and economists who think big and ignore the costs of displacement and disaffection.

Sustaining rural livelihoods requires a return to support policies for smallholder agriculture and the restoration of services and legal frameworks for nomadic pastoralism, as well as a renewed focus on rural non-farm employment, given the long dry season characteristic of the north and increasing land scarcity (Meagher 2001). A stronger policy focus on supporting education and apprenticeship in rural areas, both through public and Islamiyya schools, would go a long way to improving basic skills and literacy within limited budgets, while upgrading of rural social and physical infrastructure is key to the ability of rural areas to retain and productively employ populations. This dovetails with the need for entertainment and stimulating activities in the countryside, including film parlours or video clubs, football clubs, talks by visiting politicians, preachers and health educators, creating much needed fora for discussion and debate to immunize youth against indoctrination. Creating and running such activities offers opportunities for job creation as well as local stimulation, generating a sense of engagement and belonging for rural dwellers. Even in the context of ecological crisis, small-scale fishing, farming and trading communities are undermined as much by state neglect as by drought, thus swelling migration flows into deprived urban settlements.

In the urban context, Meagher and Hassan (Chapter 9) draw attention to the dangers of employment policies that treat the informal economy as an endless sponge for surplus labour. Instead of addressing the stresses of poverty and market saturation within the informal economy, standardized youth employment packages try to channel even more youth into informal enterprise, intensifying competitive pressures. The contribution by Meagher and Hassan is a cautionary tale about the costs of ill-informed policy approaches that actually worsen rather than alleviate radicalizing pressures (see also NSRP 2014). The authors emphasize the need for more differentiated employment programmes that consider the strained absorptive capacity of the informal economy and the varied needs and aspirations of northern youth.

Instead of addressing drivers of conflict and disaffection, standardized entrepreneurship programmes and micro-finance schemes intensify entry into the informal economy, creating new ethnic, regional and religious tensions in struggles over access to dwindling informal opportunities. The entry of over-educated and better-capitalized youth into lucrative niches within the informal economy are squeezing out skilled apprenticeship-trained operators, creating new pressures of youth disaffection farther down the social ladder. Similarly, the use of meagre micro-credit programmes to direct growing numbers of educated northern youth into low status informal activities at the bottom of the informal economy create alternative dynamics of disaffection by humiliating poor educated youth and squeezing out non-indigenes. Research has shown that youth violence is linked as much to demeaning and exploitative employment as to unemployment (Cramer 2010). More attention is needed to the creation of appropriate employment for different classes of northern youth in order to avoid reinforcing narratives of victimization and marginalization.

Considerable state and donor resources have been pumped into extravagant national job creation schemes, such as Sure-P, YouWIN! and YESSO, and more recently N-Power. Despite fabulous promises, fewer than 30,000 jobs have materialized from the older schemes. N-Power claims to have created 500,000 jobs at an eye-watering cost of N26 billion, while the scheme suffers from poor supervision and non-attendance of beneficiaries while continuing to collect stipends (Schoder 2017; Youth Policy Tool Box 2017; Techpoint 2017; Sanni 2019). While N-Power appears to target northern Nigerians, its main targets are graduates, and applications are done through a web portal. Other youth employment projects run by the World Bank in collaboration with the Rockefeller Foundation and various multinational tech firms offer training in online work to capture the opportunities of 'digital disruption'. While promoting digital employment has its place, in the educationally deprived and infrastructure-starved North East, it is not clear that these initiatives will bring employment where it is most needed. Even more to the point, the number of jobs created are only a small fraction of the 1.8 million youth that enter the Nigerian labour market each year, and the 40 to 50 million new jobs that the World Bank indicates are needed by 2030 to make growth adequately inclusive (Meagher 2013; World Bank 2015).

Efforts to tap the pool of educated youth and channel them into informal entrepreneurship may appeal to corporate models of engagement with the bottom of the pyramid, but they exacerbate the problems of over-saturation and unequal competition that feed dynamics of radicalization. By contrast, indigenous mechanisms of training and employment generation within skilled informal activities have been more successful in generating employment on a much wider scale at a far lower cost, and are more successful at reaching those most vulnerable to radicalization.

A more grounded approach to the mass job creation calls for greater attention to more conventional informal activities. Digital employment could be promoted alongside rather than instead of other skilled, high demand activities within the northern informal economy, such as tailoring, embroidery, leatherwork, butchers, electronics repair, the local building industry, northern Nigeria's largely Hausa-language Kannywood film and audio CD industries, and various lines of trade, providing a means of expanding employment from below. Programmes of technical upgrading and appropriate forms of small business credit would support quality improvements and employment expansion, linked to demand-led business strategies rather than unsustainable schemes. Current job creation programmes completely ignore the development and credit needs of these dynamic sectors. As discussed by Meagher and Hassan (Chapter 9), micro-finance loans are widely rejected by expanding northern Nigerian informal enterprises as too small and too short-term for small business development (see also Meagher 2018). Instead of encouraging the endless creation of new informal enterprises from above, strengthening processes of enterprise development and employment generation from within the informal economy would strengthen its ability to act as a bulwark against radicalization.

Taken together, the accounts of Borno, rural northern Nigeria and the northern informal economy show that the experience of poverty, regional and social inequality, lack of opportunity, and hopelessness create structural conditions conducive to violent radicalization, easily ignited in the volatile context of intense religious and economic competition. Not only does this require increased policy attention to job creation and a more differentiated understanding of dignified work, but it highlights the extreme vulnerability of north-western Nigeria to violent radicalization if initiatives for decent job creation and social welfare support are not extended across the whole of the far north. On the upside, there are many potential synergies between the need for job creation for different classes of northern youth and the realities of military and police understaffing, calls for increased educational and health provisioning, and the massive task of rebuilding housing and infrastructure. While partnering and contracting out may be necessary in some cases, insisting on the employment of local labour and local firms in the vast task of rebuilding offers vital opportunities for large-scale employment generation and skills development – opportunities that should not be wasted.

WOMEN AND CIVIL SOCIETY

The contribution by Usman, Taraboulsi and Hawaja (Chapter 7) has shown that women are particularly vulnerable to radicalization owing to the constraints of female seclusion and social if not always economic dependence on male breadwinners. While no more prone to radical ideologies than men, the economic and social dependence of northern Nigerian women forces many to accommodate to the radical choices of husbands and male relatives. Counter-radicalization therefore requires the explicit inclusion of women in compensation schemes. Many women have lost their homes and possessions as well as their male breadwinners in the conflict. Ensuring that unsupported women, especially those with dependents, are eligible for direct compensation is key to avoiding the risk of driving them into the arms of Boko Haram. Even where women have homes to return to, the reality of rescued women returning to Boko Haram is a stark reminder of the harsh economic conditions faced by many in the North East. Among the poor, the ability of Boko Haram to offer enough to eat and basic security is an improvement over what is available in IDP camps or impoverished villages (Moaveni 2019; Nwaubani 2018). For women as well as youth, effective counter-radicalization requires the state to show a willingness to offer at least a basic level of economic and social decency.

It has been argued that the subordinate status of northern Nigerian women pushed them into joining Boko Haram to gain greater autonomy

(Matfess 2017). However, the contribution by Usman et al. has shown that women's membership in Boko Haram represented a continuation of their dependence on men as breadwinners, rather than a bid for autonomy. Conversely, it is as forces for counter-radicalization that northern Nigerian women have asserted their agency. Northern Muslim women have stepped forward as journalists, as relief workers, as civil society activists, as traditional hunters and members of the CJTF to resist violent radicalization. It is important that counter-radicalization strategies harness this knowledge and commitment, and in the process promote locally valued role models of women's engagement in the public sphere.

In this context, taking advantage of the crisis to push an external agenda of women's rights and gender autonomy is not only inappropriate, but risks aggravating religious sensitivities. Constructive avenues involve simply supporting the constructive public roles that have been created in the context of the crisis. This would include supporting Muslim women NGOs that address the causes of radicalization through programmes of seed grants to women, vocational training for young people, rehabilitation of drug addicts, and sponsorship of orphans to pursue secular and Islamic education. The active role of women in the CJTF also provides a model for employing women from the community, not only to fight insurgents, but also to assist in local security, involving intelligence gathering, guarding public spaces, or searching people at entry points. In this way, the CJTF provides an intelligible local prototype for absorbing women into the police force or into community policing models discussed above.

Alongside the role of women in counter-radicalization, the counter-radicalizing role of northern Nigerian civil society more broadly has been emphasized in various contributions in this book. Professional civil society organizations play a vital role in countering the drivers of radicalization, including the Neem Foundation, which provides trauma counselling to rescued and escaped women and girls; Future Prowess Islamic Foundation School, a tuition-free school for Boko Haram orphans; or Jaiz Widows and Orphans Initiative which provides homes, vocational training and interest-free loans to internally displaced widows and orphans. These are all locally run organizations that direct external and state resources to engage with local values and priorities, while facing the risks of operating where the need is greatest. More community-based groups such as the *ulama*, youth groups, informal occupational associations, community protection groups and elders' fora also offer moral grounding and support systems to counter radicalization. However, as the research has also shown, civil society organizations, especially community groups, are not infinitely resilient. Just as they can be supported to foster counter-radicalization, they can also be undermined by ongoing religious competition, economic pressure, political neglect, distracting international protocols and mounting insecurity. It is important that counter-radicalization strategies strengthen rather than free-ride on these valuable institutional resources or they too will begin to unravel. Appropriate economic and institutional support is essential to preserve local civil society as an asset in the process of counter-radicalization.

Conclusion: Endgames and alternative futures

The objective assessment of insurgency endgames provided in the previous chapter deviates markedly from the bravado of political and military projections. The options of ongoing violence and banditry and the abandonment of the poorest corners of Nigeria to Boko Haram rule are alarming prospects. Worse still, it is a fantasy to believe that the chaos will remain confined to the north-eastern borderlands. Armed banditry is already spreading mayhem through the neglected parts of the North West, underpinned by many of the same pressures and deprivation that gave rise to Boko Haram.

Yet, endgame scenarios are not only about facing demoralizing facts; they are also about spurring the creation of an alternative future. As the philosopher Friedrich Nietzsche is purported to have said, 'the future influences the present just as much as the past'. The focus on security and humanitarian intervention has proven inadequate to ending the insurgency. Finding a peaceful way forward requires a quest for alternative futures that offer hope rather than ongoing hardship and social indignity to the bulk of the northern Nigerian population. In place of culturalist narratives of Islamic terrorism and gender oppression that represent society as the problem, this book argues for an understanding of the deeper causes of Islamic radicalization, opening new possibilities for engagement with northern Nigerian society as part of the solution.

Just as the forces for violent radicalization have emerged from the brutalization of society through extreme poverty, regional inequality and elite corruption, alternative trajectories can be opened up by engaging with the pervasive forces for counter-radicalization within northern Nigerian society. However, as this chapter has made clear, their effectiveness is dependent on addressing severe governance failures within the state and the military, as well as containing the negative side-effects of international intervention. The inability of the most acutely disaffected to see a future in the morass of corruption and competitive markets played a central role in making violent extremism a thinkable alternative. Turning the tide of Boko Haram will require the state to address these failures in the service of national visions that prioritize popular development needs rather than the imagined futures of foreign investors. To paraphrase an earlier reflection on drivers of conflict in African societies: 'What we are witnessing is not the triumph of [extremism], but the failure of statecraft' (Mustapha 1999, 125).

A more resourceful and inclusive statecraft demands a stronger focus on policy synergies between improved livelihoods, social justice and restitution on the one hand, and humanitarian relief, rebuilding and security on the other, underpinned by improved policy alignment to ensure coherence and avoid being drawn into external agendas. Reprioritizing a much greater share of investment to support and upgrade the mainstay of popular livelihoods – small-scale agriculture, informal production, service and trading activities, and local formal firms and trained professionals – maximizes the potential for rapid and appropriate employment generation capable of responding to the needs of those most vulnerable to extremist reimaginings.

In a country as large and geostrategically important as Nigeria, continuing with prevailing policy approaches is no longer an option. A hard look at where the current path leads makes it clear that the existing government and international strategies cannot resolve the crisis. Boko Haram cannot be defeated without overcoming the dysfunctional political and economic forces that fuel it. As this book has shown, the flames of the insurgency are not fed by the alien motivations of global terrorism, but by the broken promises of liberal modernity and market-led development, compounded by the broken promise of Sharia reforms to restore hope and social justice to the beleaguered masses. The increasingly reactionary and violent consequences of extreme inequality, elite neglect, and a deep sense of popular betrayal highlight the real costs of leaving too many behind – costs reflected in increasingly alarming populist political dynamics emerging across the globe (Hadiz 2018; Hadiz and Chryssogelos 2017). Overcoming Boko Haram is about facing the demons of political and economic injustice, but it is also about embracing the knowledge and institutional strengths of northern Nigeria's diverse Muslim majority society to build a future that leaves no one behind.

Bibliography

AfricaTech, 2019, 'Northwest Nigeria Violence Drives 20,000 into Niger – UNHCR', 28 May, *Reuters*, https://af.reuters.com/article/topNews/idAFKCN1SY0WO-OZATP, accessed 3 August 2019.

Brown, K.A. and Saeed, T., 2015, 'Radicalization and Counter Radicalization at British Universities: Muslim Encounters and Alternatives', *Ethnic and Racial Studies* 38 (11), 1952–68.

Cramer, C., 2010, 'Unemployment and Participation in Violence', World Development Report 2011 Background Paper, World Bank, Washington, DC.

Daily Post, 2014, 'Sambo Dasuki: Nigeria's Soft Approach to Countering Terrorism', 19

March, presentation by Mohammed Sambo Dasuki, National Security Adviser, on the roll out of Nigeria's soft approach to countering terrorism held in Abuja, 18 March, https://dailypost.ng/2014/03/19/sambo-dasuki-nigerias-soft-approach-countering-terrorism, accessed 15 April 2014.

Duffield, M., 2018, *Post-Humanitarianism: Governing Precarity in the Digital World*, New York: John Wiley & Sons.

Durmaz, M., 2019, 'Making Sense of Boko Haram's Comeback in Nigeria', *TRT World*, 9 January, www.trtworld.com/magazine/making-sense-of-boko-haram-s-comeback-in-nigeria-23210, accessed 19 May 2019.

Enria, L., 2012, 'Employing the Youth to Build Peace: The Limitations of United Nations Statebuilding in Sierra Leone', *Human Welfare* 1 (1), 42–56.

GCERF (Global Community Engagement & Resilience Fund), 2016, Report of the Fifth Board Meeting, www.gcerf.org/wp-content/uploads/REPORT-OF-THE-5th-BOARD-MEETING.pdf, accessed 12 April 2019.

—— 2017, Annual Report, www.gcerf.org/wp-content/uploads/2017-Annual-Report.pdf, accessed 29 April 2019.

——2018, 'Nigeria Call for Expression of Interest', www.gcerf.org/grants/core-funding-mechanism/nigeria-call-for-expressions-of-interest-2 accessed 12 April 2019.

Gould, J., 2018, 'Trump Gaffes on Attack Aircraft Sale to Nigeria', *Defense News*, 30 April, www.defensenews.com/air/2018/04/30/trump-trips-up-on-attack-aircraft-sale-to-nigeria, accessed 12 July 2019.

Ibrahim, J., 2018, 'Telling Ourselves the Truth about the Boko Haram Insurgency', *Premium Times*, 21 December, https://opinion.premiumtimesng.com/2018/12/21/telling-ourselves-the-truth-about-the-boko-haram-insurgency-by-jibrin-ibrahim, accessed 7 May 2019.

Ibrahim, J, and Bala, S., 2018, 'Civilian-Led Governance and Security in Nigeria After Boko Haram', Special Report, United States Institute of Peace, Washington, DC, www.usip.org/sites/default/files/2018-12/sr_437_civilian_led_governance_and_security_in_nigeria_0.pdf, accessed 13 March 2019.

Idrissa, R., 2017, *The Politics of Islam in the Sahel: Between Persuasion and Violence*, New York: Routledge.

Hadiz, V.R., 2018, 'Imagine All the People? Mobilising Islamic Populism for Right-Wing Politics in Indonesia', *Journal of Contemporary Asia* 48 (4), 566–83.

Hadiz, V.R. and Chryssogelos, A., 2017, 'Populism in World Politics: A Comparative Cross-Regional Perspective', *International Political Science Review* 38 (4), 399–411.

Higazi, A., 2019, 'Nigeria (Farmer-Pastoralist)', *The Armed Conflict Survey 2019*, International Institute for Strategic Studies, London.

Iorember, P.T. and Jelilov, G., 2018, 'Computable General Equilibrium Analysis of Increase in Government Agricultural Expenditure on Household Welfare in Nigeria', *African Development Review*, 30 (4), 362–71.

Kelly, F., 2019, 'ISWAP Killed "Dozens" of Nigeria and Chad Troops near Baga in July 29 Clashes', *The Defense Post*, 1 August, https://thedefensepost.com/2019/08/01/nigeria-baga-iswap-borno, accessed 7 August 2019.

Kendhammer, B., 2013, 'The Sharia Controversy In Northern Nigeria and the Politics of Islamic Law in New and Uncertain Democracies, *Comparative Politics*, 45 (3), 291–311.

Knight, W.A., 2008, 'Disarmament, Demobilization, and Reintegration and Post-Conflict Peacebuilding in Africa: An Overview', *African Security* 1 (1), 24–52.

Matfess, H., 2017, *Women and the War on Boko Haram: Wives, Weapons, Witnesses*, London: Zed Books.

Maclean, R., 2018, 'Nigerians Forced Out by Boko Haram Return to Ruins and Continuing Risk', *The Guardian*, 27 July, www.theguardian.com/global-development/2018/jul/27/nigerians-forced-out-by-boko-haram-return-to-ruins-and-continuing-risk, accessed 20 May 2019.

—— 2019, 'They Say Boko Haram Is Gone. One Mother's Terror Tells Another Story …', *The Guardian* , 2 February, www.theguardian.com/world/2019/feb/02/

election-nigeria-boko-haram-refugees, accessed 9 March 2019.

Mercy Corps, 2016, 'Motivations and Empty Promises: Voices of Former Boko Haram Combatants and Nigerian Youth', Portland, OR. www.mercycorps.org/sites/default/files/Motivations%20and%20Empty%20Promises_Mercy%20Corps_Full%20Report.pdf, accessed 29 March 2019.

Meagher, K., 2001, *The Bargain Sector: Economic Restructuring and the Non-Farm Sector in the Nigerian Savanna*, Aldershot: Ashgate.

—— 2013, 'The Jobs Crisis behind Nigeria's Unrest', *Current History* 112 (754), 169–74.

—— 2018, 'Complementarity, Competition and Conflict: Informal Enterprise and Religious Conflict in Northern Nigeria', in A.R. Mustapha and D. Ehrhardt (eds), *Creed & Grievance: Muslim-Christian Relations & Conflict Resolution in Northern Nigeria*, Woodbridge: James Currey.

Moaveni, A., 2019, 'What Would Make a Woman Go Back to Boko Haram? Despair', *The Guardian*, 14 January, www.theguardian.com/commentisfree/2019/jan/14/woman-boko-haram-nigeria-militant-group, accessed 21 May 2019.

Musa, Rear Admiral Y., 2017, United Nations High Level Conference on Counter Terrorism: Statement by Head of Delegation of Nigeria, 28–29 June 2018, New York.

Mustapha, A.R., 1999, 'Back to the Future: Multi-ethnicity and the State in Africa', in L.R. Basta and J. Ibrahim (eds), *Federalism and Decentralisation in Africa: The Multicultural Challenge*, Fribourg, Switzerland: Institut du Fédéralisme.

—— (ed.), 2014, *Sects & Social Disorder: Muslim Identities & Conflict in Northern Nigeria*, Woodbridge: James Currey.

—— 2015, Violent Radicalization: Northern Nigeria in the Light of the Experience of Southern Niger Republic', in A.R. Mustapha and Muhammad Sani Umar (eds), *On Radicalisation: Counter-Radicalisation, and De-Radicalisation in Northern Nigeria*, Publication of the National Security Advisor, Federal Republic of Nigeria, 234–74.

Mustapha, A R. and Ehrhardt, D. (eds), 2018, *Creed & Grievance: Muslim-Christian Relations & Conflict Resolution in Northern Nigeria*, Woodbridge: James Currey.

Ndujihe, C., 2018, 'Security: FG Spends 6trn on Defence in 7 Years', *Vanguard*, 29 July, www.vanguardngr.com/2018/07/security-fg-spends-n6trn-on-defence-in-11-years, accessed 12 April 2019.

Nemr, C. and Bhulai, R., 2018, 'Civil Society's Role in Rehabilitation and Reintegration Related to Violent Extremism', IPI Global Observatory, 25 June, https://theglobalobservatory.org/2018/06/civil-societys-role-rehabilitation-reintegration-violent-extremism, accessed 8 March 2019.

NSRP (Nigeria Stability and Reconciliation Programme), 2014, 'Winners or Losers? Assessing the Contribution of Youth Employment and Empowerment Programmes to Reducing Conflict Risk in Nigeria', Abuja.

Njoku, E.T., 2018, 'Strategic Exclusion: The State and the Framing of a Service Delivery Role for Civil Society Organizations in the Context of Counterterrorism in Nigeria', *Studies in Conflict & Terrorism*, www.tandfonline.com/doi/abs/10.1080/1057610X.2018.1543131, accessed 17 August 2019.

Nwaubani, A.T., 2018, 'The Women Rescued from Boko Haram Who Are Returning to Their Captors', *The New Yorker*, 20 December. www.newyorker.com/news/dispatch/the-women-rescued-from-boko-haram-who-are-returning-to-their-captors, accessed 21 May 2019.

ODI (Overseas Development Institute), 2016, 'Time to Let Go: Remaking Humanitarian Action for the Modern Era', Humanitarian Policy Group, www.odi.org/sites/odi.org.uk/files/resource-documents/10422.pdf, accessed 12 July 2019.

Olojo, A., 2019, 'Another Chance for Nigeria to get Counter-Terrorism Right', Institute for Security Studies, 15 February, https://issafrica.org/iss-today/another-chance-for-nigeria-to-get-counter-terrorism-right, accessed 19 May 2019.

Olufemi, J., 2015, 'Nigeria Spends N4.62 Trillion on National Security in 5 Years, Yet Widespread Insecurity Remains', *Premium Times*, 18 June, www.premiumtimesng.com/news/headlines/185285-nigeria-spends-n4-62-trillion-on-national-security-in-5-years-yet-widespread-insecurity-remains.html, accessed 12 April 2019.

Samuel, M., 2019, 'The Economics of Terrorism in the Lake Chad Basin', *ISS Today*, 10 July, Institute for Security Studies, Pretoria, South Africa, https://issafrica.org/iss-today/economics-of-terrorism-in-lake-chad-basin, accessed 10 August 2019.

Sanni, K., 2019, Special Report, 'How N-Power Beneficiaries Abscond from Duty, Abuse Opportunity in Three States', *Premium Times*, 14 July, www.premiumtimesng.com/investigationspecial-reports/340703-special-report-how-n-power-beneficiaries-abscond-from-duty-abuse-opportunity-in-three-states.html, accessed 7 August 2019.

Schoder, D., 2017, 'The Business Competition that Worked', American Economic Association, 20 September, www.aeaweb.org/research/nigeria-business-plan-competition-entrepreneurship-employment-innovation, accessed 21 May 2019.

Techpoint Africa, 2017, 'Everything Wrong with the N-Power Youth Empowerment Scheme', 11 July, https://techpoint.africa/2017/07/11/n-power-empowerment, accessed 7 August 2019.

The Defense Post, 2019, 'Boko Haram Factions Attack Sajeri and Auno as Buhari Acknowledges Setbacks', 8 January, https://thedefensepost.com/2019/01/08/boko-haram-attacks-sajeri-auno-buhari-acknowledges-setbacks, accessed 10 May 2019.

Thurston, A., 2018, *Boko Haram: The History of an African Jihadist Movement*, Princeton, NJ: Princeton University Press.

Tucker, D. and Mohammed, J.A., 2018, 'Through Our Eyes: People's Perspectives on Building Peace in Northeast Nigeria', Policy Paper, Kukah Centre and Conciliation Resources, April, Abuja and London.

Umar, M.S. 1993, 'Changing Islamic Identity in Nigeria from the 1960s to the 1980s: From Sufism to Anti-Sufism', in L. Brenner (ed.), *Muslim Identity and Social Change in Sub-Saharan Africa*, Bloomington and Indianapolis: Indiana University Press.Wakili, H., 2009, 'Islam and the Political Arena in Nigeria: The Ulama and the 2007 Election', Working Paper 09-004, Institute for the Study of Islamic Thought in Africa, The Roberta Buffet Centre for International and Comparative Studies, Northwestern University, Evanston, IL.

World Economic Forum, 2017, 'The Future of Humanitarian Response', World Economic Forum Annual Meeting 2017, Davos-Klosters, Switzerland 17–20 January, www3.weforum.org/docs/WEF_AM17_Future_Humanitarian_Response.pdf, accessed 25 May 2019.

Youth Policy Tool Box, 2017, 'Youth Enterprise with Innovation in Nigeria (YouWiN!!) –Nigeria', https://yptoolbox.unescapsdd.org/portfolio/youth-enterprise-innovation-nigeria-youwin-nigeria, accessed 21 May 2019.

World Bank, 2015, 'More, and More Productive, Jobs for Nigeria', World Bank Other Operational Studies 23962, The World Bank, Washington, DC.

Index